CHAUCER STUDIES XIV

CHAUCER: COMPLAINT AND NARRATIVE

# CHAUCER STUDIES

I
## MUSIC IN THE AGE OF CHAUCER
Nigel Wilkins

II
## CHAUCER'S LANGUAGE AND THE PHILOSOPHERS' TRADITION
J. D. Burnley

III
## ESSAYS ON TROILUS AND CRISEYDE
Edited by Mary Salu

IV
## CHAUCER SONGS
Nigel Wilkins

V
## CHAUCER'S BOCCACCIO
Sources of Troilus and the Knight's
and Franklin's Tales
Edited and translated by N. R. Havely

VI
## SYNTAX AND STYLE IN CHAUCER'S POETRY
G. H. Roscow

VII
## CHAUCER'S DREAM POETRY: SOURCES AND ANALOGUES
B. A. Windeatt

VIII
## CHAUCER AND PAGAN ANTIQUITY
Alistair Minnis

IX
## CHAUCER AND THE POEMS OF 'CH'
in University of Pennsylvania MS French 15
James I. Wimsatt

X
## CHAUCER AND THE IMAGINARY WORLD OF FAME
Piero Boitani

XI
## INTRODUCTION TO CHAUCERIAN ENGLISH
Arthur O. Sandved

XII
## CHAUCER AND THE EARLY WRITINGS OF BOCCACCIO
David Wallace

XIII
## CHAUCER'S NARRATORS
David Lawton

ISSN 0261-9822

CHAUCER

# COMPLAINT AND NARRATIVE

W. A. DAVENPORT

D. S. BREWER

First published 1988 by D. S. Brewer
240 Hills Road, Cambridge
an imprint of Boydell & Brewer Ltd
PO Box 9, Woodbridge, Suffolk IP12 3DF
and of Boydell & Brewer Inc.
Wolfeboro, New Hampshire 03894-2069, USA

ISBN 0 85991 277 9


British Library Cataloguing in Publication Data

Davenport, W. A. (William Anthony)
    Chaucer: complaint and narrative ——
    (Chaucer studies, 0261-9822; v.14)
    1. Poetry in English. Chaucer, Geoffrey –
    Critical studies
    I. Title      II. Series
    821′.1
    ISBN 0-85991-277-9


Library of Congress Cataloging-in-Publication Data

Davenport, W. A. (William Anthony), 1935–
    Chaucer: complaint and narrative / W.A. Davenport.
      p.  cm. — (Chaucer studies ; 14)
    Bibliography: p.
    Includes index.
    ISBN 0-85991-277-9
    1. Chaucer, Geoffrey, d. 1400—Criticism and interpretation.
    2. Complaint poetry, English—History and criticism.  3. Narration
    (Rhetoric)   I. Title.    II. Series.
    PR1933.C65D38 1988
    821′.1—dc19                                             88-11622
                                                              CIP

♾ Printed on long life paper
made to the full American Standard

Printed in Great Britain by St Edmundsbury Press, Bury St Edmunds, Suffolk

# Contents

In Memory of
My Mother and Father

Ethel Davenport (née Price)
1899–1971
and
Frank Davenport
1892–1984

# PART I: COMPLAINT AND FORMAL EXPERIMENT

CHAPTER ONE

# The Order of Complaint

However cheerful his temperament, Chaucer must have liked writing complaints. They are spread through his work from early to late and, though his complaints vary in form and function, they all show a sufficiently sympathetic response to the pity and error of things to identify a recurrent direction of thought. It is my contention that far from being an artificial rhetorical exercise of a type which Chaucer discarded as his work matured, it was a mode of expression which he went on finding useful and adaptable to a variety of purposes. The complaint tradition is, in any case, more varied than it is often given credit for, stretching from the passionate soliloquy of self-pity to the plaintiff's statement in court and the satirist's ululations. Chaucer had a go at most types and it seems appropriate to begin with his learning the very alphabet of complaint.

At the beginning of his writing career he encountered, in Deguilleville, the idea of fervent lament expressed in lengthy stanzas, ingeniously built round few rhymes, although he did not imitate these features until later; in his own translation of the prayer from *Le Pèlerinage de l'Ame* he simplified the 12-line stanza with two rhymes to an 8-line one with three. What seems to have interested Chaucer in 'An ABC of the Virgin', apart from the acrostic exercise, is the note of plangency—affective piety in long, flowing lines, with vivid, dramatic phrasing, freedom in the placing of syntactical pauses and rich imagery.[1] Chaucer's version has a greater speaking urgency than his original, well seen in the sixth stanza:

> Fleeinge, I flee for socour to thi tente
> Me for to hide from tempeste ful of dreede,
> Biseeching yow that ye you not absente,
> Thouh I be wikke. O help yit at this neede!
> Al have I ben a beste in wil and deede,
> Yit, ladi, thou me clothe with thi grace.
> Thin enemy and myn—ladi, tak heede!—
> Unto my deth in poynt is me to chace!   ('An ABC', 41–8)

3

The prayer combines a lament of the desperate sinner, characterised by line 124, 'Allas! I caityf, whider may I flee?', with praise of the Virgin; the emphasis on pity connects the poem with the central themes of the medieval Latin *planctus*, the suffering of Christ and the sorrows of Mary.[2]

A similar power to convey a troubled state of mind and emotional urgency is found in Chaucer's other prayers to the Virgin in *The Second Nun's Prologue* and in *The Man of Law's Tale*. The latter draws on the tradition of Complaints of the Blessed Virgin lamenting for her child:[3]

> 'O litel child, allas! what is thy gilt,
> That nevere wroghtest synne as yet, pardee?'
>
> (*CT*, II, 855–6)

But Mary's contrast of the sufferings of her son and that of the children of the mothers to whom she laments is inverted into a cry by Constance for Mary's aid:

> 'Thow sawe thy child yslayn bifore thyne yen,
> And yet now lyveth my litel child, parfay!
> Now, lady bright to whom alle woful cryen, . . .
> Rewe on my child . . .'    (*CT*, II, 848–50, 853)

Again it is for the effect of pathos that Chaucer alludes to the *planctus* tradition. The themes of other religious complaints, the complaint of soul against body and the regrets of old age, are similarly reflected in the speech Chaucer gave to the old man in *The Pardoner's Tale* and in *The Reeve's Prologue*.

The Christian Latin *planctus* is only one of the elements that went to make up the medieval idea of complaint. Even older is the classical tradition of complaint as a satirical form attacking 'man and his perennial frailties'.[4] The diffused influence of Juvenal and Horace as literary models is mingled with Old Testament indignation to produce a homiletic tradition of castigation of the vanity and the transitoriness of man's life presided over by Dame Fortune. John Peter distinguishes four types: complaints of corruption of classes of men (clergy, lawyers, etc.); complaints of particular vices and types (women, misers, etc.); complaints of specific abuses (dress, cosmetics); and complaints on general themes such as providence, virtue and vice, the contrast between present misery and the past, and the idea of man's inner condition as the microcosmic expression of the state of the world.[5] The classical idea of the lost Golden Age becomes tinged with Christian regret for Paradise before the Fall. Death and the Last Judgment are the means of concentrating the mind on the defects of the present. Chaucer's absorption of such themes from Christian homiletic sources, such as *De Contemptu Mundi*, meets with the current of thought in Boethius, whose *De Consolatione Philosophiae* begins in passionate lament against the uncertainties of Fortune, which echoes classical elegies of exile and distress, particularly Ovid's *Tristia*,[6] and goes on to consolatory teaching which includes much material belonging to the tradition of moral complaint of the vanity of worldly things. Chaucer reflects the themes of complaints against the vices of man in the tales he gave to the Pardoner and Parson and the themes and form of the Boethian moral complaint in his ballades 'Lak of Stedfastnesse', 'Truth', 'Fortune', and in 'The Former Age'.

4

Boethius himself looks back not only to Ovid, of course, but more significantly to Platonic and Ciceronian uses of dialogue for philosophical, didactic and forensic purposes, and to Augustine's development of the dialogue as a way of externalising mental debate. Complaint in dialogue is the stimulus to an answer, not an exercise in elegiac or condemnatory rhetoric for its own sake. The complainant may take up the stance of a litigant in the law-courts or of a challenger in a school disputation. The use of complaint in debate was interesting to Chaucer, as his use of Alain de Lille's *De Planctu Naturae* in *The Parliament of Fowls* makes clear. Alain identifies his work with the Boethian tradition by following the literary form of the *De Consolatione Philosophiae* (the Menippean satire in alternating prose and verse) and by modelling his description of Nature on the figure of Philosophy.[7] The poet begins by lamenting current contempt for Nature's laws and so prefigures the flood of rhetoric from Nature herself, as she laments how all creation obeys her laws except for man, who is misled by the irresponsibility and irrationality of Venus. The dialogue of poet and Nature is a simple pupil/teacher relationship: the element of debate is in the treatment of the nature of love by means of the contrary aspects of Nature and Venus and of the conflict of Virtues and Vices. This poetic treatise deploring the weaknesses of mankind represents several aspects of complaint: the moral theme, presented as a debating issue, the composite prose and verse form, the allegorical plaintiff seen in a dream experience.

Rhetorical tradition associated complaint mainly with the lamentation of catastrophe, as in Chaucer's best-known reference to medieval rhetoric:

> O Gaufred, deere maister soverayn,
> That whan thy worthy kyng Richard was slayn
> With shot, compleynedest his deeth so soore,
> Why ne hadde I now thy sentence and thy loore
> The Friday for to chide, as diden ye?
> (*The Nun's Priest's Tale, CT,* VII, 3347–51)

However ironic Chaucer is here about Geoffrey de Vinsauf's recommended method of lamenting death, he accepted the poetic propriety of such laments, not only in the elegy for one dead, as in *The Book of the Duchess,* but also for one facing death, especially the innocent heroine. An explicit instance is Virginia's request:

> 'Thanne yif me leyser, fader myn,' quod she,
> 'My deeth for to compleyne a litel space;
> For, pardee, Jepte yaf his doghter grace
> For to compleyne, er he hir slow, allas!'
> (*The Physician's Tale, CT,* VI, 238–41)

Chaucer here simply uses the pathos of the idea of lamenting 'against' one's death, without a rendering of the actual plaint, but in *The Legend of Good Women* he had gone further in the brief complaints, which occur in the majority of the legends, based on the lamenting letters given to his tragic heroines by Ovid in the *Heroides.*[8] Though Chaucer's versions are truncated, he sometimes catches the spirit of such poetic ceremonies of death in his choice of image or typifying rhetorical device. So Dido's letter to Aeneas encapsulates the themes of many another betrayed heroine's lament:

> 'Ryght so,' quod she, 'as that the white swan
> Ayens his deth begynneth for to synge,
> Right so to yow make I my compleynynge.
> Not that I trowe to geten yow ageyn,
> For wel I wot that it is al in veyn,
> Syn that the goddes been contraire to me.
> But syn my name is lost thourgh yow,' quod she,
> 'I may wel lese on yow a word or letter,
> Al be it that I shal ben nevere the better;
> For thilke wynd that blew youre ship awey,
> The same wynd hath blowe awey youre fey.'
>
> (*The Legend of Good Women*, 1355–65)

The situation of Dido had already drawn from Chaucer a fuller and more passionate lament in *The House of Fame* and the combination of female vulnerability, man's betrayal and the threat of death continued in *The Canterbury Tales* to be a nexus of elements apparently sought and exploited by Chaucer not merely for a local effect of pathos but to act as a focal point for the morality and feelings in a tale.

Complaint is a type of expression, or a rhetorical device ('an *apostrophe* dislocated from its circumstances', as Payne puts it[9]), not—for Chaucer at any rate—a poetic form. Thus complaint occurs in the form of ballade or other lyric pattern, or as speech inset within a longer work, with or without change of metre, identifiable at times by function and content, but not form. The nearest it came to having a fixed form in the medieval period was in the hands of courtly French poets who developed complaint as one of a number of set types of love-lyric. Guillaume de Machaut used a 16-line stanza for complaint and this was imitated by Froissart and other French poets and by Chaucer in *Anelida and Arcite*. But though complaint sometimes appears in French lists of the fixed forms of lyric poetry (such as *balade, rondel, virelai, chant royal*),[10] it was not always in such stanzas, nor always recognised as a separate type of lyric. The main idea of the courtly complaint is the lover's expression of his suffering. Chaucer was interested enough to imitate both the single separate lyric (as in 'A Complaint to his Lady') and also the more complex pattern of inclusion of complaint within a longer poem. This latter idea is based on the occurrence of complaint within a number of poems of the kind conveniently identified (following Wimsatt)[11] as *dits amoureux*; this is the concept of complaint most obvious in Chaucer's work, in *The Book of the Duchess*, in *The Complaint of Mars* and in the Complaint of Anelida in *Anelida and Arcite*.

The French courtly narrative with complaint provides patterns of combination of elements which are of interest for Chaucer. In several thirteenth-century love stories the narrator is involved in a sequence of incidents of which lament is a part. In the *Romanz de la Poire*[12] it is after the process of falling in love has been dramatised through symbolism and allegory that the lover complains; the answering advice of Reason is disdained, and the lovers reach agreement and exchange a token, despite the jealous husband. In the *Fablel dou Dieu d'Amours*,[13] a lively 'jongleur' compilation in the form of a dream, it is after a debate of birds that the lover laments when a dragon seizes his *amie*; the God of Love comes to the rescue and the poem moves on to another sad episode of a lost lover. In a related poem *De Venus la Déese d'Amor*[14] the lament has a more dominant role, though again it is simply part of a sequence of episodes including another bird-debate, the testing of the lover by Venus, a scene at the Court of Love, a lover's charter and so on. In such poems complaint is used as rhetorical ornament; it is not essential to the narrative, which is arbitrarily compiled from narrative, allegorical and lyric motifs. The complaints may be, as Wimsatt suggests, derived from short examples in *Le Roman de la Rose*.

The fourteenth-century French examples turn complaint in the *dit* much more into a central lyric set-piece. Guillaume de Machaut put lengthy examples in 16-line strophic form into the *Remède de Fortune* and the *Dit de la Fonteinne Amoreuse* and Froissart used the same form in the *Paradys d'Amours* and the *Espinette Amoreuse*.[15] These are the poems that established the poem of complaint and comfort as a courtly kind.[16] The essentials of the form are the narrative setting for the complaint, the complaint as a rhetorical lyric with its own distinct metrical form, and the process of consolation. This last element brings one back to Boethius as a source, as is clear in the *Remède de Fortune* where the poet's complaint against Love and Fortune is answered by *Esperence*, a figure modelled on the Lady Philosophy. Several other kinds of inset lyric are scattered through the poem and interspersed lyrics occur also in the two complaint and comfort poems of Froissart named above and in other French courtly poems of the mid-fourteenth century. Guillaume de Machaut's last work, the *Voir Dit* (1363–4), has numerous examples, rondeaux, virelays, complaints, as well as a lengthy exchange of prose letters. The poem of Chaucer closest to the French *dits amoureux* is obviously *The Book of the Duchess*, which is directly dependent on the above-named poems of complaint and comfort by de Machaut and Froissart; however, the idea of the mixture of narrative and lyric was more indirectly but perhaps more penetratingly influential on his composition. The poems of the lover's complaint and comfort again suggest, as do complaints against Fortune, a process of accusation and response which leads to a type of debate poetry. The combination of narrative and lyric suggests other possibilities: variation in the poet's stance, for instance, or a combination of different voices in the poem when narrator gives way to another, identifiable as sufferer or suppliant.

The several literary traditions with which complaint had historical connections suggest why Chaucer wrote in the mode so frequently. Modern commentators have often spoken of complaint disparagingly as an empty rhetorical display of conventional feeling. But there were more possibilities in the idea than has been recognised and Chaucer experimented with it, trying it out in various guises, both by itself and in combination with other literary forms and ideas. What I intend to argue in this book is that complaint was a seminal idea for Chaucer, one of his growth points, and that his ideas of both feeling and form in poetry may be identified through recognition of the recurrence of the complaint idea throughout his work, adapted to different contexts and purposes.

The French courtly poets used complaint in two main ways: first, as a separate lyric form in which a pleasing mood of melancholy could be expressed and the music of the lover's 'herte' and 'smerte' plangently attenuated; secondly, in longer poems as one of several stages in demonstrations of the etiquette and morality of love. The formal complaint presents the lover's speech as the registration of the extent of sophisticated anguish; refinement of expression and elegant variation are the subtleties offered to a knowing audience who recognise in the subject-matter familiar key ideas, a rehearsal of the principles of love's suffering. In the longer poem the complaint helps to create plot, since the intense emotion requires answer, whether in consolation or restraint or antithesis. Chaucer was interested in both these aspects of the poet's voice: the lyric voice, which speaks in the moment of feeling, and the narrative voice, which constructs some continuity out of events, variations, consequences.

His exploration of the first-person expression of the lover's moods and moral states perhaps led naturally to the expression of more general reflections in religious and philosophical lyrics; or, independently, Christian complaints and Boethius could have incited these other exercises of the lyric manner. Whatever the reasons or the order, one recognises in Chaucer, among his other imaginative enterprises, the development of a voice of feeling. This is identifiable as part of a general development of literary sensibility in the later fourteenth century. As Janet Coleman points out,[17] there was an existing tradition of social protest in poetry before Chaucer and social and spiritual complaints overlap; social issues are condemned from a religious standpoint; complaint writers constantly contrast the abuses of the age to an ideal, a sense of moral rightness. Complaints confront current moral dilemmas[18] and in the development of the mode of writing in the hands of Langland, Gower and Chaucer one can see complaint used as an instrument of moral and emotional exploration.[19] The use of the voice of the sufferer moves poetry towards aspects of individualism; love, war, betrayal, injustice and so on are expressed in a way which requires the poet to enter into the afflicted point of view and to express moral judgment. Complaint ought to be justified:

> The ordre of compleynt requireth skylfully
> That yf a wight shal pleyne pitously,
> Ther mot be cause wherfore that men pleyne . . .
> (*The Complaint of Mars*, 155–7)

The writers of religious lyric were already using emotion to draw and to develop faith. Moral and social complaints intend by accusation and attack to stimulate thought, debate, reform. Chaucer was less inclined than either Langland or Gower to the explicit moral expression of immediate social disquiet; instead he transformed it, sometimes into imagined instances, sometimes into Boethian expression of the universal theme of injustice and pain in the world. The complaint as lyric perhaps seemed to Chaucer inadequate to deal with particular circumstance, more apt to the expression of mood or general aspect or state of mind.

Perhaps some sense of the limitation of complaint as a separate form explains Chaucer's more frequent use of complaint either in combination with narrative or embedded in longer works. The narrative framework allows greater possibility of relating the protest to the conditions and it could, though it does not always do so in Chaucer's works, provide the possibility of resolution of the tension of the situation. One could say that poetic complaint is an expression of the human condition, particular or general, and that Chaucer found the idea suggestive but not complete in itself. Hence Chaucer tends to provide situations as anchors for lament or to construct a sequence of action and behaviour in which complaint focusses on intense moments.

For some poets it is the formal possibilities of complaint which justify its use, both as a separate lyric and as an inset section of dream-poems or court narratives: decoration and ceremony were a challenge to the technique of the poet and the Gothic richnesses of patterned exuberance to which a heroine's distress might give rise could themselves be seen as the source of invention and discovery in poetry. Chaucer at least entertains the possibility in *Anelida and Arcite*.

Elsewhere Chaucer seems to be trying out the various opportunities offered by the kind, experimenting with form and metre in some poems, with combinations of complaint and narrative in others, adapting, developing and contradicting complaint in longer poems and inserting its particular dramatic sharpness into narrative material. Study of Chaucer's use of complaint is inevitably also an exploration of some aspects of the development of Chaucer's ideas of literary structure.

# CHAPTER TWO

# Complaints Simple and Compound

## 1. Simple Complaints

'A Complaint to his Lady' belongs to the stage at which Chaucer thought complaint a suitable type of writing for metrical experiment and exercise in the courtly poetic idiom.[1] The four poems or fragments have been read by some as separate poems, by others as a sequence; Clemen describes them as variations on a theme.[2] Chaucer's trials of *terza rima* in the second and third passages and of a decasyllabic 10-line stanza in the fourth demonstrate his flexible adjustment of sentence-structure and phrasing; as in 'An ABC' he creates the impression of a fluent speaking voice:

> In my trewe and careful herte ther is
> So moche wo, and eek so litel blis
>     That wo is me that ever I was bore;
> For al that thyng which I desyre I mis,
> And al that ever I wolde not, ywis,
>     That finde I redy to me evermore;
> And of al this I not to whom me pleyne.
>     For she that mighte me out of this brynge
>     Ne reccheth nought whether I wepe or synge;
> So litel rewthe hath she upon my peyne.  (40–49)

The Italian influence suggested by the use of *terza rima* has led editors to think that the poem was composed in the 1380s, but whether or not it came after the dream-poems, it shows Chaucer willing to take on the voice of the plaintive lover here, even if he explicitly disclaimed it elsewhere. There is less passion in his playing the role than that of the penitent sinner in 'An ABC' but there is an elegant confidence in the combination of the voice of the sleepless poet and the fashionably sorrowful lover. The third part of the set sees him trying out a different part of the lover's idiom, the catalogue of personified qualities, to produce an effect distantly akin to Marvell's in 'The Gallery' of the lady's capacity to be seen in contrary guises in the distorting mirror of the lover's sensibility:

> Now sothly, what she hight I wol reherse.
> Hir name is Bountee, set in womanhede,
> Sadnesse in youthe, and Beautee prydelees
> And Plesaunce, under governaunce and drede;
> Hir surname is eek Faire Rewthelees,
> The Wyse, yknit unto Good Aventure,
> That, for I love hir, she sleeth me giltelees.   (23–9)

Both the speaking voice and the analysis of the lady's qualities show Chaucer going for sense rather than manner. The material is courtly commonplace but Chaucer's directness and unpretentious diction, in such lines as 'The more I love, the more she doth me smerte', produce a graceful effect from it.[3]

'Womanly Noblesse' shows a similar combination of elements: an exercise in the Deschamps pattern of ballade, with three 9-line stanzas and a 6-line envoy; the stanzas are through-rhymed using only two rhymes (*remembraunce, plesaunce* etc. and *noblesse, distresse*, etc.) with a variation in the envoy, whose last two lines repeat the opening lines of the poem. The predominantly three-syllabled rhyme words make the expression cumbersome in places, but Chaucer nicely plays off monosyllables against polysyllables in some lines:

> So wel me liketh your womanly contenaunce,
> Your fresshe fetures and your comlynesse,
> That whiles I live, myn herte to his maystresse
> You hath ful chose in trewe perseveraunce
> Never to chaunge . . .   (5–9)

The woeful stance of complaint is used to give emotional purchase on the central moral idea of remembered virtue.

The slightly impersonal quality of such capable management of diction and idiom is more effective in the moral or philosophical complaints, where the thought is of Boethian or Senecan cast, but the stylistic and formal model often again Deschamps. The ballade form in three rhyme-royal stanzas with envoy is found in 'Truth' and 'Lak of Stedfastnesse'. The element of complaint is stronger in the latter, which is built round one of the traditional themes of Latin complaint, the contrast between past and present; this is interpreted in an equally characteristic medieval vein:

> for turned up-so-doun
> Is al this world for mede and wilfulnesse,
> That al is lost for lak of stedfastnesse.   (5–7)

The detached tone Chaucer uses in such poems places the ideas before the reader in a suitably intellectual manner, suggesting the airing of a general idea for mutual perusal and converse; the idea, as has often been pointed out, is a commonplace.[4] Only in the envoy, where Chaucer turns to the imperative mode to King Richard, is there a touch of rhetorical passion. The art of this type of complaint, when presented as a single poem without a context of narrative or argument, is to persuade the reader of the justness of the speaker's view, rather than the pathos of suffering; Chaucer again shows himself capable of catching the right quality of voice, in, for example, the effect of balance and forthrightness, even an epigrammatic touch, in 'Trouthe is put doun, resoun is holden fable'. The terms Chaucer learned from Boethius prevent him falling into the vein of lightweight journalism to which Deschamps' ballades on contemporary life descend. Chaucer's expression of moral weariness[5] with his times is powerful not with the note of personal passion but rather an effect of sober, sad intelligence:

> For among us now a man is holde unable,
> But if he can, by som collusioun,
> Don his neighbour wrong or oppressioun.   (10–12)

The forthrightness and the imperative mode take over in the more often quoted and praised poem 'Truth', Chaucer's 'Balade de Bon Conseyl', addressed (if the envoy, occurring only in MS Addit. 10340, is genuine) to his friend Vache. This may belong to a much later period of Chaucer's life than the other complaints mentioned so far, perhaps with the verse epistles to Bukton and Scogan in his last years, and at first sight it has little of complaint about it. But in the line 'Her is non hoom, her nis but wildernesse' (17) is recognisable the familiar complaint motif of the world's vanity and, despite the sententious vigour of the first two stanzas, possibly influenced by Seneca as well as Boethius,[6] the theme identifies the poem as pastoral indictment of city and court. The central idea is that the courtier gives himself to the arbitrariness of Fortune and so loses control of his own fate.[7] The conjunction of ideas is partly a jest here, since the name Vache gives the image of man as a beast in its stall a comic dimension, but it belongs to a recurrent train of thought in Chaucer's writing. Palamon arraigns the gods for reducing man to the status of beast:

> 'What is mankynde more unto you holde
> Than is the sheep that rouketh in the folde?
> For slayn is man right as another beast. . . .'
> (*CT*, I, 1307–9)

In *Troilus and Criseyde* it is Fortune who is accused:

> But O Fortune, executrice of wyrdes,
> O influences of thise hevenes hye!
> Soth is, that under God ye ben oure hierdes,
> Though to us bestes ben the causes wrie.
> (*Troilus and Criseyde*, III, 617–20)

One of Chaucer's sources for the comparison of man and beast is Boethius' contrast between the downward-inclining heads of beasts and the high-raised head of man:

And, but yif thou, erthly man, waxest yvel out of thi wit, this figure amonesteth the, that axest the hevene with thi ryghte visage, and hast areised thi forheved to beren up an hy thi corage, so that thi thought ne

12

be nat ihevyed ne put lowe undir fote, syn that thi body is so heyghe areysed.

(Boece V, met. 5)

Chaucer imaginatively fuses this imagery of down/up, low/high with the figure of the pilgrim setting forth from the wilderness so that the 'heye wey' becomes a phrase with a double meaning:

> Forth, pilgrim, forth! Forth, beste, out of thy stal!
> Know thy contree, look up, thank God of al;
> Hold the heye wey, and lat thy gost thee lede;
> And trouthe thee shal delivere, it is no drede.   (18–21)

The personal turn of the envoy provides Chaucer with a neat signing-off; the solemnity of the theme is given due expression and then the wry smile of 'therfore, thou Vache . . .' twists it into affectionate intimacy leading to the neat pun on 'mede' in the penultimate line. Even in such short poems Chaucer seems to like the extra dimension, almost a framing device, which the envoy provides.

Among the 'love' complaints Chaucer uses the turn from ballade to envoy even more interestingly in his comic pastiche of the yearning lover's lament 'The Complaint of Chaucer to his Purse'. He puts on a fine show of traditional postures for the sake of his 'light' love, the 'lady dere' who can save him from his deathbed, can steer his heart, shine in his sky and be his saviour; all the seriousness of the ballade becomes mock solemnity and so the envoy is deprived of the chance of turning gravity into urbanity—there is nowhere to go but into seriousness:

> O conqueror of Brutes Albyon,
> Which that by lyne and free eleccion
> Been verray kyng, this song to yow I sende;
> And ye, that mowen alle oure harmes amende,
> Have mynde upon my supplicacion!   (22–6)

To end a comic complaint by bidding a royal patron to take him seriously is the mark of poetic confidence and experience; complaints had become second nature by the time Chaucer wrote that, near the end of his life. Far from marking the 'disintegration of the genre' as Clemen suggests,[8] it seems to confirm its capacity to renew itself, even by turning itself inside out.

Chaucer seems to have written only one separate complaint in the form of the 3-stanza ballade without envoy (the pattern used by de Machaut), the polished 'To Rosemounde'.[9] In this exercise in self-mocking exaggeration the element of complaint becomes courtly teasing and Chaucer finds a substitute for the envoy's effect of coda in the effect of crescendo, as he builds up his self-portrait from the wounded lover needing the ointment of the lady's beauty and the weeping lover filling a brewing-vat with his tears to the double climax of comparing himself simultaneously to Tristram and a cooked fish wallowing in its sauce. He captures the absurd aspect of the lover's everlasting protests in a wonderful line:

> I brenne ay in an amorous plesaunce.   (22)

The ballade's refrain-line rounds each stanza off and so even here the sense of pattern contributes to the effect. The refrain 'Though ye to me ne do no daliaunce' counteracts the effusiveness of what has gone before and so acts as a repeated check on the threat of the imagery to multiply and luxuriate.

Of Chaucer's complaints only 'The Former Age' does without the structural definition provided by refrain or envoy or some framing device. Here Chaucer depends just upon rhyme, stanzaic division and the internal rhetoric. Despite its opening with the serene image of the happy past, the complaint element is strongly in evidence:

> Allas! than sprang up al the corsednesse
> Of coveytyse, that first our sorwe broghte! (31–2)

and at the climax:

> Allas, allas! now may men wepe and crye! (60)

The exposure of the present by contrast with the peaceful, satisfied and simple life of the past is the basis of all eight stanzas but Chaucer makes the repetition a device for strengthening the effect of the poem by clever accumulation of imagery and instance. The stanza used is the same 8-line one, rhyming ababbcbc, as Chaucer used in 'An ABC', the so-called 'Monk's stanza'; the central couplet focusses the stanza—Schmidt calls it the 'keystone of the arch'[10]—flanked by the two groups of three lines. This stanza, with deca-syllabic lines, is weighty and, in combination with the unusual range of vocabulary used by Chaucer here, creates an effect of power and resonance. The myth of the Golden Age from Ovid's *Metamorphoses* is reinforced from Boethius (who was himself recalling Ovid) as a means of condemning the present.[11] The poem moves from the lovely ease of the opening:

> A blisful lyf, a paisible and a swete
> Ledden the peples in the former age. (1–2)

to the hideous piling up of horrors at the end:

> For in oure dayes nis but covetyse,
> Doublenesse, and tresoun, and envye,
> Poyson, manslauhtre, and mordre in sondry wyse. (61–3)

The transition from one to the other is effected by varied interplay between images of pastoral simplicity, awaiting what might seem desirable discovery and change ('No man yit knew the forwes of his lond;/No man the fyr out of the flint yit fond.'), and accumulation of properties more threatening, absent from the innocent life:

> No trompes for the werres folk ne knewe,
> Ne toures heye and walles rounde or square. (23–4)

Between the two are other ambiguous qualities of the civilised life, ostensibly useful and beneficial but tainted by aggressive and exploiting words:

> Unkorven and ungrobbed lay the vyne . . . (14)
> No ship yit karf the wawes grene and blewe;
> No marchaunt yit ne fette outlandish ware. (21-2)

The abuses of the age which are the core of satirical complaints are indicated obliquely by the association of luxury with tyranny and of palaces and halls, even walls alone, with insecurity, envy, disloyalty. Wantonness and pride are identified through the names of Jupiter and Nimrod, making a strange conjunction between classical and Old Testament references but remaining within the figural, mythic convention of the whole.[12] So although the poem is dealing with the Fall and characteristic medieval views of the corruptions caused by the sins in contemporary society, Chaucer has created an idiom which makes his poem a statement of regret and, by implication, of idealism, more profound and impressive than the theme might be expected (in English at this time) to produce. Moral seriousness and intensity are conveyed by the language and the consciously literary repetitions of line-openings, sentence-patterns and the insistent amassing of corroborative detail. This is complaint written for moral and sententious effect not for the effect of pathos or picturesquely elegant melancholy. Though the tone of 'The Former Age' is echoed by individual passages and lines elsewhere in Chaucer, it is, as a poem, unique and Chaucer's most forceful separate piece of complaint poetry.

Chaucer's single complaints show a surprisingly wide range of kinds and effects. At its most intense, complaint is a poignant rendering of agitation of mind, but love-complaints often seem part of a polished, fashionable game and Chaucer sounds at home in both the grave and the urbane varieties of lament. If some of his complaints seem experimental, it is because he did not produce many examples using exactly the same combination of metre, theme and form: he shows himself capable of well-turned courtly verse, but does not (unlike some of his contemporaries) go on to produce a whole calendar of ballades of lamenting love. The nearest he came to producing sequences of poems is in works which themselves seem experimental, in structure if not in sentiment. Even more than the individual complaint, the idea of combining complaint with other forms or multiplying complaints or making a pattern or design from them seems to have stimulated Chaucer to composition. The exact artistic motivation varies considerably.

## 2. Compound Complaints

*The Complaint of Venus*, *The Complaint unto Pity* and *Fortune* are all indicative of Chaucer's interest in form and structure and show how lyric can be developed into a semi-drama.

*The Complaint of Venus* consists of three ballades with a final envoy paying tribute to Granson, whose *Cinq balades ensuivans* are the source. Chaucer has adapted the first, fourth and fifth *balades* and changed the speaker from man to woman. Oton de Granson seems to have specialised in complaints rather more than other fourteenth-century French poets;[13] apart from *balades* and other short forms which express complaint themes, he also wrote eleven *Complaintes*, some of which are elaborate and lengthy. The longest is *La Complainte de Saint Valentin* which has a narrative frame, the poet lamenting the death of his lady and consolation by Amor. *La Complainte de l'An nouvel* has a bored poet offering comfort to a grief-stricken knight overheard complaining in a wood, but it may have been composed a few years after *The Book of the Duchess* and be influenced by it rather than an influence upon it.[14] Granson first visited England in 1369 after attending the wedding of Lionel of Clarence in Milan and was in the service of Edward III and Richard II until 1387 when he returned to Savoy on the death of his father; he was in England also in 1392–6. Wimsatt has recently pointed to the fifteen French poems with the letters 'Ch' between rubric and text in the late fourteenth-century University of Pennsylvania MS French 15, as possible evidence of Chaucer's involvement in the fashionable modes of court verse and of association with Granson:[15] apart from over a hundred poems of de Machaut, the MS contains a substantial number of poems by Granson including the five *balades* adapted for *The Complaint of Venus*, which were originally headed 'Complaint'.

From the five French poems Chaucer makes a tauter pattern of three: praise of the beloved, the anxiety of jealousy, the vow of unending love. The element of complaint is concentrated in the middle poem with its summing up of the lover's life:

> As wake abedde, and fasten at the table,
> Wepinge to laughe, and singe in compleynyng,
> And doun to caste visage and lokyng,
> Often to chaunge hewe and contenaunce,
> Pleyne in slepyng, and dremen at the daunce,
> Al the revers of any glad felyng.   (27–32)

But the lover's fate of being 'ever in drede and sufferyng' exists in the outer poems of the triptych in the form of threats to joy. So whereas Granson in the first poem offers the good qualities of his lady as a comfort 'Quant je ne puis a ma dame parler' and when he has 'temps, loizir et espace/De longuement en sa valour penser', Chaucer's female speaker piles up the weighty qualities of her beloved—*manhod, worthynesse, trouthe, stidfastnesse, gentilesse*—as a consolation 'When that I am in any hevynesse/As for to have leyser of remembraunce'. The possible causes of 'hevynesse' and the implication of estrangement in 'remembraunce' echo in the mind, and, in the lines that follow, the apparent confidence of the poem is disturbingly undermined by touches of over-insistence and deprecation, such as

> And not withstondyng al his suffisaunce   (17)

or

> Ther oghte blame me no creature,
> For every wight preiseth his gentilesse.   (7–8)

This is conventional poetic idiom, true, but it always creates the negative

16

undertone that perhaps some *do* blame. The same note of obligation adds a gloss to the lady's reassurances at the close:

> I am set in verrey sikernesse.
> Thus oghte I blesse wel myn aventure,
> Sith that him list me serven and honoure;
> For every wight preiseth his gentilesse.   (21–4)

The reader is beginning to suspect the emotion from which the poem is ostensibly expressed.

The central poem about jealousy confirms the suspicion; love becomes, through the bitterness of jealousy, 'sorwe ynough, and litil of plesaunce' and the joy of love is brief:

> A lytel tyme his yift ys agreable,
> But ful encomberous is the usyng.   (41–2)

This passage in the minor key is robustly thrust back by a return to resolution in the third ballade:

> Sufficeth me to sen hym when I may;
> And therfore certes, to myn endyng day,
> To love hym best ne shal I never repente.   (54–6)

But still the note of melancholy sounds in the sense of protest quelled, dissatisfaction turned, yearning restrained:

> Herte, to the hit oghte ynough suffise
> That love so high a grace to the sente, . . .
> Seche no ferther, neythir wey ne wente,
> Sith I have suffisaunce unto my pay.   (65–6, 69–70)

It may be that the envoy, addressed to 'Princesse' in two manuscripts, to the ambiguous 'Prynces' in the other six, is associated with a particular occasion which might have provided a reason for making the speaker a woman, but it fits with Chaucer's frequent association of the anxieties of love, especially the anguish of possible or actual desertion and betrayal, with female vulnerability. Chaucer claims that old age and incapacity are the reasons for his changes to his source:

> For elde, that in my spirit dulleth me,
> Hath of endyting al the subtilte
> Wel nygh bereft out of my remembraunce;
> And eke to me it ys a gret penaunce,
> Syth rym in English hath such skarsete,
> To folowe word by word the curiosite
> Of Graunson, flour of hem that make in Fraunce.   (76–82)

Chaucer seldom acknowledges his source so directly, but, as elsewhere, his modest disclaimers divert attention from the fact that he has not translated

17

'word by word' and that he has created in *The Complaint of Venus* a more pleasing pattern of poems and the hint of a suppressed narrative; both are evidence of one aspect of Chaucer's 'subtilte of endyting' if not of the purely verbal kind. The adopted woman's voice for the ballades and the switch to the poet's professional request, apology and compliment in the envoy adds to the effect of a studied semi-dramatic lyric. One reason for Chaucer's composition of complex complaints may have been that he found the single complaint thin, but another could be a sense that the voice of the grieving lover suited him less well than that of the modest poet, who could look over the lover's shoulder.

Nevertheless in *The Complaint unto Pity*, probably at a much earlier period, he attempted something much closer to the French love-complaint in the first person and, if one judges by the full array of personifications, did it thoroughly. Clemen describes it as 'court etiquette and court ceremonial translated into the sphere of poetry',[16] but it is more interesting than that, even if only in that it may be Chaucer's first trying out of rhyme royal. The poem consists of two parts, a fantasy narrative or 'allegorical episode', as Norton-Smith calls it,[17] of the poet's finding Pity dead 'buried in an herte', and 'The Bill of Complaint' which he had intended to present to her. The keynote of the poem is the second line, 'With herte soore and ful of besy peyne', which is repeated as the final line. The beginning is striking: the word 'Pite' stands waiting for a syntactical function to fulfil, but all the rest of the stanza, and the second stanza, describes the unsuccessful seeking of the long-suffering lover; the linguistic structure imitates the situation, since Pity and the lover fail to make contact and before the word 'Pite' has been found a place in the sentence, the poet finds her dead.

> Pite, that I have sought so yore agoo,
> With herte soore, and ful of besy peyne,
> That in this world was never wight so woo
> Withoute deth,—and, yf I shal not feyne,
> My purpos was to Pite to compleyne
> Upon the crueltee and tirannye
> Of Love, that for my trouthe doth me dye—
> And when that I, be lengthe of certeyne yeres,
> Had evere in oon a tyme sought to speke,
> To Pitee ran I, al bespreynt with teres,
> To prayen hir on Cruelte me awreke,
> But er I myghte with any word outbreke,
> Or tellen any of my peynes smerte,
> I fond hir ded, and buried in an herte.   (1–14)

The first three and a half lines can be read as vocative, an interrupted apostrophe, an opening in resonant complainant's voice which breaks off for the poet to qualify it all with the gloss of his second thoughts: 'this *was* my purpose, but what's the point?' The poet is ready enough with the standard lover's diction of 'my peynes smerte' and so on, but the free-flowing sentence-structure, running over the ends of lines, and the shift to a more conversational note in 'yf I shal not feyne' make this artificial language sound spontaneous and natural. The allegorical experience is thus 'naturalised' and dramatised by the sense of the poet's using two voices and speaking of two levels or moments of feeling, the original invoking of Pity and the horror of the discovery that there is no Pity to listen to him. The language registers this horror through the idiom of elegy:

> Allas, that day! that ever hyt shulde falle!
> What maner man dar now hold up his hed?
> To whom shal any sorwful herte calle?   (23–5)

But again the poet draws back from this declamatory rhetoric of exclamation and question into explanation of his feelings:

> But yet encreseth me this wonder newe,
> That no wight woot that she is deed, but I.   (29–30)

Chaucer creates the effect of a man describing a dream, the language waxing into the experiencing of the vision and waning into registration of its oddness. Since the allegorical qualities are aspects of the beloved, ruthless woman, the picture of the company of virtues around the hearse of Pity has the very odd dream-like effect of symbolising a woman as a well-attended funeral. The poet returns to the earlier time of believing that Pity might respond in the Bill of Complaint itself. This is composed in nine stanzas with the rhyming of *tweyne/seyne* and *pleyne/peyne* in stanzas 3, 6 and 9 creating a sense of pattern.[18] The last three lines return to the theme of the dead Pity and so both complete the pattern of the Bill and step outside it to round the poem off in an echo of its beginning. In the Complaint Chaucer uses an obviously rhetorical manner only in the opening address:

> Humblest of herte, highest of reverence,
> Benygne flour, coroune of vertues alle,
> Sheweth unto youre rial excellence
> Youre servaunt, yf I durste me so calle,
> Hys mortal harm . . .   (57–61)

This has as much of the appropriateness of a letter as of a complaint: C. J. Nolan suggests that Chaucer has superimposed on the pattern of love-complaint (often consisting of sadness, remedies, appeal to lady, vow of unending love) the better-marked three-part structure of the legal bill: address, statement of grievance, prayer for remedy.[19] But it is more natural to recognise simply that Chaucer combines several complaint motifs together. The Bill is partly a social complaint against the way of modern love; the decline of the world is seen as resulting from a palace revolution in which Cruelty has ousted Pity, who now fails to support Truth and Beauty. The poet thus laments Pity's own decline:

> Allas, that your renoun sholde be so lowe!   (88)

But at the same time the lover complains of his own suffering and addresses Pity as suppliant to protectress:

> Let som strem of youre lyght on me be sene
> That love and drede yow . . .
> For Goddes love, have mercy on my peyne!   (94–5, 98)

Since we know that the recipient is deaf to his cries, the more pathetic aspect of the Complaint is coloured by the ironic knowledge that the poem can only end by reaffirming that it is proper to the lover's state to 'pleyne':

> Sith ye be ded—allas, that hyt is soo!—
> Thus for your deth I may wel wepe and pleyne
> With herte sore, and ful of besy peyne.   (117–19)

Chaucer is trying to make something out of the shift of focus in poems with included complaint and something different from the French pattern of complaint and comfort. Rather than the promise of consolation the narrative part of the poem has the effect of denying the possibility of redress. Chaucer thus increases the element of hopelessness in both aspects of the complaint, its criticism and its pleading. The death of Pity is continually envisaged as a prelude to the lover's own:

> My peyne is this, that what so I desire
> That have I not . . .
> What maner thing that may encrese my woo
> That have I redy, unsoght, everywhere;
> Me lakketh but my deth, and than my bere.   (99–100, 103–5)

But the ironic pattern created by the two-part structure of the poem conveys to the reader that it is the lover's fate not to die of love but perpetually to lament that he may do so.

The dramatic element created by an imagined situation and variation of voice is even clearer in *Fortune*, possibly composed in the 1380s. This, like *The Complaint of Venus*, consists of three ballades in three stanzas each, plus an envoy, but they are arranged as a *débat* for two speakers, the plaintiff and Fortune. The dramatic quality of the rhetoric is identified by the title in the manuscripts, *Balades de Visage sanz Peinture*. This has been variously interpreted, somewhat ingeniously, for example, by James Reeves as meaning an unpainted face and hence implying 'a contrast between the straightforwardness of the Plaintiff . . . and the deceitful face of Fortune'.[20] Kolve more plausibly glosses the phrase as 'songs that paint portraits' and compares other medieval instances of the process of poetic invention being construed as a visual conception of the subject, as in pictures of the poet writing with his subject standing beside him.[21] The primary meaning is that the poet recreates a mental picture of two opposing speakers. The subject-matter, however, suggests that the title may indicate also that the theme of the poem is, as Reeves reasons, that of appearances. The material of the debate may have had its starting-point in two *balades* by Deschamps in which *Franche-Volonté* defies Fortune and is then answered,[22] but the actual words of Chaucer's poem more often reflect Boethius, not so much in close rendering of a particular passage as in intelligent use of the terms of Boethius' discussion of the nature of Fortune. Chaucer creates the complaint against Fortune out of philosophical commonplaces but gives them some force by uniting two strands: the view of one who, like the aged Egeus, has known 'this wrecched worldes transmutacioun' and who registers Fortune's mutability, lack of order and dissimulation, is combined

with the resolution of the man governed by Reason, who is sufficient to himself
and has learned from Fortune's vicissitudes to defy her:

> Yit is me left the light of my resoun,
> To knowen frend fro fo in thy mirour.
> So muchel hath yit thy whirling up and doun
> Ytaught me for to knowen in an hour.   (9–12)

The force of character formed by cultivated resistance to Fortune's power to
disconcert is one of the reactions to disaster found admirable in medieval
times, despite its secular limitation; it is associated with Stoic fortitude and
Chaucer's borrowing of Socrates from *Le Roman de la Rose* as his instance of
'stidfast' immunity to the deceits of Fortune shows his association of this
resolve with the pagan past, an association which he explored more fully in his
classical narratives, particularly *The Knight's Tale*. The emphasis of this
secular wisdom, expressed not only by Boethius[23] but also by Seneca, turns
this first ballade into a challenge rather than a lament:

> My suffisaunce shal be my socour;
> For fynally, Fortune, I thee defye!   (15–16)

This is the 'complaint' of the law-court, the pleading of a grievance seen as a
case presented more than a loss regretted.

It is through the example of Socrates that Chaucer develops the allusion to
knowing 'frend fro fo' into the theme of the contrast between appearance and
truth. Fortune is traditionally a deceiver; Socrates' indifference to her favours
and her spites enabled him to see her true nature:

> Thou knew wel the deceit of hir colour,
> And that hir moste worshipe is to lye.
> I knowe hir eek a fals dissimulour.   (21–3)

This theme is central to the second ballade, Fortune's reply: she claims that it
is to her credit, not the resolute man's, that such clarity of understanding
exists:

> I have thee taught divisioun bitwene
> Frend of effect, and frend of countenaunce;
> Thee nedeth nat the galle of noon hyene,
> That cureth eyen derked for penaunce;
> Now seestow cleer, that were in ignoraunce.   (33–7)

That experience teaches one to know true friends lies behind the refrain 'And
eek thou hast thy beste frend alyve'; if this was a specific allusion (to a patron,
to John of Gaunt or Richard II, say) knowledge of the circumstance has been
lost. But it makes sense without the extra knowledge: the plaintiff has learned
to know a true friend and has one, still alive too—what better luck can a man
have? The references to friendship are threaded into the main arguments.
Fortune must fulfil her role in the 'regne of variaunce' in which man is born

and whose laws he must obey. The plaintiff is himself the creator of illusion since his grievance is in his own mind:

No man is wrecched, but himself it wene. (25)

In contrast to his picture of a steadfast man, clear-sighted in a deceitful and shifting world, Fortune creates her own version of man needlessly woeful, striving pointlessly, ungratefully and presumptuously against the conditions of a world which has given him knowledge and which may yet bring him favour. Again Chaucer has made his ballade out of commonplaces and the basic ideas can be found in Boethius, Book II, prose 2, but an infusion of allusions to other sections of Boethius, to *Le Roman de la Rose* and to bestiary lore creates an effect of density and concentration. As complaint in the first ballade was really challenge, so here the response is simultaneously defence and counter-attack. The poem could stop there but Chaucer pursues the argument further into the third phase of Boethius' treatment of Fortune,[24] going beyond the Stoic idea that self-sufficiency protected the wise man against external evil, to develop the deeper significance of Fortune as dependent on the deity: she is not all-powerful but merely an agent of the divine providence which foresaw all events. Chaucer presents these ideas as Fortune's reply in the third ballade which is divided between the two speakers. First the plaintiff angrily rejects Fortune's teaching that 'All's for the best in the most variable of worlds' by labelling as 'adversitee' what Fortune had associated with 'governaunce', 'haboundance' and 'plesaunce'. The second theme of friendship again figures in the argument as the plaintiff contrasts Fortune's blindness with the clear sight he has learned from her which enables him to know those 'friends' of Fortune who are interested only in money; they are fortune seekers and this means they are subservient to Fortune and will be attacked in their supposed security:

Tak hem agayn, lat hem go lye on presse!
The negardye in keping hir richesse
Prenostik is thou wolt hir tour assayle;
Wikke appetyt comth ay before syknesse. (52–5)

Fortune's response is not to counter this anger but to undermine it by reasserting her essential mutability as an inevitable condition of earthly life and then to undermine her own claim to power by revealing herself as a mere name given by ignorant men to the workings of divine providence; they make the image of the tyrant because they can't perceive divine motives.[25] Chaucer's absorption of scattered ideas relevant to Fortune is most strongly demonstrated here in the concise density of the last stanza of the third ballade:

Lo, th'execucion of the majestee
That al purveyeth of his rightwysnesse,
That same thing 'Fortune' clepen ye,
Ye blinde bestes, ful of lewednesse!
The hevene hath propretee of sikernesse,

> This world hath ever resteles travayle;
> Thy laste day is ende of myn intresse:
> In general, this reule may nat fayle.   (65–72)

This stanza is headed 'Le pleintif' in the manuscripts and, though editors have always emended this, J. Norton-Smith has argued for its retention as part of a case stressing the tension between acceptance of the Boethian answer and the poet's angry response to the prospect of social isolation.[26] The textual point seems eccentric since several lines make sense only in Fortune's mouth, but the tension is certainly there. The debate is not resolved in comfort or reassurance. Fortune contrasts the 'resteles travayle' of the world with the security which only heaven possesses and this is an appropriate way of halting the dispute, but between the bitter condemnation of men as 'blinde bestes' and the civilised strength of 'My suffisaunce shal be my socour' is a gap which the envoy does not attempt to fill. Fortune can still promise favour to the princes of the world and offer prosperity as a bribe to the plaintiff to persuade him to cease 'on me thus [to] crye and pleyne'; the Christian ethic that all suffering is part of a just divine purpose should breed patience in tribulation but the point is succinctly made, not didactically stressed, and Chaucer retains the dramatic illusion in the envoy of two unreconciled opponents presenting their view to a worldly audience who may hear with cynicism.

These three complaint poems, *The Complaint of Venus*, *The Complaint unto Pity* and *Fortune*, not often ranked high among Chaucer's works, seem to me to show Chaucer working very purposefully, at different stages of his career, to make something new out of derivative or conventional material by exploring the possibilities of a composite form. In all three there are elements of an imagined situation, and the poet assumes various voices, of a dutiful but obscurely troubled woman, of an anguished lover dramatising his suffering through an allegorical charade and of man and Fortune in self-justifying debate. The different ways of exploiting the fact that complaint is a rhetorical performance add an interesting edge to the poems. Complaints in a series can explore a succession of aspects of a theme or several emotional stages; a plot structure emerges from a developed argument or the development of feeling. The framed complaint attempts to create a complex literary experience out of two facets of the subject. In these three instances one can identify both ideas and techniques which Chaucer made use of again in longer works; *Fortune* in particular is a rehearsal of the arguments and the debate strategies which were developed between Troilus and Pandarus. But, for the moment, I want to remain with structural notions and to examine what happens when complaint is combined with narrative.

CHAPTER THREE

# Dual Forms

## 1. *Anelida and Arcite*

If one approaches *Anelida and Arcite* as an incomplete work, then its dual form of narrative and complaint may be thought accidental. If Chaucer had completed the poem, the 'Compleynt of Anelida the Quene upon fals Arcite', which appears by itself in some manuscripts, might perhaps be an episode at the beginning of an English courtly *dit*. Wimsatt suggests that the completed poem was going to follow the complaint and comfort pattern of de Machaut and that it was likely to have been twice its present length.[1] Cherniss puts forward the less obvious idea that it was going to be a dream-poem with a description of the Temple of Mars followed by the appearance of Mars to Anelida in a vision.[2] Norton-Smith, on the other hand, argues that the poem is complete (and the last stanza, which, following C. S. Lewis's comment on *The Complaint of Mars*, he describes as 'nonentity yawning in 70 syllables', spurious); he sees it as a transitional work, written after *Troilus and Criseyde* and showing Chaucer on the way to writing *The Legend of Good Women* in its combination of classical material, tragic heroine and epistolary complaint.[3] All three are reacting to Clemen's critical view of the poem as falling apart as a result of the disharmony between the epic narrative style of the beginning and the rigid French formalism of the lyric section.[4] Otherwise Clemen reflects the traditional opinion that the best that can be said for it is that it is notable for the metrical virtuosity of the complaint, but he goes a little further in claiming some creation of character and feeling in the complaint. The striking mixture of artificial expression and simple, natural phrasing creates an ebb and flow of mood designed to move the reader; in the narrative too the enrichment of Chaucer's diction through the influence of Boccaccio adds to the impression that Chaucer is seeking 'new modes of expression' to produce a work which contains isolated impressive lines and passages, even if the effect of the whole is of the failure to unify the promise of great and stirring deeds with the sensitive expression of rather small passions.

The poem, as it survives, is a larger, more elaborate version of the pattern Chaucer used in *The Complaint unto Pity*, a poem in two halves, not quite equal, one narrative, the other a formal complaint. The material of *Anelida and*

*Arcite* is not allegorical though, but a mixture of grandiose classical matter (an invocation followed by narrative concerning Theseus, in the epic manner stimulated by Boccaccio's *Il Teseida* and supplied by Statius' *Thebaid*) and a story of courtly love and betrayal in the manner of the French *dits*. Wimsatt suggests two possible sources in de Machaut, the *balade* 'Je suis aussi com cils qui est ravis', in which a male narrator speaks in a state of dazed suffering, and the *chant royal* 'Amis, je t'ay tant amé et cheri', spoken by a lady whose hard-hearted lover prompts a desperate lament.[5] The actual complaint of Anelida may draw on the letter of Dido to Aeneas in Ovid's *Heroides* as well as the already mentioned French *dits* of complaint and comfort, with their inset complaints in 16-line stanzas.

The grounds for regarding the poem as an experiment in which Chaucer is seeking a 'new mode of expression' are thus not just the fact that it may be incomplete, but, first, the evidence that Chaucer was creating a composite poem from various sources, secondly the element of virtuosity in the elaborate metrical and stanzaic design of the Complaint and thirdly the puzzling questions set for the reader. Why set up such an elaborate and weighty mythological and epic machinery for a love-complaint? Why Anelida instead of a known heroine, and why 'fals Arcite' when the character of Arcita in the *Teseida* is identified with passionate commitment to love for a woman and is himself subjected to the vagaries of Fortune to a degree which could justify (and did elsewhere) a passionate complaint from him?

It looks as if *Anelida and Arcite* began from interest in classical historical material for its own sake and an ambition towards poetic grandeur. From the idea in the *Teseida* of Arcita as a rival in love, who spent part of the poem in disguise under an assumed name, Chaucer could have developed the idea of an unstable lover and then linked him with the motif of the betrayed heroine from Ovid. Though looking to the pomp and rhetoric appropriate to ancient matter, he prefers to invent a history for his heroine, picking up a mellifluous, melancholy name, perhaps from an Italian source,[6] and placing her against a background which is full of historical names, places and actions and yet also generalised into imprecision. Chaucer goes to some trouble to claim that the story is of genuine historical circumstance, both in declaring his intention

> in Englyssh to endyte
> This olde storie, in Latyn which I fynde . . .
> . . . nygh devoured out of oure memorie.  (9–10, 14)

and in invoking the aid of Polyhymnia on the grounds that

> thou . . .
> Singest with vois memorial in the shade,
> Under the laurer which that may not fade.  (15, 18–9)

Chaucer's identification of the function of the poet as the upholder of memory, and of poetry as the evergreen resilience which outlives the toothless chewings of time, *edax rerum*, is interestingly enough expressed for the reader to accept the instance of 'Quene Anelida and fals Arcite' as a symbol of a tale of old, whether it is historical or invented. Similarly, the invocation in the opening stanza of Mars and Bellona invites interest in the poet's possible purposes in honouring Mars within his 'grisly temple ful of drede' so that when Chaucer identifies his intention to write 'With pitous hert' the conjunction welds together war and sorrow as his themes. Though Clemen may, in literal terms, have some justification for his view that the first three stanzas 'are full of promises that are not kept and statements that are not true',[7] in terms of the oblique effects of poetry he is talking nonsense: Chaucer's intention to express an old story as a song of the sorrows of war is as clear as daylight.

In the narrative proper, intention is clearer too than commentators have often suggested. Chaucer intends to approach his story by the 'slye wey' (48), or 'the crooked corridor' as Henry James would later call it. He is creating perspective by apparently unrelated or merely circumstantial events. The nature of the perspective is unambiguous. Theseus' conquest of Scythia is presented as a triumph of Mars and the stanzas are scattered with images which have the quality of a 'token of glorie', people cheering, trumpets blaring, knights in their freshness, helmets in their brightness, laurel, gold, beauty. Then comes the conflict between Thebes and Greece, another work of Mars leading to the tyranny of Creon, during which Anelida, Queen of Armenia, is dwelling in Thebes to be loved and betrayed. Here Mars is seen as instigator of fiery restlessness to kill and as destroyer of people and cities:

> So desolat stod Thebes and so bare,
> That no wight coude remedie of his care.   (62–3)

Chaucer now moves to the supposedly private story of love, but the contrast of Mars in triumph and destruction is obviously a parallel to the course of the love story. Anelida is to be a likeness of the triumphant and of the desolate city; at first shining brighter than the sun, 'this lady bright' is chilled and desolated, so that

> Other colour then asshen hath she noon.   (173)

The relationship of man to woman is also seen in terms of conquest; Arcite is characterised largely through his being a knight and having the gifts of the skilful, deceitful campaigner in war. He

> Was yong, and therwithal a lusty knyght,
> But he was double in love and no thing pleyn,
> And subtil in that craft over any wyght,
> And with his konnyng wan this lady bryght.   (86–9)

Then, too, although Chaucer turns away from the epic material of Theseus' conquests in order to develop his moral, sentimental tale of woman's complete devotion, subjection and suffering, juxtaposed with man's perversity and disloyalty, the rest of the Theban story is implicit in the material. If one assumes that Chaucer's 'real' intention was to invent an English equivalent to *Il Teseida*, an epic adventure on a grand scale, then he lays himself open to criticism for shifting the scale of his treatment: why deal briefly with military triumphs and with fighting only to labour the details of an unsuccessful love

26

affair? But why should one assume that *Anelida and Arcite* is a botched shot at writing *The Knight's Tale*? The treatment of the epic matter is subordinated to the story of the Queen and merely provides setting and imagery for it. Chaucer may or may not have assumed that his audience knew the rest of the story of the *Thebaid* but he could not prevent those who did know it realising that Creon was to be attacked and defeated by Theseus and that Anelida's story is thus suspended between one bloody conflict and another. The society of which Anelida is temporarily a part is suggestively described as that of 'the olde Creon' who

> held the cite by his tyrannye,
> And dyde the gentils of that regioun
> To ben his frendes, and dwellen in the toun.
> So, what for love of him, and what for awe,
> The noble folk were to the toun idrawe.   (66–70)

So the nobles are gathered around a tyrant, threatened by the passage of years, the uncertainty of the tyrant's role, the instability of the balance of love and fear. Even if one does not read in expectation of Theseus' conquest, it is hinted that Anelida's story waits for the inevitable end of the city's present state; if one reads with knowledge then to the disbanding of the society one may add the prospect of the capture of Arcite and his eventual death, unless *that* Arcite is rigorously kept to a separate existence in the mind.

From the premonitory context of the story Chaucer passes swiftly through the initial situation of Anelida's physical and moral beauty and Arcite's conquest of her to the lengthy contemplation of the nature of Anelida's love (lines 92–140). There is no direct narration of particular events in the course of the courtship or of the affair. Chaucer conceives the story as description of a state of being and of contrasting moralities rather than as a sequence of incidents. Hence actions are treated as illustrations of typical behaviour, habitual action rather than specific, what a character would do or even would not do as much as what he or she did. The effect is to generalise the relationship into an antithesis between two moral natures, one sincere, innocent, generous, the other deceitful and mean-spirited; the contrast is painful in exposing the vulnerability of a love that gives itself so completely to the will of another. Chaucer emphasises this complete yielding several times: we are told that 'al was his that she hath', 'al that lyked hym hit dyde her ese', 'al his wil her thoghte hit skilful thing' and these are supported by other superlative expressions, such as

> Ther nas no lak with which he myghte her wite   (110)

which, like the undercurrents in *The Complaint of Venus*, is eloquently suggestive of unease within perfection. The focus is mainly on Anelida and much of Chaucer's poetic energy goes into the framing of lines which memorably capture her passionate sincerity:

> So ferforth upon trouthe is her entente,
> That wher he gooth, her herte with him wente.   (132–3)

27

At moments Chaucer reaches towards a lyric concentration on the expression of love as a state of mind:

> When she shal ete, on him is so her thoght,
> That wel unnethe of mete tok she kep;
> And when that she was to her reste broght,
> On him she thoghte alwey til that she slep.  (134–7)

But the movement towards an ecstatic absorption in love as a pure ideal of shared being is always held in check by our knowledge of the falsity of Arcite. The woman gives up her own will even before she is required to:

> Withoute bode his heste she obeyde.  (119)

But the man yields nothing and even usurps emotions beyond his will in order to add pain to conquest:

> Withoute love, he feyned jelousye.  (126)

The idea of love is thus heightened as an ideal not only by the threat of the doomed city but also in the sense of wasted sweetness. The repeated designation of Anelida as queen adds to this the motif of noble generosity from high to low; simultaneously present is an echo of Queen Dido's generous, misused love for Aeneas and of some ballad of a fine lady and a lowly suitor. Chaucer creates this latter effect by repetition of the phrase 'Anelida the quene' in various conjunctions with 'fals Arcite' as in the summing up of this section of the poem:

> Thus lyveth feire Anelida the quene
> For fals Arcite, that dide her al this tene.  (139–40)

After four further stanzas (141–68) the lines recur with the significant change of the verb, as Chaucer describes

> the helle
> That suffreth fair Anelida the quene
> For fals Arcite, that dide her al this tene.  (166–8)

This suggestion of refrain and the effect of dividing up the poem into portions consisting of several stanzas increases the reader's sense that whatever kind of poetry Chaucer thought he was composing it was not simple narrative unfolding of story. Very few incidents, consisting only of the bare outline of a sentimental history of war, love, betrayal, are the framework for moral contrast and patterned action associated with intense feeling. The treatment of man's duplicity is rather clumsy, with the image for Arcite's falsehood the most effective touch:

> Ryght as an hors, that can both bite and pleyne.  (157)[8]

28

More effective are the stanzas that complete the narrative section where Chaucer sharpens the antithesis between Anelida's vulnerability and Arcite's cynicism by creating a picture of frenzied hysteria opposite a callousness hardened by the constraint of his new lady. Chaucer has been criticised for the 'exaggerated sentimentality' and high melodrama[9] of

> She wepith, waileth, swowneth pitously;
> To grounde ded she falleth as a ston;
> Craumpyssheth her lymes crokedly;
> She speketh as her wit were al agon.   (169–72)

But that extreme note seems as necessary to the strain of intense sincerity, to show the breaking up of ordered behaviour when truth is cruelly abused, as is the contrasting note of wordly wisdom to the identification of the perversity in Arcite's behaviour:

> That for her liste him 'dere herte' calle,
> And was so meke, therfore he loved her lyte.
> The kynde of mannes herte is to delyte
> In thing that straunge is, also God me save!   (199–202)

Just as the poem began with the contrary facets of the influence of Mars, triumph and bloodshed, so both in the course of this doomed love and in the distinction between woman's truth and man's falsehood the principle of composition is that of antithesis. Quality is defined by opposition and the poet can veer from one side to the other. So he completes his 'narrative' by turning the tale of Anelida and Arcite into an example by which women may take warning, a warning which, if heeded, would turn love into a matter of resistance and constraint hardly preferable in the abstract to the matter of yielding and abuse which has been displayed in the poem; the relevance of Mars to a story of love is clear enough.

The Complaint of Anelida is the best evidence of Chaucer's command of courtly idiom and lyric delicacy. The antithetical view of the narrative is left behind and the single view, anguished, plaintive, bitter and desolate by turns, takes over. The poetry is formal both in the sense that Chaucer chooses, at least for the opening and its echo at the close, an idiom which is literary, and in the sense that the stanzaic and metrical patterning of the work contributes much to its effect. An opening and concluding stanza of nine lines, using only two rhymes, frame two sets of six stanzas, in each of which four 9-line stanzas similar to the first and last are followed by a 16-line stanza on two rhymes and a 9-line stanza with internal rhyme in each line; the 16-line, 'de Machaut' stanza rhymes aaab aaab bbba bbba, and the effect of the four quatrains of tail-rhyme is augmented by a shift from octosyllables in the first three lines of each quatrain to a decasyllabic fourth. To describe this patterning as 'rigid French formalism', as Clemen does, betrays a lack of ear. As in 'An ABC' Chaucer skilfully employs a combination of patterned expression and a dramatic lyric style which is impulsive and vivid. The courtly language establishes a sense of ceremony and significance in Anelida's acting out a rite of sorrow: complaint of this kind is a spoken aria or *scena* where feeling is intensified by a sense of order and rhythmic patterning. At the same time the poet creates a sense of change and development within the complaint, whereby feeling intensifies and relaxes, threatening at moments to break through the verse pattern, but returning to its discipline.

Chaucer begins Anelida's introductory stanza with a striking image from Dante: it is with the point of memory that the heart is pierced by sorrow's sword. This is linked with two other themes, the change from sureness to fear and Anelida's embittering realisation that 'hit availeth not for to ben trewe', to form a condensed opening statement of motifs to be expanded in what follows. In the first of the two sets of six stanzas which Robinson calls 'Strophe', Anelida's thought begins with the love that was, moves to the falsehood and lack of pity that now exists, determines to complain to and to plead with no other but the source of her sorrow and turns to direct questioning and reproach of the treacherous lover. So each of the first four stanzas is a stage in the movement from self-communing, where Arcite is 'he' and Anelida complains of him, to vocative address, where Arcite is 'ye' and she complains to him. It would be easy to point out, as commentators often have, that many of the things Anelida says are paralleled in other love-complaints and to suggest that therefore the expression is 'conventional', but Chaucer weaves simple, idiomatic expression in with the ceremonial striking of attitudes. So if, on the one hand, the rhetoric of complaint as a public performance takes over when Anelida seeks the right response:

> And shal I pleyne—alas! the harde stounde—
> Unto my foo that yaf myn herte a wounde,
> And yet desireth that myn harm be more?  (238–40)

on the other, Chaucer conveys her experience in natural language:

> [I] called him myn hertes lif, my knyght,
> And was al his, as fer as hit was ryght;
> And when that he was glad, then was I blithe . . .  (223–5)

Chaucer uses such variation of register to create a sense of a varying pulse of feeling in the complaint, as Clemen points out. Anelida's sufferings are characterised as partly from a sense of injured decorum; the wrongness of Arcite's behaviour is an offence against an accepted public standard based upon the values of courtesy and civilised consideration and Chaucer uses the standard poetic mode of the 'ubi sunt' question with nouns of courtly resonance to express this:

> Alas! wher is become your gentilesse,
> Youre wordes ful of plesaunce and humblesse,
> Youre observaunces in so low manere,
> And your awayting and your besynesse
> Upon me . . . ?  (247–51)

But the suffering is also a direct, private matter and so, in the shorter lines of the 16-line stanza, the reproach is more direct, the words mostly simpler, the rhymes more insistent, the syntax more extempore:

> But for I shewed yow, Arcite,
> Al that men wolde to me write,
> And was so besy yow to delyte—
> Myn honor save—meke, kynde and fre,
> Therfor ye put on me this wite.
> Alas! ye rekke not a myte.  (264–9)

The sixth stanza of the group becomes a patterned variation on the themes established; question, reproof and appeal to return are expressed with a fluttering anxiety created by the splitting up of the lines by rhyme and the staccato quality of the many monosyllables.

> My swete foo, why do ye so, for shame?
> And thenke ye that forthered be your name
> To love a newe, and ben untrewe? Nay!  (272–4)

Thus the variations in metrical form seem to be part of the emotional quality of the piece, not merely an external decoration.

In the second set of six stanzas, Robinson's Antistrophe, Chaucer takes the variations in Anelida's mood between sorrowful love and resentment further apart; the effect is of a gradually increasing dramatic passion. So the first stanza envisages the two extremes for Anelida, possession or death. The second is a bitterly passionate expression of sorrow and accusation, the language suddenly violent:

> Myself I mordre with my privy thoght.  (291)

and swift-moving:

> I wepe, I wake, I faste; al helpeth noght;
> I weyve joye that is to speke of oght,
> I voyde companye, I fle gladnesse.  (293–5)

The third rejects pleading with resentful recognition of its usefulness, and moves into the bitter scorn and disillusion of the fourth, which forms the emotional and thematic climax of the complaint:

> For thogh I hadde yow tomorwe ageyn,
> I myghte as wel holde Aperill fro reyn,
> As holde yow, to make yow be stidfast.
> Almyghty God, of trouthe sovereyn,
> Wher is the trouthe of man? who hath hit slayn?
> Who that hem loveth, she shal hem fynde as fast
> As in a tempest is a roten mast.  (308–14)

31

From the first Anelida had been identified with 'trouthe':

> For, as of trouthe, is ther noon her lyche,
> Of al the women in this worlde riche.   (76–7)

One whose steadfastness surpasses that of Penelope and Lucrece has earned the right to be spokeswoman for all her sex; through her Chaucer expresses the theme that interested him in *The Legend of Good Women* and in the tale of Griselda and elsewhere, the lonely pain of woman's constant virtue in a world dominated by unstable men. By creating a substantial set piece he allows Anelida to pursue her realisation of the unfairness of things as far as scornful, dismissive anger. 'Wher is the trouthe of man?' is a question that takes her wounded grief beyond the courtly complaint of love's sufferings and it is here that Chaucer suggests some philosophical dimension to the complaint, given resonance by the epic imagery of the beginning of the narrative. In the two more elaborately patterned stanzas Chaucer again, as in the first set, turns to an effect with less weight, but greater personal intimacy. Anelida retracts her anger into bewildered loss and sorrow, fearing that she has gone too far but excusing herself because 'my wit is al awaye'; the stability and meaning of her world has gone, as the placing of Anelida's society at the start hinted that it would be, and all she is left with is dreams in which she sees Arcite, clad in faithful blue, offering again to be true. This vivid, affective image gives a touching pathos to the patterned variation of the sixth stanza, where Anelida sketches a self-portrait in days of sorrow and hopelessness. In the concluding stanza, which completes the framing of the complaint by returning to the piercing point of memory in the last line, Chaucer borrows from Ovid's Dido the image of the sorrowing heroine as dying swan, lamenting that security will never return. In these closing stanzas Chaucer expresses a degree of bleak hopelessness that is deeply enough felt for one to recall the context of the narrative and its mythological and historical images. One looks for the sense in which this love and betrayal is, like the other events, a work of Mars, since the expressions of conquest, treachery, outrage, violence, anger, madness and death accumulate to give a universal scope to the story of betrayed feelings. The one stanza that promises continuation of the story is, pace Norton-Smith, intelligently relevant to the direction of the thought in the rest of the poem; Anelida is to sacrifice to Mars within the temple and to pray, possibly for revenge in the shape of Theseus' destruction of Creon's regime. Anelida's lament is an equivalent to the grief of the mourning widows in *Il Teseida* and *The Knight's Tale*; like them Anelida laments a kind of impiety and though her story is one of private passion rather than public action and duty, there is a sense running through *Anelida and Arcite* that the betrayal of woman's honour is treachery to traditional *mores*.

Whether Chaucer ceased working on the poem because the direction in which it was leading—suicidal bitterness and possibly vengeful warfare—was threatening to disturb the scope of his moral intentions can only be a surmise. It could be that he thought the poem as it stands said all that needed to be said and that the conjunction of his antithetical moral narrative and his bravura monologue of pain and sorrow satisfied him. The Complaint concentrates on poetic plangency and a sensitive combination of patterned verse and delicate expression of feeling, while the narrative enriches and enlarges the material of a courtly *dit* with historical symbolism and with moral analysis. Narrative and lyric are interestingly united not just as situation and emotion but also with a sense of different time-scales. The span of history is the natural material of narrative and the exploration of the experience of the moment that of lyric; Chaucer partly exploits that interplay here, though it is a more significant juxtaposition in some other works in which narrative and lyric are used together, but his narrative points as much to the quality of different experience, female and male, as to the passage of time or a particular sequence of actions and events. The combination has not seemed satisfactory to many readers, who have found the parts out of harmony, or the experience incomplete. The work has been undervalued, in my view. The joining of narrative and lyric is original and exploratory. Chaucer the poet has interests here, stronger than those that appear elsewhere, both in the power of poetic form to express feeling and to create a disciplined framework for it and in the possibilities of classical pagan material to give dimension to a theme of courtly sentiment and sense of dishonour. Purely as a technical experiment *Anelida and Arcite* has considerable interest. It extends the range of the simple and compound complaints by its joining rhetorical expression of passion with historical material. It is not clear where the work belongs in the chronological order of Chaucer's compositions, but it is tempting to think that this might have been a first attempt to bridge the gap between the emotional mannered rhetoric of the love-complaint and the tougher debating material of the complaint on social and philosophical themes. Whether or not this is so, it makes an interesting contrast with Chaucer's other conjunction of complaint and classical material, *The Complaint of Mars*.

## 2. *The Complaint of Mars*

Like *Anelida and Arcite* and *The Complaint unto Pity*, *The Complaint of Mars* divides into two unequal halves, one narrative (the longer part here) and the other complaint; the shift from one to the other is marked by change from rhyme royal to 9-line stanzas rhyming aab aab bcc. Both halves may be further divided, the complaint into an introductory stanza and five sets of three stanzas, and the narrative into a St Valentine's Day prologue supposedly sung by a bird and overheard by the poet and a combination of mythological story and planetary movement concerning the love affair of Venus and Mars and the interruption by Phoebus, the light of day; the bird-narrator's is the voice used for this too, though Chaucer allows it to be forgotten once the narrative begins. Though similar to the other two poems in creating a kind of diptych effect— the complaint completes the poem without a return to the classical narrative or the courtly bird, and the manuscripts divide the poem in two—*The Complaint of Mars* can also be seen as a sequence of episodes, with something of the medley quality of *The House of Fame* or *The Parlement of Foules*, or as a Prologue plus series (of 3-stanza ballades) like *The Legend of Good Women*. The poem's variousness conveys a sense that here too the poet was seeking new modes of expression. He makes a new combination of narrative and lyric, using an opening aubade to the birds and flowers to lead in to the narrative. He combines a mythological story from Ovid with medieval interest in stellar motions and French courtly love motifs. Unlike the complaints and more like the dream-poems, *The Complaint of Mars* has an element of comedy, together with a degree of philosophical seriousness in the complaint sequence which has reminded readers of Boethius and has even led to its being described as 'a miniature *Troilus*'.[10] Its range of effects is thus wider than that of *Anelida and Arcite* and so it has seemed more characteristically Chaucerian and more appealing as a poem; it is though, despite its completeness, a less consistent one.

The metrical shift into longer stanzas shows that Chaucer was still thinking of the complaint as a distinctive entity, rather than as something to be integrated into the narrative, as complaints are in *The Knight's Tale* and *Troilus and Criseyde*. But there is no suggestion that the complaint marks a stage in a moral or ethical demonstration, as it might have done in a French *dit* of complaint and comfort and as it could have done in a retelling of the Mars and Venus episode from *Metamorphoses*, had Chaucer chosen to follow the didacticism of the *Ovide moralisé*.[11] Instead it is the culmination of the work. Nor is complaint here, as in *Anelida and Arcite*, used for its emotional and dramatic possibilities, but rather for its argumentative and reflective ones. The difference is partly between Chaucer's conception of womanly complaint and a more robust and analytical manly version, but even when closest in thought to Anelida's complaint, there is greater detachment here. This is no ceremony of bitter sorrow, but a stating of a case. This is made clear by the much abused introductory stanza (quoted in Chapter One), in which the process of complaining is presented to the reader as something with its own rules. The 'pedantically fulsome and verbose'[12] lines do not seem to me intended to characterise Mars (as a bluff war-god unused to rhetorical elegance) but to emphasise the legalistic aspect of what is to come. Mars complains

> not for to have redresse,
> But to declare my ground of hevynesse. (162–3)

Even to say that compensation is *not* what is being sought sets the tribunal atmosphere. With such an introduction, it is not surprising that the qualities of what follows are not plangency and intensity but argument and irony.

The irony comes mainly from the conjunction of the subtle, probing stanzas of the complaint and the stately comedy of the heavenly liaison. But Chaucer prepares the irony right from the start with the enigmatic expression of the story as a St Valentine's Day celebration by one of Nature's choristers. Chaucer's talking birds, the Eagle in *The House of Fame*, the whole parliament in *The Parliament of Fowls*, the betrayed falcon in *The Squire's Tale*, Chantecleer and Pertelote, the crow in *The Manciple's Tale*, are apt to be argumentative or opinionated or self-dramatising; representing aspects both of divine knowledge and of human nature in simplified, emblematic form, they have to be exaggerated into their species, since their place in the hierarchy of birds and their particular observance of the law of kind has become an equivalent for a strain of behaviour. But birds collectively can simply represent the mating instinct, the spirit of spring and natural sexual energy, or they can be the means of expression of the harmony of the earthly paradise and so on. So at the end of *The Parliament of Fowls* birds are without individual identity as they join together to sing their roundel 'Now, welcom somer with thy sonne softe'. Chaucer's main source for the association of birds and such poetic effect was *Le Roman de la Rose*, where in the early parts of the poem the birds signal the joy of the season and celebrate divine service with paradisal sweetness. The association was reinforced by the use of birdsong in de Machaut's and in Froissart's *dits* (and by other French bird-debates, bird-masses, bird-messengers and so on).[13] The association with St Valentine was shared with Granson, though it is difficult to know which way round the influence was.[14] In *The Complaint of Mars* Chaucer uses an individual but unspecified bird-speaker, thus joining the general sense of birds' representation of the law of kind with suggestion both of court entertainer and of divine messenger. An exhortation to birds and flowers to rejoice in the day fulfils one role, the contrary warning to human lovers to flee the light the other. The bird's conjunction of opposite natures is then used cryptically to juxtapose the advice to all birds to choose their mates, renew their service and swear loyalty and patience, with the announcement of the subject of the celebratory song—a story of discovery, fear and separation to celebrate a feast of continuity and joining. The idea seems to be of a kind of anti-masque, a possibly cynical comment on what is in any case inevitable. By means of the bird-voice the poet may simultaneously sing to courtiers about love, like the nightingale outside Criseyde's window, and be privy to the secrets of the gods and the movements of the planets, like the Eagle in *The House of Fame*. The bird is an image of the poet as tutelary spirit, and its combination of the innocent and knowing, the natural and the artful provides a useful point of balanced detachment.

With the story itself the irony is created by the relationship of gods and planets and Chaucer's skilful dovetailing of a sense of the predestined movement of the heavenly bodies with the impression of the spontaneous acts and words of their human counterparts. Chaucer rejects the grotesque comedy of Ovid's picture of Venus and Mars caught in the act and providing laughter for the gods, and his version is, in part, a sophisticated account of a noble love:

> Who regneth now in blysse but Venus,
> That hath thys worthy knyght in governaunce?
> Who syngeth now but Mars, that serveth thus
> The faire Venus, causer of plesaunce? (43–6)

But behind the knight and his lady loom the large shadows of their planetary identities; the discreet arrangements for their meeting throw courtly etiquette onto the large screen of the heavens with mountingly comic effect, as when we are invited to imagine Venus frantically scuttling along her orbit to meet Mars, hanging about in 'hir nexte palays'. Nevertheless the poetry remains confidently, even indulgently, sympathetic to the actions described and to the figures of the gods; the comic irony is present merely in the sense that we are contemplating it all:

> And thus in joy and blysse I lete hem dwelle,
> This worthi Mars, that is of knyghthod welle,
> The flour of feyrnesse lappeth in his armes,
> And Venus kysseth Mars, the god of armes. (74–7)

The discovery, the arming of Mars, the flight of Venus and her reception by Mercury are narrated with a tongue-in-cheek seriousness which leaves the reader to appreciate the comedy of the gods in panic and to perceive that the gods themselves are at the mercy of forces beyond them. They become victims of circumstance and bewildered plaintiffs against the arbitrariness of destiny. Love written in the stars is merely human confusion writ large enough for everyone to see—so much for the 'influences of thise hevenes hye'. Their own experience of ennobling love becomes a visible sign of love's transitoriness.[15] The conjunction of comedy and seriousness and the actual course of events (the knight's forced acceptance of the lady's departure and her reception by another as 'his frend ful dere' and the knight's being left to lament) express in condensed form the material of *Troilus and Criseyde*, as several commentators have pointed out. Mars is interpreted through medieval ideas of knighthood and chivalry and Troilus' heroic, masculine aspects are expressed partly through association with Mars. Arcite in *The Knight's Tale* is a third treatment of the same linking. The Complaint in *The Complaint of Mars* has the function of expressing the theme of the bereft knight who, like Troilus and Arcite, is set by a Christian author in a pagan system of thought. The results in all three cases show Chaucer stretching his imagination to do justice to the idea of the aggrieved hero and his questioning of the purposes of life and yet to retain a sense of limitation. In *The Complaint of Mars*, because the narrative is much briefer, there is less opportunity to complicate the reader's understanding and the chosen form focusses on the complaint as the climax of the work, but, despite the brevity, Chaucer has managed to create something of complexity in that the actions of Venus and Mars are seen as comically disillusioning (even Venus is subject to the embarrassments of her own passions) and yet, because they represent a unique conjunction of planetary movements, to be taken seriously as a fulfilment of destiny. As Clemen points out, the apparent paradox illustrates the relationship between choice and compulsion, or, in Boethian terms, between free will and determinism.[16]

The complexity of perspective is mirrored in the Complaint sequence by Chaucer's exploitation of both the courtly and the philosophical possibilities of the genre; the five sections modulate from urbanity to seriousness and back again. So Mars begins with praise of the lady in de Machaut style,[17] and recognition of her power to reject the lover who then 'may not longe in joye of love endure' and who can only cry 'Who may me helpe? Who may my harm redresse?' He moves on to a questioning of God's purposes in making men subject to the transitory and misleading power of love, which echoes the same passage in Boethius (Bk I, met. 5) used by Chaucer for Arcite in *The Knight's Tale*. Then he returns to the knights and ladies, lovers among an audience of fellow-sufferers who must all complain. Similarly, Chaucer focusses on the characters of Mars and Venus at the beginning, where the power of the sovereign lady as 'such on that may me knette/ To wele or wo' is alluded to within the knowledge that Mars' lady is the very power of love itself. The courtly hyperbole becomes ironically true:

> This is no feyned mater that I telle;
> My lady is the verrey sours and welle
> Of beaute, lust, fredom and gentilnesse,
> Or riche aray.  (173–6)

From the dozens of ladies of whom poets have said such things, here is the one lady for whom it may honestly be claimed. Even more explicitly, at the end

Mars identifies the knights in the audience as 'of my devisioun' and claims their sympathy and allegiance, then calls on the ladies to partake in the desolation of 'youre emperise/ Negh ded for drede'. So all human nature is subsumed in the pairing of Mars and Venus, knight and lady and 'ye lovers' to whom the whole poem is addressed. Between the opening and the close, however, the focus shifts from the particular (if inclusive) case to general points of argument and principle. So in the second ballade the speaker moves from desperate questioning to rueful recognition that it is the lover's chief virtue, fidelity, that makes him vulnerable to sorrow. This prepares the way for the theoretical probing and metaphysical intellectualism of the third and fourth sections. These, together with the polished urbanity of the last, are among Chaucer's most mature, elegant pieces of writing showing the same control of tone, idiom and verse movement as that other sophisticated piece of ironic comment, the Envoy to *The Clerk's Tale*.

At first the voice, no longer explicitly that of Mars, questions and observes, dispassionately yet insistently:

> To what fyn made the God that sit so hye
> Benethen him love other companye?
> And streyneth folk to love, malgre her hed?
> And then her joy, for oght I can espye,
> Ne lasteth not the twynkelyng of an ye,
> And somme han never joy til they be ded.
> What meneth this? What is this mysthihed?
> Wherto constreyneth he his folk so faste
> Thing to desyre, but hit shulde laste?   (218–26)

The skilful variation in the length of the syntactical groups here creates a satisfying interplay between the verse-patterns and rhythms of natural speech; the rhetorical liveliness that results draws one in to the speculative mood. Having engaged one's attention the speaker argues more closely in what follows:

> And though he made a lover love a thing,
> And maketh hit seme stedfast and during,
> Yet putteth he in hyt such mysaventure
> That reste nys ther non in his yeving.
> And that is wonder, that so juste a kyng
> Doth such hardnesse to his creature.
> Thus, whether love breke or elles dure,
> Algates he that hath with love to done
> Hath ofter wo then changed ys the mone.   (227–35)

Here the syntactical units tend to be longer, more often occupying the whole line or two lines, in comparison to the first stanza's mixture of lines and half-lines. The rhetoric has moved from question to assertion, the connectives from *what, and then, what, wherto* to *though, yet, that, thus*. The balance between what God compels and its unreliability runs through both stanzas, but the tentative qualifications (*malgre her hed, for oghte I can espye*) and plaintive questions through which the disparity is identified, are replaced by positive condemnatory words (*mysaventure, hardnesse*). The effect is of a toughening of the stance, a more purposeful engagement with the issue and a bleaker view of love and life. This middle stanza puts all the weight of its nine lines into making a point, and a point which moves beyond the range of love-complaint into complaint of the conditions of being. The third stanza maintains the posture but returns to a lighter quality of expression, with more pauses, through imagery and a consequently more mixed diction:

> Hit semeth he hath to lovers enmyte,
> And lyk a fissher, as men alday may se,
> Baiteth hys angle-hok with som plesaunce,
> Til many a fissh ys wod til that he be
> Sesed therwith; and then at erst hath he
> Al his desir, and therwith al myschaunce;
> And thogh the lyne breke, he hath penaunce;
> For with the hok he wounded is so sore
> That he his wages hath for evermore.   (236–44)

The combination in the image of the relationship of love and the lured lover and that of God and his bewildered creatures broadens the range of reference; the image stands for the general condition of man lured by desire into mischance and left to pay for his folly. But Chaucer holds back the moral weight of the thought by leaving it all as speculation: 'Hit semeth' and 'may se' allow it to be read as a case being put forward, hypothetical rather than assertive, allowing the reader freedom to limit its application to the immediate circle of reference if he chooses. The passage skilfully raises questions about the justice of having endowed human beings with moral responsibility and suffering but Chaucer makes it possible to return to the sphere of love-complaint by allowing detachment to exist alongside response. From the beginning of the Complaint Chaucer left open the possibility of judging it ironically. The narrating bird's injunction 'paciently taketh your aventure' is not accepted by one who complains:

> I yaf my trewe servise and my thoght
> For evermore—how dere I have it boght!   (167–8)

The superlative praise and vow of devotion of lines 174–90 are violently reversed in the impatient questions and regrets of the second movement:

> Alas! that ever lovers mote endure,
> For love, so many a perilous aventure!   (198–9)

So Chaucer has entered a reservation which makes his exploration of the state of mind of Mars, as with his equally adventurous explorations of others who question providence, Troilus, Arcite and Palamon, Dorigen and so on, a conditional one, controlled perhaps by a medieval Christian view of the pagan past or simply by an intelligent artistic tentativeness about material outside the range of experience, material which is as much fantasy as history.

A similar balancing act is performed in the fourth ballade, the only place, I think, where Chaucer, for a moment, might be taken for Donne. In two stanzas the unlucky brooch of Thebes and the effect of its beauty is set as a case before the mind, culminating in the argument that it is not in the object but in the artificer, and, to a lesser extent, in the deluded coveter, that the cause of disaster lay. This argument offers a vivid symbol of the deluding power of beauty and the analogy between a jewel and a beautiful woman is a chilling exemplum of the idea of human beings as toys in the hands of the gods. I think that is the way it works the first time one reads it: if one considers the maker and the desire the ones to blame, then by analogy the lover's misfortune is caused not by the lady's beauty but by her creator and by the lover's own folly, as the third stanza states:

> She was not cause of myn adversite,
> But he that wroghte her, also mot I the,
> That putte such a beaute in her face,
> That made me coveyten and purchace
> Myn oune deth; him wite I that I dye,
> And myn unwit, that ever I clamb so hye.  (266–71)

But there is more to it than that. In this section, by means of the allusion to Thebes, Chaucer begins to turn back from general argument to the pagan past. He has made his brooch of Thebes by transforming Statius' description of the necklace which Vulcan made as a poisonous gift for Harmonia, the daughter of Mars and Venus, at her marriage to Cadmus.[18] Chaucer transfers the maker's responsibility from Vulcan, the vengeful cuckold, who made the jewel, to the Creator of the lady and allows the classical allusion to remind the reader only of the doomed history of Thebes, but even so the idea of the artificer as cause of subsequent evil cannot be quite the same once one recognises this source. The argument begins to look like a specious allusion to the idea of Aristotelian causes (specious because only part of the system of causation is referred to).[19] Chaucer is using intellectual ingenuity to create a kind of conceit which has to satisfy logic only long enough for the comparison to be made. The classical allusion leaves lurking the sinister suggestion of vengeful malice in God's treatment of man, but the touch of word-play in the last two lines ('him wite I that I dye/ And myn unwit . . .') again leaves the serious meaning not pinned down but allowed to float off in a witty turn.

The end of the poem continues the return to the voice of Mars and the reference to Venus suggested at the end of the 'brooch of Thebes' passage, and enlarges the touches of urbane wit. When Mars himself is so humbled, the knights in his audience should take warning and join him in complaint. When Venus herself can not manage her affairs, the ladies too should weep. The tone has returned to that of direct social address, elegantly tongue-in-cheek, with touches of humour in the exaggerations and reservations and in word-play in the punning on the two senses of *emperise*, 'empress' and 'courage' in lines 285–9. Finally all lovers are addressed, as they were in the warning of the coming of dawn at the beginning: all must complain.

> Compleyneth her that evere hath had yow dere;
> Compleyneth beaute, fredom, and manere;
> Compleyneth her that endeth your labour;
> Compleyneth thilke ensample of al honour,
> That never dide but al gentilesse.  (293–7)

39

To complain has become the natural human lot. The comic discomfiture of Mars and Venus has put all lovers to flight as the light of day is shone upon their dealings. Complaint has exposed the power of love to tame and to shame and to cause bitter sorrow—wounds which it is only just possible for witty urbanity to plaster.

*The Complaint of Mars* is thus a work which demonstrates Chaucer's flexibility in creating poetry out of a medley of matter and ideas. Not only a combination of narrative and complaint, but also bringing in elements of dream fantasy, classical myth and allegory, the poem describes an arc from lightness to seriousness and back again to urbane assurance. It is a more sophisticated, more artfully self-protective piece than *Anelida and Arcite* but it shows the working out of a similar interest in material of mixed origin and a similar impulse to extend complaint from an expression of love's suffering to a protest against the injustices of the mutable scheme of things.


### 3. *The Squire's Tale*

Like *Anelida and Arcite*, *The Squire's Tale* breaks off with a flourish of classical gods, leaving only a promise of an unknown story. Like *Anelida and Arcite* again, what does exist falls into two sections, the first a narrative of distant courts and adventure, the second mainly a lament of woman's betrayal by unfaithful man; true, *The Squire's Tale* presents this latter episode as narrative with dramatic speeches, not as formal lyric, but the story is similar, except that the betrayed female is not a foreign queen but a different kind of exotic, a distressed falcon confessing to a Tartar princess. Reactions to the tale have stretched from Spenser's and Milton's wish that Chaucer had completed it to the impatience of some modern readers with its Oriental magic, its talking bird and its narrator's apologies for the inadequacy of his skill to narrate the wonders of his tale;[20] gratitude that it is no longer, even to the extent of taking it as a parody of romance broken off like *Sir Thopas*, has focussed particularly on the promise at the end of Part II of what is to come:

> How that this faucon gat hire love agayn
> Repentant, as the stori telleth us,
> By mediacion of Cambalus . . . .   (*CT*, V, 654–6)

Even less to the taste of some is the promise of a return to 'aventures' and 'batailles':

> wol I telle yow of Cambyuskan
> That in his tyme many a citee wan;
> And after wol I speke of Algarsif,
> How that he wan Theodora to his wif,
> For whom ful ofte in greet peril he was,
> Ne hadde he ben holpen by the steede of bras;
> And after wol I speke of Cambalo,
> That faught in lystes with the bretheren two
> For Canacee er that he myghte hire wynne.   (*CT*, V, 661–9)

The threat, as it seems to some, of a vast series of episodes running to thousands of lines has seemed enough to justify a reading of the tale as a joke against the incompetence of the youthful, amateur story-teller; it has become almost orthodox to assume that the Franklin's compliment to the Squire is a deliberate interruption, bringing the tale to a stop, though the lines could just as well be taken as intended to go at the end of the tale, when written (and in the Hengwrt MS the lines are given to the Merchant anyway). With *Sir Thopas* and *The Monk's Tale* Chaucer makes the interruption clear; by comparison *The Squire's Tale* appears simply not to go on. Its incompleteness seems rather to belong with that of *Anelida and Arcite* and *The House of Fame*. Charles Larson suggests that all three belong to a period of experiment in the 1380s and that Chaucer realised that their combination of elaborateness and pointlessness represented an artistic dead end.[21] All three have found modern commentators who have suggested that they are in some sense complete, even if unfinished. So Jennifer R. Goodman argues that *The Squire's Tale* is a new and unfinished romance intended as 'a mirror of a young man's mind', a young man who like his tale is 'to be continued'; Chaucer, in her view, thus expands the generic variety of *The Canterbury Tales* without unbalancing the whole work by completing a lengthy romance—merely a sample of 'a young man's imaginary world' is enough.[22] It is interesting that the early fifteenth-century manuscript of *The Canterbury Tales* MS Lansdowne 851 contains an attempt to plug the gap:

> Bot I wil here nowe maake a knotte,
> To the time it com next to my lotte . . .

This intelligent idea that a long tale could be told in instalments might have been a possibility contemplated by Chaucer at the stage when he was envisaging four tales for each pilgrim. Since he presumably changed his mind and decided to end his sequence at Canterbury instead of back at Southwark, perhaps the incentive to complete his long serial tale went.

So the tale leaves the problem to the reader of how it should be judged, as a deliberately broken-off fragment, as work in progress, as an instalment, or even as what might have been. The tale pleases me and the thought of another 10,000 lines or so about magic horse, mirror and sword is a good deal more alluring than some parts of the tales that did get written; I think Spenser and Milton got it right. Chaucer has provided enough information for it to be clear what kind of whole tale he had in mind, whether or not he ever seriously meant to write it. The Oriental setting, the mixed nature of what was completed and the summary of the rest identify the type of romance which modern literary historians have dubbed 'Composites of Courtly Romance'.[23] These late fourteenth-century and fifteenth-century works use segments of earlier romances as building-blocks, attempt to rival French prose romances in multiple plot-lines, cater for an interest in marvels and the sensational, pay attention to the niceties of court life and show a fondness for exotic, especially Oriental settings. The main examples, *Sir Degrevant, Generides, Partonope of Blois, Eger and Grime, Ipomadon, Valentine and Orson, The Squire of Low Degree, Clariodus,* display a variety of aspects which are of interest for *The Squire's Tale*. Nearly all of them show a liking for the picturesque qualities and the trappings of courtliness and weave together several plots, either by having two heroes as in *Generides, Eger and Grime* and *Valentine and Orson*, or by a lengthy sequence of episodes and phases. The majority have magic objects, such as the magic brass

41

head and magic horse in *Valentine and Orson*, or fairy elements in the plot. Most are set in foreign lands, Oriental in *Generides*, France and Byzantium in *Partonope*, Italy in *Ipomadon*. At least two, *Partonope* and *Ipomadon*, show sophistication in the narrative method comparable to the self-consciousness Chaucer uses in *The Squire's Tale*. In terms of material and setting *Generides* affords the most interesting comparison, with settings in India, Persia, Syria and Thrace, two intertwined stories for heroic father and son, and many conventional motifs—prophetic dreams, a spying steward, disguise as a leper, a wicked queen, a fairy princess and so on. In terms of method and manner the tail-rhyme *Ipomadon* is a suggestive analogue, with interest in courtly breeding and gallantry and a tendency to analyse emotions and conflicts in soliloquy and complaint.

Other late medieval examples of sophisticated, manufactured romance thus enable the reader to place *The Squire's Tale*; at least some aspects of the material and manner of the work result from Chaucer's setting his hand to a known type of compositeness as part of his seeking narrative variety within *The Canterbury Tales*. Other less surely identifiable features confirm the composite nature of the work. The combination of human and animal characters suggests the memory of dream-poems, debates and mixed allegories, as well as being another possible area of Oriental influence. And the combination of narrative and complaint in Chaucer's own work is recalled by the two-part nature of what exists—a selective, rather mannered narrative of public events followed by a second part which turns to dramatic speech with a strong lyric element and stress on private feeling.

In the narrative there are several striking features: on the one hand, the presentation of a rich, elaborate court scene, which seems purely in the spirit of aristocratic romance, and the magic motifs which are to form the starting-point for adventures, but, on the other, frequent use of *occupatio*, with its implications of detachment from a full rendering of scene and event, and other touches of distancing and self-consciousness about the audience's readiness to accept the material of the tale.[24] The shifting from the first kind of writing to the second comes to form a recognisable pattern which it is interesting to examine.

Just as the narrative in *Anelida and Arcite* begins with the triumph of Theseus and Mars, so *The Squire's Tale* begins with the great conquering king of a distant land. The opening section is a flourish of praising words for Cambuskan: *hardy, wise, riche, pitous, just, sooth, benigne, honourable, stable, yong, fressh, strong, desirous in armes, fair, fortunat*. He is presented as a model both of king and of man, combining the qualities of the young warrior and of the mature governor. To pass from this, through a rich cluster of proper names, to the beauty of Canacee seems a natural continuation of the picture of an ideal aristocratic world. So the first example of the narrator's withdrawal from finding the words to convey is very much in tune with the familiar technique of enhancing an ideal by means of the describer's modesty.

> But for to telle yow al hir beautee,
> It lyth nat in my tonge, n'yn my konnyng;
> I dar nat undertake so heigh a thyng.
> Myn English eek is insufficient.
> It moste been a rethor excellent,

That koude his colours longynge for that art,
If he sholde hire discryven every part.
I am noon swich, I moste speke as I kan.   (34–41)

This combines indirect commendation of Canacee's beauty with an exagger-
atedly humble stress on its unavailability; this heroine will have to stay on the
top shelf only dimly seen in outline. The identification of the description of the
heroine as a literary set piece which the poet is not going to embark on calls up,
in passing, memories of stock responses to artful catalogues of colour and
shape, but snatches them away. The placing of the subject as 'so heigh a thyng'
identifies 'low' style as a matter of inadequacy rather than appropriateness to
humble subject matter; the metaphor of levels, here between the high level of
the matter and the low level of the expression, recurs later.

Chaucer repeats the effect of the opening section (ll. 9–27) in the lines that
follow (42–75), first by enhancing directly (formality and ceremony, astrology,
scene-setting in spring, Cambuskan in full rig in his palace) and then by
withdrawing:

> his feeste . . .
> . . . in this world ne was ther noon it lyche;
> Of which if I shal tellen al th'array,
> Thanne wolde it occupie a someres day;
> And eek it needeth nat for to devyse
> At every cours the ordre of hire servyse.
> I wol nat tellen of hir strange sewes,
> Ne of hir swannes . . .
> I wol nat taryen yow, for it is pryme,
> And for it is no fruyt, but los of tyme.   (61–8, 73–4)

Here there is a suggestion of bulk, weight, richness of material, measured in
the imagined passing of a whole long day in its telling; at the same time the
poet conveys the otherness of the world and consequently the disparity
between the values which the teller attributes to the fictional world and to his
audience. *Now*, in the audience's present time, there is consciousness of
passing minutes, of worthy ways of using time, of the pressures of life, but *then*
it mattered that things were properly done, ceremonious and adequate; 'it is no
fruyt' has its irony since the passage is about food—what was fruit then in both
senses is now profitless detail. Within the device of *occupatio* there is a con-
cealed complaint of the ways of the modern world. Chaucer's use of the
rhetorical strategy seems to me very sophisticated: it asks for our interest and
yet allows us to limit it, assess it, recognise its ironies.

In the second phase of the narrative (76–188) more attention is given to the
material, but the self-consciousness is still present in concern with style and
decorum. The details of the particular events—the arrival of the stranger on
horseback, the magic gifts—are quite quickly covered, but more space is given
to the courtesy of the strange knight and emphasis on his stylistic polish
naturally leads to the exclusion of the narrator from the knight's level of skill:

> He with a manly voys seith his message,
> After the forme used in his langage,
> Withouten vice of silable or of lettre;

And, for his tale sholde seme the bettre,
Accordant to his wordes was his cheere,
As techeth art of speche hem that it leere.
Al be it that I kan nat sowne his stile,
Ne kan nat clymben over so heigh a style,
Yet seye I this, as to commune entente
Thus muche amounteth al that evere he mente . . .    (99–108)

The pun *stile/style* gives a self-conscious humour to the distinction, again one of levels of skill; only the purport can be conveyed by a narrator (it is implied) who can only creep along the ground. The stress on rhetorical skill, the art of speech and Arthurian courtesy functions in the manner of Mandeville's accounts of civilised distant courts and instances of reverence, reason and delicacy in alien peoples; beneath the apparent naivete is a touch of satirical intent, since these literary fantasies show to the audience how things ought to be and the fulfilment of ideas to which, perhaps, only lip-service is paid in practice.

The knight's speech (110–67) falls into four divisions each describing the properties of one magic gift and the handing over of the gifts completes the set-piece of the initial idea of the tale. The material here takes precedence, interesting in itself and the basis of the episodes to follow, and Chaucer concentrates on explanation with no flourishes of style or fussiness of manner. But in the third phase (189–262) there is as much attention given to the audience's possible view of the matter as to the matter itself. The sheer space devoted to the idea of the crowd's comments on the marvels makes it a major passage in this first part. The horse comes first and sets the pattern for the rest: it could not be amended by nature or art and it towers above the crowd 'for it so heigh was'—the difference of level is now pictured literally so that one visualises a pigmy mob judging 'diversely' and buzzing like a swarm of bees; even 'thise olde poetries' merely enable them to make 'skiles after hir fantasies'. The moral judgment is clear enough:

Of sondry doutes thus they jangle and trete,
As lewed peple demeth comunly
Of thynges that been maad moore subtilly
Than they kan in hir lewednesse comprehende.    (220–3)

The effect of this whole passage is curious. In my view the reader tends to identify with the narrator's voice, not with the 'lewed' folk; by appealing to intellectual snobbery Chaucer has managed to make the audience accept his marvels; we can understand things made with subtlety even if they can not. This complicates the idea of two levels, that of the wonderful matter and that of the prosaic narrator, of which the reader has so far been made aware. Now one has to recognise a yet lower level of sensibility represented by the crowd's inability to imagine things beyond experience, beyond literal fact and already known instances. This requires us to qualify our sense of the story-teller; despite his limitations the narrator's view is one that extends as far as appreciating subtlety even if he lacks the words to convey it. The narrating voice has now turned against the limitations of an ordinary level of appreciation of which he had seemed to be the spokesman.

The details and instances used in the passage act as images which explore several aspects of the marvels. The threat of the inexplicable is expressed both through the Trojan horse and the idea of mere illusion:

> An apparence ymaad by som magyk,
> As jogelours pleyen at thise feestes grete. (218–19)

The possibility of historical precedent at one end of the scale of rationality and conjuring tricks at the other add to the threats (of war, of treachery) already envisaged by the powers of the magic gifts; as with the prospect of the doom of Thebes in *Anelida and Arcite*, Chaucer sets up uncertainty as one of the conditions for romance and feeling. At the same time wonder and rarity are extended by the seeking of parallels and the multiplication of instances, memories and myths; references to Moses and Solomon as magicians and to classical precedents elevate the magic while apparently trying to place it. There is a similar, but more ironic effect, produced by the seeking of scientific explanations: these folk are not all that 'lewed', since they have an idea of optics and 'speken of Alocen and Vitulon,/ And Aristotle' who are authorities on 'queynte mirours and of perspectives'; these are the educated doubters who can not accept the marvellous and inexplicable, intellectual literalists rather than ignorant fools. So there are even different levels of 'janglyng' and speculation:

> As soore wondren somme on cause of thonder,
> On ebbe, on flood, on gossomer, and on myst,
> And alle thyng, til that the cause is wyst. (258–60)

By the end of the passage the effect is that the importance of the marvels has been increased and the reader has in some sense accepted them. With great richness of imagination Chaucer has used the apparent debunking of magic to attach it to experience.

Thus when the reader comes upon what is perhaps the most curious passage in *The Squire's Tale*, which I see, as does David Lawton,[25] as a key passage in the work, the mixture of elements is one for which the rest of the tale has prepared: first the elevation provided by the astrological references, placing Cambuskan's passage to his audience chamber in the context of heavenly movements, and making the courtly dance, observed apparently by Venus, comparable to them, and then the gap between the quality of life and the inadequacy of the narrator's wits:

> This noble kyng is set upon his trone.
> This strange knyght is fet to hym ful soone,
> And on the daunce he gooth with Canacee.
> Heere is the revel and the jolitee
> That is nat able a dul man to devyse.
> He moste han knowen love and his servyse,
> And been a feestlych man as fressh as May,
> That sholde yow devysen swich array.
> Who koude telle yow the forme of daunces
> So unkouthe, and so fresshe contenaunces,

Swich subtil lookyng and dissymulynges
For drede of jalouse mennes aperceyvynges?
No man but Launcelot, and he is deed.   (275–87)

This is the most striking instance of Chaucer's use of a voice which is specifically 'not Squire', since 'a dul man' who has not known 'love's service' and is not 'a feestlych man as fressh as May' is most explicitly contrary to just those features which Chaucer offers as characterising his youthful pilgim. This voice has nothing to do with a 'dramatic' method of telling the tales of Canterbury, but belongs to the 'material-derived' aspect of narration in the work, necessary to Chaucer's idea of the balance of elements within the tale. The reasons for inadequacy are twofold: the lack of the right experience (so the courtly delight of the scene is beyond his range of knowledge) and lack of fine discrimination (so 'swich subtil lookyng and dissymulynges' are beyond his notation). Just as earlier Gawain was a standard of excellence by which courtly speech could be judged, so now Lancelot is needed as an adequate measure of courtly delight; the evocation of the old world of romance heroes asks the audience to go beyond its practicality and the knowledge of nowadays, but at the same time the narrator's inability to be a part of that world turns it into a distant dance of phantoms and shadows of the imagination, ghostly dancers in a sophisticated court who leave just a fleeting image of the strange knight and Canacee dancing amid courtiers exchanging subtle glances, beginning a love story which the poem does not manage to express. This is another moment of magic in a passage ostensibly excluding the reader from the magic and the moment. This is a characteristic piece of Chaucerian suggestion. To argue that such passages of *occupatio* are clumsy, or intended to expose the inadequacies of the narrator misses the knowing, nostalgic quality of the composition; it is just in these passages that Chaucer's late fourteenth-century subtlety and self-awareness are expressed. David Lawton makes an illuminating comparison with Ariosto,[26] which is another way of bringing out the mixed quality of the writing, allusive, patchy, arbitrary and yet richly evocative, a quirky kind of narrative not fully engaged with its material and yet poignant, vivid, suggestive. It is a kind of answer to the problems visible in *Anelida and Arcite* and *The Complaint of Mars*, where the narratives are equally odd in their different ways, displaying a mixture of voices and contrary directions. Looking further afield in Chaucer's writings one can see that running through his compositions is an interest in affective narrative—imagined, historical or distant circumstances within which the poetic interest is in the discovery of feeling.

Part II of the tale shifts its ground to an individual episode and is therefore selecting from possible elements, one magic object from four and one main figure. For this purpose Chaucer finds the strange means of a touch of allegory; the personification of sleep provides a new technique for turning figures into puppets or distant images. The narrator continues the effect by imagining his figures dreaming, singling out Canacee as one who is 'ful mesurable' and had chosen her own behaviour of retiring early to dream not wild, drink-induced fantasies but a vision stimulated by the magic mirror; her own taste, her pleasure, her moderation, her imaginative response to magic lead her to rise and stir her household companions. This is a modified, feminine version of the beginning of a romance quest; the personal impulse, the distinguishing virtue, the desire to put magic to the test, the ordering of the lives of subordinates, the going forth in the early morning, the description of the morning mist and the birdsong, all announce to the reader a scene or episode of courtly narrative. The narrator points the 'announcing' function of the passage explicitly with one of his insistent, ponderous comments which with exaggerated frankness displays the workings of the narrative machine; with this completion of the introductory material the tale passes from general to particular, from birdsong to a bird's lament.

The falcon is first presented as an image of violent sorrow, self-destructive and vocal, combined with beauty and delicacy: a lamenting bleeding falcon in a white tree, piercing herself like the pelican, stirring even the pity of a tiger, seems part of a tableau of Kynde and her creatures. Canacee takes her place as a 'faire kynges doghter' in a stance of pity, spreading her lap wide. Her speech offering aid is full of courtly association: references to the causes of 'wo', to the 'gentil herte', grace, help and compassion; the adverbs *verraily*, *pitously*, *wisly*, *hastily* summarise the ethics and convey the tone. The note of feminine chivalry sounded earlier continues in the heroine's immediate response to evident sorrow, the display of the right impulses of the errant, virtuous noble. But that it is a bird she encounters takes us into the world of dream-poem, fable or lyric (such as the overheard lament of 'Revertere'); the level of discourse has changed from that of the romance quest pure and simple to the literal/allegorical mixture, variously used by Chaucer also in *The Nun's Priest's Tale* and in *The Manciple's Tale*, where moral exemplum seems to be the mode identified by the means, but where resistance is set up by the tone. Here Chaucer seems both to take his fable seriously and to let the reader see the elements of absurdity through exaggeration. The shrieks and swoons announce an episode of sentimental melodrama and the first of the bird's speeches has the effect of a didactic prologue, promising an example by which others may be warned. But it also quite seriously emphasises the 'gentil' qualities of Canacee, the 'pitee' which is, as Chaucer so often notes, readily stirred in the 'gentil herte', and the

> verray wommanly benignytee
> That Nature in youre principles hath set.  (486–7)

So Chaucer identifies the teller's purpose as growing out of the listener's readiness to respond—a suggestive conjunction communicating not only the quality of sensibility in the poetry, 'feelynge his similitude in peynes smerte', but also the idea of the mutual dependence of poet and audience, as complaint is evoked by pity.

The bird's longer speech (499–620) begins as a narrative of youth and love, but once the meeting with the one who 'semed welle of alle gentillesse' is accomplished, the bird-fiction and the narrative manner give way to human terms and the rhetoric of vituperation and complaint, as male hypocrisy is made the theme of a demonstrative contrast between trusting faith and cynical pretence. Again seriousness and touches of detached awareness seem both to be present. On the one hand familiar complaint motifs are expressed with some bite: emphasis on the antithesis between outward *trouthe*, *plesance*, *peyne*, and concealed *treson*, *falsnesse* is sharpened by images of false-dyed colour, of serpent beneath flowers, of handsome tomb concealing corpse. On the other the hint of burlesque in the picture of the feigning lover on his knees is absorbed into the self-aware irony of describing him as 'this god of love' and the scorn in the portrayal of this illusion of joyful courtesy:

> His manere was an hevene for to see
> Til any womman, were she never so wys,
> So peynted he and kembde at point-devys
> As wel his wordes as his contenaunce.   (558–61)

The echo of *Troilus and Criseyde*, II, 637 (Troilus riding from battle seen by Criseyde) gives an ironic twist since this lover seems thereby a false semblance of the 'trewe knight Troilus'. The vivid delineation of a lover putting on an act develops the tale's distinction of different levels of behaviour; here it is the imitation of a pattern of ideal conduct instead of the earlier contrast between distant ideal being and the everyday inability to describe or to have time to appreciate it. It is, in a way, Chaucer's most powerful presentation of a philandering lover, a brilliant picture of arrogant cruelty opposed to self-effacing gentility. The piling up of elaborate words connected with the etiquette of love—*cerymonyes, obeisances, observaunces*, 'That sownen into gentillesse of love'—give a satirical flavour to the complaint, echoing various passages elsewhere in Chaucer, the attack on Jason in *The Legend of Good Women*, the picture of Fortune's deceptions in *The Book of the Duchess*, the Eagle's promises in *The House of Fame*.

Burlesque and suggestions of mock-heroic are more clearly indicated by the animal comparisons ('this tigre, ful of doublenesse') and the citing of Jason explicitly, and of Paris and Lamech; both require the reader to have forgotten the identity of the speaker or else to recognise the comic bombast. Literary tone and references are similarly ambiguous, as in:

> Ne koude man . . .
> Countrefet the sophymes of his art,
> Ne were worthy unbokelen his galoche,
> Ther doublenesse or feynyng sholde aproche . . .   (553–6)

The use of John the Baptist's words about Christ in 555 was perhaps less striking then than it seems now, but the disparity between instances is uneasy. Chaucer seems to be protecting his matter with touches of self-parody from the audience's possible resistance, while calling on our sympathetic response. The height of direct lyrical expression of lost love is reached in 562–73 as the falcon describes her complete submission:

> . . . my wyl was his willes instrument, . . .
> Ne nevere hadde I thyng so lief, ne levere,
> As hym, God woot! ne nevere shal namo.   (568, 572–3)

This leads into the intense grief of parting and the speaker's bitterness at the betrayal of sincere feeling which followed. In the behaviour of the lamenting falcon, however absurd the instance and the rivalry of a passing kite, is combined the experience of grief as sharp as the pains of death, and the ability of good breeding to make 'vertu of necessitee' and to accept, as Dorigen must in *The Franklin's Tale*, that love must give way to honour. The bitterness of recognition is expressed by particularly pointed use of the balanced expression of the heroic couplet:

> What he answerde, it nedeth noght reherce;
> Who kan say bet than he, who kan do werse?
> Whan he hath al wel seyd, thanne hath he doon.    (599–601)

The world-weary recognition of the inevitability of man's desire for novelty in which the speech ends picks up a proverbial turn of expression from earlier; love-complaint broadens into moral generalisation ('Men loven of propre kynde newefangelnesse') and Chaucer returns to the bird level by means of his illustrative example of reversion to nature, the pampered cage-bird leaving behind the elegances of nurture for the worm of instinct.

The total effect of the bird's speech is mixed: at times dramatic, intense and poignant in expression with some forceful condemnation of faithlessness, the speech is also sententious and expository, asking the reader to see the account as illustrative case rather than shared experience. The elements of complaint are present but Chaucer, though covering very similar ground to that of *Anelida and Arcite*, does not here concentrate on bravura rhetoric or metrical variation or effects of plangency. The quality is less poetically demonstrative of passion and resentment, but Chaucer conveys the impression of a report of experience, a penetrating and yet ironic portrait, since the disparity between human and animal worlds means that personal sorrow is viewed from a worldly distance. Canacee's care for the bird by placing her in a pen by her bed covered in blue velvet gives us another emblematic picture, an image of fidelity set within a frieze of painted birds representing falsehood. So there is another odd conjunction of the supposed real bird symbolising woman and the painting of birds from bestiary lore presenting a cartoon commentary on treachery and reproach; the painting emphasises the sense of outer and inner meanings, the falcon is bird without but human feeling within, the heart in 'mewe'.

The suspension of this story until a later stage and the turning to more conventional romance matter are the main points of emphasis in Chaucer's summary of what is to come. The story one might expect is that of the love of Canacee and the strange knight from the court of the King of 'Arab and of Inde'; their dancing together at the feast seems an appropriate starting point for romance. But Canacee is caught in the results of Chaucer's compositeness; the natural heroine is displaced into the role of confidante by the introduction of an episode centred on complaint in the de Machaut tradition—the bird representing noble fineness and self-destructive sorrow. Canacee becomes observer and consoler, while the bird takes over the lamenting heroine's role of pitiable innocence. Chaucer's leaving behind of self-aware comments by the narrating voice after lines 401–8 represents a significant change of style in the second part of the tale; commitment to rendering confession and complaint in direct speech changes the balance. Had Canacee's womanly quest to use her magic gift to reconcile love and honour achieved completion, then Chaucer perhaps could have been seen to have worked together the material of lyrical *dit* and of romance; as it is, the episode is left dangling between stools. So too, of course, is *The Squire's Tale* itself, an experiment, perhaps, in variegated narrative which got no further than the dual impulse already visible in Chaucer's earlier narratives with complaints.


## 4. Duality

So, although the two-part structure of *The Squire's Tale* may be, as with *Anelida and Arcite*, an accidental product of its incompleteness, the conjunction is suggestive of Chaucer's sense of the two faces of romance and of other dualities through which these may be expressed—the opposition of Mars and Venus, Fortune's opposite gifts of triumph and disaster, the contrary nature of masculine and feminine senses of virtue and so on. The three works discussed here combine narrative and complaint in a way which has them pulling against one another. The poet sets up a current of history, a movement of the heavens, a stirring set of circumstances and objects but all they lead to is a monologue of regret and frustration. They all three contain suggestions that things can not stop there, but, for whatever reason, they do. Taken together they express a strain in Chaucer's thinking that connects martial triumph, pomp, circumstance, and the outward observance of courtly forms with distress and dismay. At some stages in his writing this was as far as he could take it. One mood answered another and he could not find the way, or he ran out of the wish, to resolve the tension he had created. In *Anelida and Arcite* there is a suggestion that he found the idea of intense emotion between periods of war interesting, as if the time between disasters is a kind of suspension in which suffering is distilled. The same situation obtains in *Troilus and Criseyde* and the sense of a doomed Troy adds poignancy and irony to the treatment of happiness and sorrow; the fact that all is temporary is inevitably present in the mind. In *The Complaint of Mars* the pre-ordained movements of the planets create a comic impression of the actors in the drama unwillingly on the move; as Mars settles to complain, already Venus is half gone from the range of his vision, and he too can lament only in a suspension of inevitable time and motion. The falcon's lament in *The Squire's Tale* occurs in another suspension, that of the normal relationship of human and animal worlds; magic creates an experience stolen from the usual current of being and this betrayed grief too is left hanging in the air with a mere promise that in time all may be resolved.

In other places Chaucer found ways, if not of resolving the problem of human suffering, at least of not leaving oppositions quite so obviously to be resolved later. But the traces of the patterns of thought visible in these three narratives with complaint may be seen, even if transformed, in several other works besides *The Knight's Tale* and *Troilus and Criseyde*, both of which I intend to examine in later chapters.

One striking dual pattern Chaucer made use of elsewhere is that of tale plus prologue or epilogue within *The Canterbury Tales*. Obviously this can apply only when the prologue or epilogue is substantial enough to be more than a functional lead-in to the story or more than a transition from one tale to the next. Also the effect of duality created by a tale's having some link with a preceding or following passage is clearly different from the occurrence of such structures in isolation, since in *The Canterbury Tales* Chaucer was overlapping several devices of linking and cross-reference and the perspective created by a prologue or epilogue sometimes has more relevance to a wider context of morality, theme or character than to the particular tale to which it is attached. This is the case with the reaction of the Host to the tale of Melibee which functions as an epilogue, though occurring in the *Prologue* to *The Monk's Tale*. With reference to *Melibee* this passage is one instance of Chaucer's using the Host to demonstrate the common 'lay' judgment of fiction simply in terms of its relevance to one's own experience. The Host judges the lesson of Prudence to be one from which his wife, Goodlief, might benefit and goes on to portray her as Prudence's contrary; if this may be said oddly to confirm the tale's lesson of patient suffering of adversity by showing its opposite as a grotesque caricature of wifeliness, it contributes more to the reader's sense of the running comedy of husband/wife relationships in *The Canterbury Tales* than to any modification of an idea of the tale itself. On the other hand, it reminds one of Chaucer's Envoy to that other piece of praise of perfect, patient womanhood, *The Clerk's Tale*, and suggests a recurrent dual pattern of idealism and comic envoy, which may seem to undercut, but which is really alternative to, rather than critical of, the ideal form.

Another place where Chaucer uses the transition between one tale and another to give a retrospective, contrary glance is in *The Reeve's Prologue*. As with the Host's reaction to *Melibee*, the Reeve's expression of the bitterness of old age contributes to a larger theme running through *The Canterbury Tales*, that of the Ages of Man; the obvious representative of youth, the Squire, and the various aspects of middle-aged maturity, worldliness, covetousness represented in the Franklin, Man of Law and Physician together suggest in the General Prologue that Chaucer has in mind that scheme in which all mankind is comprehended. The monologue of the Reeve fits well into a design whereby the range of moral types among the pilgrims acts as a scaffolding for the exploration of relationships within the tales. The Reeve's irritation at the Miller's mistreatment of carpenters thus helps to identify more clearly what the reader has half-perceived, that the figures in *The Miller's Tale* were playing a generation game and that, beyond that, the figures in *The Knight's Tale* were arranged to represent youth, middle age and old age, and, further, that in *The Merchant's Tale* and *The Pardoner's Tale* the contest is to recur. But the Reeve's complaint does also make its particular comment on *The Miller's Tale*, since the recognition that old men 'hoppen alwey whil the world wol pype' and that 'Oure wyl desireth folie evere in oon' are comments too apt to the situation of John the carpenter to be ignored. The tale ends with John's discomfiture; his injury is seen entirely as a joke; he is believed mad and cuckolded by his lodger. As far as the story is concerned that is the end of the matter:

> This tale is doon, and God save al the route! *(CT*, I, 3854)

But there is still room for a glance back from outside the tale, from the one among the audience who is ready 'to grucche', to complain, and hence to reject the view of life offered in the story:

> The sely tonge may wel rynge and chymbe
> Of wrecchednesse that passed is ful yoore;
> With olde folk, save dotage, is namoore! *(CT*, I, 3896–8)

As with other complaints added to narrative, there is a sense that confidence is checked; the Host may dismiss 'this sermonyng' but Chaucer has enriched and humanised the perspective from which the reader sees the comedy of old age outwitted.

Something similar but more difficult, because a serious tale is involved, is achieved in the Envoy to *The Clerk's Tale*. Here Chaucer not only concludes the tale, as does Petrarch, by recognising the literal unacceptability of the example of Griselda and by translating it into moral allegory, but he goes further and steps right outside the story, separating it from his audience's actual experience of human behaviour, and going on to make a tonal volte-face from the 'heigh stile' of his imitation of Petrarch into as polished a piece of courtly lyric cynicism as he ever penned. As with the Complaint of Anelida, Chaucer makes a shift of metre too, from rhyme royal into six 6-lined stanzas, through-rhymed and forming a kind of sestina. The relationship between this concluding 'song' and the tale is the most testing of Chaucer's enigmatic dual structures and critics have often expressed unease in knowing how to read the work.

It is clear that Chaucer took the tale seriously. He made a careful close version of his original,[27] changing and adding only now and then to intensify a touch of pathos in connection with Griselda and, more particularly, to emphasise the aspect of arbitrary tyranny in the behaviour of Walter. Chaucer's story is moving and painful to read because he resists the tendency to abstraction in the exemplary nature of the fable and makes the literal relationships, particularly of husband and wife, the focus of his attention. It is not possible to read the tale with the extenuating thought that Walter is a type of the divine tester of the errant sinner, and if one is to see the action as an exemplification of a religious ideal then it has to be accepted in a most difficult form. For human marriage to work as a metaphor for the relationship of God and the soul, one must accept that the wife's role is to represent an innocent vulnerable capacity for complete subjugation and self-sacrifice, because only through suffering can be generated that redemptive power of love, which will convert the tyranny of the almighty ruler's transmission of power through the instruments of Fortune into the protective love of lord and father of his people. The tale must move the reader into acceptance and Chaucer's enhancing of the Scriptural and pathetic imagery associated with his heroine shows that that is what he intends.[28] But just as the triumphs of Mars brought into Chaucer's mind the contrary image of disaster and dishonour, so the moving image of patient suffering is accompanied by the unacceptable human face of the tyrant who imposes the suffering on others; hence the story must be both accepted and rejected. The moving image of 'vertuous suffrance' is uninjured by the poet's shift of stance. The comic twist both serves to remove the reader's reservations about the story, by conceding that part of the mind may gloss the behaviour of the characters in a worldly light, and it also enhances the intense delicacy of the presentation of Griselda by its obviously concessive move into a less discriminating diction and manner, and by the allusion to the Wife of Bath.

The final sestina is a wonderful example of Chaucerian urbanity, expertly polished in its management of metre and rhyme and, as in 'To Rosemounde', playing off the verse pattern against a luxuriance of imagery and reference that borders on wild fantasy: so Chichevache the gaunt cow, Echo, camel and tiger make their appearance and culminate in the comic picture of husband as mailed knight, vainly sheltering behind visor and breastplate as wifely darts find the weak spots and turn him into a cowering quail. That the tale of Griselda should conclude with the advice to wives

> Be ay of chiere as light as leef on lynde,
> And let hym care, and wepe, and wrynge, and waille!
>
> (*CT*, IV, 1211–12)

is a supreme irony. To attempt to *explain* it (as part of the characterisation of the Clerk, as part of a subtle game of conformity to the Host's commands, and so on) is really unnecessary, since one can see that it is a characteristic piece of Chaucerian two-handedness.[29] The appeal to the audience in a spirit apparently contrary to the *sentence* of the tale works even more forcefully than Harry Bailly's picture of his rampant Goodelief to underline the ideal example as a standard by which the world may be judged. Both bring the release of laughter at the end of a solemn story and both purposefully shift from the view of life developed within a fiction to a recognition that real experience is different, but Chaucer has worked harder with Griselda than with Prudence to implant in one's mind the image of steadfast virtue, the innocent girl fetching water from the well plucked from the current of her life to become the testing ground for God and Fortune. The result is that Chaucer's handling will not settle into one fused picture but remains dual.

*Melibee* is part of another teasing dual pattern which has left modern readers uncertain of the right reaction, the pair of tales which Chaucer devised for himself in the Canterbury series. If *Sir Thopas* is a successful joke at the author's expense, is *Melibee* a contrary joke that misfires?—or a serious attempt at worthy tale-telling which worked well enough in its time but now finds little response in an audience deaf to sententious prose? R. F. Green interestingly considers the two tales as a reflection of the contrary aspects of the court author in the period.[30] *Melibee* can be placed with Book VII of Gower's *Confessio Amantis* as sound political and moral instruction for the young Richard II and thus identified with the role of poet as adviser to princes and with court respect for the practical value of literature. *Sir Thopas* belongs with an older tradition of the kind of entertainment expected of the court-minstrel and perhaps surviving in Richard II's time outside the sophisticated circle of the king. Green suggests that Chaucer's

> position as court entertainer, successor to generations of professional minstrels, is belittled in the self-mockery of *Sir Thopas*, but as the adviser to kings the author of *Melibee* writes essentially without irony . . . it was through such works as *Melibee* that the writer in the *familia regis* might hope to demonstrate his particular worth and claim for himself a more substantial role than that of a mere amateur entertainer.[31]

On the other hand Chaucer may be thinking only in terms of the game he has created, and be using the author figure as a suitable mouthpiece for two kinds of narrative. The terms of the tale-telling contest in *The Canterbury Tales* provide a pointed antithesis in the Host's calling for 'tales of best sentence and moost solas'. In *Sir Thopas* Chaucer shows by exaggeration where writing only for 'solas' can lead: escapism without sense is a logical extreme of the avoidance of serious purpose in narrative. *Melibee* represents the other extreme, 'sentence' without much 'solas'. There is support for this way of viewing the tale within *Melibee*, when 'oon of thise olde wise' among Melibee's friends offers unwelcome advice against war:

> And when this olde man wende to enforcen his tale by resons, wel ny alle atones bigonne they to rise for to breken his tale and beden hym ful often his wordes to abregge. For soothly, he that precheth to him that listen nat heeren his wordes his sermon hem anoieth.   (*Melibee*, 1042ff.)

In the light of what follows this is a reproof to the impatient audience, rather than a criticism of the speaker and the tenor of the rest of the tale is to lay stress on the worth of judicious counsel, with little regard to what is pleasing to the hearer. One might also suggest that *Sir Thopas* is a comic comment on what can happen when a poet ranges freely and uses his 'imagination' and inventive capacity. Instead of the liberation of the poet's creative powers, one gets randomness and mere unrealised archetype. At the other extreme the writer is tied to his source: Chaucer accepts the text of the French version of the *Liber Consolationis et Consilii* of Albertanus of Brescia as a task for translation, and renders it word for word in places. The two tales thus comment on one another: if the sober accuracy and moral earnestness of *Melibee* are an object-lesson for the author of *Sir Thopas*, the irresponsible verbal comedy and skipping metre of the poem cock a snook at the plodding sentences of the prose. The most significant thing about the double act, apart from the brilliant joke of *Sir Thopas*, is simply the demonstration of Chaucer's self-awareness as a literary artist and his drawing the variations in his audience's literary taste into a subtle literary game. Other evidence of such exploration of the purposes, meanings and methods of literature is scattered through *The Canterbury Tales* and other critics have examined Chaucer's interest in the 'professed literary tastes and aspirations of a small group of especially self-conscious literary performers among the pilgrims'.[32]

*Sir Thopas* and *Melibee*, like the tales of Miller and Reeve and of Friar and Summoner, only form a dual pattern in a loose, informal fashion. One tale comments on the other and in this particular pair Chaucer jestingly displayed contrary faces of the writer's art.[33] If one considers the two tales in the company of Chaucer's narratives with complaints, then one may observe that here too is an uncompleted tale of chivalry paired with a lengthy expression of the moral problems of injustice. But whereas Anelida, Mars and the falcon cry out against their fate and remain unsatisfied protesters against providence, in *Melibee* the spirit of complaint is strongly resisted:

> For the poete seith that 'we oghte paciently taken the tribulacions that comen to us . . .'   (1495)

and again:

> Salomon seith, 'The angry and wrathful man maketh noyses, and the pacient man atempreth hem and stilleth.'   (1513)

In so far as *Sir Thopas* comically expresses a kind of self-indulgence on the writer's part, then the pair may be seen to provide a completion of that pattern left unfinished in *Anelida and Arcite*; both narrative and lyric indiscipline are firmly controlled by a withdrawal into severe moral fable and the repeated *sentence* of patience and self-control.

In the case of prologues and tales a closer relationship of two parts is presented and, judging from the frequency of references in his work to the Wife of Bath, it appears that Chaucer was particularly satisfied with the effect he had created in the two types of expression he devised for her. The dual element is strikingly present in the conjunction of prologue and tale and in aspects of the content. Here is a prologue which grossly outruns the extent of its function by being twice as long as the tale to which it leads. Chaucer makes sure one grasps this point of interest by having the Friar comment explicitly upon this 'long preamble of a tale'; it seems as if the tale itself might never be reached and the reader begins to suspect that Chaucer is producing a new version of one of his old formulae, a personal complaint offered instead of an achieved narrative. But here he has found a way of not leaving his antithesis between the complacent, pre-ordained tendency of tales and the disruptive, unsatisfied note of protest hanging in the air. He achieves the narrative but distorts it to demonstrate the warping effect on narrative detachment of the complainant's personal motives. So from long preamble he moves to the subtle display in *The Wife of Bath's Tale* of the effects of unsympathetic narration on the believability of a romance fable of quest and magic transformation. The story becomes merely a perfunctory framework for a demonstration of aggressive tale-teller's mannerisms, from the comic refusal to accept the tale on its own terms at the beginning to the identification between the speaker and the women in the tale, the random digression into the story of Midas and the lengthy diatribe of the old hag on gentility, poverty and old age. And yet the tale is not a mere extension of the prologue. The references to King Arthur and the familiarity of the folk-tale motif of transformation of the old woman into beautiful, young and faithful wife have a strong enough identity to be able to resist, to some extent, the teller's distortions. The logic of the prologue and of the Wife's rejection of the magic of 'th'olde dayes of the Kyng Arthour' is that of the current of present, passing time, of the numbered sequence of marriages, of the lessons of experience and of the acceptance of age:

> But age, allas! that al wole envenyme,
> Hath me biraft my beautee and my pith.
> Lat go, farewel! the devel go therwith!
> The flour is goon, ther is namoore to telle;
> The bren, as I best kan, now moste I selle.
>
> (*CT*, III, 474–8)

But the tale's logic is that of reversible time and of escape from the consequences of experience: knight solves both the hard questions; coarse old hag becomes courteous young beauty and all is well. Chaucer's imaginative linking of self-justifying, argumentative prologue and twisted romantic tale opens up a suggestive range of possibilities to the reader's mind. One can read it as a demonstration of narrative as wish-fulfilment or as a subtle piece of anti-feminist irony because Chaucer has once again created literary richness by placing two aspects together, not by subordinating one to the other.

The dual nature of Chaucer's idea of the Wife of Bath is interestingly expressed within the *Prologue*:

> For certes, I am al Venerien
> In feelynge, and myn herte is Marcien.
> Venus me yaf my lust, my likerousnesse,
> And Mars yaf me my sturdy hardynesse;
> Myn ascendent was Taur, and Mars therinne.
> Allas! allas! that evere love was synne!   (*CT*, III, 609–14)

That Chaucer thought of his character as a child of just such a planetary moment as was ruefully lamented in *The Complaint of Mars* suggests a mental connection with his other explorations of the Mars/Venus relationship in *The Knight's Tale, Anelida and Arcite, Troilus and Criseyde* and *The Complaint of Mars* itself. By the time the tale has been added to the prologue, it is clear that Mars and Venus relate not only to the combination of bold strength and desire within the character of the Wife but also to the battle between the sexes and, as in these other works, to the nature of knighthood and the potential for conflict in its allegiance to honour in battle, fame and the pomp of ancestry, on the one hand, and to tenderness and virtue on the other. In the prologue Chaucer cleverly mingles together the two sides of the character to temper the bold exploitation of her husbands with generosity and humour, to complicate reaction to her egoism with sympathy for her zest and resilience and even, eventually, for her vulnerability, and to bring the interplay of planetary forces (and of clerical arguments) into the perspective of a believable local, social and physical form. Chaucer handles many familiar motifs from anti-feminist writing and from *Le Roman de la Rose*, but in inventing the Wife as the battle-ground on which the old conflicts are replayed, he has transformed the themes from theses into impulses, comic self-dramatisations and moments of inhibition and uncertainty which convincingly simulate the natural current of experience. In the tale knighthood is submitted to judgment entirely through women's eyes: the knight offends against women, escapes condemnation through women's mediation, must learn to know and understand women and eventually to accept their rules for his own life. While Chaucer still leaves it open to the reader to accept this with a knowing smile as the narrator's manipulation of fable to reflect her own preferences, he gives, in the final scene between husband and wife, some dignity to the husband's learning of his lesson, which allows one also to take seriously the course of humanisation of the brutal Martian impulses of knighthood. In learning woman's right to sovereignty the knight releases virtue and love, and the transformation, even in this comically distorted telling of the old tale and even with a final ambiguous flicker, manages to produce a moment of magic for the reader.

The dual pattern of dramatic monologue as prologue and of a tale chosen and handled so as to reflect the themes of the monologue proved for Chaucer one of his most absorbing and subtle literary forms. It is, in a sense, an imaginative reversal of the pattern of narrative with complaint. In *Anelida and*

*Arcite* and *The Complaint of Mars* a situation was created from which lament and argument could arise. Here the complaint comes first:

> Experience, thogh noon auctoritee
> Were in this world, is right ynogh for me
> To speke of wo that is in mariage.  (*CT*, III, 1–3)

And speaking of woe leads to a complaint which unites argument with lament; the Wife presents her case against clerks and against men and at the same time laments the passing of time and 'that evere love was synne!' The double strain prevents the argument from becoming strident and the lament from becoming plaintive. The tale fulfils the function of exemplum in so far as the prologue has its elements of sermon and the tale of the knight's learning what women most desire proves the point. But the ingeniously complex gloss which Chaucer's humour and sympathy add to the case-history makes the tale more than a demonstrative exemplary fable; it combines the instance of the argument with a kind of answer to the lament and the 'wo that is in mariage' is replaced by the perfect joy of this marriage and the recipe for the career of contented wife:

> And thus they lyve unto hir lyves ende
> In parfit joye; and Jhesu Crist us sende
> Housbondes meeke, yonge, and fresh abedde,
> And grace t'overbyde hem that we wedde;
> And eek I praye Jhesu shorte hir lyves
> That wol nat be governed by hir wyves;
> And olde and angry nygardes of dispence,
> God sende hem soone verray pestilence!
>
> (*CT*, III, 1257–64)

In *The Wife of Bath's Prologue* the transformation of complaint into confession, even self-justification, leads to a wider range of rhetorical effects and to a much more naturalistic idiom than was appropriate in the lover's complaint. By drawing in Scriptural and anti-feminist authorities Chaucer sets the character within a context of ideas and principles. The complaint thus combines the qualities of the satirical complaint based on observation of the follies of men and the abuses of the world, with the sentimental personal history and its emotional appeal to the reader's sympathetic response. The tale ruthlessly converts old myth into present-day use but out of an original mixture of deflating realism, of digression, of perfunctory tale-telling, and narrative bias Chaucer still manages to create a narrator's voice which accepts the function of completing the sequence of the tale and acting out the roles of the characters. The relationship between complaint and narrative perhaps works better this way: in *Anelida and Arcite*, *The Complaint of Mars* and even *The Squire's Tale* the promise of amplitude implied in the narrative opening seems narrowed into a channel of lyric suffering. With the prologue and tale the effect can, even in such an odd example as *The Wife of Bath's Prologue and Tale*, be that of an individual history being enlarged by narrative, which detaches the voice from its own circumstances and gives it the opportunity to dramatise itself in metaphors supplied by an imagined time and place.

This is the case with *The Pardoner's Prologue and Tale*, where what might be a limited, if effective, satirical picture of an avaricious exploiter of men's bad consciences, becomes a subtle exploration of the morality of art, of the relationship between appearance and intention and of the death of the spirit, by means of the tale added to the confessional prologue. The prologue which, compared to *The Wife of Bath's Prologue*, more convincingly fulfils the prefatory function in providing the circumstances for the tale and in preparing the audience's mind for the points of interest in it, turns the tale itself into a self-consciously rhetorical performance. The effects of irony, both within the tale and in the audience's awareness of the preacher's acquisitive intentions, are neatly prepared and carried out. The double level of effective moral tale and disconcerting access to the preacher's private thought works soundly to provoke direct and oblique reactions from the reader and to stimulate debate about the possibility of good being done by evil men, of powerful serious moral ideas being expressed by means of a shallow, self-seeking preacher, of the nature of the truth of a tale whose teller is lying. There is no enigmatic uncertainty here about the dual pattern. To the already composite form of sermon and exemplum, that is of direct and indirect presentation of moral instruction, Chaucer has added a perverse version of the 'modesty' prologue; here is the one pilgrim who does not apologise for his rhetorical inadequacy for the task in front of him, but boasts of his professional skill and gives the audience enough information for them cynically to mark all of his insincere flourishes in what follows. Chaucer, of course, cheats by being a good deal cleverer than the character he portrays but nevertheless the tale becomes, after that alerting introduction, a tour-de-force in its combination of vivid moral exhortation, demonstration of the wickedness of sin, sinister imagining of the horror of old age and the tight inevitability of its fulfilment of the moral pattern which exemplifies the Pardoner's perpetual theme *Radix malorum est cupiditas*.

To the possibility in the narrative plus complaint of extending history and situation into personal suffering and protest Chaucer has here, as in *The Wife of Bath's Prologue and Tale*, added moral depth by using the tale to extend the range of reference of the moral instances presented in the prologue. So the figures of the three rioters and of the old man, the bleak pictures of tavern life, the brief moments of fantasy as one is invited to contemplate the satisfying of gluttony by the grotesque ingenuity of cooks or the promise of 'myrthe and joliftee' in eight bushels of 'floryns fyne of gold', and the stark economy of the narration in contrast to the verbose flourishes of the preacher's condemnations and reproofs have all been imagined in terms of the Pardoner's intention. This becomes clear when one examines the material of the Pardoner's homily and compares its treatment with Chaucer's use of it elsewhere. The teaching on gluttony is based on the same source material as *The Parson's Tale*, where Chaucer sticks to the methodical definition of sins, authoritative denunciation of them and classification of aspects of sin in turn:

Glotonye is unmesurable appetit to ete or to drynke . . . This synne corrumped al this world, as is wel shewed in the synne of Adam and of Eve. Looke eek what seith Seint Paul of Glotonye: 'Manye,' seith Seint Paul, 'goon, of which I have ofte seyd to yow, and now I seye it wepynge, that been the enemys of the croys of Crist; of which the ende is deeth, and of whiche hire wombe is hire god, and hire glorie in confusioun of

hem that so devouren erthely thynges.' He that is usaunt to this synne of
glotonye, he ne may no synne withstonde. He moot been in servage of
alle vices, for it is the develes hoord ther he hideth hym and resteth. This
synne hath manye speces. The first is dronkenesse . . .   (*CT*, X, 817ff.)

Chaucer's use of this material in *The Pardoner's Tale* is virtually a translation
into a different language. First the general condemnation is turned into
repeated apostrophe:

> O glotonye, ful of cursednesse!
> O cause first of oure confusioun!
> O original of oure dampnacioun,
> Til Crist hadde boght us with his blood agayn! . . .
> Corrupt was al this world for glotonye.   (VI, 498–501, 504)

Then Paul's teaching is not only quoted but used to pump up the rhetorical
level again to a high pitch of exclamatory oratory:

> The apostel wepyng seith ful pitously,
> 'Ther walken manye of whiche yow toold have I—
> I seye it now wepyng, with pitous voys—
> That they been enemys of Cristes croys,
> Of which the ende is deeth, wombe is hir god!'
> O wombe! O bely! O stynkyng cod! . . .   (VI, 529–34)

And so it goes on with Chaucer creating a high-flown performance, exagger-
ated, emotional and melodramatic; the moral argument has been re-imagined
as an aspect of character and a demonstration of method.

The ostentatious rhetoric displayed here is the nearest that *The Pardoner's
Prologue and Tale* comes to the verbal techniques of the complaint. Chaucer
did not manage in *Anelida and Arcite* to resolve the problems of the relationship
between historical matter and the rhetorical expression of emotion. The con-
junction of story and exclamation undergoes an interesting transformation in
*The Pardoner's Prologue and Tale* where, because the rhetorical expression is
attributed to a calculated piece of oratory, it can be more easily enjoyed; it is a
convincing demonstration of how to turn didacticism into effective dramatic
speech. Through such imagining of the way that discourse would be trans-
formed, distorted and manipulated, by an unscrupulous exploiter of an
audience's manoeuvrability, Chaucer has extended his Pardoner beyond the
psychological case-history that many commentators have found into a complex
representation of the artist-performer, who tells us the tricks of his trade and
still makes them work powerfully on our sensibility to words, ironies and
narrative patterns. The duality of narrative and complaint seems for Chaucer
always to have had in it some relevance to his own awareness of the complexity
of the role of poet, with the double duty of conveying moral teaching and of
entering into experience outside his own convincingly enough to stir an
audience's reactions. Like the other self-conscious narrators among the
Canterbury pilgrims, the Pardoner represents an aspect of Chaucer, who is all
the time turning on the rhetoric, neatly tying up the ironies and expecting to
take in the Harry Baillies among his hearers.

Dual forms are thus often conjunctions of rhetorical flourishes of various kinds with some creation of contextual history or moral perspective. They are also nearly all composites of disparate material. In *Anelida and Arcite* Chaucer linked material from Statius with ideas from de Machaut; in *The Complaint of Mars* he put Ovid with Boethius and in *The Squire's Tale* joined an Oriental romance with the material of a pathetic *dit*. In *The Clerk's Tale* he passes from Petrarchan narrative to courtly chanson. *Sir Thopas* and *Melibee* unite in the repertoire of one narrator the trash of minstrel romance with the moral earnestness of sententious allegorical fable. In the prologues and tales of the Wife of Bath and the Pardoner Chaucer adapted matter from confessional speeches in *Le Roman de la Rose* to Arthurian magic tale and homiletic address. These are not the only places where Chaucer composes from a mixture of sources, of course, and the kind of duality that exists in some of these instances is inherent in the narrative method that Chaucer chose for *The Canterbury Tales*. But by giving the prologues of the Wife and the Pardoner sufficient independent life for them to act as fictions of which the tales become an aspect, by writing an unusual envoy to the tale of Griselda and by directing attention to the contrast of *Sir Thopas* and *Melibee* through adopting them as his own, Chaucer isolates these particular instances and presents them as deliberate juxtapositions. The combination of compositeness of material and variation of rhetorical stance gives them an identity beyond the accidental.

CHAPTER FOUR

# Sequence and Series

## 1. Episodic Dream Sequences

Chaucer's first ventures in using narrative to enlarge lyric may well have been the dream-poems. The poetic impulse in the development of the French courtly *dits* may be seen as an embroidery of poems of yearning and pleading into exempla and debates illustrating the ethics of love.[1] The narratives envisage situations and attitudes which provide a context for inset lyrics. Whether using a dream or the similar fiction of overheard situations, the poems are usually framed by an initial and concluding expression of theme. In the dream form the waking narrator's introduction and conclusion surround the dream, which may consist mainly of dialogue or of an allegorical scene or a journey or a narrative of comfort after complaint or some combination of such elements. Guillaume de Machaut's *Dit dou Vergier*, written in the 1320s, furnishes one sort of example: the opening passage, where the narrator in a garden on a beautiful May morning thinks of his lady and falls into a trance, is balanced by the close, where, after a contest between personified aspects of love, the God Amours wakes the dreamer by shaking dew in his face and the waking lover resolves to follow the instructions he has received from the God in the dream. While most of de Machaut's *dits* do not use a dream framework, he did return to it nearly forty years after the *Dit dou Vergier* in the *Dit de la Fonteinne amoreuse*, from which Chaucer in *The Book of the Duchess* probably derived the example of Ceyx and Alcyone, the promise of a feather-bed to Morpheus, the situation of confidences between two men, one the poet, the other a distressed noble (Jean, Duc de Berry in de Machaut's case) and the basic narrative pattern of complaint and comfort.[2] In this poem de Machaut creates a more complex and episodic narrative but the dream experience of Venus' comfort of the lamenting lord is enclosed between lengthy opening and closing sections dealing, in realistic detail in places, with the poet's initial learning of the lord's distress at the prospect of separation and his final account of helping the lord towards resolution and the preparation for his journey. Another French source for *The Book of the Duchess*, Jean Froissart's *Paradys d'Amours*, begins with a melancholy and sleepless narrator and ends with his waking, thanking Morpheus and others for the dream, which is seen as poetic

61

material: in the dream the poet takes up the role of Amant who complains and curses Love but learns patience, sees a hunt of love and a carole of famous lovers and heroes in the grounds of Amour, woos and wins his lady, singing a ballade to the daisy in response to her chaplet; the narrative, though episodic, like that of many French *dits*, moves clearly along a line of development and learning in the lover towards the poet's enlightened awakening.

The fountain-head of this stream of poetry, *Le Roman de la Rose*, presents a less clear-cut pattern because of its length and its diffuseness and the switch from Guillaume de Lorris to Jean de Meun. The introduction to the dream is brief but its speculation on the value of dreams stuck in Chaucer's mind as a possible prologue and its nature is clearly extra-visionary. On the other hand Jean de Meun allows dreaming and waking life to merge and the waking up is a mere signing off in the last line. Many of the French *dits* of the thirteenth and fourteenth centuries were not in the form of dreams at all, and many were, like the early parts of *Le Roman de la Rose*, sequences of scenes or episodes rather arbitrarily linked together by means of the narrator, who is sometimes the central participant, sometimes the observer who overhears or witnesses the significant moments of others' experience. Like the dream-poems, some of these are clearly structured as main episode framed by an opening and closing passage, but others, like *Le Roman de la Rose*, are more concerned with the speeches, scenes, lyrics generated by the situation than with formal shaping. Among those of the former type are some other *dits* of de Machaut almost certainly known to Chaucer. So the *Dit dou Lyon* (1342) has a central scene of a court in a garden where true and false love are expounded and the crowned Lady whose court it is explains the allegorical significance of the tamed lion who has led the poet through brambles and wild beasts to the fair meadow; this is framed by the opening praise of his lady by the poet in spring and the concluding relation of his adventure by the poet to others. However, de Machaut's last and longest *dit*, the *Voir Dit* of the 1360s, is a loose auto-biographical account of an affair containing numerous interspersed lyrics and a series of prose letters, where no conclusion is reached and where the characterisation of the unheroic, hesitant, aging lover (who takes up a book to relieve ennui and so may be the source of that Chaucerian idea) is the main point of interest. The earlier *Remède de Fortune* (1340s) shows de Machaut already going down that path, turning the allegory of *Le Roman de la Rose* into literal scenes of courtly games and pastimes and using these as settings for rhetorical complaints, lyrics in praise of the lady, ornamental set-pieces of didacticism and so on.

Between the clear structure of the framed allegory or court scene and the diffuse sequence, one finds among the French *dits* an intermediate type consisting of an introduction followed by a narrative in several stages and a brief return to the poet. So de Machaut's unusual bird-allegory the *Dit de l'Alerion* (1340s) begins with an introduction to the parallel between falconry and love in the form of the poet's knowledge of birds but rounds off the sequence of bird-relationships simply with an acrostic identifying the poet. The *Jugement dou Roy de Navarre* (late 1340s) has a lengthy realistic introduction where Guillaume considers the decay of the times during a period when he is confined to his house by plague before the summoning of the poet to be accused of treachery to women (in saying in the *Jugement dou Roy de Behaigne* that the Knight suffered more from the betrayal by his lady than the Lady from the death of her knight); Guillaume answers the examples of tragic death cited by his accusers (Bonneurté and twelve other female personifications) with his own of women's inconstancy and earns the adverse judgment of the King in the lengthy conclusion; the penance imposed of writing a lay, a chanson and a ballade returns attention to the poet but this conclusion is also the natural culmination of the judgment scene.

Thus *Le Roman de la Rose*, de Machaut's *dits* and other French courtly poems provided Chaucer not only with material which he copied, combined, rehashed and juxtaposed with other matter from classical and medieval Latin sources, but also with a number of possible shapes for poems. Other fourteenth-century English dream-poems show that a variety of forms was in use at the time when Chaucer was writing. The careful symmetry of *Pearl*, where a significant closing passage presenting the awakening from dream as a dramatic return to realisation and assessment balances the opening presentation of the narrator's troubled grief, makes *The Book of the Duchess* look very unbalanced with its nearly three hundred lines of pre-dream rambling about sleeplessness and Ovid and its eleven lines of return to waking in an unseemly dash to finish the thing off. On the other hand *The Parliament of the Three Ages* shows the same loose structure, with its long naturalistic poaching scene at the beginning and a very perfunctory conclusion. The three early dream-poems of Chaucer together indicate that Chaucer was not very interested at this stage of his writing in conclusions or in symmetry or a sense of careful design or even of clear unity. The end of *The Book of the Duchess* brings a long process to a sharp, quick end, effective in its way, though unexpected. Instead of identifying the poet by an acrostic as de Machaut might have done, it identifies the main character by puns and allusions and then very briefly adds the professional writer's conclusion that this was the material for a poem. It does not fulfil any idea, certainly not explicitly, that the process of dream leads to comfort for the sorrow which is the poem's subject, nor that the process of revelation has been educative. The end of *The House of Fame* is not there at all, or, if one considers the existing text, it is a mere breaking off in mid-scene. *The Parliament of Fowls*, a much shorter poem than either and one in which Chaucer manages to create an impression of compact, well-planned treatment despite the varied material, has an effective close in the song of the birds and the poet's being aroused to return to his initial interest in acquiring knowledge from books, but this ending too is conspicuous by its lack of concluding assessment or culmination or achievement.

As to the actual material of the poems, the first impression again is that Chaucer was not much interested in concentrated, close treatment of a single situation or theme or source. The extraordinary compositeness of *The Parliament of Fowls* suggests that Chaucer constructed merely by stringing one thing after another; the *Somnium Scipionis*, *Le Roman de la Rose*, the *Teseida*, *De Planctu Naturae* and a bird debate from the *dits amoreux* are neatly dove-tailed so that the joins hardly show, but the art seems nearer that of compiler than of author.[3] *The House of Fame* branches out, develops and spreads itself, including complaint, dialogue, allegory, social satire and philosophical and literary exploration in a bewildering mixture of at least three styles of poetry. Though *The Book of the Duchess* may seem a more unified performance because of its elegiac, celebratory central purpose, it too, by the side of Chaucer's other dream-poems, reveals itself as a string of items—narrator, Ovid, picturesque

63

mystery, complaint, love story, dialogue; one thing leads to another in a way which seems casually not purposefully organised and which eventually stops rather than ends. The critical view of these composites of mixed matter and the form Chaucer created has varied from condemnations of disunity to defences of their underlying philosophical or literary purpose, but a recent editor of *The Book of the Duchess* sums up the situation fairly enough:

> All three are episodic in structure. None of them makes explicit the argument or conclusion which is to be drawn from the series of episodes it presents. It is for the reader to draw a pattern of argument from the sequence of experiences through which the narrator-dreamer passes, with their parallels and contrasts, variety of textures and literary echoes.[4]

Looking for a structural rationale in such poems may seem pointless, since the French *dits* provide models for episodic structure and for mixture of naturalistic and non-naturalistic subject-matter, for lyric and narrative, allegory and autobiography, but Chaucer's dream-poems manage to be odder than any of the more predictable mixtures of de Machaut or Froissart or Watriquet de Couvin. Robert Payne looked to the idea of a thematic thread which was interpreted, amplified and ornamented in a variety of ways to form a 'combinative' structure, of which the three main components were book, experience and dream.[5] Helen Phillips declares simply 'The basic method is juxtaposition', with the narrator as the unifying element.[6] Spearing sees the structure of Chaucer's dream-poems both as sharing with other medieval dream-poems the ambivalence, exuberant ornamentation and tendency to love of ingenuity and disguise of late-Gothic taste, and as showing Chaucer's individual interest in the way actual dreams work; so he sees Chaucer using the method by which superficial disorder and abrupt transitions disguise the deeper level of intricate order and full intelligibility.[7] This produces a kind of reading, which many other commentators have engaged in with reference to these poems, which consists of a claim to reveal concealed cohesive principle. Some have found cohesion in the obvious themes of sorrow in *The Book of the Duchess*, reputation and rumour in *The House of Fame*, love in *The Parliament of Fowls*; others have interpreted the three as stages of development in Chaucer's use of the dream convention to examine larger philosophical issues, such as the relationship between authority and experience or the poet's sense of his craft and of the materials out of which poetry may be made.[8]

These poems are full of suggestions of a poet experimenting in joining things together and, though *The Book of the Duchess* and *The House of Fame* are both, in my view, inferior as examples of poetic achievement to *The Complaint of Mars* or 'The Former Age', even in some senses to *Anelida and Arcite*, they are longer and so include more, and in doing that express a wider range of ambitions and interests; they have a larger place in one's sense of Chaucer's development as a writer since they show him moving on from translations and from lyrics through the form of the dream-poem towards the full-scale narratives of his later period. There were several ways from short units, such as the complaint, towards larger, more far-reaching poetic expressions: one way was by facing the problems of retreating a major subject such as Chaucer found in *Il Teseida* and *Il Filostrato*, but before that another way was by building up poetic forms out of units imitated from a variety of French, Latin and Italian sources. So duality of form led naturally to episodic dream sequences consisting of a larger number of units strung together on a theme line.

*The Book of the Duchess* is generated from the idea of the complaint as a major motive in the courtly dream, though the function of the complaint is here deflected from the purpose one would expect in a French *dit*. It is not just a framed love-complaint but a combination of elegy and eulogy; no comfort, other than that of the relief of telling his story to another, is offered to the knight. Yet Chaucer's allegiance to the French motif is clear enough from comparison of *The Book of the Duchess* to French examples from the thirteenth century which established the lover's complaint as a rhetorical ornament in the *dit* and from the lyric set-pieces in the fourteenth-century examples by de Machaut and Froissart which acted as a direct source.[9] The knight's initial 'maner song' is a complaint with its own rhyme scheme, like the intercalated lyrics of so many French poems, and the whole of the early long speech of the knight (560–709) is a monologue of complaint sharing themes, attitudes and images with such passages as Amant's complaint against Love and Fortune in the *Remède de Fortune* and the Knight's complaint of betrayal in the *Jugement dou Roy de Behaigne*, combined with the sorrow at the death of the beloved expressed by the Lady in the same poem, and the dreamer-poet's listening to the noble lord's complaint from the *Fonteinne amoreuse*. Even the comparison with Alcyone's learning of death through dream has its parallel in de Machaut, and the narrator's sleeplessness, the reading of the book, the comparison of his dream with the dreams of Pharaoh and Scipio, these too are all culled from books and stirred into the pot-pourri.

Any sense of individuality in the work can only come from the poet's sensitivity in interpreting and in combining these borrowed parts. But, unexpectedly, the treatment of the knight's complaint is much less concerned with sensitivity of feeling than one would expect from the theme of bereavement. The initial lay is a rather blunt statement of the knight's state of mind, more in the manner of a text for the rest of the poem to explore, than a lyric statement, complete in itself:

> 'I have of sorwe so gret won
> That joye gete I never non,
> Now that I see my lady bryght,
> Which I have loved with al my myght,
> Is fro me ded and ys agoon.
>    Allas, deth, what ayleth the,
> That thou noldest have taken me,
> Whan thou toke my lady swete,
> That was so fair, so fresh, so fre,
> So good, that men may wel se
> Of al goodnesse she had no mete!'
>           (*The Book of the Duchess*, 475–9, 481–6)

What this reveals is the inadequacy of rhyming octosyllables as a suitable vehicle for plangency, without much enjambement and varied phrase length, which is how Gower sometimes brings off the effect. With Chaucer it is only when he gives the knight a long speech, with its longer periodic effects of building up repetitions, echoes and patterns, that the idiom seems adequate to the formal expression of courtly emotion:

> 'But whooso wol assay hymselve
> Whether his hert kan have pitee
> Of any sorwe, lat hym see me.
> Y wreche, that deth hath mad al naked
> Of al the blysse that ever was maked,
> Yworthe worste of alle wyghtes,
> That hate my dayes and my nyghtes!
> My lyf, my lustes be me loothe,
> For al welfare and I be wroothe.
> The pure deth ys so ful my foo
> That I wolde deye, hyt wolde not soo;
> For whan I folwe hyt, hit wol flee;
> I wolde have hym, hyt nyl nat me . . .
> For whoso seeth me first on morwe
> May seyn he hath met with sorwe,
> For y am sorwe, and sorwe ys y.'   (574–86, 595–7)

Even here Chaucer finds that fervent, speaking voice of 'An ABC' or of Anelida's Complaint only in occasional phrases or lines; the poet's intention is rather to create an ornamental expansion of the initial song and a symbolic picture of grief, identifiable by traditional topics such as that of death escaping the grieving seeker and, in the passage that follows, of the reversal from joy to sorrow:

> 'My song ys turned to pleynynge,
> And al my laughtre to wepynge . . .
>                   . . . my wele is woo,
> My good ys harm . . .
> To derke ys turned al my lyght,
> My wyt ys foly, my day ys nyght,
> My love ys hate, my slep wakynge,
> My myrthe and meles ys fastynge . . .'
>                   (599–600, 603–4, 609–12)

Such reversals lead aptly into the part of the speech which has greatest force, the complaint of the treachery of deceitful Fortune which combines vigour of utterance with visual and moral images—the game of chess, the squinting yet straight-looking, laughing, weeping figure of Fortune, the monster's head concealed in flowers, the hypocrite scorpion and the unstable wheel—to amass an indictment of the mutability of things which has sufficient bite to make up for the limp expression of personal grief. This is part of the effect of deflection which I mentioned earlier. The Black Knight's complaint by itself hardly works to arouse the reader's sympathy, but as an echo of what has gone before it has greater resonance.

For what Chaucer has managed to do by making a collage of borrowed

66

material is to create several layers of complaint. He begins with the narrator's complaint of his own numb discomfort:

> For I have felynge in nothyng,
> But, as yt were, a mased thyng,
> Alway in poynt to falle adoun;
> For sorweful ymagynacioun
> Ys alway hooly in my mynde.   (11–15)

Here complaint is used as motive; the initial state of the poet is, it is implied, to be changed by what follows. The longing for sleep and dream leads to material for the poem and so to the sense that the grief of the Black Knight, when it is expressed, is part of the satisfaction of the poet's unrest. Then he moves on to his classical instance of the power of dream to satisfy sorrowing desire, the story of Ceyx and Alcyone. The complaints of Alcyone are brief cries of grief, 'Alas!', 'A! mercy! swete lady dere!', and so on, but the summary of the tale conveys the idea clearly enough of the lamenting of the death of a loved one as an instance of the sort of material to which the imagination responds. So when the Black Knight's lament of death arrives it offers the path of entry into another's experience and hence into the main themes of the poem, lost love and beauty, the waywardness of Fortune, the fragility of earthly love and happiness. The knight's complaint thus functions not as simple elegy but as the culmination of a sequence of areas of thought and of words. As other French courtly *dits* use complaint to lead to resolution of love's difficulties or sympathetic exploration of the state of love and separation, so Chaucer in *The Book of the Duchess* uses complaint in layers to lead to celebration of the beauty of woman and young love, made more poignant by loss. The end makes it clear that this is all: beauty and love existed, now they are gone; this is itself apt subject for verse.

As in *The Complaint of Venus*, Chaucer's interest in *The Book of the Duchess* is partly in expressing several phases of the lover's life, combining praise of the beloved with feelings of anxiety and loyalty. Again, as in *The Complaint unto Pity*, he finds the change of focus from the element of criticism and protest in complaint to pleading an interesting aspect of the courtly love poem. Both are for most of the time expressed as hopeless and, despite the success of the knight's courtship, the emphasis is, as in *Fortune*, on the lack of comfort or reassurance. In the combination of aspects which elsewhere he linked with complaint Chaucer found a suitable way of lamenting and celebrating a dead duchess. There is no possibility of redress or promise of consolation but with the 'poynt of remembraunce' the sword of sorrow pierces the heart and so the knight's recalling of his love, more than the proclamation of his sorrow, fulfils the poet's search for the symbolic 'hert', the responsive impulse adequate to the expression of another's grief.

Underlying the veneer of the courtly *dit* which Chaucer gave to *The Book of the Duchess* is the interesting evidence of Chaucer's encounter with classical poetry and the broader concepts of supernatural experience which Ovid's *Metamorphoses* provided transform the poem. By inviting the reader to compare the Black Knight with the bereaved Queen the poet extends the figure beyond a courtly archetype playing out some de Machaut parlour-game into a poetic symbol of love blasted by death.

A striking feature of all three dream poems is the heterogeneous nature of the sources which Chaucer fused together. Dream was a useful device by means of which Chaucer could transfer his allegiance temporarily to alien worlds and beliefs. He does this explicitly in *The Book of the Duchess* as he offers gifts to Morpheus and Juno in return for sleep. Although hitherto 'I ne knew never god but oon' he is ready, 'in my game', to open his mind to other divine powers for personal need. The normal world, including religious belief, is inadequate to resolve his fretfulness and so he needs to go into another state for relief; this state combines Ovid and dream as a way of understanding the human heart and so opens the way to images, emblems and allegories as keys to feeling. Even the comic reference to Joseph and Macrobius has the effect in the early part of the poem of suggesting the opening up of the mind to new possibilities, of the dream's revealing the future or providing a picture of the ordering of the world. As in his other dream-poems Chaucer seems to associate the beginning of the dream with speculation, a readiness to accept and respond, not to prejudge according to a fixed evaluation of dream experience.

The scene of the dream draws on the richness which comes from combining material from several origins. It has the conventional elements of *Le Roman de la Rose*, the May morning, birdsong, specific reference to the poem and so on, which identify the world of allegorical vision, an emblematic representation, as in de Lorris, of the springtime of life with all the picturesqueness of a romanticised aristocratic setting. To this Chaucer added religious overtones: the song of the birds is characterised as the 'moste solempne servise' and the painted walls and the stained-glass windows create the scene of an elaborate chapel, even though the scenes depicted are the secular ones of the Fall of Troy and parts of the *Roman* itself. The effect is to sanctify the moment and give it special significance in the poem. The sound of the hunting horn and the poet's exit from the chamber with his horse is the real beginning of the poem's main subject-matter and Chaucer creates a most suggestive, unexplained effect of the poet's hitherto being enclosed indoors, enclosed in melancholy at first and then enclosed in the story and the picture. Now he is released to find the object of his hunt, a young man in black, lamenting beneath an oak tree: this, the poem seems to be saying, is what sleepless poets seek, this is the heart of things, a grieved young man in the act of complaint. Though it celebrates the object of the young man's grief vividly and gracefully, the rest of the poem says little beyond that.

By the time he came to write *The House of Fame* Chaucer's idea of what was at the heart of poetry had changed somewhat, as had his sense of the possibilities of dream poetry and his technical command over the octosyllabic couplet. Chaotic as *The House of Fame* may seem at times, its verse moves rapidly and purposefully, now mock-heroic, now quickly summarising, allusive, satirical and plain by turns, with little of the flaccid diffuseness and fussy detail for its own sake that blurs *The Book of the Duchess*. Complaint is here only one element in a long and varied work, but Chaucer's use of it is nevertheless a clear connecting thread with earlier and later poems.

The complaint of Dido is the centre-piece of Chaucer's presentation of the story of the Aeneid, supposedly depicted on the walls of the Temple of Venus in Book I of the poem. As with his treatment of Dido in *The Legend of Good Women*, whose complaint was quoted in Chapter 1, Chaucer found in the story a powerful conjunction of the three motifs to which he returned at intervals throughout his writing, woman's vulnerability, man's deceit and the threat of death. To these in *The House of Fame* is added the theme of *Fama*, reputation and rumour. So Chaucer first narrates Aeneas' betrayal of Dido, sententiously and proverbially, emphasising man's artful use of false appearances and woman's innocent folly. The Complaint is divided into four sections in a passage of sixty lines (300–60). First Dido bitterly identifies men's fickleness and their frivolous and cynical attachment to women but for a short time or even to three women at once, one for reputation, one for friendship and one for sexual pleasure. But in contrast to this satirical, almost caustic, opening, the complaint then veers from the attacking stance to the dramatic pathos of direct plea to Aeneas for mercy:

> 'Have pitee on my sorwes smerte,
> And slee mee not! goo noght awey!'
> *(The House of Fame*, I, 316–17)

In the longest continuous passage (320–60) this pleading is first enlarged and then moves on to the familiar motifs of the betrayed heroine's lament, protestation of innocence, reproof of man's deceit and the brevity of their love, self-accusation and the rueful but self-justifying recognition of women's simplicity:

> 'Allas, that ever hadde routhe
> Any woman on any man!
> Now see I wel, and telle kan,
> We wrechched wymmen konne noon art.' (332–5)

In the final movement Dido turns to lost reputation and the destructive power of Fame:

> 'O, wel-awey that I was born!
> For thorgh yow is my name lorn,
> And alle myn actes red and songe
> Over al thys lond, on every tonge.
> O wikke Fame! for ther nys
> Nothing so swift, lo, as she is!' (345–50)

As with other complaints Chaucer completes the passage by making clear its utter fruitlessness:

> Al hir compleynt ne al hir moone,
> Certeyn, avayleth hir not a stre. (362–3)

Although not the central subject of the *Aeneid*, this episode of Dido's suffering dominates Chaucer's summary of the work, showing the influence of Ovid, of course, but also identifying Chaucer's focal point, the use of a striking instance of pathos to effect a sympathetic entry by the reader into the imagined world of his poem and of a striking instance of fruitless protest against the workings of Fame to introduce the main moral theme of the work. The elaborate construction of the complaint in its various stages makes the instance not too obvious a piece of didactic symbolism. The veering from the pain of desertion to bitter comments on the way of the world are psychologically plausible but that seems less Chaucer's aim than the combination of the sense of suffering with the idea of the instability of reputation and love. The quality of the complaint has often been attacked, particularly by those who make inappropriate comparisons with Virgil, but Chaucer puts it at a remove from the reader by its setting: it becomes a kind of quotation, where its force as instance matters more than its force as poetry adequate to express a great emotion. The irony that this exemplum of fame's loss and of rumour's working and of the shaming of innocent womanhood is blazoned on the wall of Venus' Temple as a bitter tribute to the power of poets to convey a kind of immortality on their subjects is all suggestive of the material which Chaucer set himself to explore in the rest of the poem.

Chaucer placed this classical instance within the dream, unlike that of Alcyone in *The Book of the Duchess*, and this seems to me a more fruitful device. Again the beginning of the poem is speculative and exploratory, asking the reader to be aware of the variety of dream experience and, through the disputes over its significance, to be open-minded about its possibilities. The first exercise for this open-mindedness is to accept the complaint, within its Temple setting, as a significant entry point to exploration of a theme, to a journey and a sequence of sights and experiences. Even more explicitly than with the ornamental chamber of *The Book of the Duchess* the setting is, though a pagan temple, described as a religious place, where special significance is attributed to its appearance:

> Yet sawgh I never such noblesse
> Of ymages, ne such richesse,
> As I saugh graven in this chirche.   (471–3)

So the secular pieties of the past are endowed through the responsive imagination with a splendour to be revered, through which knowledge and understanding may grow. That at least is the apparent implication and, if one takes only the serious aspects of what follows in Books II and III, then perhaps that is what occurs. Chaucer, the ignorant dreamer, is taken on the wings of thought and philosophy through the realms of universal knowledge to the allegorical source-houses of human memory and information, where reputation and news are created; so all is revealed, the arbitrariness of earthly fame, the role of poets and historians, the multiplicity of men's activities and so on. But this poem is not the wide-ranging, philosophical work that it would seem from a list of its contents and allusions.[10] Chaucer uses the episodic sequence of pictures and experiences that he learned from de Machaut and Froissart to construct an intellectual kaleidoscope of bits and pieces from Dante and Ovid, Nicole de Margival[11] and others. The poem is full of pleasing local effects. Chaucer makes the journey of the dreamer in the company of a guide into a brilliant parody of the instruction of the inexperienced hero; the ludicrous physical image of poet dangling from instructor's claws translates the metaphor of the creative mind seized by thought into vivid action; the disparity between the teacher's lengthy speeches and the hearer's terrified monosyllables pushes the imbalance of medieval teacher-pupil dialogues to a nice extreme; the knowledge of the universe generously made available exposes the idiotic

70

aspects of all dream-poems, in which we can all sign our names in the heavenly visitors' book alongside Isaiah, Scipio, Nebuchadnezzar and the rest. In the third book he creates a succession of vivid pictures: the rock of ice, the castle with its minstrels and heralds, Fame's court and the whirling House of Rumour. Particularly interesting is the clever contrast which Chaucer builds up between the Hall of Fame and the House of Rumour; the former is identified by castle walls, massy pillars, gold plate, spacious, ordered, where Fame is permanently installed, holds court and, despite railing like a fishwife from time to time, observes some ceremony and hierarchy and draws heavenly harmonies in her honour; the latter by antithesis is completely unstable, made only of wicker, ever-moving, and crowded and crammed, without order, noisy and with all classes jumbled together in discord and jangling.[12] But all of this is brilliantly superficial, producing a cabaret of a poem, which can find no place to stop.

The idea that has appealed most to commentators on this exercise in unfinished variety is that Chaucer was exploring the art of poetry and the question for himself of the proper stuff of literature.[13] Even more explicitly than in *The Book of the Duchess* Chaucer uses the pattern of the dream-poem to express the idea of the poet-narrator moving out from an enclosed, limited environment into the vast possibilities of the poetic imagination and from a narrow conception of court culture out into the wide world of human activity: the touches of comic autobiography in Book II, 641–60 invite the reader to apply this also to his career as writer as opposed to his career as civil servant. Particularly tempting is that picture of the House of Rumour as a house

> ful of shipmen and pilgrimes,
> With scrippes bret-ful of lesinges,
> Entremedled with tydynges,
> And eke allone be hemselve . . .   (III, 2122–5)

since it can be read as a momentary glimpse of an idea of the Tabard Inn and of a medley of stories. But of that, as of the themes and traditions it refers to, *The House of Fame* is merely the glossy brochure; that is, much of the poem consists of never-to-be-substantiated promises of wonder and knowledge. It is full of possibilities for Chaucer's later work because so many things are mentioned without being pursued. The Eagle is an ideal courier on this quick guided tour and even the Temple of Venus makes the impression of a holy art-gallery that one whips through before catching the next flight to the Milky Way.

As there is no consolation at the end of *The Book of the Duchess*, so here there is no suggestion that, even if the poem went on, it would reach a point of revelation. Knowledge of love is promised but never arrives; there is only the confusion of Fame's arbitrariness and the chaos and turbulence of Rumour. Love, like the rest, is compounded of truth and lies. The Dreamer has learned only by observing and listening and accumulating impressions. He has been shown some of the confused rules and ways of life but has achieved no certain stance from which to view them.

Compared to *The Book of the Duchess* and *The House of Fame*, *The Parliament of Fowls* is a more compact and organised piece of writing and, despite the extraordinary variety of the material which Chaucer combined together within it, and despite its being a string of disparate episodes linked one to another with little explicit indication of the logical connection between them, it manages to create the impression of purposeful direction and process as well as to provide vivid images in the descriptive portions and lively dialogue in the parliament itself. Instead of using the complaint as a linking principle between the dissatisfied narrator and the main theme of the poem, as in the other two, Chaucer here puts the note of plangency back into the courtly setting of the demande d'amour and uses it for the pleas of the rival lovers for the female's hand. So rather than the female cries of loss and betrayal, Chaucer here takes up the motifs of l'Amant from the French *dits* and the tone of rhetorical protestation of intensity of suffering combined with requests for pity:

> 'For certes, longe may I nat lyve in payne,
> For in myn herte is korven every veyne.
> Havyng reward only to my trouthe,
> My deere herte, have on my wo som routhe.'
> (*The Parliament of Fowls*, 424–7)

However cliché-ridden this courtly language could seem in a series of ballades, it is given new life by the dramatic conflict among the three eagles in this poem and by the subsequent greater contrast between this courtly language and the variously practical, insensitive, sentimental and aggressively colloquial reactions of the lower-class birds. Complaint and plea become associated with a particular culture and ethic which asks to be judged on ideal principle not in terms of practical decision.

> 'Of long servyse avaunte I me nothing;
> But as possible is me to deye today
> For wo as he that hath ben languysshyng
> This twenty wynter, and wel happen may,
> A man may serven bet and more to pay
> In half a yer, although it were no moore,
> Than som man doth that hath served ful yoore.'   (470–6)

Chaucer provides the material from which the reader can imagine the debate of a refined court of love concentrating entirely on balancing the claims of one sort and degree of love against another. That is not the debate that happens but by using the conventional language of complaint and plea Chaucer draws sufficient stock response to form a context in which the irreverence of goose, cuckoo and duck is particularly startling and comic. Chaucer's association between complaint and fruitlessness is neatly turned into this contrast within Nature's hierarchy between those who plead and those who mate. The Troilus/Pandarus antithesis is obviously inherent in this comic juxtaposition.

Lying behind Chaucer's brilliant demonstration of varieties of loving is the shadow of the more philosophical version of the same theme found in Alain de Lille's *De Planctu Naturae*.[14] By naming 'the Pleynt of Kynde' as his source for the description of Nature, Chaucer invites the reader to view the juxtaposition of the Temple of Venus and the St Valentine's Day assembly of the goddess Nature in terms of Alain's poem, but the theme is not explicitly identified. As with the imitation of the language of the courtly lyric for the eagles' speeches,

Chaucer wants the play of possibilities to be present, but does not wish to turn this in the direction of didactic certainties, despite his earlier summary of the *Somnium Scipionis*. The memory of Nature's complaint against Venus' irresponsibility and encouragement of perversion and crime illuminates the antithesis between the two. Alain's excommunication of man who has sinned against Nature explains in an oblique way why Chaucer's poem populates Venus' Temple with personifications, divinities and famous tragic lovers but Nature's assembly entirely with birds, and the idea that Nature, God's deputy, the holder of Boethian balance between the elements of the universe, is, in her parliament, enacting the Law of Kind suggests that the whole poem may be coloured by Nature's moral complaint against man's disobedience to that law. But all is left to juxtapositions and covered over with a connecting net of comedy and irony, not with a mastering sententious purpose. From his compound complaints and his dual poems of narrative and complaint it seems that Chaucer liked to create perspective by unexplained contraries. In this more complex sequence of elements he develops the technique into a virtuoso flourishing of enigmatic juxtaposition. He wants to be seen as a poet who explores but does not judge. He knows that Alain condemns man as the only part of creation to disobey Nature; he then explores the disharmony among Nature's own obedient creatures, ending the poem in compromise, temporary joy and harmony and the promise that more, different books may provide more, different views and knowledge.

In all three dream-poems complaint thus plays a part, although only *The Book of the Duchess* is characterised by it as a whole. Elements of sorrow and protest are present in all three, of loss, betrayal and longing on the one hand and, on the other, at the instability of life and the contrariety of fame, fortune and man. Chaucer turns from the seriousness of elegy in the earliest poem towards comedy and variety in the other two, but all three show complaint used in antithesis to positive expressions of principles of love and harmony. Common elements in the three suggest several recurrent aspects of Chaucer's thinking. All start from the idea of the limitations of life though this is expressed in the different guises of sleeplessness and melancholy in *The Book of the Duchess*, the boredom and restriction of everyday affairs in *The House of Fame* and the frustration and uncertainty of the questioning poet in *The Parliament of Fowls*. The gateway which represents some sense of escape from this limitation is, like the gate to the garden in *The Parliament of Fowls*, twofold, though the two sides do not necessarily contradict but may augment one another; one side is the literature of the past, the other his own imagination, represented by the activity of dream. The world of dream consists of a great variety of scenery of which the confused dreamer is given some sort of quick guided tour; in *The House of Fame* and *The Parliament of Fowls* these tourist views of a strange world are clearly identified as activities which broaden the mind and open out the subjects of fame and love, satisfying a curiosity which is associated with the mind of the poet seeking understanding of experience and of the relative values of what is to be learned from books. Though no clear didactic principle is established, there is a sense that each phase of the poem modifies what has gone before.

Comparison with the French *dits amoreux*, which provided the episodic pattern of these poems, reveals Chaucer's most significant departure from his model as the omission of an authoritative figure who enlightens or instructs or judges. Chaucer's guides lead him to places and leave him to get on with the business of observing (in *The House of Fame* and *The Parliament of Fowls* after indicating that he is dim and probably incapable of doing so intelligently). As to the other figures, the Man in Black is sufferer not answerer and reduces the dreamer to the level of confidant, though he tries to act at times as if he were consoler; even in this serious elegiac poem there is a comic ironic element in that the reader recognises that the Dreamer's inadequacy is a disguise for the poet's indecent appetite for the other's sorrow as the subject-matter of his poem. The Eagle comes nearest to fulfilling the role of divine instructor but he offers simply information (not always wanted and with some dubious reasoning in it) rather than moral instruction. The various goddesses are symbolically pictured displaying the signals of their nature, holding court, but they have no direct contact with the Dreamer and are presented critically or at best with some ambivalence. It is an inevitable consequence of this lack of authoritative figures that no goal is reached. The Dreamer observes and is led to share experiences but he still needs to read on. So Chaucer repeats the pattern of making a metaphorical journey into literature and imagination, taking the lonely, anxious and ignorant poet out of his isolated book-reading into a wider sphere of experience, ranging in imagination over past and present, the world and beyond, but eventually returning to the limits, the business of writing and reading and being uncertain. There is no sense of transformation. He has simply read, looked, listened, examined, with a naive eye asking truth to reveal itself.

It would seem therefore that Chaucer was interested in the process he found in French *dits amoreux* and interested in their mixture of lyric, narrative and allegory, but not in imitating their moral framework or their assumptions as to where a poem was leading. He uses the situations without the judgments, the complaints without the comfort, symbolic figures who do not provide answers and a sense of poetry as exploring without necessarily any sense of discovery. If anything positive is established it is of a general philosophical kind about the subjects themselves. If *The Book of the Duchess* registers that the heart of poetry is a young man lamenting his lost love, it registers also the poet's curiously prying, even predatory, role. *The House of Fame* registers that contrary aspects of the same general force in human life paradoxically both ensure that Dido's tragedy is enshrined in memory and in her own experience helped to destroy her honour and her name. *The Parliament of Fowls* registers that love harmonises and divides. The complaints in the three poems are central to each of these themes.


## 2. Prologue and Series

*The Legend of Good Women* is often treated as if it were a regression to a cast-off, youthful way of writing. The dream prologue allies the poem to Chaucer's earlier explorations of the matter and the manner of the French *dits*; the courtly set-up of the God of Love and the Queen Alceste creates for it a literary ambience much less appealing than the 'lifelike' sphere of reference of the Canterbury pilgrimage; the Ovidian tales hark back to *The Book of the Duchess* and *The House of Fame*. Yet there is much that is sophisticated and intelligently experimental about the work, not least in Chaucer's use of the decasyllabic couplet; it is not only the accusation of the poet's unfairness to women that identifies it as produced after *Troilus and Criseyde*.

The basic narrative structure of both *The Knight's Tale* and *Troilus and Criseyde* was provided by Boccaccio. Chaucer changed the proportions in both by the different techniques of abbreviation and amplification; he varied and sharpened the experiences within the narrative by the judicious use of passages of now stylised, now naturalistic conversation, of lyric, of debate, of narrator's comment; he glossed the endings by adding new material. In the course of these shifts Chaucer demonstrated over and over again the usefulness of the lamenting or protesting speech. But his application of the mode of expression was within a determined pattern of action. Though this is always likely to be so in a period when narrative is seen as a use of known stories for demonstrative purposes, Chaucer had shown in *Anelida and Arcite* an interest in using a new combination of narrative elements as a springboard for the dramatic apostrophe. *The Legend of Good Women* shows that interest to be still working in his mind.

Here the narratives themselves are borrowed, variously from Ovid's *Heroides*, *Metamorphoses* and *Fasti* (in order of frequency), from the *Aeneid*, from Boccaccio, Plutarch, Guido de Columnis, the *Ovide Moralisé*.[15] They are not much amplified; more often they are curtailed into summaries of the bare outline of complex actions with varying shifts of emphasis. In most of them, especially those echoing Ovid's format in the *Heroides* of the distressed heroine's letter, the tragic virtuous woman complains of her own situation. The qualities of experiment are, first, in the combination of abbreviated story with selected focal points of intensified treatment, and, secondly, in the combination of narratives into a set, or sequence of likeness, preceded by a dream prologue, which is a sequence of a different kind.

It is possible that after the large-scale Boccaccian narratives Chaucer was looking for a more individual form of writing, one which allowed him to re-tell known narratives but which also allowed him to manipulate them, to take up an independent stance towards them, to cut them to the bone, rather than have to become merely the servant bearing the burden of a heavy weight of matter. Although *The Legend of Good Women* may seem the very opposite of this, since the Prologue creates a fiction that the narratives are imposed upon the poet, rather than chosen by him, in effect (and more logically than in his 'as myn auctour seyde' mood in *Troilus and Criseyde*) the narrator can register his sense of the imposition by selective, even at moments irresponsible, treatment of the material, by irony and by subversive intentions, all of which are apparent at different points.[16] It is the selectivity of treatment that Chaucer identified as left (by the God of Love) to the poet's discretion in his longer, earlier version of the Prologue:

> 'I wot wel that thou maist nat *al* yt ryme,
> That swiche lovers diden in hire tyme;
> It were to long to reden and to here.
> Suffiseth me thou make in this manere,
> That thou reherce of al hir lyf the grete,
> After thise olde auctours lysten for to trete.
> For whoso shal so many a story telle,
> Sey shortly, or he shal to longe dwelle.'
>
> (F Prologue, 570–77)

This passage brings to an end the first version of Chaucer's bookish intro-
duction. Unlike his practice in the earlier dream-poems, here Chaucer does not
use one book from the past to provide an authoritative point of reference, but
lumps all books together as a potential source of knowledge which is outside
the normal range of experience:

> And yf that olde bokes were aweye,
> Yloren were of remembraunce the keye.
> Wel ought us thanne honouren and beleve
> These bokes, there we han noon other preve.
>
> (F Prologue, 25–8)

Thus the ideas of the poet's subject-matter and the relationship between source
and treatment are dealt with in a more general way than in earlier poems—no
longer through the individual themes of sorrow, fame, love, but by means of
antithesis between the poet's enthusiasm for books, his readiness to give them
'feyth and ful credence', and the contrary impulses symbolised by springtime
and the daisy which lure the poet away: 'Farewel my bok, and my devocioun!'
(F Prologue 39).

This antithesis may be interpreted variously. It is in part a separation of
sense and sensibility. The bookish zeal, the basis of accurate knowledge,
expresses the poet's intellectual, academic engagement in the absorption and
transmission of the fruits of past thought; this is displaced by, even perhaps to
some extent in conflict with, the spontaneous, natural response of the sensi-
bility to beauty and the world. In a passage based on the opening stanzas of *Il
Filostrato* in the F Prologue, the daisy, which in the dream is later meta-
morphosed into Queen Alceste, the poet's defender and emblem of wifely
virtue (that is simultaneously patron and subject), is addressed as Muse and
sovereign lady:

> She is the clernesse and the verray lyght
> That in this derke world me wynt and ledeth.
> The hert inwith my sorwfull brest yow dredeth
> And loveth so sore that ye ben verrayly
> The maistresse of my wit, and nothing I.
> My word, my werk ys knyt so in youre bond
> That, as an harpe obeieth to the hond
> And maketh it soune after his fyngerynge,
> Ryght so mowe ye oute of myn herte bringe
> Swich vois, ryght as yow lyst, to laughe or pleyne.
> Be ye my gide and lady sovereyne!   (F Prologue 84–94)

The explicit reference to the idea of the inspiration of poetry, in the vivid
image which Chaucer introduces of the poet as harp fingered by the controlling
hand and the idea of the selection of the appropriate voice from the poet, all set
up the terms of a debate between the poet's conscious knowledge and his
power to express, in preparation for the accusation of the poet in the dream. In
this later fantasy transformation of his waking experience the poet is given his
subject-matter as a penance at the culmination of a process of trial. In the F

version of this Chaucer puts emphasis on the possible defences of the poet
against the accusation of slandering love and women. The debate is, as a result,
rather one-sided, but the point at issue is clearly enough the degree of
responsibility of the writer. One of the significant shifts in the later G Prologue
is Chaucer's cutting down the defensive, muse-inspired aspect of the debate
and his strengthening the accusation and the references to authority.[17] So
before the dream begins the poet announces his intention:

> But wherfore that I spak, to yeve credence
> To bokes olde and don hem reverence,
> Is for men shulde autoritees beleve,
> There as there lyth non other assay by preve.
> For myn entent is, or I fro yow fare,
> The naked text in English to declare
> Of many a story, or elles of many a geste,
> As autours seyn; leveth hem if yow leste!
>
> (G Prologue, 81–8)

This is a clearer indication than in F both of the authoritative purpose and of
the maintenance of an independent view—'leveth hem if yow leste!' The
weight of authority is also in the G Prologue attributed to Chaucer's accuser,
the God of Love, who virtually dictates a book-list to the poet in which he can
find better subject-matter:

> 'Why noldest thow as wel han seyd goodnesse
> Of wemen, as thow hast seyd wikednesse?
> Was there no good matere in thy mynde,
> Ne in alle thy bokes ne coudest thow nat fynde
> Som story of wemen that were goode and trewe?
> Yis, God wot, sixty bokes olde and newe
> Hast thow thyself, alle ful of storyes grete . . .'
>
> (G Prologue, 268–74)

The God then goes on to name Valerius, Titus, Claudian, Jerome, Ovid and
Vincent of Beauvais as likely sources. In both versions the poet's defence of his
practice is divided between Alceste and Chaucer himself: Alceste offers the
weaker arguments that he may be so in the habit of writing that he hardly
notices what he is saying or that he may be writing at the bidding of another
and so not be responsible for the sentiments; Chaucer's voice offers the
stronger defence of an honest purpose which is being misunderstood:

> 'what so myn auctour mente,
> Algate, God woot, yt was myn entente
> To forthren trouthe in love and yt cheryce,
> And to ben war fro falsnesse and fro vice
> By swich ensample; this was my menynge.'
>
> (F Prologue, 470–74)

But the defending Muse is not any more sympathetic than the accusing Deity:

> . . . she answerde 'Lat be thyn arguynge,
> For Love ne wol nat countrepleted be
> In ryght ne wrong; and lerne that at me!'
>
> (F Prologue, 475–7)

So there is no choice of subject-matter and no choice of meaning: women are to be virtuous and men false—so get on with it! Hence Chaucer embarks on his series of narratives offering the 'naked text', or at least the main bits of it, in 'swich vois, ryght as yow lyst, to laughe or pleyne', with no more guidance to the reader than the warning: 'leveth hem if yow leste!'.

The purpose of this highly self-conscious prologue (Chaucer's anxious interest in it conveyed by the fact that this alone of his many unfinished or complete works survives in variant versions) is to solve the problem of the relationship between narrative material and expressive treatment which Chaucer shows to be a recurrent question for him in many places, in the incompleteness of some works, in the shifts between disinterested recording and partial pleas and judgments in *Troilus and Criseyde* and in the amplification of parts of *The Canterbury Tales* by means of diverse dramatic monologues, within and without the narratives. The incomplete works suggest, among other things, that Chaucer did not find the combination of narrative and complaint enough to form a satisfying literary structure. In the longer narratives based on Boccaccio he made substantial use of the intensifying power of complaint within a framework of war and rivalry, but to both *The Knight's Tale* and *Troilus and Criseyde* he felt it necessary to add a passage of moral resolution. The Prologue to *The Legend of Good Women* is looking again at the problem of bringing together narrative and the poetry of feeling, with which the poet's own sense of the significance of his material is associated. Must inspiration coincide with authority for the theme to be satisfactorily realised? What if the poet (or the audience) does not believe the story? Can inspiration's power to suggest to him the right voice in which to make the material work solve the problem?

The matter of *The Legend of Good Women* shows Chaucer still thinking that there was some mileage left in the combination of narrative and complaint, if only he could find the right proportions or the right voice. Stirring, violent stories of the past which involved intense feeling and the conflict of virtue and vice must remain one of the main subjects for poetry: how to convey them so that their exemplary force is passed on but the poet is not merely 'and nothing I' (F Prologue 88)? Chaucer appears to accept the pattern of tragic narrative with its (often brief) element of lament in *The Legend of Good Women* but he has given it form by creating a series and placing it within a frame. The series of tales implies that truth is proved by the accumulation of instances and the repetition of moral assertion; the pattern recurs and declares the essential similarity of every one of the tales. The framing device of the Prologue, on the other hand, even while providing the ostensible cause and justification for the series, indicates that the evidence is rigged. The pattern is predetermined, not one that emerges but one that is imposed. The more stories there are (and the more differences and variations of circumstance, motive, character, time, place and so on), the more absurd the moral patterning seems. The formula Chaucer devised provides a clever combination of subservience and independence: the material is imposed but the handling of it may (despite Alceste's instructions) provide a sub-text which is disruptive, ironic, laconically aloof. The few parts of the series which were completed provide several types of evidence of complexity of intention.

The first tale of Cleopatra shows what happens when the poet sticks to his brief of an outline of main events. The story has been set, like a holiday task, by the God of Love and the fact that it is the least suitable of the stories to 'prove' the moral point is not, one presumes, accidental. Chaucer produces a story of no character or rendered life but one treated simply as instance: because Cleopatra cast herself naked into a snake-pit for love of and loyalty to Antony, her case is recorded, with an outline of history. It is almost impossible to follow if one does not know the story already and little attempt is made to animate it:

> The weddynge and the feste to devyse
> To me, that have ytake swich empryse
> Of so many a story for to make,
> It were to longe, lest that I shulde slake
> Of thyng that bereth more effect and charge;
> For men may overlade a ship or barge.
> And forthy to th'effect thanne wol I skyppe,
> And al the remenaunt I wol lete it slippe.  (616–23)

Apart from the irrelevant amusement of thinking how Shakespeare was to 'overlade' Cleopatra's barge, this passage is an indication that the number of tales will provide the weight of the piece and its logic; this opening tale is apparently setting a standard whereby only an outline is appropriate. Chaucer of course does not stick to this standard in all the other tales. There is no insistence on the 'sentence' of the tale (though again some later tales do explicitly insist): the example is enough. What registers on the poet and consequently on the reader in this otherwise laconic telling is a picture of battle and a queenly death speech; that is what it means to the poet's eye—war and sorrowful faith. The account of the battle of Actium provides the image. The vividness has reminded some readers of contemporary accounts of sea-battles, such as Froissart's version of the battle of La Rochelle in 1372,[18] and Robinson points out the resemblance in the use of alliteration and anaphora to *The Knight's Tale* with its particular contemporary battle perspective. The effect is to generalise the defeat of Antony into the culmination of a succession of typifying acts of sea fighting.

> With grysely soun out goth the grete gonne,
> And heterly they hurtelen al atones
> And from the top doun com the grete stones . . .
> In with the polax presseth he and he;
> Byhynde the mast bygynneth he to fle,
> And out ageyn, and dryveth hym overbord;
> He styngyth hym upon his speres ord;
> He rent the seyl with hokes like a sithe.  (637–9, 642–6)

Cleopatra's speech to the dead Antony combines the function of complaint, as she records

> 'That nevere wakynge, in the day or nyght,
> Ye nere out of myn hertes remembraunce,
> For wele or wo, for carole or for daunce.'   (685–7)

with the fulfilment of a vow to suffer what he had suffered; so

> 'that shal ben wel sene
> Was nevere unto hire love a trewer quene.'   (694–5)

Without any gesture towards the Roman or Egyptian background or the character of Antony, Chaucer renders down the tale to a moving picture and a speaking moment. The technique is a kind of impressionism and it results in the tale's being the briefest of the nine narrative sections.

In the version of the story of Pyramus and Thisbe *occupatio* is again much in evidence and it provides the most vivid line, even while the poet is protesting his inability to render 'How kysseth she his frosty mouth so cold!' (878). But the dominating features here are the dividing wall, to which Chaucer devotes a sixth of the narrative, and Thisbe's final speech which, like Cleopatra's, combines lament with self-proclamation, a kind of tragic labelling to bring the demonstration that 'a woman can/ Ben as trewe in lovynge as a man' to a close. Over the space of thirty-five lines the wall generates a succession of images of stolen moments, such as:

> And with a soun as softe as any shryfte
> They late here wordes through the clifte pace.   (745–6)

The joint accusation 'Alas, thow wikkede wal!' yields a touching effect of pathos in duet:

> 'Yit woldest thow but ones let us mete,
> Or ones that we myghte kyssen swete,
> Thanne were we covered of oure cares colde.'   (760–2)

The traditional complaint against Fortune here is transformed into a lament against the physical object that determines their condition; there is a kind of absurdity about it but absurdity is an apt means of displaying the arbitrariness of the fathers' opposition. Thisbe's final speech duly reproaches the 'wrechede jelos fadres oure' and achieves a pathetic dignity in her promise to the dead Pyramus, the only male figure in the series who earns credit:

> 'Thow shalt no more departe now fro me
> Than fro the deth, for I wol go with thee.'   (898–9)

Between the symbol of division and the heroine's threshold-of-death speech Chaucer covers the narrative in swift glimpses of actions far removed from the battle of Actium; perhaps the modern reader can not avoid seeing an aspect of pantomime in this particular tale, but Chaucer could be said to be juxtaposing

80

stories with an intention of varied mood, despite the repeated exemplification of the central moral idea of the series.

There is certainly a difference in the section devoted to Dido, the longest and most elaborate narrative. Chaucer signals the shift of mood by opening flourishes of literary tribute and intention:

> Glorye and honour, Virgil Mantoan
> Be to thy name! and I shal, as I can,
> Folwe thy lanterne, as thow gost byforn,
> How Eneas to Dido was forsworn.
> In Naso and Eneydos wol I take
> The tenor, and the grete effectes make.   (924–9)

In this tale there follows a much more sustained realisation of what Chaucer meant by 'making the great effects'. The narrative itself, as elsewhere, is reduced to summary and the account of the Fall of Troy and the history of Dido and Carthage might well remind the reader that 'the naked text' is all that is being promised, but then Chaucer begins to enlarge and creates a sequence of vivid pictures. This begins with the impression made upon Dido by Aeneas:

>                    that he was lyk a knyght
> And suffisaunt of persone and of myght,
> And lyk to been a verray gentil man . . .   (1066–8)

The generous welcome she thinks suitable produces a rich evocation of courtly luxury:

> To daunsynge chaumberes ful of paramentes,
> Of riche beddes, and of ornementes,
> This Eneas is led, after the mete,
> And with the quene, when that he hadde sete,
> And spices parted, and the wyn agon,
> Unto his chambres was he led anon
> To take his ese . . .   (1106–12)

A list of the appurtenances of the noble life of leisure and wealth follows, so that Dido's liberality is fully rendered in the telling and makes its moral point as well as contributing to the effect of romance. Chaucer carefully identifies the developing moods, Dido's bemused fascination with Aeneas' narrative of Troy and her growing passion, to build towards the hunting scene with an impression of passing time and cause and effect. The hunt is full of splendour, colour and lively detail, Dido brilliant as the day in gold on a red saddle, Aeneas like Phoebus on 'a courser startlynge as the fyr', the cries of the huntsmen, the zest of the young men. This vivid, mimetic picturing of incident gives animation and visual aspects which Chaucer used only in brief moments in the two preceding narratives; it is a narrative style inconsistent with the intention merely of citing instances of virtuous wronged women, though one more sympathetic to the reader looking for drama, movement and character. What it communicates is the poet's freedom, even within the narrow confines of his stated literary purpose in The Legend of Good Women, to imagine and to

81

envisage when he feels the impulse. The greater range of expressiveness does in fact lead to the strongest expression in any of the episodes of the theme of the work. The storm, Aeneas' successful wooing of Dido and the immediate malice of 'wikke fame' provide sufficiently striking occasion for the narrator's identification of morality to have a justified base:

> O sely wemen, ful of innocence,
> Ful of pite, of trouthe, and conscience,
> What maketh yow to men to truste so?
> Have ye swych routhe upon hyre feyned wo,
> And han swich olde ensaumples yow beforn?
> Se ye nat alle how they ben forsworn?   (1254–9)

In the later stages of the narrative Chaucer finds his focal point in Dido's distress, and instead of creating a major impassioned lament, he gives a greater dramatic force by means of several short outbursts of feeling: 1303–8, 1316–24, 1338–40 and her final letter 1355–65. In this sequence reproaches addressed to Aeneas develop naturally into expressions of misery and into a complaint which is offered as a mere extract from Ovid's full account, but which expresses in ten lines the themes and feelings of many a longer lament, as I suggested earlier when quoting it as representative of the type of betrayed heroine's lament.[19]

It is in this episode that one can best judge what Chaucer thought he could achieve in the abbreviated narrative. It will, of course, not satisfy the reader who thinks that Virgil's epic is being given short shrift, but it is an intelligent selection of effects, working with economy and point as in Dido's reproach to Aeneas:

> 'Allas! what woman wole ye of me make?
> I am a gentil woman and a queen.'   (1305–6)

or the sharp picture of her degradation:

> She falleth hym to fote and swouneth ther,
> Dischevele with hire bryghte gilte her,
> And seyth, 'Have mercy! and let me with yow ryde!'   (1314–16)

One is reminded of Chaucer's evaluation of 'olde bokes' in the opening lines of the poem, as providing the key of remembrance: if we as readers want fully to experience the old tale we are sent back to Virgil and to Ovid; Chaucer honours and follows them, taking the 'tenor and the grete effectes' and here it works. We already know the story and merely need it recalled to our minds; its richnesses we can augment from our own store—the poet has tactfully and sensitively provided some mnemonic keys. His independence lies in the choice of keys and Chaucer goes for a few brightly coloured pictures and typifying gestures and words. The effect is of riches in a little space.

The subversive aspect of his detachment is more apparent in the bold opening of the fourth section and the linking together of the stories of Hypsipyle and Medea. The address to Jason echoes the direct vocative to Virgil at the beginning of the preceding tale but in contrary spirit; honour and praise are replaced by dishonour and scorn. The idea of using the stories of two heroines to expose Jason attributes to the source-material the quality not just of old examples but of the documents in the case, authoritative records to be cited in court. And though the idea of revealing the heartless untruth of the man in the case may seem to serve the cause of the whole work and leads on naturally from the tracing of Aeneas' passage from chivalrous knight to artful deceiver and heartless deserter, nevertheless the spirit of the attack on the hero is so zestfully vengeful and spiritedly gleeful that the poet's role of humble subservience is left behind. This is the best piece of writing in *The Legend of Good Women* and one of Chaucer's finest bravura passages. It has some common quality with the Envoy to *The Clerk's Tale* in the ironic conjunction of the theme of suffering virtuous womanhood and a tone of polished, satirical worldliness. It is only here that the poet's adopted voice of virtuous woman's defender sounds the note of challenge:

> Yif that I live, thy name shal be shove
> In English that thy sekte shal be knowe!
> Have at thee, Jason! now thyn horn is blowe!   (1381–3)

This vigorous expression of the poet's taking on the reputation of a dead hero of the ancient past adds comic resonance to the poem's theme of present-day awareness of old authorities; it is not the impressive models offered by the victims but the chance for the writer of a verbal combat that is the point of inspiration. The result is that the poet does the heroines' job for them and produces a vehement complaint against masculine faithlessness.

> Thow rote of false lovers, Duc Jasoun,
> Thow sly devourere and confusioun
> Of gentil wemen, tendre creatures,
> Thow madest thy recleymyng and thy lures
> To ladyes of thy statly aparaunce,
> And of thy wordes, farced with plesaunce,
> And of thy feyned trouthe and thy manere,
> With thyn obeysaunce and humble cheere,
> And with thy contrefeted peyne and wo.
> There othere falsen oon, thow falsest two!
> O, often swore thow that thow woldest dye
> For love, whan thow ne feltest maladye
> Save foul delyt, which that thow callest love!   (1368–80)

If only the betrayed heroines spoke in such tones then *The Legend of Good Women* might be a great collection of poetic tirades, but in this particular poem Hell hath no fury like a tongue-in-cheek poet. The fact that the most morally condemnatory passage in the poem is also, in the mocking voice of the poet, irresistibly funny gives an ironic twist to the procedure of the whole; such irony promises much, if only Chaucer had found a way of building on it. As it is, one has an illuminating gesture, showing that when the poet's partisanship for his heroines inspires him to speak like a wronged Anelida, or Dido, or whoever, the game of interpreting ancient sources takes wing and becomes an interesting clash between the language of one age and the heroes of another.

By lumping together the stories of Hypsipyle and Medea, telling them both briefly and eschewing the imaginative possibilities for enrichment and complication (particularly obvious in Medea's case), Chaucer maintains the impetus of this opening flourish of ironic gusto. The telling is arbitrary and he even ceases to trouble to tell the story, leaving it to the false lovers in his audience to supply the hero's treachery:

> As wolde God I leyser hadde and tyme
> By proces al his wowyng for to ryme!
> But in this hous if any fals lovere be,
> Ryght as hymself now doth, ryght so dide he,
> With feynynge, and with every subtil dede.
> Ye get namore of me, but ye wole rede
> Th'origynal that telleth al the cas.   (1552–8)

So the tale of Hypsipyle becomes a kind of do-it-yourself narrative, even an anti-narrative as it fades into the poet's refusal to be bothered. Because there is potentially more, the story of Medea seems even more extremely laid aside, reduced to support for the opening statement for the prosecution, drawing breath only for an extract from Medea's Ovidian letter of lament, which ends with something of the bite which the arraignment of Jason requires:

> 'O haddest thow in thy conquest ded ybe,
> Ful mikel untrouthe hadde ther deyd with the!'   (1676–7)

The tales as dramatic experience barely exist, Chaucer here preferring the demonstrative allusiveness of his ironic role as historical prosecutor on a circuit of classical betrayal.

Although the story of Lucrece is also reduced to its bare bones, the fifth section represents another kind of contrast. Beginning with brief pointed encapsulation of the scene of praising wives and of the visit of Tarquin and Collatine to the latter's house, Chaucer evidently then became interested in the unusually detailed treatment of Tarquin's state of mind which he found in Ovid's *Fasti*. He produces a lengthy passage combining interior monologue with the all-seeing narrator's description: the result is one of the most convincing presentations of mental processes in medieval English writing. The reader is given time to absorb and consider it, as the poet moves from Tarquin's immediate observation of Lucrece:

> Tarquinius, this proude kynges sone,
> Conceyved hath hire beaute and hyre cheere,
> Hire yelwe her, hire shap, and hire manere,
> Hire hew, hire wordes, that she hath compleyned . . .   (1745–8)

to his recalling of this image on the next day:

> Amorwe, whan the brid began to synge,
> Unto the sege he cometh ful privily,
> And by hymself he walketh soberly,
> Th'ymage of hire recordynge alwey newe:

> 'Thus lay hire her, and thus fresh was hyre hewe;
> Thus sat, thus spak, thus span; this was hire chere;
> Thus fayr she was, and this was hire manere.'   (1757–63)

and then to the reverberations within his mind:

> And as the se, with tempest al toshake,
> That after, whan the storm is al ago,
> Yit wol the water quappe a day or two,
> Ryght so, thogh that hire forme were absent,
> The plesaunce of hire forme was present . . .   (1765–9)

The passage could belong to an account of a worthier love and Chaucer has to check his response to it for its own sake in order to get back into the condemnatory voice. The rest of the narrative takes on an intentness from this passage and the vivid image of Lucrece's feeling the weight on the bed, the dialogue between Tarquin and Lucrece, the comparison to wolf and lamb and the description of the rape are clear and forceful:

> What! shal she crye, or how shal she asterte
> That hath hire by the throte, with swerd at herte?   (1802–3)

In the scene of sorrow and suicide Chaucer prefers indirect narration of Lucrece's confession to complaint, except for two lines. The over-all effect is a sober, concentrated narration leading to a serious, powerful conclusion. The story emerges as one of

> the stable herte, sadde and kynde,
> That in these wymmen men may alday fynde.
> Ther as they kaste hir herte, there it dwelleth.   (1876–8)

The declaration that of men even the 'trewest ys ful brotel for to triste' is more readily acceptable here than in the story of Jason's betrayals. The evidence suggests that, though within a limited compass, Chaucer was in *The Legend of Good Women* looking to create some variety of effect.

These three central stories in the series, of Dido, Jason's betrayals and Lucrece, show an interesting range of tone, of uses of narrative and complaint, of the combination of summary, embellishment and epigrammatic point. There are suggestions within them of Chaucer's discovering possibilities in his material and his methods as he went along. The placing of the comic attack on Jason between the dramatic pictures from the Aeneid and the sobriety of the story of Lucrece creates a most accomplished succession of effects, from splendour to satire to seriousness; here Chaucer shows how to make the series as a literary idea into a combination of reinforcement and variety. The complaint of the heroine becomes merely one of the possible devices to give rhetorical point to the tales; the poet may take up the accusatory stance and express indignation on their behalf, reminding the reader that these stories are not re-animations but present-day perusals of the past. Even the condemned male characters in their shared role of betrayer are treated variously: the splendour of Aeneas explains the susceptibility of Dido but the lures of the seducer in Jason's case receive only scorn, while with Tarquin the internal process of the growth of desire is examined and persuasively imagined.

Something went wrong after that. The story of Ariadne reverts to the method of one or two selected focal points. The image of the two sisters, Ariadne and Phedra, overhearing in the moonlight the lamenting imprisoned Theseus is one and the final dramatic rendering of the deserted Ariadne, groping for Theseus in the empty bed and passionately complaining is the other. Between the two is a muddle of stilted speeches for Phedra (who plans the whole killing of the Minotaur), Ariadne and Theseus. The most interesting touch is, as with Dido, the division of Ariadne's lament into short, staccato snatches. Here these outcries are effectively woven in with images of landscape and loneliness:

> And to the stronde barefot faste she wente,
> And cryed, 'Theseus! myn herte swete!
> Where be ye, that I may nat with yow mete,
> And myghte thus with bestes ben yslayn?'
> The holwe rokkes answerde hire agayn.    (2189–93)

The poet explicitly avoids any complaining which might be 'long' or 'hevy', but the impression is conveyed. Chaucer seems to find no interesting angle in the story of Philomela, though the opening cursing of Tereus reverts to the grand rhetorical addresses to Virgil and Jason. In the tale of Phillis he does include substantial passages of complaint, revealing a closer following of the pattern of expression in Ovid's *Heroides*. There is some sense of structure in the division of the complaint into two parts, one expressing reproach of and protest to Demophon, the other progressing through self-pity to self-reproach and judgment of the betrayer, but the over-all effect lacks force and character and the uncertainty of tone is confirmed by Chaucer's final undermining comic gesture:

> She for dispeyr fordide hyreself, allas!
> Swych sorwe hath she, for she besette hire so,
> Be war, ye wemen, of youre subtyl fo,
> Syn yit this day men may ensaumple se;
> And trusteth, as in love, no man but me.    (2557–61)

The uncertainty of tone, betraying loss of conviction on the poet's part, continues through the final, incomplete tale of Hypermnestra, where the speech of the heroine's father sounds as if he is leading up to the suggestion of incest rather than murder, which comes almost as a relief. The soliloquy of the heroine distraught on her wedding night provides the last coloratura variation on virtuous distress before the series peters out.

Nevertheless, there are sufficient positive qualities within *The Legend of Good Women* for it to be seen as an interesting venture which, like many other of Chaucer's works, did not go right. As with the racy variety of *The House of Fame* or the plangent classicism of *Anelida and Arcite*, the poet sounds confident and polished within his chosen style at particular points of the poem. The series of stories is not merely a monotonous repetition of effects, even if the insistence on feminine virtue and masculine caddishness threatens to become constricting. There looks to be an attempt to combine serious and ironic treatment and so to exploit the element of choice of voice which is indicated in the Prologue. The choice of an abbreviating style of narrative could well have been a reaction against the lengthy, ample works which had developed from his response to Boccaccio. However, summary tends to reduce varied stories to their lowest common denominator and this works against Chaucer's interest in variety of effect. The combination of narrative and complaint continues to be a useful structural design, but it is turned inside out in the attack on Jason, it is varied by splitting up lament into more naturalistic spurts of moment-by-moment feeling, and it is consciously restrained in the repeated passages of *occupatio* which Chaucer uses to modulate his complex games of poet and ancient source, from apparent reverence to cavalier omission and disrespect.

This combination of subservience and independence is perhaps the most fruitful idea to survive from *The Legend of Good Women* into *The Canterbury Tales*. In the latter unfinished series of narratives there is the same sense for the reader of encountering a series in which it is difficult to reconcile the interesting impulses of the writer with a single view of the work. Chaucer's ability to vary his stance towards his material is so marked a feature of *The Canterbury Tales* that it has often seemed a point of difference from the earlier poem, a lesson learned from the mistake of trying to make a tale-collection out of moral instances all illustrating the same idea; but variation is apparent both in attitude and treatment within *The Legend of Good Women*. Some debate about woman's innocence and vulnerability is inherent in the undercutting touches of worldly cynicism. Deliberately to abbreviate narrative is to draw attention to the processes of selection and emphasis. Chaucer developed both ideas into more effective literary tools in *The Canterbury Tales*, the first by attributing the variety of views to a variety of voices and the second by shifting the literary genre of his tales. The only significant element which he jettisoned from his notion of prologue and series as a structural design was the idea that the prologue defined a moral function for the narratives to fulfil. The tales in the Canterbury series do not have to prove a point; they should have one but what it is can be part of the movement of thought within the poem. But the rationale of *The Legend of Good Women* presumes a defined moral intention. The poet's review of the pathetic cases of virtuous wronged heroines from the past will accumulate into an act of reparation. Complaint (by the virtuous martyr) will answer complaint (against the unjust poet). The prologue with series comes nearer to resolving Chaucer's repeated self-questioning about the best way of combining feeling and argument, narrative and complaint, history and empathy, than the sequence of episodes in the dream-poems.

# PART II: COMPLAINT IN NARRATIVE

# CHAPTER FIVE

# Complaint in Narrative I: The Knight's Tale

## 1. Introduction

In the second half of this book I intend to concentrate on three major works in which Chaucer made substantial use of complaint, *The Knight's Tale*, *Troilus and Criseyde* and *The Franklin's Tale*. All three are based on works by Boccaccio and Chaucer's interpretation of his source-material is as much my theme as his inclusion of rhetorical lyric sections within his narratives. In all three the addition of complaint to the epic or romance material, or the high-lighting of complaint already present in it is a significant key to the purpose and quality of the whole. The device has an obvious, superficial appropriate-ness to courtly narrative involving intense feelings and the shifts of Fortune's favour, because apostrophe and addresses to the gods are clear characterising features of poetry in the high style. But Chaucer's recourse to complaint within narrative goes further than that, as I hope to demonstrate in detailed examina-tion of the three works.

Of the three, *The Knight's Tale* is the one that has most in common both with Chaucer's dream-poems and with his pairings of narrative and complaint. It shares the Temple of Venus with *The House of Fame* and *The Parliament of Fowls*, Arcite and Theseus with *Anelida and Arcite*, Venus and Mars with *The Complaint of Mars* and other works, and more generally courtship, love, loss and chivalry with *The Book of the Duchess* and so on. The elements of lyric, *demande d'amour* and debate link it to the French courtly *dits*, formal speeches about Fortune and Providence to Chaucer's Boethian moral complaints. It is, on the other hand, the poem which can most readily be seen as an ambitious turning-point in Chaucer's creative life, where he rose to the challenge of rendering into English an impressive, serious narrative, which had in Italian combined classical material with modern idiom and fused martial epic with romantic adventure. The tools which he had to use to transform this material into an English poem were the ones he had originally learned from French poets and which he developed in dream-poem, ballade, complaint and the rest. *The Knight's Tale* records a creative encounter between Boccaccio's matter and style and Chaucer's existing patterns of thought and expression.

Boccaccio's *Il Teseida* is not a masterpiece, but it is ambitious in combining several literary intentions. The Italian poet's imitation of the 12-book structure and the exact number of lines of the *Aeneid* give an authoritative outer shape to his declared aim of composing the first vernacular poem to challenge ancient treatments of the deeds of Mars. But the full title he gave to the work, *Il Teseida delle Nozze d'Emilia*, shows that he was not fully committed to recreating classical epic in modern language; epic is the frame, but romance the content, as Boccaccio's description of his subject makes clear:

> I discovered a most ancient story which was unknown to most people and was attractive both in the subject it dealt with—namely love—and those it spoke of, who were noble youths of royal blood . . . both noble Thebans . . . though kinsmen, they came into conflict through their exceedingly great love for the lovely Amazon Emilia; and as a result of that one of them lost his life.   (*Il Teseida*, trans. N. R. Havely,[1] Book I, Stanzas 4–5)

His provision of a pseudo-autobiographical prologue addressed to Fiammetta, the suggestion of personal ardour in offering love as a theme of shared interest and his hint that Fiammetta is intelligent enough to understand the allegorical aspects of the work provide directives to the reader similar to those at the beginning of *Il Filostrato*; these seem far from the epic purpose which is otherwise established in the full-scale invocation of Book I, the sonnets prefacing each of the books and the vigorous engagement in the opening books in the historical matter of Theseus' conquests. A further literary element was added in the form of a commentary on the text; in these explanatory glosses, or *Chiose*, Boccaccio interprets his narrative at some key points in fully allegorical terms. In imitation of the annotated manuscript he knew of Statius' *Thebaid* he takes up the tools of the medieval scholar to moralise the material of the classical past; so Venus and Mars are interpreted as the destructive passions (*concupiscibile* and *irascibile*, respectively) which need controlling by reason. Boccaccio displays another characteristically medieval literary attitude in places, an encyclopaedic interest in fullness for its own sake: he embarks on over 1000 lines in the first two books to narrate Theseus' war against the Amazons, conceding in his gloss that this material may seem unnecessary but justifying its inclusion as explaining the origin of the situation and also describing something which 'is rather strange to most people, and therefore more interesting' (Gloss on Book I, Stanza 6).

*Il Teseida* offers a good range of possibilities to the adaptor, a choice of styles, material suitable for excision (some of which is actually identified by the author), literal, natural behaviour woven in with the historical strangeness of the matter, a dual story of sad and happy outcome, exotic pictures and noble speeches, moral, religious and philosophical themes. Chaucer explored some parts of this range of opportunities on several occasions. He used it for the descriptive set-piece of the Temple of Venus in *The Parliament of Fowls* and, though he may not have had a text of *Il Teseida* with the *Chiose*, he shows that he had grasped the moral allegory beneath the surface by turning Boccaccio's sympathetic presentation of the sensuous beauty of Venus into a suggestive, rather sinister evocation of the spirit of *luxuria*.[2] The opening of *Anelida and Arcite* is modelled on the *Teseida*'s stylistic grandeur and its composite genre could be an abbreviated version of Boccaccio's mixture of war and love. In

*Troilus and Criseyde* the invocations and classical references echo the high style of the *Teseida* and the use of Arcita's posthumous view of the triviality of worldly concerns for Troilus shows Chaucer absorbing the double perspective of pagan and Christian thought which he chose to subdue in *The Knight's Tale*. The *Teseida* was a storehouse as much as a lavish, imitable model of sophisticated urban culture and of classical knowledge. *The Knight's Tale* reflects its mixed nature even in its uncertainties and the question of Chaucer's dependence and independence, though it has often been discussed, remains complex and interesting.

The main features of Chaucer's treatment are well known.[3] He reduced the twelve books of the *Teseida* to about a quarter of its original length by discarding epic invocations, by dealing briefly with Theseus' battles in the first two books, by omitting the wanderings of the exiled Arcita, by cutting out the lengthy list of warriors from Book VI and using only two representative figures, by cutting out accounts of individual exploits in the tournament; he also omitted most of the passages about Emilia's thoughts and feelings, thus reducing her role to that of an idealised, symbolic figure, and removed many of Boccaccio's mythological, pseudo-classical allusions. The result was often described in the past as Chaucer's turning Renaissance epic into medieval romance and this idea has support in evidence of Chaucer's insertion of specific details of 'feudal realism', references to the attributes of medieval court-life, battles, tournaments and chivalry. Other commentators have seen Chaucer's fusion of classical supernatural machinery with medieval astrology and Boethian philosophy as the most significant refocussing of the material,[4] which turns the poem into an examination of the relationship between gods and men.

The division of *The Knight's Tale* into four parts is usually followed by modern editors; this division depends on the Ellesmere manuscript. The Hengwrt manuscript divided the tale into a prologue (first 34 lines) and three unequal sections: Part I consists of Ellesmere's Parts I and II; Part II of the equivalent of lines 1883–2742 in the Ellesmere text; Part III of the last three hundred odd lines from Arcite's deathbed onwards. The other manuscripts and early prints do not have divisions at all.[5] Thus, although the structural similarity between the familiar arrangement of *The Knight's Tale* and *Sir Gawain and the Green Knight* (taken with the evidence that Chaucer made use of the techniques of alliterative poetry at several points in *The Knight's Tale*) is particularly intriguing,[6] one has to be conscious that it is probably the preferences of scribes and editors which have accentuated the likeness. The division into four parts is convenient and makes one kind of sense, but the pattern of the Hengwrt version of a short prologue, one long sequence of episodes (tracing the course of the fortunes of Arcite and Palamon from capture to interrupted duel), balanced by a different kind of long sequence (a leisurely, grandiose presentation of preparations for and the holding of the tournament which is to settle their rival claims for Emily's hand) and completed by a shorter coda (dealing with the tragic aftermath and the resolution), also makes a plausible and meaningful structure. Chaucer may have been thinking simply of the natural divisions of the narrative, but he went out of his way to emphasise symmetrical patterning in the part of the poem dealing with the temples and prayers, in the paralleling of the situations of the two heroes and in the conflicts among men and gods. The tale is highly patterned, however one divides the printed text.

The Hengwrt prologue is indicative of Chaucer's priorities in the initial stages. He places Theseus in the forefront as governor and conqueror, praised for 'his wysdom and his chivalrie', but immediately, by the use of *occupatio*, a device which becomes one of the keynotes of treatment, he withdraws from full narration of Theseus' history; the past must be taken for granted—the treatment is to be selective. The poet's justification of this (too much matter, limited resource) is fused with the contextual one of not wanting to delay the tale-telling contest for the free supper. This is the only reference to the Canterbury setting in the tale and it looks very much like Chaucer's one gesture towards harmonising a previously written tale with his subsequently devised series. Both the omission of the reference to Arcite and Palamon as the main subject and the example of the kind of material that he is excising suggest that the quality that Chaucer is looking for is that of epic on a reduced scale, but that is not quite the effect he produces once the tale gets under way. Rather than summarising Theseus' exploits, Chaucer seems, in the early part of the tale, to be finding in particular moments and episodes qualities which he can turn into emotional focal points. In the latter part of the tale the attention of writer and reader is differently directed. The Hengwrt division is a clearer indication of this than the Ellesmere structure.

## 2. Complaint and Debate: Hengwrt I, Ellesmere I and II

In the first episode, Theseus' meeting with the mourning widows of Thebes, Chaucer takes a symbolic picture from the current of historical narrative in *Il Teseida*. Boccaccio's emphasis is on the return of Theseus to Athens in triumph; hence a striking point in his presentation of the ladies is their unkempt appearance, unfitting to the occasion, and Theseus' perception of their underlying nobility. Chaucer reduces the ladies to a formal, black-clad tableau of lament in which the idea of propriety is expressed only in terms of the propriety of verbal rhetoric. The eldest lady, the widow of Capaneus (Evadne, but Chaucer characteristically removes her individual name) responds to the rebuke that their cries disturb the time of rejoicing with the first of the work's complaints against Fortune, which she claims is fittingly addressed to one who is now favoured by Fortune and hence an appropriate source of 'mercy and socour'. The request raises the question of fittingness both with reference to the appropriate treatment of women of noble station brought low by Fortune's wheel and of the bodies of the noble dead, conquered in battle. Theseus' reaction and his subsequent actions illustrate his qualities of noble pity and courtesy as well as his heroic stature, and after the antithesis between Fortune's misused victims and a favoured prince comes another contrast between Theseus and the tyrant Creon 'that hadde his death ful wel deserved'. The portrait of Theseus as a 'trewe knyght' who fought with Creon and slew him 'manly as a knyght/ In pleyn bataille' establishes the noble conqueror, 'this worthy duc', simultaneously as a fulfilment of the ideals of medieval chivalry and a historical figure from the pagan past with Mars on his banner and the Minotaur on his pennon. This vivid episode is necessary to the main plot of *The Knight's Tale* only to explain how Arcite and Palamon came to be captives of Theseus but it is a significant and memorable beginning, indicative of several features of the whole. Chaucer conveys the tone of his epic source mainly in dignified speeches expressing morally fine attitudes, without devoting much space to accounts of epic deeds. Pictorial elements and rhetorical speech are his preferred modes, and feminine pathos his point of entry into the morality and feeling within the material. He is, at this point, writing not so much reduced epic as something not unlike his combination of complaint with narrative setting in *Anelida and Arcite*, giving more attention to the contrasting pattern made by the figures than to balanced sequence of action or clear indication of a central narrative thread. The main pattern of contrast is between power and weakness; it is established through the complaint of the weak, the noble pity of the strong. The entry of Arcite and Palamon into the story is handled similarly and the contrast between them in prison 'in angwissh and in wo' and Theseus

> With laurer crowned as a conqueror;
> And ther he lyveth in joye and in honour
> Terme of his lyf . . . (1027–9)

shows that dramatic juxtaposition takes precedence over any gesture towards naturalistic consistency in the presentation of the figures. The treatment of the two young captives is part of Theseus' absolute conquering power and Chaucer cuts out of his source the details which help to build up a picture of Theseus as a humane and rational ruler. Boccaccio describes the two as of princely rank, something which was apparent in their haughty demeanour 'which made them seem in their anger to be defying God'; Teseo finds their scorn and pride indicative of honour and courage, has their wounds treated, considers putting them to death because they might become powerful enemies but commutes this unjust verdict and treats them honourably. By omitting any reference to their characters Chaucer removes the idea that fear of them is justified and by omitting details of Theseus' motives makes his actions appear arbitrary. Chaucer's concern to move quickly and to give only an outline sketch of the situation with a clear antithesis between conqueror and conquered produces an alienating effect of the callousness involved with pity and of the price of war, when cousins of royal blood are merely a linked pair in a heap of bodies, the spoils of war to be torn from the heap and put in a dungeon. 'What nedeth wordes mo?', says the narrator; Theseus wins, they lose. Chaucer, that is, creates the arbitrariness which is one of the themes of the work by his abbreviation of the narrative and his turning to images and rhetorical outbursts rather than an historical account of events.

Although Chaucer does not moralise upon the theme, the opening section of the tale has the effect of an illustration of the ups and downs of Fortune. The widows kneeling, catching Theseus' bridle, swooning, and the two knights lying wounded, 'Nat fully quyke, ne fully dede', then imprisoned in a tower, present images of supplication and subjection in contrast to Theseus' enactment of the generous and the punitive aspects of reigning power; all are recognisable as instances of the phases of Fortune. The simplified moral diagram is fleshed out with persuasive speech and colourful detail and once the story begins to develop it becomes merely an aspect of a tale which combines some qualities of realism with elements of abstraction. But from the start the figures are treated as representative ones, standing for rather than being.

This is even clearer in the passage dealing with Emily, Palamon's and Arcite's falling in love with her and the debate between them (1033–1186).

Although Chaucer goes directly to the presentation of Emily, omitting a passage on the despair of the two prisoners and three stanzas about spring, it is only to give a symbolic, unindividualised picture of her. He removes any awareness on Emily's part of the knights' observing and admiring her and any suggestion of the girlish vanity attributed to her by Boccaccio. Instead Chaucer blends Emily with the May season to combine in her the natural and the divine; she is a flower at sunrise, an angel singing in a garden; she is the embodiment of refinement and sensitivity, as 'fyner', 'gentil', 'subtil' indicate; she rivals the lily in fairness, May in freshness, the rose in fineness. The delicate, evocative idea of the spirit of femininity is linked with a detached, superhuman innocence which requires that she be unaware of her own beauty and of her admirers. Readers have often compared this ethereal 'conventional' figure unfavourably with Chaucer's vivid sensual description of Alison in *The Miller's Tale* but the presentation of Emily is just as good an instance as the other of Chaucer's ability to adjust his style to his material. Emily is obviously no longer a character as she is in *Il Teseida* but a poetic image with enough of the natural to inspire Arcite's physical love of her and enough of the divine to inspire Palamon's 'affeccioun of hoolynesse' and enough of suggestive, never-to-be-defined ambivalence to instigate the debate between them. Chaucer reverses the order of their seeing her and this is part of his reduction of the role of Arcite (Arcita is given more attention than Palemone in *Il Teseida* and treated more sympathetically—this order of preference does survive in some parts of Chaucer's tale). Chaucer combines the two contrary devices of making the two heroes more nearly equal in prominence and sharpening the rivalry between them; in the Italian they remain comrades in love and console each other in their wounded state.

The most striking quality of effect in the passage as a whole is that by his omission of descriptions of naturalistic behaviour and by turning repeated action over a period of time into a single May occasion, Chaucer shifts the expression from narrative to speech; indeed he gives the impression that the situation is used mainly to generate speech. Apart from Palamon's startled 'A!' the speeches are dignified and rhetorical and arranged as an emotional debate gradually increasing in intensity. Arcite's repeated questions and providential consolation (1081–91) stimulate Palamon to a response in the style of a literary lyric (1093–102, 1104–11), using the language of the mind, eye and heart, the relationship of 'bane' and the lady's fairness before moving into direct address to Venus whereby Emily is elevated to goddess while he abases himself into a 'sorweful, wrecched creature' imprisoned by tyranny, begging for compassion. This archetypal expression of a medieval lyric theme, full of the image of the lover as the wounded, sorrowful, awed suppliant seems a much more significant indicator of the essential core of Chaucer's initial concept of the work than associations with medieval visual emblems (pace Kolve).[7] Chaucer is thinking in terms of rhetorical stances, the characteristic linguistic modes of lover, rather than thematic images. Lovers are metaphorically prisoners; it seems a logical reversal that prisoners should become lovers, if only to give to the words describing their literal situation an appropriate poetic resonance, as when Palamon begs Venus:

'Out of this prisoun help that we may scapen.' (1107)

In the two main speeches of rivalry (Palamon 1129–51 and Arcite 1152–86) the dramatic intensity increases when Palamon turns to attack rather than self-expression. The theme of kinship and sworn brotherhood's implications of obligations of honour leads to a crescendo in the antithesis between words associated with pride and words associated with shame: so in Palamon's address one strain builds up in *honour, sworn, never, death, love, trewely, ooth, conseil, ybounden, knight, helpen* while running counter are the reproofs in *false* (three occurrences), *falsely, traitour, darst not, withseyn*; the pride words are more varied and the shame words used more often which adds an effective counterpoint of richness of association against insistence. Also repeated are the ideas of mutuality and obligation to help; the word *oother* occurs three times and the sound-link with *ooth* adds to its claims; *forthre(n)* occurs three times, *conseil* twice. The terms of address and identification of the other, *brother, cosyn, knight*, are all reminders of obligation. The linguistic pressures add intensity to Palamon's final claim:

> 'I loved hire first, and tolde thee my wo
> As to my conseil and my brother sworn
> To forthre me, as I have toold biforn.
> For which thou art ybounden as a knyght
> To helpen me, if it lay in thy myght,
> Or elles artow fals, I dar wel seyn.'   (1146–51)

Arcite's response begins in pride with a return of the accusations of falsehood and Palamon's emotional rhetoric of accusation and moral blackmail, but turns to a more philosophical morality and argument about love and law, using the exemplum of the dogs quarrelling over a bone being robbed by the opportunist kite. The more literal quality in the language reflects the distinguishing note Chaucer attributes to Arcite of Palamon's loving Emily as a goddess while he loves her as a living being. The effect of reasoning is conveyed by the phrasing, syntax and methods: the debater's phrase 'I pose that . . .' is backed up by rhetorical questions ('Wostow nat wel . . . ?', 'who shal yeve a lovere any lawe?') and the sententious assertions and reference to 'positif lawe'. The outlook is more sternly practical and worldly wise:

> 'And therfore, at the kynges court, my brother,
> Ech man for hymself, there is noon oother.'   (1181–2)

This is in essence a denial of that mutuality, that recognition of the rights of the other, on which Palamon had insisted. The two are separate beings and each may choose his way: Arcite's way is a combination of Stoic, fatalistic resolve and readiness to 'take his aventure'.

Chaucer's simultaneous paralleling and contrasting of the two thus creates debate out of what was in Boccaccio a conversation of shared bewilderment and frustration. The polarising effect of debate prevents our continuing long to consider the two an identical pair. Although he is not so specific that we need to see them as personifications (whether of the Active and Contemplative Man, or of Boccaccio's concupiscence and irascibility), Chaucer is building a more consistent association between Palamon's acts and words and his allegiance to

Venus and those of Arcite and his allegiance to Mars. But more immediately apparent is the sharpening effect of antithesis. If Palamon's idealism is exposed as folly by Arcite's realism, Palamon's (unjustified) association of love with hope of escape is enhanced by Arcite's vehement self-interest and touches of bitter fatalism. Chaucer's rounding off of this phase of the poem is expressed in terms which identify situation and literary form:

> Greet was the strif and long bitwix hem tweye. (1187)

As individual speeches may be read as variations on courtly lyric motifs, so the whole section of speeches between the two may be read as 'strif', a literary contention reminding the reader of other medieval debates of Heart and Eye, of Knight and Clerk as lovers, even of Body and Soul. Chaucer's way of encapsulating the interest of *Il Teseida* is not to produce a romance narrative of sequential adventure, but to focus on emotional contrasts, expressions of lament, misfortune, dispute.

The reduction of the function of narrative to that of providing the framework for rhetorical speech is again apparent in the rest of Ellesmere's Part I (1187–1354) where the passage describing Arcite's release from prison makes some notable omissions and seems merely to be devised to lead on to the major set piece of this first phase of *The Knight's Tale*, the two parallel complaints of Fortune. The main excisions are Boccaccio's descriptions of the physical appearance and the temperaments of the two heroes and the detailed, circumstantial account of the meeting of Pirithous and Arcita and Teseo in prison and of Arcita's thoughts on the occasion. All is turned by Chaucer into dramatic rhetorical address: his basis is the scene where Arcita goes to say goodbye to Palemone—they part with good will and a kiss, consistent with Boccaccio's continuing expression of the affection between the two. Chaucer detaches his speeches from the particular occasion of meeting; Arcite speaks after the event, but still addresses Palamon; Palamon speaks after 'Arcite was agon' and yet still directly to him. Thus Chaucer heightens the poetic abstraction of the passage by presenting the complaints as soliloquies, which are also addresses to the rival in his absence and to the gods. They are like stage speeches in which characters address both the audience and the characters within the stage world; they speak both within the immediate situation and of the larger condition of things. This simultaneous effect adds to the patterned antithesis on which the subject-matter of the speeches is already based.

The first of the two, Arcite's speech, is announced in terms which declare its status as complaint:

> He wepeth, wayleth, crieth pitously;
> To sleen hymself he waiteth prively.
> He seyde, 'Allas that day that I was born!' (1221–3)

He first laments the situation, with extremes of feeling characteristic of the genre, elevating the speaker's passion above the level of practical commonsense. Arcite would prefer prison; he has been in purgatory but at least that was continuing and finite—now it is changed for the eternity of hell. In his words Chaucer epitomises the idea of unfulfilled yearning as a kind of bliss in comparison to the end of hope:

> 'Oonly the sighte of hire whom that I serve,
> Though that I nevere hir grace may deserve,
> Wolde han suffised right ynough for me.'   (1231–3)

In the distorted thinking of Arcite's distress, prison is now paradise and Palamon the victor in their contest; it is the sight of the beloved which is the sign of Fortune's favour and which provides the opportunity for Fortune's workings; his own lot is that of the exile 'bareyne/ Of alle grace'. This creation of a dramatic picture gives body to the courtly language: to describe Palamon as 'a knyght, a worthy and an able' is to develop a likely fate for such a one, contrasted to the despairing outcast, already imagined at the point of farewell and death:

> 'Wel oughte I sterve in wanhope and distresse.
> Farwel my lif, my lust, and my gladnesse!'   (1249–50)

The signal word 'Allas!' (1251) renews the strain of complaint in order to move into the more general phase of Boethian moral complaint concerning Fortune. Here, it is, in a sense, an anti-complaint, since Arcite in his perverse state of feeling, which rejects good fortune as bad, accuses men of error in preferring their own free choice to the situations God or Fortune provides; desired riches are causes of murder or disease; desired release from prison leaves a man to be slain by his own household. Human beings are seen as ignorant creatures, lost in this world, drunken men seeking the way home. So Arcite who thought that escape would mean 'joye and parfit heele' finds that, when it comes, it ironically means exile and hopeless death. Chaucer turns the particular case into ironic general reflection on the vanity of human wishes with the aid of Boethius, Book III, prose 2 which is about man's idea of 'sovereyn good' and 'al the purposede forme of the welefulnesse of mankynde: that is to seyn rychesses, honours, power, glorie and delitz'. Men seek the sovereign good

> . . . with a dyrkyd memorie; but he not by which path, ryght as a dronke man not nat by which path he may retourne hom to his hous.'

In the speech as a whole Chaucer expresses the sense of discontent through contrast, antithesis, alternation and denial: prison is contrasted with paradise, what was hoped for with what is. The speech is threaded through with strings of related words and phrases that bind it together to convey an impression of intense, dense feeling: the references to *now* and *then*, to what was had, might have been had, would have been had, to *thyn* and *thee*, to absence and presence, distress and gladness. The pairings and echoings and the return to words used at the beginning of the speech emphasise its studied, carefully wrought quality.

Palamon's parallel complaint (1281–98, 1303–33) is uttered 'Upon that oother syde'; Chaucer's choice of words fuses together the reference to Palamon's whereabouts (though it could represent the opposite end of a cell, the prison tower as opposed to Thebes where Palamon imagines Arcite walking 'at thy large', or the opposite side of a medieval law-court or debating chamber) and the sense that his speech is an answer to Arcite's, a view of the other side of the question. The brief picture Chaucer gives is certainly of Palamon alone after Arcite has gone, a symbolic, larger-than-life image of emotion, the huge tower echoing with his cries, his fetters wet with tears. His opening words both identify the complaint mode, like Arcite's, and respond, like the response in a debate or a musical form. There is thus no observation of literal realism: Arcite's words, literally unheard by Palamon, are, in a dramatic and rhetorical sense, available for his use:

> 'Allas!' quod he, 'Arcita, cosyn myn,
> Of al oure stryf, God woot, the fruyt is thyn.'  (1181–2)

The first half of Palamon's complaint corresponds to the middle section of Arcite's speech; Palamon too creates an imagined picture, here of a free uncaring Arcite in Thebes leaving him in sorrow 'that sterve here in a cage,/ For I most wepe and wayle . . .'. The woe of prison is doubled by that of love. If to an exiled Arcite prison and proximity and Palamon's knighthood together produce an image of Palamon and Emily united through his exclusion, so to an incarcerated Palamon freedom and opportunity and Arcite's knighthood give birth to the contrary image of Arcite and Emily joined through his sorrowing immobility. The parallelism and antithesis create a fascinating expression of the feelings of love in a stylised pattern. Chaucer elaborates a conceit in which conventional poetic metaphor is animated and exploited by dramatic situation. The use of two heroes in the tale is given its poetical justification through the sense of love as a theme for debate; two heroes enable the terms to be varied in the way that story-tellers use twins to explore variations in the relationship between nature and situation. Both are love's captives and prison represents their being held by Emily's fair image. But to be held has contrary facets. Whether to be held by the eye (representing the whole idea of the physical origin of love, the dart and the wound, and so on) is better or worse than to be held by the fetter (representing the lady's power to command and inhibit, the social need for discretion, and so on) is as productive a debater's question as the measuring of degrees of grief which Chaucer had encountered in de Machaut. Intense feeling is played off against images of restriction, variously supplied by Fortune and social convention. So imprisonment/freedom are balanced against presence/absence: the best is freedom plus presence but that is not possible at this stage, though the state to which the heroes aspire and to which they gradually move from different developments in their relationship with Theseus; the worst is imprisonment and absence but that extreme at least can be ruled out except as a threat to even the present fragile grounds of hope; only the two middle states of imprisonment with presence and freedom with absence occur; both are unsatisfactory but which is worse? The problem is made by Chaucer into a literary game of torture and the measuring of gradations of joy and despair is finally identified as a formal game, a *demande d'amour* of the Lover and the Prisoner, by Chaucer's summing up of the situation and his offering the problem for the judgment of the lovers in his audience. We can have no doubt at this point that *The Knight's Tale* is an exercise in sophisticated court poetry. But Chaucer has already gone beyond

100

expression of the sentiments appropriate to a lovers' debate over extents of suffering by giving a moral, Boethian dimension to Arcite's contemplation of the changes in his and Palamon's fortunes. Palamon's state in prison is even closer to that of the confined Boethius and Chaucer turns the second half of Palamon's complaint, with material from Boethius (Book I metrum 5 and Book III prose 7) into a serious questioning of the nature of man's life on earth.[8] The combination of the lover's passion and youthful vehemence with accusations of divine injustice gives to the passage a greater depth and power to disturb than can be accommodated within the idea of 'medieval romance'.

In these complaints Chaucer is not merely finding debating points as a means of rhetorical dramatisation of his lovers' rivalry; he raises expectations that the rest of the work will develop a serious treatment of moral and philosophical themes. He uses the voice of Palamon, who is to be the survivor of the two heroes and therefore in a position to consider in this life his own fate in comparison to Arcite's, to express man's resentment at the hard and cruel rule of the gods, their arbitrary treatment of men and the injustice of the disparities in men's fate:

> 'O crueel goddes that governe
> This world with byndyng of youre worde eterne,
> And writen in the table of atthamaunt
> Youre parlement and youre eterne graunt,
> What is mankynde moore unto you holde
> Than is the sheep that rouketh in the folde?' (1303–8)

As Elizabeth Salter puts it, Chaucer here turns an occasion of lament in Boccaccio into one of protest.[9] The motifs of the instability of Fortune and the enmity of the gods are already present in *Il Teseida* but are handled with detachment there; Chaucer enlarges the whole subject by bringing in the planets and giving more substance to expression of the idea by his use of Boethius to bolster the Italian. The immediate situation becomes more interesting and the dramatic antithesis between the two (not a feature in Boccaccio) more pointed, but Chaucer goes beyond the local and dramatic to envisage man as no better than a beast and to develop the picture of the imprisoned Palamon into an emblem of man in the dungeon of this world.

The internal rhetoric of Palamon's speech sees Chaucer continuing from Arcite's speech the use of *thow* as an emphatic directive of emotion in balance with references to himself; this turns in the second part of the complaint into a general antithesis between the power of the ruler and the weakness of the ruled; the vocabulary groups itself into two, one group associating divine power with prevention and rigid fixity and the other associating men and beasts with innocent obedience and suffering. The difference between Boccaccio's rendering of personal feeling, pathos and yearning and Chaucer's stress on the representative aspects of the situations is as clear in such details as in Chaucer's omissions and abridgements.

Chaucer continues to loosen logical connections in his account of Arcite's despair, dream and disguise, Palamon's escape and the meeting between them. Instead of particular times and places (Arcita's visiting Thebes, his hearing of the death of Emilia's betrothed), Chaucer places Arcite in an emotional, supernatural limbo, offering a perspective of feeling rather than history with

101

description of his mood and his prophetic dream. He is portrayed as a type of desperate lover, suffering like Tristram and Lancelot the lover's madness:

> Nat oonly lik the loveris maladye
> Of Hereos, but rather lyk manye,
> Engendred of humour malencolik,
> Biforen in his celle fantastik.  (1373–6)

The striking shift of register here into a combination of the literary and the scientific marks the moment and the feeling as beyond the conventional, though that too is present:

> His eyen holwe, and grisly to beholde,
> His hewe falow and pale as asshen colde,
> And solitarie he was and evere allone,
> And waillynge al the nyght, makynge his mone.  (1363–6)

The treatment of Arcite's disguise is another instance of the removal of plausible, realistic circumstance; in Boccaccio Emilia has been aware of Palemone and Arcita and thus it is consistent that she alone recognises Arcita as Penteo. Chaucer has left Emily unaware and so naturally there is no recognition of the disguised figure, who is not named until he has become Emily's page; the name Philostrate allies Arcite with Troilus and although Chaucer does add some details of Philostrate's career, these are not touches which relate to verification of plot or situation—rather they outline a romance rise, based like Havelok's on nothing but youth and strength, from nobody to court somebody.

While Arcite is temporarily cast into the role of archetypal romantic hero, Palamon is demoted into that of plotting rival, but Chaucer similarly directs attention to crucial states of mind rather than to details of plot; he changes the order, omits the minor figure of Pamfilo (Palemone's servant who overhears Arcita complaining in the grove and motivates Palemone to escape), and makes Palamon's escape another arbitrary action, dependent not on reason but 'aventure or destynee' (1465). The reader sees that it is necessary for the pattern that Palamon should escape; it is no triumph over constricting circumstance through the melancholy crescendo of the hero's frustration, but a requirement of the narrative design. The whole business is reduced to bare outline, and though the cutting through the material has the effect of speeding up, it also lessens the weight of Palamon's experience and difficulties in comparison with those of Arcite. Interestingly this part of the tale is one of the places which Robinson lists among the 'main correspondences' between Chaucer and Boccaccio,[10] and in a sense Chaucer could be said to follow the source, though abbreviating, and because this is a phase where circumstances change, Chaucer is writing in a mode which is superficially concerned with plot and narrative succession, but comparison in detail with *Il Teseida* reveals a consistent blurring of rationality, a loosening of temporal, motivational and sequential connections, and a consequent increase in the sense of men at the mercy of the irrational. Again the reader perceives that it is Chaucer's excisions which have created a world in which irrational forces determine outcome.

Continuing to turn repeated action into single occasions Chaucer follows his picture of Arcite as demented lover with one of him as May hero, 'lusty', full of the joy of spring, like Aeneas 'on a courser, startlynge as the fyr'; he fills the gaps with 'Fortune had brought him in the snare' and this and reference to 'aventure' suggest that the removal from the city is a removal into a place of chance, of spontaneous feeling and a kind of freedom, but also of risk. Arcite's love complaint springs out of the increased uncertainty, as if protest is the corollary of the speaker's unstable state. Arcite's complaint (1528–73) is well within the type characterisation of Arcite as 'woful lovere'; here Chaucer stresses the quixotic shifts of lovers' moods with the Fortune image of 'Now up, now doun, as boket in a welle', while maintaining a slightly comic detachment in 'As doon thise loveres in hir queynte geres' (1531). This note of narrator's withdrawal is an early stage in the resistance to the lovers' extremity of grief which is to culminate in Theseus' humorous assertion of a commonsense view of their situation. Chaucer is preparing his contrary movement of thought, but in the immediate moment it tends to draw attention to the elements in Arcite's speech which are not merely the 'queynte' extremes of those with 'overcaste' hearts. The material of Arcite's complaint is generally drawn from passages in *Teseida* Book IV, mingling Arcita's grief over the desolation of Thebes and Juno's enmity with later protests in conversation with Palemone. By fusing together elements from two scenes, Chaucer replaces Boccaccio's general complaint against 'wretched Fortune' by Arcite's simultaneous blaming of Juno, Mars and Love who together have brought him to the point of death. The effect is to make the results of love part of the determinist view of the historical events. The love-complaint is thus more tightly woven into the view of events in general than in Chaucer's dual compositions *Anelida and Arcite* and *The Complaint of Mars*; Arcite protests not just against the injustices of love, but against love as a type of the injustices of history and fate—the actual weapons that slay him (the eyes of Emily and the darts of love) are extensions of the anger of Mars. The influence of Mars carries over into the meeting and challenge between Arcite and Palamon. Chaucer has already developed the rivalry between the two and left behind the good feeling of comradeship which is still here expressed by Boccaccio; Chaucer conflates events, bringing out the coincidence of the meeting and its dramatic violence:

> He stirte hym up out of the bushes thikke,
> And seide, 'Arcite, false traytour wikke,
> Now artow hent, that lovest my lady so . . . '   (1579–81)

Palamon's speech is intensified and particularised; in this aspect of the tale Chaucer is actually more circumstantial to give dramatic vehemence to the speech. The enmity of Palamon is expressed as less than generous or heroic, even with a note of petulance:

> 'Thou shalt nat love my lady Emelye,
> But I wol love hire oonly and namo;
> For I am Palamon, thy mortal foo.'   (1588–90)

Arcite's response has more dignity, depth of feeling and honourable observance of decorum and reminds Palamon of the standards of knightly behaviour; as in some earlier passages Arcite is the more seriously treated as representative of youth and honour; Palamon is conveyed in briefer impressions, though with moments of vividness, as when he 'thoughte that through his herte/ He felte a coold swerd sodeynliche glyde' (1574–5). The contrast is made simply and strongly with one main speech for each.

So by removing detail and fusing together occasions and speeches, Chaucer directs sharpened attention to the contrast between and the similarity of lover and rival. Though Chaucer follows regular procedure in the duel of fighting with spears and then with swords, he does not attempt an account of the incidents in the fight: where Boccaccio has Arcita thinking he has killed Palemone and lamenting, then Palemone reviving and insisting on resuming and their discovery by Emilia, Chaucer prefers a succession of dramatic pictures—apprehension in the leafy grove, intent arming and bestial violence. For the first of these he brings forward from later in *Il Teseida* (the approach of the warriors to the amphitheatre in Book VII) the apprehension and the comparison with hunters; the image of lion or bear crashing through the undergrowth links with the later comparison of the two men fighting to lion and tiger and to wild boars and to their discovery by the hunting Theseus to form a significant ironic echo of the earlier complaints of man's bestial state. The current of events which has brought Palamon and Arcite to this moment has, except for details here and there, occupied Chaucer's attention less than the striking shift from the initial picture of the two 'bothe in oon armes' to their passionate enmity as each thinks:

> 'Heere cometh my mortal enemy!
> Withoute faille, he moot be deed, or I;
> For outher I moot sleen hym at the gappe,
> Or he moot sleen me, if that me myshappe.' (1643–6)

Even the gesture towards comradeship in their helping each other to arm has an inevitable tang of bitterness; to treat a man as if he were one's 'owene brother' is so close to treating him as a mortal enemy or an animal. The description of Theseus' appetite for hunting is shadowed not only by the emphasis on Destiny and God's purveyance, but also by the irony developing from the earlier imagery. For Boccaccio the royal hunt has echoes of Virgil and the mythology of Diana; Chaucer, though conscious of this, thinks of the word-play in describing Theseus as 'the grete hertes bane' and the men in the wood fighting 'as it were bores two'.

Once the discovery is made the poetry adopts the manner of French courtly allegory. Theseus halts the duel with the gesture of a court sergeant-at-arms and decorum and gentlemanly conduct are immediately established as criteria. Theseus' authority displays its several faces; imperious anger and quick judgment melt into noble pity in response to womanly sorrow and pleading. In contrast Palamon's conduct is exposed as vengeful and excessive in its despair, lacking in noble frankness. The formal rhetorical cast given to Palamon's speech by the opening and closing acceptance of death, marks this as Palamon's equivalent to Arcite's earlier 'woful lover' complaint. Chaucer combines in it the lamenting plea for death of one in despair and the protesting complaint against an enemy of one wronged; any remnant of the chivalrous spirit of brotherhood is dispersed by the mean-spirited element which strikingly highlights Theseus' ultimate generosity. The softening of Theseus' anger is an important stage in the moral situation, interestingly expressed in a kind of reported speech soliloquy with switches to direct interior monologue (1767–81). As reason counteracts anger within Theseus, by means of a reminder of the power of love and the way men will be prompted by it and then of women's sympathy and pity and the fitting nature of a ruler's distinguishing between treatment of the repentant and treatment of the defiant, so the current of feeling in the tale turns from anxiety and complaint towards 'compassioun', 'mercy', 'discrecioun' and the ideas associated with reason and justice. The expansive, humorous quality which Chaucer gives to Theseus' speech to the lovers vigorously asserts the values of common-sense in resistance to those of passionate lamentation. Chaucer's having kept Emily in ignorance of the two knights' love becomes a useful means of representing Arcite's and Palamon's behaviour as an unreasonable, absurd game; love has brought them into folly and danger and turned them into bleeding victims of passion, and

> 'this is yet the beste game of alle,
> That she for whom they han this jolitee
> Kan hem therfore as muche thank as me . . . '    (1806–8)

Through irony the lesson is delivered and the courtly 'strif' is thereby, in a sense, concluded; the reasonable, middle-aged voice, characterising the heroes' behaviour as 'al this hote fare', combines sympathy with regulation of conduct in a way which satisfies the needs of the courtly *demande d'amour*, shaped around complaint and debate, which Chaucer had seen in *Il Teseida*. It is appropriate to such a literary structuring of the material to conclude with a judgment and a symbolic act, and Theseus' announcing a tournament (though, of course, it leads on into the second half of the tale) provides a suitable chivalrous resolution for the rhetorical contrasts and moral stances of the first half of the tale. The idea of the lists being specially built suggests the foundation of a temporary order of chivalry to fulfil a vow (one of the 'Votal Orders').[11] So experience and social custom resolve the disturbance to rationality associated with youth and love. Theseus is present at beginning and end, conditioning the experience of the lovers by both the arbitrariness of power and its controlling benevolence. From the early impression of an arbitrary world in which the protesting voice of the prisoner represents the sympathetic note, Chaucer has moved on to counter complaint with judgment and the processes of settlement. The adventures of Arcite and Palamon are contained (in this first half and, in a broader sense, in the tale as a whole) by the governing power of Theseus to decide their fate, to regulate their behaviour, to give and to withhold. Because Chaucer develops for both the young knights some expression of the help-lessness of man within the arbitrary power of Fortune and the gods and because his abridgements endow Theseus' own conduct with arbitrariness, the role of Theseus becomes ambivalent; as governor he both creates and resolves tensions—a human image of God's power to give and to take away and certainly of the power later attributed to Saturn to punish mankind but to preserve some principle of cosmic order. This first half of *The Knight's Tale* works as a unit in the sense that the complaints, protests and conflict of the young heroes are halted and put into perspective by the voice of Reason. As in Book I of *Troilus and Criseyde*, Chaucer interprets the Italian material through his experience in writing dream-poems and other imitations of the French courtly *dits*.

## 3. Courtly Narrative

In the second half of the tale Chaucer finds other aspects of interest in his material and shifts his attention to symbols and to action, displaying other dimensions of the court poet's sense of his repertoire and his audience's likely responses, but producing, as a result, a less unified effect. The symmetrical structure of Ellesmere's Part III (with its three temple descriptions, the arrival of the guests dominated by the parallel depictions of Lygurges and Emetreus, and the three prayers to the gods) masks the divisions within the narrative, but the reader begins to identify two strands (at least) in the writing: one builds on the earlier complaints and protests in the prayers to the gods, and later in the scene of Arcite's death-bed and in Theseus' final speech; but the other responds to the epic quality of *Il Teseida* with positive enthusiasm for flamboyant description, symbolic tableaux, the paraphernalia of the tournament and Theseus' role as host and prince. This latter aspect of *The Knight's Tale* makes it look like an extravert piece of court display more than a selection of emotional and moral phases.

Many touches spread through the tale indicate that the composition of a court narrative was one of Chaucer's purposes; perhaps some sense of disparity between courtly show, knightly activities, fighting and ceremony on the one hand and paired complaints, conceits and refined feeling on the other may find an explanation in terms of fourteenth-century court history. The main area of Chaucer's adjustment of the material of *Il Teseida* in the direction of medieval court interests is in the treatment of Boccaccio's pseudo-epic combats as examples of medieval fighting;[12] such examples of medieval feudal realism are characteristic of romance's tendency to bring old matter up to date, but, as Pratt pointed out, Chaucer 'never destroys the illusion that the events took place far away and long ago.'[13] It may be that the idea of the ancient pagan past did not conflict with the intention to feature aspects of knighthood and courtly tournament because for a poet writing in the 1380s these were particularly associated with the interests of Edward III's court; the idea of a more sophisticated, detached view developing in association with the quality of interest in chivalry at the court of Richard II fits aptly the combination that one finds in *The Knight's Tale*.

Editors and commentators have at different times pointed out a large number of parallels between *The Knight's Tale* and historical events, occasions, characteristics. Among these is the possible reflection of Chaucer's personal experience in his account of Arcite's career, in his disguise as Philostrate, first as 'page of the chambre' to Emily and then as squire of the Duke's household.[14] The historical allusions include the general sense that the poem celebrates Edward III's enthusiasm for the ideas of chivalry, the possible reflection in the building of a symbolic fortress for a mustering of knights of Edward III's building enterprises at Windsor Castle (particularly the 280 foot circular space, enclosed by two concentric walls, occupying the upper bailey),[15] the foundation of the Order of the Garter,[16] the design of St George's Chapel and such possible references to specific events as Brewer suggests could be present in the echo of Queen Philippa's pleas for the burghers of Calais in the scene where Hippolyta and Emily plead with Theseus to spare Arcite and Palamon and induce the flow of pity from his 'gentil hert'.[17] As Brewer goes on to say 'the portrait of the fiery, magnanimous, chivalric Theseus' has many of the traits of Edward III in his prime. There is a possibility that Chaucer knew Jean de le Mote's lament for Queen Philippa's father, 'Li Regret Guillaume, comte de Hainaut' (1339), a rhetorical dream-poem of thirty lamenting women each personifying a chivalric quality,[18] and was recalling it in the account of Theseus' meeting with the mourning widows of Thebes. The idea of Theseus' final speech, though the material is a mixture of Boccaccio and Boethius, echoes the fatalistic spirit of one of Edward III's mottoes 'It is as it is', a motto prominently displayed and used in the special bed-covers and costumes (with a design of *rotulis*—possibly wheels of Fortune) commissioned for the betrothal of Prince Lionel to Elizabeth, later Countess of Ulster, in 1342; Chaucer's service in their household could have brought into his experience other people's memory of such an occasion and the elaborate tournament held to celebrate it.[19] Even closer resemblances to *The Knight's Tale* are found in the Chandos Herald's Anglo-Norman verse life of the Black Prince (*c.* 1386), where the reception of the Prince after his victories resembles Theseus' triumph and where the dead hero is celebrated as model of courtesy and prowess.[20]

*The Knight's Tale* is a reflection of the main literary interests of the fourteenth-century court too. Among the works possessed by most medieval European courts, high on the list of frequency are Vegetius' *De Re Militari* (seen as a standard work on knighthood, despite its fourth century origin) or some derivative of it, such as Ramon Lull's *Livre de Chivalrie*, and Boethius' *De Consolatione Philosophiae*, perhaps possessed so widely, as R. F. Green suggests, because readily applicable to the uncertainties of authority in the Middle Ages.[21] One could hardly imagine a narrative poem better devised than *The Knight's Tale* to appeal to a courtly taste nurtured on the rules of chivalry and the consolations for Fortune's unruly whims. An interesting aesthetic possibility is that Chaucer's sight of wall-paintings in Italy,[22] or even of paintings in England in the Lombard style in St George's Chapel, Windsor and St Stephen's, Westminster may be reflected in his envisaging the 'speaking pictures' of the walls of the Temples. More allusions, echoes, resemblances could easily be added;[23] wherever one looks, *The Knight's Tale* seems to contain elements of the literary, social and cultural values of the court civilisation of its time. Even the touch of satire present in Arcite's comment on the court is within a recognised courtly mode.

Links between a poet's work and his audience are tricky things to be certain about, particularly when one knows comparatively little about Chaucer's exact circumstances in relation to court patronage. Recent discussion of the question has produced an interesting and plausible picture, even if it does depend upon some surmise. Paul Strohm points to evidence of social mobility in the later medieval period (for example, groupings of knights among the *mediocri* with esquires and merchants) as part of his argument that the audience to which Chaucer's identifying tone of sophisticated intelligence was directed was a mixed group of knights, esquires, lawyers and Chancery figures, most of whom were 'new men', born in the middle class or petty gentry, moving between worlds of London business, country landholdings and the world of their noble masters. He suggests that such men would have gained a capacity for complexity of response and that this is the key to Chaucer's liking for exploring contradictions, for unresolved debate, for subtle qualification of expected responses.[24] Derek Pearsall argues similarly that, although only a few of Chaucer's works are directly addressed to a royal audience (*The Legend of Good Women*, 'Lak of Stedfastnesse') or have aristocratic connections (*The Book of the Duchess*), he is nevertheless a court poet in the larger sense of writing for a mixed audience of household knights and officials, diplomats and civil servants—men for whom learning was part of their lives and necessary to their profession;[25] Chaucer's role as *translateur* and as innovator relates to this changing court milieu. R. F. Green makes a more direct attack on some old clichés, scotching the notion that the 'middle-class' pilgrims in *The Canterbury Tales* see the aristocratic life with distant, escapist longing—as far as literary taste is concerned, they are all one—and rejecting the old idea of a 'new reading public': the court itself was the origin of the literary vogue for moral instruction and for historical information. Green puts particular stress on the importance of the *Camera Regis*, the King's Chamber, which had a staff and a social life of its own and which was the place for the display of social graces and for entertainments and accomplishments: here was the focus for the shift in court culture, a shift from literature for the hall and entertainment by minstrels to works for an intimate audience, commissioned works of art and the elegant exercises of the amateur courtier poet. Deschamps' *Art de Dictier* makes the social distinction that 'musique naturele' (spoken verse, as distinct from song) is the preserve of the gentleman, and poets and authors regularly form part of the nobility from the fourteenth century. Consequent upon such social changes were changes in the relationship of poet and audience:

If the old minstrel literature was a literature of performance, the new courtly verse might be characterised as a literature of participation.[26]

On the other hand the subjects preferred by the two courts of Edward III and Richard II show a contrary movement. In the earlier part of the century the evidence of books possessed and bequeathed, of commissioned, possessed, recorded works of literature, painting and architecture and so on show a sustained pattern of literary interest throughout Edward III's reign, as Juliet Vale demonstrates.[27] The occurrence of the *Secreta Secretorum*, Vegetius and Mandeville's Travels among the possessions of Isabella the Queen Mother identifies a characteristic court interest in advice to princes and 'practical' knowledge and the inclusion among goods recorded at her death (1358) of six to ten panel paintings including three from Lombardy is evidence of Italian influence early in the century. As significant is the connection of one of Edward's major areas of artistic patronage, St George's Chapel, with a specifically chivalric impulse. Chivalry and culture are seen as inextricable, as accounts of royal celebrations and tournaments make clear: the inspiration for costumed masques or 'disguisings' was often both literary and topical—Arthurian romances, the story of Troy, the Nine Worthies, the chansons de geste, travel literature are all reflected in court *ludi*, but figures could also reflect current political situations, as in the Smithfield tournament of 1343 which alluded to current animosity towards papal influence. The resemblance between items provided for the Christmas *ludi* of 1352 and details of costumes described in *Winner and Waster* is a specific instance of connections between court literature and social life.[28] Thus, though the movement of court literature may be from enjoyed performance towards courtiers' participation and the idea of light social poetry as part of genteel education, at the same time, the literary activity most typically associated with the court of Edward III is that in which courtiers re-enact literary roles in the context of chivalric pageantry and expensively dressed court games. In a different way informative and practical literature has a continuity with the actual duties and practical interests of the royal court. By contrast Richard II, though he continued the court attraction of practical literature (history used as example, handbooks for rulers), had little interest in participating in chivalric games; he preferred the role of observer; cautious and unwarlike, he did not hunt or take part in tournaments, but liked to watch. So while the society of the hall and the minstrel's songs and tales may have been gradually replaced by courtiers' coteries and games of love, there is a shift from a robust celebration of chivalric honour to a more observant interest in the art of the activity. To some this shift was offensive: Thomas Walsingham in *Historia Anglicana* (1387) describes the knights of Richard II's court as 'knights of Venus rather than knights of Bellona, more valiant in the bedchamber than on the field, armed with words rather than weapons, prompt in speaking but slow in performing the acts of war.'[29] V. J. Scattergood presents an interesting picture of the literary culture of Richard's court as showing some division between the preferences of courtiers for Latin and French works on serious subjects, with romance (perhaps in the vernacular) for entertainment, and the tastes of the professional men, more open to new, serious-minded poetry in English dealing with philosophy and love.[30] Scattergood supports this with a quotation from an attack in 1391 by one of the 'new men', though his Lollard sympathies may make him extreme on the point, Sir John Clanvowe; his subject is the court's high valuation of extravagant conquerors and men anxious to defend their worship in the world and their reputation after death.

And of swyche folke men maken bookes and soonges and reeden and syngen of hem for to hoolde þe mynde of here deedes þe lengere heere upon eerthe, ffor þat is a þing þat worldely men desiren greetly þat here naame myghte laste loonge after hem heere upon eerth.

(*The Two Ways*, 493–9)[31]

*The Knight's Tale* could be read as such a work, though Chaucer uses the hope of leaving a great name behind as a characteristically pagan belief and though Chaucer could be said to be trying to bridge the gap between the courtiers' interest in the niceties of knighthood, tournaments, hunting and ceremony and the professional men's taste for philosophy and debate.

Some sense of gap is nevertheless visible in the second half of the tale. Between the description of the three Temples, which Chaucer has brought forward, and the accounts of the respective prayers of Palamon, Emily and Arcite to their patron deities, Chaucer has inserted his version of the next stage of the narrative, the recruiting of supporters by the two young men and their arrival for the tournament (2095–208). At first Chaucer creates a general impression of activity, people and multiplicity. The effect comes from repeated references to numbers and groups of men, and the idea of many vying to be included or being chosen; there are several expressions referring to part/whole or some/others. The passage is full of large numbers with general group attitudes and, at the same time, of the thoughts of individuals, as in the following extract:

> For every wight that lovede chivalrye,
> And wolde, his thankes, han a passant name,
> Hath preyed that he myghte been of that game;
> And wel was hym that therto chosen was.
> For if ther fille tomorwe swich a cas,
> Ye knowen wel that every lusty knyght
> That loveth paramours and hath his myght,
> Were it in Engelond or elleswhere,
> They wolde, hir thankes, wilnen to be there,
> To fighte for a lady, benedicitee!   (2106–15)

Many expressions refer to free choice (*his thankes, chosen* etc), so that threaded through the impression of activity and life are suggestive attitudes which imply a society which makes them possible. In contrast to the Temple descriptions, dominated by foreboding images of the extremes to which uncontrolled passion, whether of love or war or even virgin modesty, may lead, and giving an over-all impression of human beings in the power of irrational divinities, here Chaucer is animating an approving picture of the chivalrous activity of the tournament, seen as an expression of free will, drawing enthusiasm, ambition, lively spirit. To love 'paramours' is to have stirred one's fighting pluck and manly zest for reputation.

The passage can be seen as part of Chaucer's medievalising of the material, but it is not just the local colour of armour and the group version of that conventional motif, the arming of the knight, that one perceives, but a more specific delineation of a secular order of chivalry and the heraldic quality which authenticates its observances. Courtly readers would be likely to see in the story a celebration of contemporary noble ideals and courtly public entertainment, and both aspects are indicated in Chaucer's use of such expressions as 'that game' and 'It were a lusty sighte'. Some readers have tried to link the description of the two kings, which follows, to contemporary instance, especially Emetreus who has been identified with both Richard II and Henry, Earl of Derby, or to medieval symbolism (Lygurges as Saturnian, Emetreus as Martian and so on).[32] But it is the general quality of colourful panache that most strikes the modern reader. As a substitute for Boccaccio's more specific list of heroes, Chaucer has worked up an antithesis, inventing Emetreus to balance Lygurges and adding visual detail (using bits of Agamemnon and Evandro) to the brief picture in *Il Teseida* and inventing parallel detail for Emetreus to make a striking contrast of physical types. Both figures are bizarre and the flamboyant images of warlike masculinity act as another kind of externalisation of the qualities of Arcite and Palamon. These two exist in the story as stylised depictions of young lovers, carried along by powerful destiny, but not as dominant figures; victims or suppliants, guilty, imprisoned, disguised, anxious, grateful, their heroic virtues or passions are either abstract, supernatural forces or, as here, displaced into others. The two kings play no significant role in the battle that follows; they are present simply as images of splendid public bravado. The stress in the picture of Lygurges is on size and strength, ferocity and rich, shining blackness. The portrait is admiring (*pace*

110

Spearing's identification of 'bestial' qualities),[33] but there is no suggestion that it is within the idea of 'lusty chivalry' adumbrated in the previous passage. The picture is exotic. Lygurges seems some wild Tartar (or Macedonian or Cretan) belonging to the world of Mandeville or Oriental romance, or, at the nearest to a chivalric court, to the idea of a visiting foreigner such as Palomides in *Le Morte D'Arthur*. Here is something of the dangerous glamour of war that is strikingly absent from the tapestry of images in the Temple of Mars. Opposed to blackness and sleekness are the curly yellow ringlets, gleaming sunlike, of Emetreus who is compared to Mars himself. The emphasis in this picture of a blonde King of India is on wealth, youth and a tawny vigour and brightness uniting fiery Mars with animal strength; despite the reference to India this is a more European courtly image, leading to the more general picture of the armed knights with him 'gadered in this noble compaignye/ For love and for encrees of chivalrye.'

After this virtuoso display of splendid extravagance it is not surprising that Chaucer has recourse to occupatio in the summary of Theseus' welcome and feasting of the knights, but Boccaccio is himself general at this point so that Chaucer is not in fact summarising a more detailed passage in his source; he is simply using this way of suggesting yet further luxury and entertainment and civilised court life beyond the reach of his pen, with just a flicker of humour at the suggestion that he might have told us the name of the hawks and hounds and painstakingly have listed everything. There is in occupatio a quality of choosing from a mass of material which adds here to that earlier impression of a freely choosing society and the part/whole distinctions which suggest range and multiplicity.

In Ellesmere's last section (divided in Hengwrt into the completion of its Part II and an epilogue) Chaucer covers a lot of ground and makes some significant omissions—the apotheosis of the dead Arcita, the marriage of Arcita and Emily, the ceremony and passion of the closing stages. Chaucer produces a mixture of public panorama and private tragedy, falling into a number of distinct phases and shifting ground as he dodges from following his source to drastic changes of interpretation and emphasis; this is particularly obvious at the division point in the Hengwrt text, line 2742 in Ellesmere, where, despite Arcite's accident, Theseus brings the tournament to a hospitable, harmonious end, but Chaucer, by omitting Palemone's presentation of himself as prisoner and the marriage scene, turns Arcite's deathbed into the aftermath to form resolution and judgment. The effect is almost of two endings, one to the epic/romance picture of court and battle, the other to the moral debate.

In the handling of the tournament itself one sees the rival claims on Chaucer's attention. Avoiding Boccaccio's epic flourishes of invocation and grandiose imagery, Chaucer provides a chivalrous court prelude in a romance style (2483–522) conveying the excitement and 'plesaunce' of the occasion in 'the lusty seson of that May', with a bustle of activity from 'many a route/ Of lordes upon stedes and palfreys', the clatter of weapons, trumpets and drums, the audience assembling. It is one of Chaucer's most vivid pictures, appealing to the courtly hearer through the language of the accoutrements of chivalry:

> The sheeldes brighte, testeres, and trappures,
> Gold-hewen helmes, hauberkes, cote-armures;
> Lordes in parementz on hir courseres,

> Knyghtes of retenue, and eek squieres
> Nailynge the speres, and helmes bokelynge;
> Giggynge of sheeldes, with layneres lacynge
> (There as nede is they weren no thyng ydel);
> The fomy steedes on the golden brydel
> Gnawynge, and faste the armurers also
> With fyle and hamer prikynge to and fro . . .   (2499–508)

Activity, anticipation, contemporary detail, together convey enthusiastic involvement, which carries over into the description of Theseus' rules for and supervision of the ordered ceremony (2523–98).

> Duc Theseus was at a wyndow set
> Arrayed right as he were a god in trone.   (2528–9)

Where Boccaccio makes the distinction between battle for a serious purpose and a dispute 'for love alone' in which there was inadequate reason for kinsfolk to kill each other or princes to lose their lives, for Chaucer the chivalrous tournament needs no special justification or explanation and Theseus' decree about non-mortal combat has as its reason simply the avoidance of 'destruccioun/ To gentil blod'. The terms of combat are closer to Froissart than to Boccaccio. The whole passage is a sympathetic treatment of a secular order of chivalry, and related attitudes and atmosphere, submitting the 'ancient' literary material to a fourteenth-century sense of occasion. It is one of the most explicit passages of one kind of court poetry anywhere in Chaucer.

For the fighting Chaucer concentrates on a panoramic battle scene, somewhat in the style of alliterative poetry (2599–662).[34] The effect in a Chaucerian context is more archaic than it would be in, say, the *Alliterative Morte Arthur*; the tournament suddenly becomes a battle rather than a game. Yet the passage is forceful and economical, employing a clever alternation of plural and singular statements (which is Chaucer's replacement for Boccaccio's more detailed account of individual exploits) and giving the impression of darting here and there and of taking at one moment a broad view, at another an exact one of a complex scene. Many of the plural statements are impersonal ones about the weapons and other accompaniments of battle (*trompes, speres, shaftes, steedes* and so on), giving the impression of battle as mechanical action, with objects moving, making noise, breaking, destroying. The only identified human groups are the heralds and observers. The singular statements are personal but anonymous; they describe individual acts, mainly of suffering, though the anonymous 'he' presents them as typical instances:

> In goon the speres ful sadly in arrest;
> In gooth the sharpe spore into the syde.
> Ther seen men who kan juste and who kan ryde;
> Ther shyveren shaftes upon sheeldes thikke;
> He feeleth thurgh the herte-spoon the prikke.   (2602–6)

Despite the preliminary build up of anticipation and sense of the chivalrous pleasure of the tournament, here there is little attention given to aspects of vigorous enjoyment or youthful challenge; all is violence and injury and this carries over to the references to Arcite and Palamon that follow. Chaucer had to choose between two of his interpretations of *Il Teseida*; he was, on the one hand, building up the chivalrous, court aspect, but, on the other, intensifying the personal rivalry and here the intensity and bitter enmity win. In the general passage the effect is more of a realistic recognition that battle is bloody and that risk and pain are accepted, but the particular depiction of the heroes makes a shift into Homeric comparison, which in the bloody context becomes heavily ironic:

> Ther nas no tygre in the vale of Galgopheye,
> Whan that hir whelp is stole whan it is lite,
> So crueel on the hunte as is Arcite
> For jelous herte upon this Palamon.
> Ne in Belmarye ther nys no fel leon,
> That hunted is, or for his hunger wood,
> Ne of his praye desireth so the blood,
> As Palamon to sleen his foo Arcite.
> The jelous strokes on hir helmes byte;
> Out renneth blood on bothe hir sydes rede.   (2626–35)

Under the flourish of showy names, there is not all that much difference in the actual acts of Arcite and Palamon from their duel in the grove; the 'dignity' of the tournament looks thin here. The absence of any intimate sense of the young men's feelings and the omission of passages about Emily reduce the tournament to two unrelated tableaux of enjoyment and of violence. Perhaps Emilia's reflection in *Il Teseida* that Theseus would have done better to let them fight it out alone has coloured the passage, even if Chaucer omits it.

Chaucer jumps to the end, continuing in the same vein, not allowing any sense of triumph or glory except in the muted sense of Palamon's being unable to avoid defeat and of retaining 'his hardy herte'. Chaucer communicates discomfort to the reader by concentrating on the defeated knight; whereas earlier he had treated Arcite as the representative 'woful lover', now the stress has shifted to Palamon—'Who sorweth now but woful Palamon?'. By cutting out Arcita's triumphant circuit of the arena, his thanking his supporters, and his marriage, Chaucer moves more swiftly to disaster, and though this may prepare for the eventual ending, Chaucer loses the effect of demonstrating Fortune's fickleness; there is too little of joy and splendour at this point for deprivation and death quite to make the appropriate sudden reversal. Hardly is Arcite's victory registered than the narrator is heavy-handedly warning us to pay attention (2674–5). Emilia's feelings of joy and immediate love for Arcita are reduced to a mere glance and a worldly narrator's comment (2681–2). It is only with the accident itself that Chaucer seems to settle again into a natural-sounding voice after this fit of throat clearing; he omits Venus' Fury, serpent-crowned, sulphurous, with a scourge of snakes, and makes it sound like some accident of the field—a man ditched unceremoniously from his horse, lying as if dead:

> His brest tobrosten with his sadel-bowe.
> As blak he lay as any cole or crow . . .   (2691–2)

With effective economy now he jumps to the eventual consequence of the accident and links the fall with thoughts of Arcite's eventual death and his sorrow as he is brought back to the palace in a bed:

> For he was yet in memorie and alyve,
> And alwey criynge after Emelye.   (2698–9)

This all represents a major change on Chaucer's part, characteristic of his reduction of epic panoply and of emphasis on Arcita as hero in the latter part of *Il Teseida*; of Arcita's recovery from unconsciousness, his return on a triumphal chariot with Emilia at his side, the procession to the Temple of Mars, thanks for victory, riding through the city with Palemone as captive, the comforting of Palemone by Teseo who speaks to him and his followers of divine providence, of many more details leading to the marriage of Arcita and Emilia, of all this, one might say, Chaucer 'maketh now no mencioun'.

In the omitted material are interesting seeds which grew into passages elsewhere, especially Theseus' final speech which has elements from his comforting of Palamon's men at this point. But the reduction of the roles of Arcite and Emily and of the extent of their commitment to each other clearly leaves the conclusion freer of emotional complication. Whereas in some parts of the tale Chaucer intensifies and even adds realism of feeling, here what he chooses is consistent with his lower-toned, 'medieval', court treatment of the tournament and the impression of a smaller scale; this is not the presentation of a great imperial theme but a more domestic affair. He reassures the reader that none were killed and that wounds, even, men hope, Arcite's, can be healed; defeat did not mean loss of honour or any accusation of cowardice:

> Ne ther was holden no disconfitynge
> But as a justes, or a tourneiynge . . .
> For fallyng nys nat but an aventure . . .
> It nas arretted hym no vileynye;
> Ther may no man clepen it cowardye.
> (2719–20, 22, 29–30)

Given the general abbreviation in this section, it is striking that this idea is so fully treated; concern for chivalrous honour replaces all the source's narrative of the rewards of valour and the triumph, even if temporary, of courage and love. Chaucer has extrapolated this element from Teseo's comfort of Palemone while postponing the consolatory aspect until later.

Just as he had created a chivalrous prelude, so now Chaucer forms an epilogue justifying the tournament (despite the treatment of the actual fighting, where there was little evidence of the comradeship and honour of the chivalrous ethic) almost as a thing in itself, separate from the actual fate of the heroes through whom it came into being:

> For which anon duc Theseus leet crye,
> To stynten alle rancour and envye,
> The gree as wel of o syde as of oother,
> And eyther syde ylik as ootheres brother;

And yaf hem yiftes after hir degree . .
And hoom wente every man the righte way.
Ther was namoore but 'Fare wel, have good day!'

(2731–5, 2739–40)

The good feeling expressed here is one end of a range of feeling about fighting in *The Knight's Tale* which is more directly articulated than the feelings attributed to the main characters in this part of the story. It suggests, as do many other details, that within the poem there is a subsidiary narrative going on which relates obliquely, sometimes confusingly, to the central theme of the work.

## 4. The Great Effect

Woven in with Chaucer's mainly commendatory treatment of chivalry and court ceremony is his extension of the complaining strife between Arcite and Palamon into a conflict among the gods. The pictures of the gods act both as a symbolic externalisation of the forces which motivate Arcite, Palamon and Emily, and as a confirmation of the earlier protests by the heroes against the injustice of the gods' treatment of men. It is difficult to reconcile the implications of the two (even without the further complications of the 'have good day!' variety) and Chaucer's rearrangement of the material to give prominence to the Temples and to establish what they stand for before the actual scenes where the characters pray to their patron deities makes a strange impression. The amphitheatre itself is presented as a social and moral symbol, the product of 'the dispence/ Of Theseus', noble, costly, combining elegance with usefulness. The Temples function partly to support the idea that the amphitheatre encompasses human social life, is 'a noble theatre' where the drama of love and rivalry is to be acted out and so on, but Chaucer's use of the tradition of the Children of the Planets in his descriptions of the varied human activities that can be attributed to the influence of the planet allows the descriptions to open out beyond their immediate function into an exploration of pagan gods which is partly satirical in effect.

With the Temple of Venus the direction in which attention is pointed is to the melancholy, undisciplined and corrupting aspects of love. First comes an impression of fervent desire and lament:

The broken slepes, and the sikes colde,
The sacred teeris, and the waymentynge . . .  (1920–1)

Then allegorical personifications (some taken from Boccaccio) represent the changeable attributes of love, good and bad, together with associated conditions, symptoms and results. The four lines of names (1925–8) build up a pointed piece of satire. In the first line 'Plesaunce and Hope, Desir, Foolhardynesse' the sting is in the last of the quartet, which casts a shadow of reckless folly back and undermines the other three. 'Beautee and Youthe, Bauderie, Richesse' neatly sets the two pretty conditions of picturesque love against the actuality so often found as beauty and youth fade. 'Charmes and Force, Lesynges, Flaterye' shows the balance shifted from three good qualities and one bad in the first line; now the charm, sweetness and youthful romance

115

of love is gradually drowning in intrigue, the rapist's greed, the libertine's deceits. Finally 'Despense, Bisynesse and Jalousye' sees love as entirely a matter of arrangements and anxiety. Some further general impressions of 'Lust and array, and alle the circumstaunces/ Of love' lead into classical instances of the power of love, illustrating the moral that:

> wysdom ne richesse,
> Beautee ne sleighte, strengthe ne hardynesse,
> Ne may with Venus holde champartie,
> For as hir list the world than may she gye.   (1947–50)

Love is seen as powerful and picturesque, rich in association, but touches of mockery do not allow the reader to attribute wisdom to love's servant; if Palamon submits himself to love it is because he can do no other and so his allegiance is an instance of human beings' weak vulnerability to unreliable divinities. Inevitably the role of love's servants is to lament:

> Lo alle thise folk so caught were in hir las,
> Til they for wo ful ofte seyde 'Allas!'   (1951–2)

The visual impression is strong throughout the description of the Temple of Mars as Chaucer combines the supposed observation of paintings on the wall with reminiscence of the actual Temple of Mars in Thrace. From Boccaccio's successive use of allegory and general impression Chaucer forms a mingling of personifications, individual type-figures (the pickpurse, the smiler with the knife, and so on) and images and classical *figurae* (Julius, Nero, Antony); the ideas become more exact either through the historical name or the individual picture. The whole passage is a surprisingly vivid panorama of images seen by an eye darting to and fro, and the repeated shift from allegory to instance effectively acts out this idea; references to placing in the midst of the rapid list suggest the eye forming multiple images into an over-all picture, as with 'Amyddes of the temple sat Meschaunce' (2009) or 'And al above, depeynted in a tour,/ Saugh I Conquest' (2027–8). The imagination creates some multi-figured fresco such as a Last Judgment scene.

   In neither description is there any specific reference to the allegorical interpretations in Boccaccio's glosses, but there is a sense that Chaucer sees an allegorical picture which demonstrates the destructive power of the divinity. If Venus represents the power that 'causes all kinds of lust to be desired', then Mars was, for Boccaccio, the appetite 'which troubles a man when he loses or is prevented from gaining the objects of his enjoyment'. As with the distinction between two Venuses, one representing 'all worthy and legitimate desires', the other lust, so a just, reasonable Mars was conventionally contrasted with an unjust, irrational one. Theseus' marriage to Hippolyta and his undertaking just wars may be seen as representing the good aspects of Venus and Mars respectively, but the moral interpretation is not made explicit by Chaucer. Instead he omits the glory of war and adds images of accident, violent death, the hypocrisy of enmity, of sharp weapons, of the slaughter of great men. Whether the picture conveys moral disapproval of Arcite's actions is open to question, but it certainly prefigures Arcite's death in the service of Mars, among those 'Who shal be slayn or elles deed for love' (2038) and creates a menacing

116

perspective within which the human role is inevitably that of bootless protest. If Palamon's allegiance to Venus is obliquely shown as the folly of weakness, then Arcite's allegiance to Mars is shown as dangerous, a submission of self to the destructive powers of violence; love has unloosed the dogs of war and the sudden fury that destroys him is symbolically shown as inherent in the force on which he relies—he will, in a sense, be eaten by the wolf.

Though shorter, less sharply characterised and lacking the touches of satire present in the other two, the picture of the Temple of Diana again conveys the power of the abstract forces of the goddess's various aspects—chastity, the chase, woman's physical nature—to overmaster individual instances; personal desire is controlled by stronger forces. Diana's aspects are presented so as to suggest variously Emily's role as victim. Again the symbolic picture makes the ordered construction of the stadium and its chapels mock rather than resolve human yearnings and conflicts.

The effect of Chaucer's staying away from Arcite and Palamon as individual actors, instead externalising the elements in their natures into symbolic figures and buildings, is apparent when the prayers are reached. In place of the passionate, rhetorical statements of the first half of the tale these are merely private annexes to the main public effect of the allegorical pictures. The supernatural is a matter of personal portents in response to the prayers. The speeches combine elements of complaint, as each speaks of his or her own desires and fears, with aspects of ceremonious expression of allegiance to the particular deity. Palamon's address to Venus is, for obvious reasons, the nearest to a love-complaint, but instead of Palemone's mighty pangs and intense yearning Chaucer stresses the bewildering effect of love, with an echo of *The Parliament of Fowls*:

> 'I am so confus that I kan noght seye
> But "Mercy, lady bright, that knowest wele
> My thoght, and seest what harmes that I feele!" ' (2230–32)

Palamon's inadequacy of language 'to telle/ Th'effectes', conventional in itself, is appropriately linked to the idea of his recklessly abandoning all to Venus; he gives total commitment but leaves the means to greater powers. Chaucer effectively encapsulates the tenor of the prayer in a final line:

> 'This is th'effect and ende of my preyere:
> Yif me my love, thow blisful lady dere.' (2259–60)

Similarly Chaucer condenses the core of Emily's rejected prayer, sandwiched between the two accepted ones, in her wish:

> 'to walken in the wodes wilde,
> And noght to ben a wyf and be with childe.' (2309–10)

Arcite's prayer to Mars moves to a final plea 'Yif me the victorie, I aske thee namore' after a speech fuller of Mars and strength than of the complaints of love, though that element is present:

> 'she that dooth me al this wo endure
> Ne reccheth nevere wher I synke or flete.' (2396–7)

117

These prayers have nothing like the powerful verbal force of the patterned, antithetical speeches in the first half of the poem. They signal the helplessness of the characters, which earlier formed the subject for protest for the two young men, and the transference of the debate at the centre of the poem from human to divine level—a level at which Chaucer sounds unhappy. The prayers lead directly to the conflict between Mars and Venus and to the speech of Saturn identifying his own vengeful power over human life:

> 'I do vengeance and pleyn correccioun,
> Whil I dwelle in the signe of the leoun.
> Myn is the ruyne of the hye halles,
> The fallynge of the toures and of the walles
> Upon the mynour or the carpenter . . .' (2461–5)

With a grinding gear shift at line 2470 Saturn becomes the comforter of the lamenting Venus and the preacher of reconciliation. When he comes to complete this divine debate Chaucer manages the transition more successfully by paralleling comments on Palamon and Venus and envisaging both in the stance of complainant:

> Who sorweth now but woful Palamoun,
> That moot namoore goon agayn to fighte? . . .
> What kan now faire Venus doon above?
> What seith she now? What dooth this queene of love
> But wepeth so, for wantynge of hir wille,
> Til that hir teeres in the lystes fille?
> She seyde, 'I am ashamed, doutelees.' (2652–3, 2663–7)

The weeping Venus is a reminder of love's association with lament and the appropriateness in love's knight having to win his lady after difficulty and pain. In three more lines of Saturn's reply, fulfilling his earlier promise to Venus, the supernatural passage is swiftly concluded. Chaucer both reduces the moment (especially Venus' part in it) and adds Saturn's role, making love appear ineffectual and in need of the executive power of time, Fortune and other manipulative agents. The contraries in Saturn's nature identify the problem which faces Chaucer at the end of the tale and which he exacerbates by major omissions which expose the difficulties. The Hengwrt structure suggests that one idea Chaucer had was to convey at the end of the tournament a sense of completing at least the symbolic occasion in a celebration of chivalry and courtesy, and putting a much abbreviated version of the death of Arcite and the marriage of Palamon and Emily into an epilogue.

The handling of the deathbed scene is a clear instance of Chaucer's giving much greater tautness and economy of effect; he channels the material of successive scenes between Arcita and Teseo, Arcita and Palemone, Arcita and Emilia, all into a single speech (2765–97) addressed by Arcite to Palamon and Emily jointly, preceeding this speech by a medical passage (2743–64) and following it with an account of Arcite's death and reactions to it (2798–852). The unexpectedly detailed and technical account of the poison in Arcite's system includes no really obscure vocabulary, but the cumulative effect of *clothered, veyne-blod, ventusynge, vertu expulsif, pipes of his longes, lacerte, vomyt, laxatif* is to bring the sick-room rather than the deathbed of a hero into the reader's consciousness and the disconcerting abruptness of

> And certeinly, ther Nature wol nat wirche,
> Fare wel phisik! go ber the man to chirche  (2759–60)

has to be read in this context of 'leechcraft', which has both stressed the corruption of nature and the ineffectuality of 'thilke vertu cleped naturel' on the one hand and, on the other, identified the 'phisik' that is equally inadequate since 'Nature hath now no dominacioun'. Chaucer has not included any sense of recovery or the passage of time in his handling of Arcite's injury and so can proceed directly to death, but the passage creates a kind of syncopation, slowing down for the medical detail, then dismissing it as useless. For Boccaccio's dignified sense of the proper care of a learned physician Chaucer substitutes the domestic summary of symptoms and treatment and the sense of the doctor closing up the case-notes with sharp folk wisdom. The passage supports acceptance of the inevitable, through which Chaucer attempts to harmonise Arcite's death with the conventions of romance.

Arcite's deathbed speech combines farewell, complaint and commendation, and combines also stylistic effects of touching intimacy with the high-flown repetitions and conventional phrases of rhetorical lyric. The high strain is used with intelligence and point, as here:

> 'Allas, the wo! allas, the peynes stronge,
> That I for yow have suffred, and so longe!
> Allas, the deeth! allas, myn Emelye!
> Allas, departynge of oure compaignye!
> Allas, myn hertes queene! allas, my wyf!
> Myn hertes lady, endere of my lyf!'  (2771–6)

The language of the distressed lover makes death seem at home, the rhetorical final effect of 'peynes stronge', and the passage achieves a kind of irony from being uttered by an actually dying man, as metaphor becomes literally true. Arcite here resumes the earlier role of the woeful lover, the one who has actually paid the price so often expressed but so seldom seen as anything but rhetorical threat or emotional blackmail; his case makes love seem more serious and deepens the feeling in the tale retrospectively; the fact that love can kill justifies the rhetoric and adds to the poignancy of the eventual happy ending. The high strain is visible too in the rhetorical questions of the famous lines that follow, though the words now echo Boethius as much as the troubadour's voice:

> 'What is this world? what asketh men to have?
> Now with his love, now in his colde grave
> Allone, withouten any compaignye,
> Fare wel, my swete foo, myn Emelye!'  (2777–80)

The lyric lover's note is kept up in 'my swete foo' and its irony in context gives it a piercing aptness. The phrase 'allone, withouten any compaignye' occurs in *Melibee* as well as in *The Miller's Tale*:

> 'And if thy fortune change that thou wexe povre, farewel freendshipe and felaweshipe; for thou shalt be alloone withouten any compaignye, but if it be the compaignye of povre folk.' (*Melibee*, VII, 1560)

Chaucer is again revivifying a formula by making the context supply its conditions with literal finality.

Counterpointing the lyric rhetoric is a more direct note of simplicity which gives to the speech the effect of real feeling betrayed:

> 'To yow, my lady, that I love moost . . .
> . . . softe taak me in youre armes tweye,
> For love of God, and herkneth what I seye.' (2767, 2781–2)

The latter part of the speech turns to commendation of Palamon and the ideals of the chivalrous life. Arcite defines 'alle the circumstaunces trewely' that appertain to a 'servaunt':

> 'That is to seyn, trouthe, honour, knyghthede,
> Wysdom, humblesse, estaat, and heigh kynrede,
> Fredom, and al that longeth to that art.' (2789–91)

We accept this more as a statement of an ideal than a description of Palamon (who has shown little wisdom except in picking the right god to pray to), but the closing words 'Foryet nat Palamon, that gentil man' are touching and dignified. Chaucer continues his discriminating treatment of the scene (in comparison with Boccaccio's excess) in the economical account of the death itself (2806–8). Less immediately communicating sureness of taste are lines 2809–16, though they are illuminated by *Il Teseida*; this is Chaucer's substitute for Boccaccio's description of the journey of Arcita's spirit, so that Chaucer is in effect rejecting Boccaccio's claim of knowledge when he says:

> His spirit chaunged hous and wente ther,
> As I cam nevere, I kan nat tellen wher. (2809–10)

Some readers have seen burlesque beginning here and it is possible that Chaucer indicates other differences from Boccaccio by flippancy; Boccaccio is emotional and Italian here and wallows in the whole of this death episode. Chaucer prefers, as with the funeral later, not to follow that path. His later use of occupatio indicates clearly a detachment from tragic intention, and this passage too indicates an unreadiness to express which usefully restricts the fictional view. Certainly Chaucer relies on generalisation, platitude, occupatio and abbreviation to make the transition to the funeral. He adds the 'keening' cliché in lines 2834–5 and attributes to Theseus' 'olde fader Egeus' platitudes about the world, memorable ones perhaps, but platitudes nevertheless:

Joye after wo and wo after gladnesse . . .
'This world nys but a thurghfare ful of wo,
And we ben pilgrymes, passynge to and fro.'

(2841, 2847–8)

The content of the speech echoes both Theseus' consolation of Palamon and,
more specifically, the opening of his speech proposing the marriage of Palamon
and Emily, but the attribution makes it clear that Chaucer saw the sentiments as
moral commonplace and that he wanted to free Theseus of that aspect and to
exaggerate the worldly-wise note by identifying the speaker as one who:

knew this worldes transmutacioun,
As he hadde seyn it chaunge bothe up and doun.   (2839–40)

The passage as a whole both expresses the extremity and uniqueness of loss and
yet diminishes it by assimilating it to commonplace moralising about life's ups
and downs and the ordinariness of death. Rather than burlesque, Chaucer
creates ambivalence, an uncertainty of tone which serves the narrative very well,
neither indulging morbid sentiment, nor mocking tragedy, but holding grief and
acceptance in balance.

Because Chaucer has so greatly reduced the emotional scenes surrounding
Arcite's actual death, he increases the effect of the funeral's seeming more
significant than the death itself: hence the further evidence that it is the dignity
of externals that the world of the narrative is most positive about. Chaucer's
handling of the funeral is, nevertheless, his most explicit putting aside of the
heroic aspect of *Il Teseida*: all the pomp and circumstance, the heightened
rhetoric of the celebration of death and the cult of the ancestral and military
epic of history, all this is registered but put into an annexe. The lengthy
occupatio functions as a kind of poetic museum or a series of lantern slides of
some once stirring event. While summarising the scene the poet seems to be
indicating the limits of the reader's concern with it. He finds his own focus in
irony and concentration on Theseus. So the grove is identified as the place
where Arcite's complaint had been uttered and the choice of the place for the
funeral emphasises that ironic relationship between love and death mentioned
above.[35] The irony is expressed through the conjunction of the fires of love and
of the funeral pyre:

. . . in that selve grove . . .
Ther as he hadde his amorouse desires,
His compleynte and for love his hoote fires,
He wolde make a fyr in which the office
Funeral he myghte al accomplice.   (2860–4)

The irony goes further in the imagination than merely to register the contrast
between Arcite's hopes and his actual fate; the fires of love have consumed his
manhood and martial spirit and reduced his deeds of arms to ashes. The use of
*he/his* in the passage quoted for Arcite and Theseus without specific distinction
makes a comparison, almost a fusion of the two; the *he* in 2863–4 is obviously,
from one aspect, Theseus, the organiser and accomplisher of the funeral, but

121

could, from another viewpoint, be Arcite who can accomplish dying and being burnt more effectively than he accomplished 'his amorouse desires'; Arcite would 'make a fyr' too, but differently from Theseus. The continuation of the use of *he* as agent in the subsequent lines gives the impression that Theseus almost makes the preparations single-handed. One effect of this is to reduce the scale of the operation; the funeral arrangements are almost personal tributes and comments, evidence of Theseus' own mourning as much as the Duke's ordering of a fitting public ceremony, though that sense is there too. From that point the scene is allowed gradually to fade away, from the suitable procession and observances into the passage of occupatio and the sense of drawing things to a close which leads to the final speech of Theseus.

This speech is changed in function by the passage of 'certeyn yeres' and the brief political reference; it is not the grief of immediate bereavement that has to be countered and so, even if Chaucer had not already given Theseus' consolatory platitudes to Egeus, he would have had to shift the direction of the speech. The shift is to the moral philosophy of Boethius, with material taken from *De Consolatione* Book II, metrum 8, Book IV, prose 6 and metrum 6, Book III, prose 10, and a general reflection of other passages such as Book III, metrum 9. Comparison with *Troilus and Criseyde* suggests that Chaucer found that Boccaccio's endings needed strengthening. In *The Knight's Tale* he leaves out Arcita's view of the vanity of human wishes but feels the need to end on a philosophical note. Perhaps at this stage of his development, and having left some works unfinished, he was looking to moral ideas to resolve and conclude and to provide the *sentence* which his reading taught him was one of the justifications of literature. Within his treatment of *Il Teseida* the introduction of passionate questionings at an earlier stage created a need for the conclusion of the work to make some sort of answer. Other elements in the tale—the contradictions in the nature of Saturn, the debate within a romance fable between heroic courage and committed love as chivalry's motives— could be seen as raising expectation of a theoretical resolution. But, when one has recognised all that, one needs to observe that the line of thought in Theseus' speech is still based on *Il Teseida* and that those who have seen the material from Boethius as importing a different, deeper philosophy have exaggerated. The speech as a whole is designed to support the central idea:

'Why grucchen we, why have we hevynesse,
That goode Arcite, of chivalrie the flour,
Departed is with duetee and honour
Out of this foule prisoun of this lyf?' (3058–61)

The Boethian justification of the mutability of this life is not incompatible with the 'foule prisoun' view and though the pragmatic nature of

'Thanne is it wysdom, as it thynketh me,
To maken vertu of necessitee,
And take it weel that we may nat eschue . . .' (3041–3)

expresses a kind of wisdom which is 'practical wisdom about how to live in *this wrecched world*' rather than Boethian metaphysics,[36] the opening section simply finds in Boethius a more elevated and less cliché-ridden way of saying what Boccaccio too is saying at this point. Chaucer has diverted Boccaccio's

122

platitudes about living and dying, but 'the faire cheyne of love' has bound man within the limits of time and mortality, finding endurance in the ideas of succession and continuity rather than eternity. The words Chaucer uses to evaluate the First Mover's creation of the corruptible world of Nature, within which the elements are chained in harmony are:

> Greet was th'effect and heigh was his entente.   (2989)

But the justification of mortality which goes with this intent says no more in essence than that man's life has its natural term.

Theseus' speech, that is, is not really a moral statement of the meaning of the tale. Chivalry is honoured, acceptance of the uncertainties of life in as good a light as possible is exemplified, transition is made from tragedy and sorrow to acceptance of consolation and prosperity. Because Chaucer has drastically reduced the role of Emilia and has no place for the marriage ceremony, the beauty of the bride, the virility of the bridegroom and all Boccaccio's indulgence in diffuse flashiness, the speech has to become a performance, a rhetorical set-piece to take the place of other ceremony. This is the main reason for the Boethian elevation and the combination of homiletic and dramatic in the tone; Theseus as master of ceremonies, as much as *deus ex machina*, brings down the curtain with a suitable display of authority, nobility and order. Emphasis on the content of the speech tends to attribute too much explicit theory and argument to it and consequently to the work as a whole. Chaucer's treatment has on the one hand illustrated and praised secular chivalry and on the other dramatised the states of mind of characters in the hands of the gods; forces of irrational passion and destructive violence take hold of man and are at work within the tournament, even though the tournament itself is seen as a noble ordering of such passions. Chivalry and honour are in tune with Theseus' call to acceptance and reconciliation; Arcite's death is a regrettable instance of the mutability of things, but the essence of mutability is that life must go on:

> 'I rede that we make of sorwes two
> O parfit joye, lastynge everemo.
> And looketh now, wher moost sorwe is herinne,
> Ther wol we first amenden and bigynne.'   (3071–4)

Here is the perfect note of the tragicomic ending, creating a play-like effect, a final focussing of narrative through speech and occasion. In looking for a replacement for Boccaccio's public debate and grand ceremony in order to build up the impressiveness of the movement towards harmony and joy, Chaucer has found his way, as in the first half of the tale, through rhetorical speech. True, the Boethian answers are less impressive than the earlier Boethian questions, but the real conclusion of the speech is not in philosophically large statements but in courtly feeling, the stirring of Emily's 'wommanly pitee' for one who has served her 'with wille, herte and myght':

> 'Syn he hath served yow so many a yeer,
> And had for yow so greet adversitee,
> It moste been considered, leeveth me;
> For gentil mercy oghte to passen right.'   (3086–9)

Here Chaucer brings his courtly narrative to its appropriate anchorage and here, rather than in the Boethian generalisations, lies whatever strength the conclusion may be said to possess.

The varied evidence, particularly in the latter part of the work, suggests that in *The Knight's Tale* Chaucer was trying to do several things at once: first, to write a grand court poem, celebrating chivalry and displaying an English poetic style dignified enough to render this pseudo-classical tale with a variety of pictorial and dramatic effect; secondly to draw the response, by means of lyric, debate and allegory, of the sophisticated modern generation of intellectuals in his audience to a moral examination of the relationship between the contrary impulses within the chivalric ideal and between men and gods; thirdly perhaps, though not really separable from the last, to explore his own interest in the pagan past.

The result of Chaucer's complex intentions has been to leave his modern readers in some doubt as to how to take the tale. The courtly urbanity of his appeal to fellow-sophisticates among his hearers, especially insofar as it shows itself in moments of flippant detachment, has seemed to some to get in the way of serious intentions. Others have found that the lyric intensity and the vehemence of the questionings he attributed to Arcite and Palamon raise expectations of serious treatment of serious issues which are not satisfied by the consolatory mode of Theseus' final speech, often thought lacking in sublimity. Of course, some readers are even less in sympathy with the work and have sought to justify their own lack of interest in medieval concepts of chivalry and honour and in Chaucer's ambitious attempt to create a style of English poetry capable of treating passionate emotion and classical themes by dismissing it as ironic and satirical.

A focal point in differing interpretations has been the character of Theseus. The traditional view of him[37] as the earthly agent of order, resisting Fortune's tendency to disorder, or of Reason counteracting the excesses of youthful passion, has been challenged by debunking readings which see him, for example, as a 'brilliant political opportunist' and the whole tale as a comic treatment of human folly: 'Man in the tale does not learn much by age and experience.'[38] Others have condemned Theseus as a tyrant.[39] A contrary current of opinion is set up by such criticisms to produce a view of Theseus neither idealising nor condemning but explaining him in terms of medieval views of leadership and military discipline. So Reidy gives us a view of the poem as 'a mirror for magistrates' in which the education of Theseus is the main theme:

He is a successful soldier, acting by a code honourable in the world's eyes, and really so; he is proud, confident, quick, hasty, and usually decisive in action, but unwittingly he brings great distress on his two prisoners. His presumed control over events finally fails, and a great disaster ensues; from it he has the strength of mind to recover, retains his dignity, and increases in wisdom.[40]

Reidy depends on the writings of Keen, who has himself counteracted the debunking of the Knight (rather than his tale) by Jones with evidence of the continuing force of the ideal of chivalry and the respect for knighthood and courtesy at the court of Richard II; this also acts as a perspective from which

Theseus may be viewed.[41] Another ambivalent picture emerges from Minnis's view of Theseus and the other characters from the point of view of Chaucer's interest in pagan antiquity. So, although 'This is the closest Chaucer ever got to portraying a hero', according to Minnis, the tale exposes the weaknesses in Theseus' pagan philosophy by showing that the 'spurious eternity of human fame' is the limit of his response to a recognition of earthly mutability. Chaucer's interest in the idea of the virtuous pagan has led him to present a sympathetic but detached view of the 'strengths and weaknesses of Theseus' philosophy of life'.[42]

The problem is partly that Chaucer does not treat his figures as characters at all.[43] They consist of speeches and actions which fulfil the narrative, rhetorical and moral needs of the moment. Chaucer inherits the division of interest in *Il Teseida* between an epic poem which centres on Theseus as hero in the mould of Aeneas and a romantic narrative centring on two young heroes who are to illustrate the contrary faces of Fortune. By abbreviation Chaucer makes some of the shifts from one interest to the other more abrupt and inexplicable; so Theseus at one moment shows his 'gentil herte', at another his conqueror's power, and at different times mirrors Aeneas, Edward III, Middle Age, Reason, the Marshal-at-Arms and the Lady Philosophy. Fusing these together into a single impression falsifies the multiplicity in the tale.

A different kind of debate and attempt to unify the elements in the poem is found in various 'schematic' readings, such as the view of Arcite and Palamon as Active and Contemplative Life, or Curry's reading of the tale in terms of the planetary influences which Chaucer added to Boccaccio's pagan gods.[44] More recently Brooks and Fowler have argued that the tale's psychological content is expressed through emblematic symbolism and have refined Curry's identification of Lygurges as Saturnian and Emetreus as basically Martian with Solar attributes into a melancholic/choleric scheme interlocking with the scheme of the Four Ages of Man; *The Knight's Tale* thus appears an interesting intellectual pattern in which the compass of human life is symbolically represented and in which Arcite is clearly the moral inferior (self-seeking, licentious, violent attributes of the extreme choleric complexion) of Palamon (decorum, perseverance, readiness for completion of experience of the sanguine temperament).[45] Kolve's use of dominant images works in a somewhat similar way; he sees the poem much as many other modern critics, as a treatment of human limitation by means of a treatment of the pagan past imagined from within,[46] but he argues that the idea of this pagan past is communicated through the two images of prison/garden and amphitheatre.

> The amphitheatre is to the theme of order in the poem what the prison/ garden is to the theme of freedom.[47]

Though comparison to medieval pictorial symbols is illuminating to particular passages in the tale, as a way of 'reading' the tale it is somewhat forced— another 'scheme' of medievalism. Kean's lengthy analysis of the poem puts Chaucer's knowledge of the Children of the Planets tradition to more flexible use: the composite scene shows ways in which the gods are implicated in the detail of human life; though the influences described in the poem are unfortunate, the planets are seen as ultimately a force for order and even Saturn has the aspects of Wisdom and Time to support his function as a controller of strife.[48] (Minnis, however, rejects this view, seeing Chaucer as scornful and ironic about the pagan gods.)[49] Kean sees the work not so much as a Boethian study as a study of the effects on human life of disorder and unreason opposed to the binding chain of order from First Mover downwards. The 'grete effect' of the ending of *The Knight's Tale* combines the disorder of Arcite's death with the principle of order present in Saturn's resolution of the problem; the idea of marriage as the binding force of unity and perfection for humanity is more significant than Theseus' Boethian rhetoric.

Salter presents a vigorous and interesting view of the tale as a poem 'well endowed with incentives to thought' and an experimental poem of some distinction, despite the fact that she finds the contrary impulses in the work eventually at odds. These contrarieties stem from the 'uneasy treaty' between the elaborate surface and simple theme of *Il Teseida* and the reduced decoration with increased thematic content of Chaucer's work. The result is tension between Chaucer's enlarged dramatic representation of the bewilderment and anger of man's suffering at the dictates of the gods and his attempt to provide adequate reasoning for ending with reconciliation—Boethius' rejection of worldly values is not really consistent with romance's need for a worldly happy outcome.[50] Pearsall's skilful account of the poem[51] is more wide-ranging than most, covering many aspects of the tale and its reception by others, but essentially he too thinks Chaucer unsuccessful in finding loftiness and serenity in Theseus' final speech adequate to match the earlier vehemence and passion:

> . . . the language of consolation betrays an eschatological rather than a cyclic view of things . . . Chaucer's hesitancies and inconsistencies are entirely understandable, given that he is writing a serious poem . . . not a classical charade.[52]

Chaucer's experimental ambition strains the fabric of the tale, moving in contrary directions, as in making the poem simultaneously more realistic and more remote. By making Arcite's dying speech into an act of penitence, he leaves room for Theseus' speech to fulfil only the function of epilogue.

These various readings (and many more could be cited) are testimony to the work's richness and the power of Chaucer's rhetorical language to arouse and of his colourful poetry to create pictures in the mind. For the work of a poet who had virtually to create the type of poem and the idiom in English, *The Knight's Tale* is impressive in its ambition and its characteristics, whether or not one considers it a fully achieved work. Apart from the interest of its themes and its possible allusions to past and present court life, the poem has considerable interest in terms of structure and method. Here Chaucer set himself to perform one of the tasks well within the traditional ideas of medieval rhetorical theory, to reduce a source-text without losing qualities admired in the original (and finding room to develop and add qualities desirable to the second author). Chaucer shows signs of conducting a self-conscious exercise in selection and encapsulation. The use of long summarising passages of occupatio are striking and it is significant that this is the tale in which Chaucer makes most frequent use of indications of intention and of questions which cut off the reader's continuing involvement:

What sholde I al day of his wo endite? (1380)

These usually act as accelerations as the poet moves from feeling to plot.

A less obtrusive way of performing the same act of changing pace was achieved by use of the word *effect*, which occurs particularly frequently in this poem. Early in the tale the word is associated simply with the poet's explanations of his abridgements:

> Greet was the strif and long bitwix hem tweye,
> If that I hadde leyser for to seye,
> But to th'effect. It happed on a day . . .    (1188–90)

It similarly indicates the essence or nub of the matter in 1487 and, in conjunction with occupatio, in 2207. Twice in Palamon's prayer (2228, 2259) and once in Emily's (2366) Chaucer uses the word in a reductive way to indicate the outcome, result or conclusion and the description of the rest of Egeus' moral maxims as 'muchel moore/ To this effect' (2850–51) reinforces the idea of *effect* as a useful brief indicator of amplitude restrained. It is, though, a word with a wider range of meaning than these passages alone suggest. Chaucer made much use of it in his *Boece* to indicate 'performance', 'execution', 'attainment'. Particularly interesting is the following passage:

> For ryght as a werkman that aperceyveth in his thought the forme of the thing that he wol make, and moeveth the effect of the werk, and ledith that he hadde lookid byforn in his thought symplely and presently, by temporal ordenaunce; certes, ryght so God disponith in his purveaunce singulerly and stablely the thinges that ben to doone.
>
> (*Boece*, IV, prose 6)

The idea of the accomplishment of a form previously conceived in the mind links artist and God, and the same link is suggested by Chaucer's use of *effect* in *The Knight's Tale* to refer, first, to his own movement towards the culminating action and hence to the achievement of his design for the work:

> Now wol I stynten of the goddes above,
> Of Mars, and of Venus, goddesse of love,
> And telle yow as pleynly as I kan
> The grete effect, for which that I bygan.    (2479–82)

Secondly, he refers to the First Mover's achievement of his purpose:

> The First Moevere of the cause above,
> Whan he first made the faire cheyne of love,
> Greet was th'effect, and heigh was his entente.
> Wel wiste he why, and what therof he mente.    (2987–90)

The limitation of human life, which is part of that 'entente', and the result of its being carried into effect, thus becomes suggestively associated with the completion of the literary work. The author's 'grete effect' is to achieve the narrative, to reach the consequence of the acts in it, and to draw its moral gist from it, but to complete the work is also finally to recognise its limits; this means reaching the end of the exercise of the poet's imaginative life and

127

acknowledging the limiting elements demonstrated by the story—Arcite's tragic end, the theme of the brevity of life and even the making the best of a bad job, which is the only way of reconciling characters within the tale and of reconciling the audience to the tale's outcome. To make a virtue of necessity is too pragmatic a conclusion to stir the heart and mind, but it is an attitude which comes to seem characteristic of Chaucer. The undercurrents of his use of the word *effect* suggest that endings were awkward and retractive things for Chaucer, an idea which other works by him confirm.

What Chaucer's great effect amounted to was a perception in *Il Teseida* of the dichotomy of complaint poetry. His over-all interpretation presented the fable as a process of complaint and consolation; from his restoration of widows' rights to his final speech Theseus is made the instrument of reassurance by exemplifying the patterns of providence. But in uneasy relationship to this resolution of protest is the double experience in the narrative of the hero who dies and the hero who remains to be consoled; alongside the providential aspects of the tale runs the current of pathos, protest and injustice, leading to the death-bed, the non-consolation, the tragic combination of human weakness of body with generosity of spirit whereby in Arcite complaint is not answered but transcended. In *Troilus and Criseyde* Chaucer displayed within one figure both the Arcite and the Palamon halves of the experience. Troilus achieves love and comfort for his sorrow, but his wounds are re-opened by Fortune's playing on human weakness. Chaucer could resist the dominance of lament only by finally contradicting it by means of the heavenly apotheosis which Theseus's presence had suppressed in *The Knight's Tale*.

# CHAPTER SIX

# Complaint in Narrative II: Troilus and Criseyde

## 1. Complaint and Comfort

Even more clearly than in *Il Teseida* Boccaccio's leaning in *Il Filostrato* was towards the sentimental aspects of historical material. His pretended auto-biographical prologue and epilogue suggest not merely, as in *Il Teseida*, that an ancient love story expresses a theme of shared interest between poet and beloved, but that personal anguish is the motivation for seeking out this story of tragic love and that retelling it is a way of expressing men's vulnerability to the fickleness of women. For Boccaccio, writing in his early twenties, this sorrowful cynicism was perhaps a posture designed to give a sophisticated edge to the material: the colourful combination of ancient warfare and a love story added to the tale of Troy by later writers was to be interpreted by a modern sensibility. For Boccaccio, seeking 'a disguise for my secret and passionate suffering',[1] the 'ancient legends' are adequately supplied by Benoit and Guido; ostensibly his interest is in writing melancholy Florentine verse where even Troiolo's happiness is present in order the better to understand 'the extent and nature of his ensuing sorrow'. In fact, as David Wallace points out, the style of *Il Filostrato* is a mixture of the robust, energetic, credulous story-telling and the use of popular idiom of the Italian *cantare* and the interest in motivation and inner debate of the twelfth-century French romance.[2] This combination, as much as the subject matter, probably explains Chaucer's interest in Boccaccio's poem, though, as I suggested with reference to *Anelida and Arcite*, the midst of episodes of war makes an apt setting for the idea of the temporary nature of happiness, and this aspect of *Il Filostrato* no doubt also took Chaucer's eye.

Chaucer's expression of his intentions is not, in some ways, an accurate guide to the effect of *Troilus and Criseyde*. The distinction between an English poet in his forties and an Italian one twenty years younger explains some of the quality of difference between the two works and Chaucer's adoption of the role of detached, historical poet is no mere pose; he does bolster the material from Benoit, Guido, Joseph of Exeter and elsewhere. However, he accepts the main lyric impulse of the Italian, which relegates the siege of Troy to the status of suggestive background. Chaucer does not, as he in various ways does in *Anelida and Arcite*, *The Complaint of Mars* and *The Squire's Tale*, promise narrative amplitude and then narrow into complaint, but clearly disclaims the intention of creating epic effect and proclaims sorrow as his main theme. The theme of war, the prophecies of disaster, the registration of Troilus' heroic qualities, the conjunction of Troilus and Mars, all are present in Chaucer's work and sometimes augmented and made more specific than they are in *Il Filostrato*, but essentially these things provide merely the conditions within which the emotional phases of the story are shaped. The attraction of the subject was the idea of the love-stricken hero and the stimulation of Boccaccio's handling of it lay largely in the opportunities he suggested for lyrical elaboration of feeling and for debate, both internal and external, along lines which Chaucer had thoroughly learned from de Machaut and the French courtly *dits* and had augmented from Boethius.[3]

This lyrical elaboration may be seen most obviously in the 'inset' lyrics in *Troilus and Criseyde* which give to the poem the effect of a long amorous *dit*. Payne conveniently lists ten clear-cut examples of 'the system of lyric and apostrophe, set within the structure of the narrative proper' in *Troilus and Criseyde*.[4] In Book I Chaucer adds the first *Canticus Troili* (400–34) based on a Petrarch sonnet; in Book II Antigone's song (827–75) based on motifs from several poems of de Machaut;[5] in Book III Criseyde's aubade (1422–42) and Troilus' two aubades (1450–70, 1702–8) expand brief exclamations and reports in *Il Filostrato* and Troilus' hymn to Love (1744–71) brings more substantially into the poem the material of Boethius II, metrum 8, already drawn on by Boccaccio for the song which Chaucer turned into the proem to Book III; in Book IV Boethius also provides the material for Troilus' predestination soliloquy (958–1082); in Book V Chaucer creates a lyric soliloquy for Troilus (218–45) from what had been a speech to Pandaro in the Italian, expands an image into Troilus' apostrophe to Criseyde's empty palace (540–53) and, in the last of Payne's examples, the second *Canticus Troili* (638–58), takes over a 'song' passage from Boccaccio but substitutes a compact address to the star by which he can no longer steer for Boccaccio's rambling 5-stanza *canzone* of love and death. Payne sees these instances of apostrophe as something akin to a sonnet sequence, 'a kind of distillation of the emotional progress of the poem',[6] but he sees them as 'interrupting' the action, creating pauses for evaluation. I see them rather as part of a substantial continuous process in *Troilus and Criseyde*, whereby Chaucer focusses his fiction through a sequence of monologues and dialogues which define the action of the poem more than the external events which shift the situation. This sequence has similarities to the structure of dream-poems and of other courtly *dits* in the construction of narrative in a linked chain of lengthy speech, lyric apostrophe, dialogues of grief and response, interspersed with passages of debate, and of comment and structural direction from the poet. The difference from the courtly *dits* is in the historical matter. As in *The Knight's Tale* Chaucer has found suitable material for development in Boccaccio, but the tools with which the development is effected are those of already acquired rhetorical processes.

Compared to *The Knight's Tale*, *Troilus and Criseyde* is less concerned with narrating events and with scenic effects. Though Chaucer uses the pagan setting of temples effectively and creates a sense that discreet private life must be snatched by subterfuge from the social life of households, friends and family, nevertheless there is some truth in William Godwin's characterisation of *Troilus and Criseyde* as failing to generate 'visible images in the reader' or to excite 'his imagination with pictures of nature and life'.[7] What excites the imagination is an ebb and flow of attitude and relationship. Complaint is a central element in the poem, mainly because the stricken hero and his double sorrow is the main theme, but also because the expressive lyric utterance of sorrow becomes part of the debate between philosophies of life which Chaucer explores through Troilus, Pandarus and Criseyde. Complaint is the starting-point of *Troilus and Criseyde* and it is the finishing point of Troilus' story, though Chaucer chose to add to that story the apotheosis of Arcita from *Il Teseida* and the moderating perspective of an author's epilogue. But, within the five-book pattern which Chaucer created, complaint has a shifting significance, which is clear from a study of the five books in sequence and of what Chaucer added to his source.

What Chaucer really did to *Il Filostrato* is richly complex and may be characterised in a variety of ways[8] according to which qualities one selects, but in each book one can distinguish a number of main emphases and in the work as a whole a shift of centre. For Boccaccio the development from Troiolo's falling in love to the consummation was swift and straightforward, and was accomplished in the first three of the nine sections of *Il Filostrato*. Separation, betrayal and grief are the phases to be drawn out and they occupy from Part 4 to Part 8 of the work, leaving the ninth section for the poet to instruct his poem to try with its mournful guise to move the noble mistress to pity. Chaucer uses roughly one section of *Il Filostrato* for each of Books I to IV (except that Book I takes in the first quarter of Boccaccio's second section) and then condenses Boccaccio's Parts 5 to 8 into his Book V, substituting his own 'Go litel book' and his closing complexities for Boccaccio's last section. Chaucer thus gives greater emphasis to the process of courtship before the consummation, creates a symmetrical Boethian structure of the rise and fall of Troilus' fortunes in love, pivoting around the happiness described in Book III, and makes the opening and closing sorrow of Troilus correspond to form a meaningful design; so must all vain hopes—so the poem's structure implies—return to the apprehension from which they began. The sense of Chaucer's deliberately shaping the poem into a significant design is present from the opening words of the work and is renewed in the invocatory prologues to the subsequent books. At the beginning Chaucer dispenses with Boccaccio's pose of personal motivation and declares his interest in the double sorrow of Troilus, lodging the over-all design in the reader's mind and commencing the movement towards an inevitable end. The sense of seeing it as a whole, the 'conscious articulation of the narrative' as Windeatt describes it,[9] is markedly different from the sense in *The Knight's Tale* of embarking on a narrative which has a life of its own, only partly to be reported in the poem. Not merely does Chaucer put aside the events of the Trojan war by focussing on Troilus' adventures in loving, but the lyric bias is communicated by the repeated emphasis on feeling and response; the idea of sorrow and torment, the narrator's inadequacy, the need for the audience's sympathy, all contribute to engaging the reader's imaginative interest in the articulation of emotion more than in chronicles of ancient rivalries.

In the first of his five books Chaucer moves the narrative of *Il Filostrato* in the direction of complaint and debate. His major additions to the source suggest that he saw in this phase of Troilus' story parallels to the narratives of complaint and comfort in the *dits* of de Machaut and Froissart. In the first half of the book he gives most attention to a much elaborated account of Troilus' falling in love. The purpose of the elaboration is to make the reader see the whole process of love's coming to the hero, the change it effects upon him, the processes of human life which it demonstrates. If he adds to the unsympathetic first impression of the hero by augmenting Troilus' smugness in sneering at the lovers among his companions, this, it becomes clear, is to enhance the impact of the sudden reversal brought about by Cupid's arrow. Animating what is merely metaphor in *Il Filostrato*, Chaucer makes Troilus into the victim of the God of Love; he had called his companions 'veray fooles, nyce and blynd' and to punish him for folly and pride he is reduced to plucked peacock and a mere tool in the hands of greater power. So 'Troilus is clomben on the staire' and the blindness of lovers is swallowed up in the blindness of the world itself, an inherent condition of human life. Chaucer's addition of lines 218–66 directs attention to Troilus as an illustrative case, limited like a beast to the instability of nature, and, even though he is a prince, unable to escape punishment for pride or to avoid love's revenge. There is an interesting ambivalence in the passage; seeing his earlier behaviour as a fault means that Troilus' falling in love is, in a sense, wise, while at the same time the effect of love describes an inevitable pattern of folly; supernatural forces are bringing love about and love is 'vertuouse in kynde', but the common lot is the giddy circling of Fortune's wheel. The antithetical play of values indicated by the passage continues in different guises throughout the poem. In describing Troilus' sight of Criseyde Chaucer emphasises inner activity by elaborating his reactions; the effect is of inner life suddenly quickening:

> And of hire look in him ther gan to quyken
> So gret desire and swich affeccioun,
> That in his hertes botme gan to stiken
> Of hir his fixe and depe impressioun . . .   (I, 295–8)

The language moves both towards the idea of mental and emotional activity (the heart spreading and rising and so on) and towards apprehensions of death; the result is a disturbing intensity of feeling. At the same time Troilus' inner acknowledgement of emotional change makes it necessary for him to disguise his feelings and so his outer behaviour has to become a mask. Chaucer again augments the idea by the addition of a mocking speech (I, 330–50) which does not any longer work against the reader's sympathy with Troilus because of its irony; Troilus speaks now against himself and his experience will prove true some of the points he makes. So Chaucer's heightening of the reversal in Troilus brought about by love makes an association between love and concealment from the start, even before the courtly etiquette of discretion comes into play. Love for Troilus is coloured by guilt and unease, weakness and folly; confidence is a mere veneer to conceal sorrow and bewilderment. Through the traditional idea of the power of love utterly to possess Chaucer undermines his hero (and, in varying degrees, his other main characters in turn); he is a hapless being played on by images and forces.

Thus Chaucer establishes his complex perspective, whereby the inner mental and emotional activity of the hero is imaginatively expressed, with sufficient sympathy and appeal to common experience to induce a sympathetic response, while the hero's behaviour is seen as a typical demonstration of a common pattern of moral and rational weakness in human kind. But it is Troilus' anxious solitude which at first occupies the foreground of the reader's attention. In the passage dealing with Troilus alone (I, 358–546) which completes Boccaccio's first section Chaucer mainly follows his source, adding intensity at moments such as the one where Troilus makes 'a mirror of his mind' in which he sees the image of Criseyde again, and augmenting the figurative language in places, as in the suggestive image with which Troilus rounds off his determination to conceal his desire:

> Rememberyng hym that love to wide yblowe
> ʒelt bittre fruyt, though swete seed be sowe.    (I, 384–5)

His major addition is the Petrarch sonnet, Troilus' first complaint, and it is significant that this insertion comes not long before *Il Filostrato* itself contains a passage of complaint which Chaucer renders at lines 505–39. Chaucer presumably wished even further to intensify the expression of Troilus' contemplation of his feelings in privacy and his choice of a sonnet dealing with the paradoxes of love stresses the idea of uncertainty and fluctuation between extremes. Chaucer's treatment of Petrarch's text brings it into harmony with the context, since, as with his treatment of *Il Filostrato* at this stage, he gives more impression of the inner thoughts of the speaker, and adds touches of figurative language and illustrative symptoms to expand each of the quatrains into a rhyme royal stanza. The sestet is converted into one stanza only but Chaucer emphasises the figures, giving physical vividness to the image of the 'sterelees' boat with the word 'possed', making the winds constantly fixed in contrariety and augmenting Troilus' many allusions to death by the addition of the final 'I dye'. The main effect of the song is to dramatise the association between love and anxiety, which Chaucer takes as a main motif of Troilus' early experience in love. Any sense of joy or that which is 'savory' is perversely rooted in woe. The poem is a complaint which simultaneously laments the confusions of love and criticises lamenting itself; to complain is contrary to consent and so an element of debate is set in train between willing acceptance of love, with happiness implied, and the despairing protest of the hapless lover tormented by uncertainty:

> 'And if that at myn owen lust I brenne,
> From whennes cometh my waillynge and my pleynte?
> If harme agree me, wherto pleyne I thenne?'    (I, 407–9)

To set complaint within a context of debate is one fruitful way of developing from what may otherwise become at length mere indulgence in the rhetoric of self-pity and this is an idea which Chaucer later substantiates, but first the impression of Troilus as sensitive lover must be thoroughly established. Chaucer follows his *Canticus Troili* with an idealistic rendering of Troilus' vow to the God of Love (422–34) in which the hero's life-and-death commitment takes on the pattern of 'a kind of feudal service',[10] reversing the social standings of hero and heroine according to the allegiances of love:

> 'For myn estat roial I here resigne
> Into hire hond, and with ful humble chere
> Bicome hir man, as to my lady dere.'    (I, 432–4)

Here Chaucer identifies another of the ambivalences involved in his material. Troilus' role as lover has already been expressed as both that of wise man and fool. Now the paradox of prince and humble servant elaborates the sense of contraries. Troilus' status as lover in the poem depends much on his rank and importance in Troy but he voluntarily does Fortune's work for her and renounces that royal state in the sphere of love to become liegeman and suppliant. Again the terms out of which debate may develop are being suggestively planted in the reader's mind.

Continually adding touches consistent with his sensitising Boccaccio's treatment of the hero, such as the reference to death in 469, to madness in 477 and 499 and the bleeding heart in 502, Chaucer moves to Troilus' second complaint (505–39). Here he suppresses the idea that love is unsuited to the time of war, augments the references to death and strengthens the metaphor of snaring: from Boccaccio's 'or se nel laccio preso, il qual biasmavi / tanto negli altri ed a te non guardavi' ('now you are caught in the snare you so much scorned others for being trapped by, and you couldn't watch out for yourself'),[11] Chaucer derives:

> 'O fool, now artow in the snare,
> That whilom iapedest at loves peyne;
> Now artow hent, now gnaw thin owen cheyne;
> Thow were ay wont eche lovere reprehende
> Of thing fro which thow kanst the nat defende.'     (I, 507–11)

Windeatt compares the reference to marriage as a chain in the 'Envoy to Bukton'[12] but the effect here is more pessimistic; love itself is seen as endless imprisonment and Fortune's chain in which Dorigen feels herself wrapped seems a more apt comparison.[13] The effect of this complaint is to combine self-reproach at exposing himself to others' scorn with the conviction that he will be destroyed by love. So Troilus reinforces both the sense of love as folly and the evidence of love's fatal power. Whereas Boccaccio's Troiolo hopes for response, Troilus seems merely to want Criseyde to know of his love until the formal plea; convinced of her coldness, while love's burning will consume him, Troilus prefers to die soon rather than to suffer both the 'languishing in drede' and being known as a fool, and so the end becomes an appeal to save him from death. The passage thus fulfils the idea of complaint as a lyric form giving plangent expression to strong feeling, appealing to the lady's pity and pathetically exposing and ritualising the lover's distress, but it continues the idea of contrary forces from the earlier Petrarch lament and combines self-condemnation with abasement and pleading.

In the first half of Book I Chaucer uses various means to sharpen the focus on Troilus' sorrow and to increase its intensity, the disturbing contrary emotional impulses within it and the experience of inner debate. In the latter part of Book I he brings forward the first scene of Boccaccio's second section with the effect of counteracting this initial impression, but before that he augments the sense of psychological disturbance in Troilus' language, especially by references to death, and in his situation, particularly by distinguishing between outer and inner life; he doubles the occasions of formal rhetorical complaint and complaint becomes a sign of the hero's sensibility—to lament is to feel, and feeling, it is implied, is of value.

Chaucer tends to simplify or to concentrate other elements in Boccaccio's first section which might draw attention away from this central subject. The treatment of Criseyde, in particular, limits her to a sequence of images of abstract womanhood, seen distantly through the sensibility of others or the narrator's uncertainty. From the opening situation of Criseyde 'allone/ Of any frend' the tale moves to the scene with Hector where she is described indirectly as beauty in distress; Hector speaks while she is merely reported but even Hector's words channel the reader towards Troilus since his later reaction to Criseyde is implicit in his brother's noble pity. A second static picture of Criseyde is presented at the feast (169–82), a combination of modesty and assurance, of matchless beauty enhanced by sober covering, a bright star under a black cloud. A third picture is seen through Troilus' eyes (281–94), womanly and shapely, with aristocratic manner and expressive face. The three pictures form a series suggestive of feminine variety, of vulnerability and sexual appeal but also of reserve and independence. But Chaucer marks the sense of distance from which she is viewed; she is 'She, this in blak' and all one knows of her words is either what her appearance suggests,

> for she let falle
> Hire look a lite aside in swich manere
> Ascaunces, 'what, may I nat stonden here?'   (I, 290–2)

or a mere idea of what is appropriate to the occasion:

> On knees she fil biforn Ector adown
> With pitous vois, and tendrely wepynge,
> His mercy bad, hir selven excusynge.   (I, 110–2)

To present Criseyde thus is to implant in the reader's mind the idea of a figure whose nature exists only as circumstances dictate or as others see. She comes with association of treachery, vulnerability and uncertainty: she is the sort of daughter abandoned to picturesque pleading by a clever, unscrupulous father who picks her up later when opportunity offers, the sort of wife whose husband has gone leaving her picturesquely in black, even (Chaucer suggests by deliberate vagueness) the sort of mother whose children may or may not exist. To counteract these disconcerting implications are the qualities of an idealised image of woman—heavenly beauty, appealing helplessness, aloof self-assurance. Once Criseyde appears directly on the scene in Book II the impression changes, but at the beginning this evocative distance creates an image for Troilus to be hypnotised by and a concealed identity for Pandarus to uncover.

In the immediate context of Book I Chaucer creates a symbolic figure to be the object of courtly complaint, the embodiment of womanhood, the apparent image of nobility and peerless queen of beauty in need of a heroic champion. She, the victim of circumstance, is presented as the pre-existing condition through which Troilus is to become the central 'plaintiff' of the poem, the hero doomed to sorrow first and last and therefore doomed to express himself in apostrophe and lament. With the arrival of Pandarus Chaucer begins to show how much further he could pursue the study of complaint in a lengthy complex narrative than he could in a framed complaint, or short pairing of narrative and complaint, and how complaint can be made to develop interestingly into dramatic narrative, debate and philosophical analysis.

The entry of Pandarus leads to a lengthy scene where Chaucer at first follows *Il Filostrato*, Part 2 fairly closely, expanding some stanzas, giving Pandarus a knowing, semi-comic exaggeration in his way of treating Troilus and adding a 5-stanza speech for him (631–65) and extra stanzas later (687–700). The effect of the scene is of a drawing out of Troilus from isolated sorrow in stages; Pandarus plays the part of confidant more effectively than does the Dreamer in *The Book of the Duchess* but the process is recognisably related to that earlier exercise in the style of the French *dit*. Sullen rejection and self-pity, in which Troilus sees himself 'refus of every creature' (570) and claims 'I mot nedes deye/ Therefore go wey' (573–4), can still defend itself against the accusation of cowardice and be led on to admit to love, even if coloured with thoughts of death and concealment. Chaucer's expansion of Pandarus' persuasive rhetoric identifies his role as that of contrary spirit to Troilus. He argues that 'By his contraire is every thyng declared'; he uses his own lack of success in love and the double instance of Oenone's complaint to Paris and the allusion she makes (in the *Heroides*) to Apollo's love for the daughter of Admetus as multiple examples of the bitter lessons of experience with which to resist the naivete of Troilus' extreme despair. Complaint is thus converted into an instrument of warning by a preacher of self-awareness and the need for some mean of behaviour (another instance, that of Niobe, is added in support) in trusting others. Hence the process of consolation present in *Il Filostrato* is enriched, so that when Chaucer rejoins the text of his source (at line 701) Pandarus' pleading is a more significant expression of a contrary attitude to life than it had been for Boccaccio:

> 'Lat be thy wepyng and thi drerynesse,
> And let us lissen wo with oother speche;
> So may thy woful tyme seme lesse;
> Delyte nat in wo thi wo to seche,
> As don thise foles that hire sorwes eche
> With sorwe, whan thei han mysaventure,
> And listen naught to seche hem other cure.'    (I, 701–7)

In *Il Filostrato* this leads directly to Troiolo's confession, but Chaucer delays this process to make more of the debate between the two. In 729–854 he leaves his source and uses the situation to generate speech and to explore the process of persuasion. At first we are shown Troilus' inner thoughts (743–9) and his attempt to fend off Pandarus and to maintain his death-bound secrecy, rejecting Pandarus' proverbs and examples:

> 'Ek I nyl nat ben cured, I wol deye.
> What knowe I of the queene Nyobe?
> Lat be thyne olde ensaumples, I the preye.'    (I, 758–60)

Pandarus fights against this partly by scorning his attitude as that of a coward, and preaching active pursuit of love, and partly by exposing Troilus' gloom as folly. Although the mixed perspective of the poem will allow us later to view

Pandarus' attitude as itself 'folly' in its own fashion, here Chaucer makes him an attractive practical figure who expresses the spirit of anti-complaint. The debate of contrary temperaments is focussed in the exchange about Fortune (834–54) in which Troilus' 'wel fynde I that Fortune is my fo' (837) is strongly countered by Pandarus' argument (based on Boethius) that 'Fortune is comune/ To everi manere wight' (843–4) and that 'Paraunter thow hast cause forto synge' (854). Chaucer's additions thus invite the reader to see the two speakers as representative voices in a dialogue between pessimism and optimism.

The process of comfort is, according to the conventions of the *dit*, achieved when Troilus consents to be advised, wishes to make known to Criseyde his virtuous intent and gives his defiance to the Greeks and his full trust to Pandarus:

> 'But thow wis, thow woost, thow maist, thow art al.
> My lif, my deth, hol in thyn honde I leye.'   (I, 1052–3)

With the addition at the end of Book I of Pandarus' use of Geoffrey de Vinsauf's metaphor of the architect's premeditation and of the transformation of Troilus through the power of love, Chaucer skilfully begins the next phase of the poem while completing the first, but the emphasis on Troilus in the closing stanzas conveys a sense of completion of a significant stage in a process. The rhetoric of complaint represented by Troilus has, for a time, found its answer; the strain of antithesis to complaint expressed in the debate and the juxtaposition of serious and comic in *The Parliament of Fowls* is here embodied in a figure who combines the consoling rhetoric of folk-wisdom, literary examples and the lessons of personal experience with a mischievous, goading scorn, associated with active curiosity, interference and insistence on positive resistance. Chaucer possibly saw the story of Troilus at first as illustrating the power of love: as with *The Book of the Duchess* there is a quality in the early part of the poem that suggests the idea that he saw the young man lamenting alone as a focal point for intense poetry. He clearly has a psychological interest in the process of drawing out secret feeling by means of persuasion and of exploring the implications of that feeling: that love is disaster, is guilty, is a punishment, is a kind of death, even while it also quickens and inflames. Chaucer's identification at the start of the double sorrow of Troilus as his theme tells the reader that the association between love and foreboding is essentially right; all will turn out badly and Troilus will suffer and will die, if not of it, in some sense through it. But before that the painful and foolish journey into happiness must be made and the means by which this journey is accomplished inevitably require the poet's mind to enter imaginatively into the forces which run counter to this opening insistence on the tragic pattern. From the role of confidant, necessary to the plot, Chaucer develops in Pandarus a contrasting rhetoric of persuasion towards action, and so creates a motivator towards narrative change who resists the lyric impulse to dwell in the moment and leave situations as they are. Without his insistence that

> 'Swych is delit of foles to bywepe
> Hire wo, but seken bote they ne kepe'   (I, 762–3)

there could be no development and Chaucer's animation of Pandarus is partly a functional narrative device; the translation of Geoffrey de Vinsauf at Book I, 1065–71 indicates that Chaucer is thinking of Pandarus as an artist figure who is plotting the poem for him, leaving Chaucer himself free to detach himself when he chooses. Hence the note of sympathetic understanding with his stand-in present at many moments when the reader is shown Pandarus' thoughts and manipulations. But while Chaucer's narrative designs are being furthered through this figure, the lyric sense of stasis remains as a resistant force towards which the poem must be drawn back, since sorrow is its ultimate goal, no matter how far it may apparently move towards action and drama. However, at the end of Book I the aspect of Troilus as l'Amant from a courtly *dit* is essentially completed, since the remedy is now implied. The lover's complaints have registered the anguish of love, but the challenge to the idea of an inherently malign Fortune has rebutted it and now all thought is directed to the attempted manipulation of Fortune in Books II and III.

## 2. Complaint as Strategy, Protest and Uncertainty

In Book II Chaucer invents much more freely and the proem to the book, the most complex and sophisticated of the five introductory passages, is an indicator of his more independent purpose, despite the pretence of merely translating and his apparent defensiveness. The opening use of the image of boat and waves strengthens the understanding that in this poem the power of love and the despair of Troilus are the disruptive, Titanic forces; all other things (until the ending, that is) are more rational, practical, mundane. For the moment steering is just becoming possible, with the aid of the Muse most sympathetic to narration, fact and detail. And it is in the spirit of Clio that Chaucer seems to begin to invent, since the long additions to the scene between Pandarus and Criseyde strike the reader first as a clear instance of Chaucer's filling out the narrative in the interest of realism. Boccaccio says that Pandaro and Criseida 'spent some time over the kind of laughter, pleasantness, cheerfulness and familiar talk that relatives often indulge in'[14] and it seems natural for a translator to be stimulated to imagine the pleasantries and to create an amusing plausible scene of teasing intimacy. But Chaucer's use of the situation to spark off speech is not explained by a narrative poet's liking for verisimilitude. Design and thematic purpose begin to show in Pandarus' inner thought (II, 267–73) and the self-consciousness of the persuasive strategy it implies. Chaucer is continuing his interest in using Pandarus to show artful persuasion in action. Throughout Book II frequent speeches by Pandarus dominate the poem: in a book with a high proportion of direct speech[15] the fact that Pandarus speaks on seventy two occasions and utters nearly two fifths of the 1757 lines of the book is a measure of Chaucer's building up of the character.[16] The process which he imagines is parallel to Pandarus' earlier treatment of Troilus, except that here he does not just comfort existing distress, but creates the distress at the same time as supposedly calming it; but as he both consoled and reproached Troilus, so with Criseyde he disconcerts her by a confusing mixture of practical rationality and feigned exaggerated emotion. As the unequal partner in this manufactured dialogue, Criseyde is moved, like Troilus, from an initial reaction of fear and uncertainty towards willingness to hear more and, after Pandarus has gone, to an acceptance of the idea of love and of Troilus as potential lover.

In this tracing of the stages of reaction Chaucer again makes significant use of complaint to focus the contrast between the two speakers. For Pandarus complaint and apostrophe, however strongly resisted in others, are useful devices of emotional blackmail and Chaucer elaborates the speech in which he reveals Troilus' identity to Criseyde with ready bewailings to stir her pity:

> 'Allas, he which that is my lord so deere,
> That trewe man, that noble, gentil knyght,
> That naught desireth but ʒoure frendly cheere,
> I se hym deyen . . .' (II, 330–3)

In an even higher rhetorical key moral lament too may stimulate guilty yielding:

> 'Wo worth the faire gemme vertuelees!
> Wo worth that herbe also that dooth no boote!
> Wo worth that beaute that is routheles!' (II, 344–6)

Thus complaining is used as part of the spurious persuasive arts of the skilled orator and later Pandarus is possibly even more unscrupulous as he conjures up the scene when Troilus ·'gan hym forto pleyne' and quotes the supposed actual words of Troilus' complaint (523–39) as evidence. Whether this scene is supposed to be 'true' or not hardly matters. Pandarus' invention elsewhere makes it clear that he uses the version of reality which will best serve occasion, and this complaint is the right sort of thing for the lover to have said; it creates an image of Troilus for Criseyde's sensibility to react to and the complaint in another's mouth becomes part of the puppet-master's performance, whether or not one identifies it with what one has been told earlier of Troilus. This indirect use of lyric expression by Pandarus on Troilus' behalf offers a nice example of Chaucer's liking for a layer of protective irony. Troilus' quoted words

> 'For certes, lord, so soore hath she me wounded,
> That stood in blak, with lokyng of hire eyen,
> That to myn hertes botme it is ysounded,
> Thorugh which I woot that I moot nedes deyen' (II, 533–6)

leave the reader hardly knowing whether to remember the scene at the temple with poignant sympathy or to smile at the performance of Troilus that Pandarus is giving.

Interwoven with this craftsman's self-conscious use of complaint as a device is a strand of complaint expressing and interpreting Criseyde's experience of the situation. Chaucer delays Criseyde's reaction to Pandarus' news that it is Troilus who loves her in order to expand Pandarus' emotional playing on her feelings (323–85). When Criseyde does react, it is not with the restrained tears and modest reproof given to her by Boccaccio as she remembers her dead husband and determines on a life of retired chastity, but with a frantic cry of distress and a bitter complaint against the falsity of the world:

> 'allas, for wo why nere I deede?
> For of this world the feyth is al agoon.
> Allas, what sholden straunge to me doon,
> Whan he that for my beste frende I wende
> Ret me to love, and sholde it me defende?' (II, 409–13)

Chaucer's addition of a further protest against 'This false worlde, allas, who may it leve?' to the argument of Boccaccio's Criseida that Pandarus would have reproved her if she had professed love for Troilus, leads on to a fine climax of protesting rhetorical questions:

> 'What! is this al the ioye and al the feste?
> Is this ȝoure reed? is this my blisful cas?
> Is this the verray mede of ȝoure byheeste?
> Is al this paynted proces seyd, allas,
> Right for this fyn?' (II, 421–5)

What Chaucer has Criseyde reject is the falsity of Pandarus' words; as soon as the facts of the case are clear she sees through the 'paynted proces' and the effect of her speech is to identify moral protest about truth and honesty in relationships as of a superior order to manipulations of emotion and the artful glosses of persuasive speech. In the light of what follows, this inevitably acquires irony since the painted process is, with reinforcements, enough to win Criseyde over, but in context it works to sharpen the dialogue, as in Book I with Troilus, into a debate between contrary values. So from the antithesis of complaint and anti-complaint in Book I, Chaucer moves on to explore the relationship of different kinds and levels of complaint here. Setting Boethian complaint and lover's complaint in tandem or in antithesis is part of what Chaucer does with Troilus (and with Arcite and Palamon). Criseyde at different times shares in the various attitudes: in Troilus' readiness to lament, in a philosophical protest at the instability of the world and in a resistance to complaint as self-indulgent escapism from necessary action. In this early phase her role as one manipulated by others is identified both by this protest against what is happening to her and also by a vulnerability to persuasion by emotional language and exclamatory lyric rhetoric.

In the passage dealing with her thoughts after Pandarus has left her, Chaucer shows Criseyde moving towards acceptance through a series of stages. First Chaucer invents her sight of Troilus in the street (610–51), elaborating the experience of looking at him and contemplating him before she actually meets him. Chaucer contrives a second ride-past for Troilus later (1009–22), this time planned by Pandarus. Both derive from the brief description of Troiolo passing in *Il Filostrato* Part 2, Stanza 82, but Chaucer makes each scene a significant moment.[17] It is as if Criseyde is able to rehearse the possibility of Troilus as lover by being presented with him at a remove. As with the treatment of Criseyde in Book I so here with Troilus, an image of manhood is formed from his appearance and demeanour. In the first scene the image is of 'a man of armes and a knyght' explicitly compared with Mars. The signs of dangers risked and survived, the hacked helmet, the shattered shield, serve to enhance the soldierly modesty of cast-down eyes into an allegorical image of martial courage free of vanity. It is the intoxication of this first direct apprehension of Troilus as princely warrior that in Chaucer's treatment gives rise to Criseyde's contemplation of her situation and stimulates in her the possibility of allowing change. It is image rather than action that moves on the narrative to a new stance for mental debate and lyric monologue, but before that stage is reached Chaucer puts the reader on guard (666–79) by rebutting supposed criticisms of the speed with which Criseyde is apparently falling in love. The reader would have been unlikely to have such a thought, especially given the *coup de foudre* effect already attributed to Troilus' earlier sight of Criseyde, but Chaucer skilfully attaches to Criseyde implications of instability, a suspicion that she 'so lightly loved Troilus' on the one hand and on the other the disconcerting reassurance that Troilus' 'manhod and his pyne/ Made love withinne her herte forto myne' (II, 676–7). So she is either naturally shallow or has been undermined; in either case there is no possibility of a permanently rooted growth. The effect of the narrator's intrusion is, as with Pandarus' citing of Troilus' complaint, to offer the following passage of Criseyde's inner thoughts to the reader as quoted evidence to be analysed for its sincerity factor. In tune with this, Chaucer gives prominence in the first phase of Criseyde's soliloquy (703–63) to worldly thoughts of Troilus' status as the king's son and the honour of being loved by him; thoughts of her own beauty and the independence of her position complete the Pandarine half of her meditation. In the second phase (771–805) she moves into a more Troiline frame of mind and into the idiom of complaint:

> 'Allas, how dorst I thenken that folie?
> May I naught wel in other folk aspie
> Hire dredfull ioye, hire constreinte and hire peyne?
> Ther loveth noon that she nath wey to pleyne.'     (II, 774–7)

And so Chaucer, by echoing the style associated in Book I with the two male characters, develops the impression of Criseyde as dependent upon others and dramatises her situation; she is not only the subject of debate but herself the ground on which debate is being argued out. The impulse towards practicality and the exploitation of Fortune is balanced by the self-conscious verbal elaboration of meditation on love's troubles, disturbance, jealousy, malice, instability and transitoriness:

> 'For evere som mystrust or nice strif
> Ther is in love, som cloude is overe that sonne.
> Therto we wrecched wommen nothing konne,
> Whan us is wo, but wepe and sitte and thinke;
> Oure wrecche is this, oure owen wo to drynke.
>
> Also thise wikked tonges ben so preste
> To speke us harm, ek men ben so untrewe,
> That right anon as cessed is hire leste
> So cesseth love, and forth to love a newe;
> But harm ydoon is doon, whoso it rewe:
> For though thise men for love hem first torende,
> Ful sharp bygynnyng breketh ofte at ende.

141

How ofte tyme hath it yknowen be,
The tresoun that to wommen hath ben do;
To what fyn is swich love I kan nat see,
Or wher bycometh it whan it is ago.
Ther is no wight that woot, I trowe so,
Where it bycometh; lo, no wight on it sporneth:
That erst was no thing, into nought it torneth.'  (II, 780–98)

Here the strand of masculine lover's complaint, in which Chaucer was interested in *The Book of the Duchess* and some of his shorter lyric complaints and which is a main motif in *Troilus and Criseyde*, meets the Boethian questioning of the purpose of love used in *The Complaint of Mars*, and the theme of the vulnerable woman's lament at her mistreatment by men which Chaucer explored in *Anelida and Arcite* and which is a recurring motif in *The Legend of Good Women* and various of *The Canterbury Tales*. The striking use of conceit and pithy proverb in the final lines of the three stanzas marks the passage as another piece of inset lyric. Chaucer found in Criseyde's weighing up of the pros and cons of taking on Troilus as lover in *Il Filostrato* the starting point for a free development of complaint motifs set in an ironic frame by his distancing device of making the reader look askance at Criseyde's motives. At each step he finds a mould into which her thought can be poured. At this stage Chaucer generalises her voice into that of spokeswoman for her sex and then into a demonstrator of debating points about the nature of love. So although Chaucer is here using the device of inner debate, he chooses, by distancing his reader from Criseyde and offering her for our judgment, not to suggest any depth to her thinking comparable to that of Troilus' musing in Book I; touches of glibness and archness in argument reinforce the effect. By such differences Chaucer makes it clear that, despite his appearance at times in a representative role, it is Troilus who is his protagonist; Criseyde is merely the material out of which the themes are expressed and through which Troilus' experience is shaped. Complaint is thus part of a process rather than a statement of principle and temperament, as it is for Troilus. Complaint is put in the scale opposite rational perspective and practicality and so echoes the earlier dialogue with Pandarus. Chaucer continues the process with ingenious variations by developing Antigone's song out of the chanson-complaint style of de Machaut as further persuasion towards love,[18] and then adding the twilight song of the nightingale to continue wordlessly the weaving of a mesh of love-lines around Criseyde. Antigone's song is another rehearsal for Criseyde, expressing the state of mind towards which Pandarus has been urging her, speaking of a life of 'ioie and seurte', of serving and of grace, of truth and bliss, and so hypnotising Criseyde into accepting the thoughts as her own. The dream of the white eagle tearing out her heart is Chaucer's powerful way, richly suggestive in its symbolism, of showing the reader that she has unconsciously consented to be taken over.

Thus the first part of Book II combines elements of realism with an echoing of the pattern of complaint and debate in Book I, but whereas there Chaucer was using the design of complaint and comfort as his organising structure, he is now allowing the poem to spread and introducing a variety of colours into his design. He uses Pandarus as his connecting thread and takes him alternately to

142

Criseyde and Troilus (and later to Deiphebus), so that the book is filled with conversation and a sense of his bustling activity. He plays his two fish skilfully with alternating strategies of instruction and persuasion. Chaucer allows him to dominate at this stage. He tells Troilus to write a letter and then instructs him in the proper way of writing (1023–43), but Chaucer suppresses the letter itself and substitutes reported speech. In the second scene with Criseyde Chaucer again replaces the verbatim letter in reply to that of Troilus by reported speech but gives full play to Pandarus, as in his nudging Criseyde to response to the second appearance of Troilus in the street outside her house. The physical image is a more important representation of the lovers to each other than verbal exchange; the puppet-master supplies most of the words. By use of Troilus' appearances Chaucer increases the effect of a staged series of events, a painted process. In the latter part of Book II Chaucer stops following *Il Filostrato* all together and makes little use of the end of Boccaccio's second section. What Chaucer invents in its place is lengthy speech for Pandarus (1359–93) leading to the plot involving Deiphebus and the pretence of Troilus' illness. This part is the nearest in the poem to a fully presented 'dramatic' scene, with an impression of activity and new characters introduced, but speech still occupies a major place and even Deiphebus and Helen contribute to the poem's strain of lament as they deplore Troilus' supposed indisposition.

Pushed for the first time into a subordinate role, Troilus is kept in focus in the reader's mind partly through the element of anxious plaint, as in his first reaction to Pandarus' news of his interview with Criseyde:

> 'But lord, how shal I doon, how shal I lyven?
> Whan shal I next my deere herte see?'   (II, 981–2)

It becomes a defining characteristic associated with his dependence on Pandarus and the recurrent picture of him alone in his bedroom:

> But to Pandare alwey was his recours.
> And pitously gan ay to hym to pleyne.   (II, 1352–3)

This sense of complaint as a natural state for the hero is dignified (and ultimately justified) by the fact that it is continually rebuffed and 'cynicised' by Pandarus, who sees it both as pointless and as artificial rhetoric to be turned on like a tap when occasion requires. So what sounds like a note of sympathy and attempt to cheer—

> 'lord and frend and brother dere,
> God woot that thi disese doth me wo.
> But wiltow stynten al this woful cheere . . .'   (II, 1359–61)

soon turns into the less likeable argument that he should employ it on a better occasion:

> 'It is oon of the thynges forthereth most
> A man to han a layser forto preye,
> And siker place his wo forto bywreye;
> For in good herte it mot som routhe impresse
> To here and see the giltlees in distresse.'   (II, 1368–72)

Even more explicitly Pandarus later instructs Troilus to use his complaining as part of his strategy:

'Now spek, now prey, now pitously compleigne;
Lat nought for nyce shame or drede or slouthe.
Som tyme a man mot telle his owen peyne;
Bileve it, and she shal han on the routhe;
Thow shalt be saved by thi feyth in trouthe.'

(II, 1499–1503)

The echo of Christ's words in Luke 8, 48 and 18, 42 in the last line here augments the hideous irony of the advice. So Troilus' complaining in which it is clear he 'bileves' without being instructed, comes to possess a truth and moral integrity by being seen in the light of optimistic, pragmatic Pandarus' willingness to measure all things in terms of their effectiveness in achieving ends.

Chaucer thus expresses both his sympathetic interest in love's suffering and the observer's view of lovers; out of the two he produces antithesis and debate in which the contraries of idealism and pragmatism are illustrated. The domination of Pandarus in this phase of the fiction distances complaint into an activity to be countered by common sense, to be overcome as unproductive and needless or to be employed as part of persuasive rhetoric, but this alternative to bootless sorrow is identified with the manipulation of emotion and circumstance as Pandarus weaves his webs of compromise.

Other changes of emphasis by Chaucer in Book II augment these effects. Chaucer surrounds Criseyde in particular and Troilus to some extent with a sense of a household and society which act as a constraint; it is, as it is not in *Il Filostrato*, difficult to have a word with Criseyde without getting rid of other listeners. As a result much more is made of the whole business of arranging a meeting between the two. Another suggestive shift is Chaucer's stress on Troilus' role as warrior and prince; though no space is given to the narration of events in the war, nevertheless the image of Troilus as brave knight at arms and the idea of his martial courage are both used to enhance his potentiality as lover and the idea of his being ennobled by love. Accompanying this, and providing an antithesis to it, is the repeated picture of Troilus in bed, visited by Pandarus as a physician visits a patient. Thus Troilus represents in himself the contraries of love, both strong and weak, bravely active and fearfully anxious, impatient and passively hopeless, the mirror of both Mars and Venus. Out of this contrast is Pandarus' appeal to Criseyde made; this hero is he who dies for love and the figure who at one moment is displayed in his glory in the street is to be directly presented first to Criseyde in bed, to appeal to compassion by pathetic complaint.

Chaucer's imagining of Book II thus combines as main elements a strong interest in the rhetoric of complaint and persuasion, a narrative which consists mainly of circumstantial details of plausible sense of occasion, the texture of conversation, the perspectives of experience and proverbial wisdom, and images, especially of Troilus as hero, as eagle, as Mars, but also as languishing lover, as courage threatened by anguish, as manhood lamenting. At the end the suspense is characteristically not one of action but of rhetoric: now that we are on the theshold of the lovers' meeting the question is 'O myghty god, what shal

144

he saye?'. This seems a natural question with which to close a book which is two-thirds direct speech and which includes so much consideration of how to address oneself to love and to a lover. On the other hand it is as significant that, despite the large part given to Pandarus in Book II, it is made clear at the end that Troilus is the real point of reference. Similarly, of the ten passages of any length in Book II not in direct speech, only one is devoted to plot material and to Pandarus' doings (1541–70). Two of them (619–51 and 1257–74) are descriptions of Troilus' appearance and behaviour and Criseyde's impression of him. Two present summaries of the letters exchanged, with Troilus given the more substantial passage (1065–90). In the early part of the book Chaucer uses several narrative passages to distance and develop the implications of Criseyde's reaction to Pandarus' news in comments on her state of mind (596–610 and 670–700) and the description of her household (809–26) and her sleep and dream (900–38). In the later part Chaucer summarises the growth of Troilus' love and desire and his observances and state of mind (1321–58). It appears that Chaucer interprets the function of the narrative voice as primarily to present mental and physical images of his two main figures, both in isolation and as seen by others. Speech moves from the quick exchanges of scenes of practicality and teasing, persuasion, questioning and so on to the mental and emotional definition of stylised complaint, monologue, instruction and illustration relating to aspects of love and anxiety. Enclosing this dominating effect of a poetic texture of spoken immediacy are not, as one might expect, passages of narrative movement (which is effected by brief transitions) but passages of observation, placing and distillation of mental states.

### 3. Complaint as Undercurrent

Although it may seem perverse to see Book III, the part of *Troilus and Criseyde* devoted to a positive celebration of love and the happiness of the lovers, as designed to continue the note of complaint, nevertheless this does seem to me to be the case. Of course, Chaucer stresses the power of love by bringing forward Troilus' hymn to Venus to act as Proem to Book III; the hero's allegiance becomes the inspiring force for the whole book, the theme of its action. And again, when he comes, towards the end of Book III, to the point at which this song occurred in *Il Filostrato*, Chaucer goes back to Boccaccio's source material and creates a new Boethian song in praise of love, hailing its harmonising, controlling and stabilising power, and then brings the book to a close on a note of peace and delight.[19] (Boccaccio chooses to insert a note of warning at the end of his third section, which Chaucer places at the beginning of Book IV.)

> My thridde boke now ende ich in this wyse;
> And Troilus in luste and in quiete
> Is with Criseyde, his owen herte swete.   (III, 1818–20)

But, though Chaucer may enclose the lovers' joy in a framework of harmony and the other positive aspects of love, within that outline he places love repeatedly in antithesis to uncertainty, heightening its beauty by making it fragile, delaying its fulfilment by turning quickly from the lovers' joining to thoughts of separation.

In the first half of the book Chaucer's main change from Boccaccio's telling of the story is his delaying of the consummation scene. He makes the movement of the lovers towards their affair a much more formal, stylised and arranged business, which serves to emphasise the idea of love as part of a social code and to give more importance to the observance of etiquette and hence to the processes of courtship. So Troilus' sincerity is communicated to the reader by a neat contrast between his thoughts before Criseyde arrives, as he plans to move her by his plaintive address, and his overwhelmed wordlessness when she actually comes to his bedside and speaks to him. Gradually he stammers out a few words, then progresses into a modest speech, which leads eventually to an idealised vow of love (127–47) and to a speech of acceptance from Criseyde (159–81). These exchanges form a kind of consummation in speech which is a necessary stage of love and is made to seem a more significant act than the later physical consummation. When it comes to the love scene words are inadequate, but words are the essence of these earlier formal undertakings. The non-physical (not exactly passive but non-active) aspects of Troilus as lover are thus promoted in importance. The later comic moments when Pandarus virtually prepares Troilus for bed and seems to have to provide the physical impulse to love expose the absurdity of this pursuit of love as a rhetorical exercise, but in *Troilus and Criseyde* as a whole Chaucer is more concerned with the giving and losing of the heart than of the body, and love as a verbal and mental activity is what he tunes his poetry most feelingly to convey. Troilus' pledge to be 'verray, humble, trewe,/ Secret, and in myn paynes pacient' and Criseyde's promise to 'Receyven hym fully to my servyse', provided that he keeps her honour and does not claim sovereignty, lead to a significant climax emphasising the shift from sorrow to joy, and the ceremony that is appropriate:

> 'And I shal trewely with al my myght
> Ʒoure bittre tornen al into swetenesse;
> If I be she that may ʒow do gladnesse,
> For every wo ʒe shal recovere a blisse.'
> And hym in armes took and gan hym kisse.
> Fil Pandarus on knees and up his eyen
> To heven threw and held hise hondes highe.
> 'Immortal god,' quod he, 'that mayst nought deyen,
> Cupide I mene, of this mayst glorifie;
> And Venus, thow mayst maken melodie;
> Withouten hond me semeth that in towne
> For this merveille ich here ech belle sowne.'   (III, 178–89)

Here with hero and heroine exchanging vows and Pandarus taking on the role of celebrating priest is the culmination of the movement from woeful solitary complaint to united feeling of satisfaction and joy; the moment has the effect of a marriage ceremony.

Chaucer's separation of this meeting and exchange of vows from the consummation scene at Pandarus' house by nearly a thousand lines gives him the opportunity further to complicate the reader's sense of the relationship of the three characters and of the nature of the joy that has been created out of woe. Pandarus, who has been allowed the dominant part in Book II, continues to arrange and to take advantage of Fortune's opportunities, but, though he may fulfil the necessary roles of master of ceremonies, persuader, love's priest and confidential adviser, our sense of him changes once he identifies his function to Troilus:

> 'for the am I bicomen,
> Bitwixen game and ernest, swich a meene
> As maken wommen unto men to comen—'   (III, 253–5)

The prospect of happiness in the coming love-scene is tainted by the manipulations and lies on which it is based. Though Troilus clears him of the imputation of playing the bawd, his offer of one of his sisters to Pandarus in return adds to the ambivalence.[20] Pandarus teaches Troilus on the subject of secrecy in love in a substantial passage added by Chaucer (288–343) which brings in thoughts of 'meschaunce in this world', of 'wommen lost' who lament 'weilawey, the day that I was borne'. Perhaps a necessary lesson to the prospective lover about discretion and the lady's honour, the passage also reminds the reader of the threats to joy, and of the less attractive aspects of secrecy, the need to be furtive, for Troilus to 'kepe the clos' while Pandarus 'thi proces set in swych a kynde . . . that it shal the suffise' (334–5). Already the strain of complaint begins to come again to the surface, despite the current towards love and joy.

A similar effect of perusing the situation and seeing its contradictions and uncertainties is conveyed in the lengthy passage of narration (441–546) where Chaucer ceases to follow *Il Filostrato* and contrasts Troilus' day-time existence 'in armes as a knyght' and his anxious, lonely, sleepless nights. Chaucer's summary of the period of courtship displays Troilus' active use of 'all his fulle myght' in 'Martes heigh servyse' as the justification for Criseyde's acceptance of him as a 'wal/ Of stiel and sheld from every displesaunce' (479–80). But his fervent, pleading, 'Venus' aspect reveals the disparity of true, intense, virtuous love. In action it is the eagle seizing the heart, the sparrowhawk catching the lark, the warrior wounded and wounding, willing to kill and eventually killed in battle; love is a force for domination and destruction. But in feeling and intention love is worshipper and sufferer, bed-ridden, plaintive, fervently reverent and abased, veering from one intensity to another; the sensibility which is a prerequisite for this experience is alien to the enactment of love's conquering, protective aspect. Only cynical, endlessly flexible and varied natures can love according to both sets of values. Thus Chaucer prepares for the long scene at Pandarus' house by setting in motion contradictions and when the central part of Book III is reached it proves to be as concerned with exposing disparity and anxiety as with fulfilment and joy.

If, as Chaucer moves 'to the grete effect', the two prospective lovers are 'stondyng in concord and in quiete' and all arrangements have carefully been made, still all is to be accomplished by artful feigning and is subject to the whims of greater powers. It is here that Chaucer reminds the reader, in the narrator's voice, of his other strain of complaint:

> But O Fortune, executrice of wyerdes,
> O influences of thise hevenes hye,
> Soth is that under god ʒe ben oure hierdes,
> Though to us bestes ben the causes wrie.   (III, 617–20)

Pandarus' bold manoeuvrings are counterpointed by Troilus' fervent prayers to Venus, to the planetary gods and to the Fates; Chaucer places in antithesis the two levels of apprehension, whereby the forthcoming events are to Troilus matters to be shaped with heaven's aid, while to Pandarus they are matters of here and now, of back-stairs whisperings and physical details:

> 'ȝet, blisful Venus, this nyght thow me enspire . . .
> O fatal sustren, which er any cloth
> Me shapen was, my destine me sponne,
> So helpeth to this werk that is bygonne.'
> Quod Pandarus, 'Thow wrecched mouses herte,
> Artow agast so that she wol the bite?
> Why, don this furred cloke upon thy sherte,
> And folwe me, for I wol have the wite;
> But bide, and lat me gon biforn a lite.'
> And with that word he gan undon a trappe,
> And Troilus he brought in by the lappe.   (III, 712, 733–42)

The humour of anti-climax has a pleasing local effect of vivid realisation of character, but the long-term implication is continually being developed by Chaucer. The split between the practical necessities and moral and emotional truth continues to widen as Pandarus' lies to Criseyde about Troilus' jealousy lead to Criseyde's two laments, first to Pandarus and then to Troilus, and to Troilus' swooning. The manipulator's ingenious feignings are taken seriously and used as the point of irritation into intensified rhetoric, regrets, reproofs and passionate shame which come almost to the point of destroying the outcome to which the pretences were designed to lead. Complaint is the mode associated by Chaucer with 'unrealism'; it communicates a level of intensity and sincerity too extreme for practicality.

Criseyde's first complaint (813–40) is a Boethian monologue on the falsity and mutability of worldly happiness. Already before the lovers are brought together, the joy they may have is condemned:

> 'O brotel wele of mannes ioie unstable!
> With what wight so thow be or how thow pleye,
> Either he woot that thow, ioie, art muable,
> Or woot it nought, it mot ben oon of tweye.
> Now if he woot it nought, how may he seye
> That he hath verray ioie and selynesse,
> That is of ignoraunce ay in derknesse?'   (III, 820–6)

Neither the man who realises the transitoriness of happiness nor the ignorant man has a chance of true joy; the conclusion that 'Ther is no verray weele in this world heere' is one that should freeze all further action. Complaint again contributes assessment and judgment of the value of action, which the poem's active 'meene', Pandarus, continues to encourage, ferment and galvanise, but which comes to seem increasingly vain. His cry is repeatedly

> 'O tyme ilost, wel maistow corsen slouthe!'   (III, 896)

but when the lovers are brought together the time is again devoted at first to lengthy speech, as Criseyde addresses Troilus (988–1050) and includes in her protest against jealousy a second complaint in a Boethian strain, this time invoking Jove:

> 'But O thow Iove, O auctour of nature,
> Is this an honour to thi deyte,
> That folk ungiltif suffren hire iniure,
> And who that giltif is al quyt goth he?
> O, were it lefull forto pleyne on the,
> That undeserved suffrest ialousie,
> Of that I wolde upon the pleyne and crie.'    (III, 1016–22)

Troilus' sense of implication in the shame of causing Criseyde's distress leads to his swoon and so, with a mixture of comic exasperation, anxiety and pathos, to the casting of an unconscious Troilus into bed and the joining of the lovers. The very consummation is thus engineered in terms of the creation and dispersal of protest and anxiety, of guilt expiated, of pain forgiven, and these emotions seem readier to the poet's tongue than the expression of joy as Chaucer approaches the narration of the lovers' bliss, it seems, with reluctance:

> Though that I tarie a ʒer, som tyme I moot,
> After myn auctour, tellen hire gladnesse . . .    (III, 1195–6)

The suggestion that Chaucer finds his material in some way disturbing allows in the reader's mind an odd fusion of the vision of Criseyde as the helpless victim of Troilus and circumstance and of the poet seized by the need at last to face the consummation scene:

> What myghte or may the sely larke seye,
> Whan that the sperhauk hath it in his foot?
> I kan namore . . .    (III, 1191–3)

The implication seems to be that poetry is adequate or appropriate only to sorrow; faced with gladness it acknowledges something beyond itself, outside control, and, as elsewhere, not in the poet's experience. After this it seems only right that the quality of gladness should be expressed by antithesis to prior sorrow, that Criseyde should be compared to the startled nightingale finding her song again and Troilus to the condemned man unexpectedly rescued. Chaucer has now reached the point where he can rejoin *Il Filostrato* and he describes the pleasure of the lovers with imaginative enthusiasm and delicacy to lead back into the general stream of Boccaccio's narrative, but it is significant that in his lengthy protraction of the processes and manoeuvrings towards this moment Chaucer has not simply been exploring aspects of courtly love etiquette; he has contrived, through complaint and debate, through instances of anxiety and protest and of pretence and bewilderment, to communicate the effect of the 'stormy life' which gives substance to the running thread of the imagery of storm, water, boats, steering and so on. Criseyde's earlier role as the voice of representative woman continues to be used in complaints which make potential joy appear as a fragile and tempororary state purchased at emotional cost.

149

Nor is the happiness allowed to remain long untroubled. A 'blisful nyght' may seem worth the poet's soul while 'daunger' and 'feere' are at bay but even at this time of greatest happiness, the lovers are characterised as unsure of the reality (and by implication of the permanence) of their experience, and misers are envisaged ready to begrudge and condemn. The blissful night too soon becomes the dawn and the poetry returns to the note of complaint as Chaucer introduces his aubades into the lyric sequence. Where Boccaccio's lovers renew their embraces, Chaucer's lament their parting. Criseyde castigates the black and 'rakle' night which too briefly and hastily performs its office, while Troilus reproves the cruel day, seen as envious spy creeping in to catch the guilty. So the 'blisful light' of the morning and evening star, attendant on the sun and apostrophised in Book III's opening hymn of love, has ironically become a thing to curse; its changing, transitory quality is now experienced as part of the unfolding plot, the running on of the sequence of time, the need of the lovers to resume their public life. The imagery figures for the reader the hopelessness of the situation of the lovers; to pray for a suspension of the current of time is to banish that very light which inspires their passion. Their relationship can only be a matter of snatched moments; complaint's theme is characteristically the conflict between passion and circumstance. The paradox of life as meaningful experience in conflict with life as continuing existence transfers the antithesis into a new balance between aspects of time:

> 'For how sholde I my lif an houre save,
> Syn that with ʒow is al the lif ich have?'   (III, 1476–7)

And again Chaucer extends the contrast between timelessness and the inevitability of the moment's passing into a new key in Troilus' questioning of the fixity of Criseyde's love and her ironical pledges of constancy.

> 'first shal Phebus fallen fro his speere,
> And everich egle ben the dowves feere,
> And everich roche out of his place sterte,
> Er Troilus out of Criseydes herte.'   (III, 1495–8)

So gladness very quickly becomes an idea fretted and stretched by the strains of time and uncertainty, and, though the lovers are to meet again, their parting after this first night of joy has the effect of the end of things; already their union has become the past, to be stored away in memory.[21]

Chaucer accordingly turns the subsequent scene where Troilus expresses his gratitude to Pandarus into a warning, which accurately predicts Troilus' eventual state of mind:

> 'For of Fortunes sharp adversitee
> The worst kynde of infortune is this,
> A man to han ben in prosperitee,
> And it remembren whan it passed is.'   (III, 1625–8)

The expression of Troilus' satisfaction and his fervent love are thus shadowed by threats, that he might 'rakle as forto greven heere' (1642) and forget that 'worldly ioie halt nought but by a wire' (1636). The subsequent meeting of the

150

lovers and the renewal of their joy is briefly summarised, so briefly as to emphasise the temporary quality of their bliss. The passage echoes, in condensed form, the pattern of the earlier love-scene, moving from the 'ioie and suerte' in which Pandarus brings them to bed and the banishing of 'every sorwe and every fiere' (1685) to the poet's commendation of their joy and then their separation by the day; the irony of the praise of love rings even more ominously:

> Felicite, which that thise clerkes wise
> Comenden so, ne may nought here suffise;
> This ioie may nought writen be with inke;
> This passeth al that herte may bythynke.   (III, 1691–4)

Even if one does not recall that 'clerkes' distinguish between true and false felicity and conclude that the reference to sovereign good is itself ironic, the sharp contrast between one stanza and the next forces the illusion of this superlative happiness on the reader's attention; this felicity that 'passeth every wit for to devyse' and that 'passeth al that herte may bythynke' also vanishes at first light, so that day becomes death and joy is replaced by woe and bitter cursing.

So although Chaucer chooses to end Book III on a note of peace and delight and though he returns in the *Canticus Troili* (1744–71) to Boethius' praise of love as a stabilising power in the universe, he has created for this ending disturbing undercurrents of ironic uncertainty. We may end with a picture of Troilus

> In suffisaunce, in blisse, and in syngynges   (III, 1716)

but the imagery of his song to the power of love continues to establish tension between the philosophical concept and the experience. So, on the one hand, is the idea of love binding together society and couples in the sacrament of marriage—

> 'Love, that knetteth lawe of compaignie,
> And couples doth in vertue forto dwelle,
> Bynd this acord that I have told and telle.'   (III, 1748–50)

This uncomfortably echoes the reference to the different binding:

> Aboute his herte of al Criseydes nette;
> He was so narwe ymasked and yknette
> That it undon on any manere syde,
> That nyl naught ben, for aught that may bitide.
> > (III, 1733–6)

Similarly love's power to hold the variable seasons and the discordant elements in a perpetual lasting bond is proved in the ordering of day and night:

> 'That Phebus mote his rosy day forth bryng,
> And that the mone hath lordshipe over the nyghtes—
> Al this doth love, ay heried be his myghtes!'   (III, 1755–7)

But the experience of love as shown earlier has questioned, rejected and cursed that ordering, wanting day for ever suspended. Troilus' celebration of love reveals the elements of perversity. The main force of the prayer is a seeking for permanence, a hope that the binding power will 'cerclen hertes alle and faste bynde'. Chaucer ends his third book with his attention devoted mainly to his hero and that seeking for permanence is consistent with his idealism, his complete pledging of himself to love and his allegiance to Venus' power. But the undercurrents from the earlier parts of the Book leave the reader to see Troilus' praise of love as an elevated structure of feeling and worship based on the shifting sands of illusion. Chaucer may claim accurately to have shown

> Th'effect and ioie of Troilus servise,
> Al be that ther was som disese amonge.   (III, 1815–16)

The book ends 'in luste and in quiete' but the very opening lines of Book IV immediately break the mood and declare the end of happiness.

It is in Book III that Chaucer significantly fixes the essentially lyric, elegiac quality of *Troilus and Criseyde*. Where love comes nearest to perfection, the sorrows, threats, pleas and anxieties connected with it make their most penetrating effect on the reader's sensibilities. Within a fairly slight narrative framework of contrived situation, Chaucer concentrates on the expression of states of mind, the attribution and assessment of value in love's own nature and in the feelings and relationships inspired by it. Even in the passages where he is not expressing his characters' thoughts and feelings in direct speech, Chaucer's concern is not much with events or incidents:

> But now, paraunter, som man wayten wolde
> That every word, or soonde, or look, or cheere
> Of Troilus that I rehercen sholde,
> In al this while . . .   (III, 491–4)

His narrative passages are summings up, comments, adjustments and transitions more than unfoldings; a few intense moments are dramatised against a blurred sense of other times and meetings. The reader perceives the celebration of love as a brave defiance of the inevitable. The opening and closing hymns of praise to Venus and to Love enclose shifting feelings with mutual gladness and joy maintained as a poetic mood for too short a span to seem anything but snatched from the current of uncertainty.

4. Complaint as Response to Fortune

At the opening of Book IV that current begins to flow more strongly as Fortune turns against Troilus and the poet tremulously takes up the strain of fear and regret. The keynote of lament is struck in the proem again and again: the poet regrets the brevity of joy, complains of the need to narrate unwelcome matter, regrets the tongues that speak ill of Criseyde and invokes the Furies, recalling his cry for Thesiphone's aid at the beginning of the poem, as those

> That endeles compleignen evere in pyne. (IV, 23)

It is not, in fact, until Book V that Chaucer brings his hero back to the state of isolating sorrow from which Troilus' adventures in loving began, and in Book IV the complaints of hero and heroine against the workings of Fortune are set in the perspective of debate, but in his opening narrator's declaration of intent he sees right to the end of his tale in his need of the Furies' aid

> So that the losse of lyf and love yfeere
> Of Troilus be fully shewed heere. (IV, 27–8)

The foreboding view of where it is all to end defines the immediate course of the narrative as the beginning of the process of loss. Chaucer follows the stages of that loss as described in *Il Filostrato*, satisfied, for the most part, with pointing the significance by short expansions. The only major addition in the whole book is the 'predestination' soliloquy of Troilus. However, even the shorter expansions contribute meaningfully to the structural design of the Book, which (after the opening narration of the bringing about of the exchange of prisoners) consists of alternating passages of soliloquy and dialogue: Troilus laments alone (250–336) before being reasoned with by Pandarus; Criseyde laments alone (743–98) before Pandarus joins her and discusses things; Troilus laments alone (958–1078) and is countered first by Pandarus and then by Criseyde, whose long dialogue with Troilus brings the book to an end. The proportion of direct speech in Book IV is high (70 per cent, even higher than Book II) and Troilus speaks more lines in this book than in any of the others, as does Criseyde.[22] Pandarus' role, on the other hand, dwindles in each book after Book II and he contributes only half as much as Troilus. The sequence may be seen, therefore, as one of alternating monologue and dialogue, with hero and heroine uttering the major part, set within a narrative frame.

The only significant addition to the narrative portion is Hector's expression of opposition to the exchanging of Criseyde (169–217) ('We usen here no wommen forto selle') and Chaucer's pointing of the irony of the mob's enthusiasm for Antenor:

> For he was after traitour to the town
> Of Troye; allas, they quytte hym out to rathe.
> O nyce world, lo thy discrecioun!
> Criseyde, which that nevere dide hem scathe,
> Shal now no lenger in hire blisse bathe;
> But Antenor, he shal com hom to towne,
> And she shal out.' (IV, 204–10)

Lurking unspoken in Chaucer's comment is the invitation to the reader to compare Criseyde's betrayal to Antenor's; this solemnly debated parliamentary decision releases two betrayers to their opportunity for treachery and all of the lengthy heart-searching that follows has this irony hanging over it. The passionate wretchedness of Troilus appears, as a result, not merely as a personal cry of deprivation; it is the beginning of the end of all things and Chaucer invites us to go beyond the loss of a mistress to envisage the loss of joy and of life itself:

> And as in wynter leves ben birafte,
> Ech after other til the tree be bare,
> So that ther nys but bark and braunche ilafte,
> Lith Troilus byraft of eche welfare,
> Ibounden in the blake bark of care.   (IV, 225–9)

The first of the book's soliloquies of lament is thus prepared for by irony and imagery. Troilus is 'like a dede ymage' until the bursting out of pent up madness and grief turns him into a wounded bull that 'of his deth roreth in compleynynge'. The frozen stillness and the bellowing of the doomed beast equally convey the hopelessness of the complaint that follows and intensify the passion of the speaker.

More insistently than in earlier parts of the poem, Book IV uses the association between complaint and extremity—extremity of rhetoric, of action, of physical expression of emotion, of fatalism. Before this first complaint of Troilus is expressed he has to go through 'the furie and al the rage' calling on death to release him. Before Criseyde in her turn laments her fate she falls as if dead upon her bed, rends her hair and wrings her hands, praying God to remedy her suffering with death. For his second and more philosophical complaint against Fate, Chaucer transfers Troilus from his own room to the temple where he prays for death. When Troilus and Criseyde meet, an excess of sobbing and bitter tears deprives each of speech until 'somwhat to wayken gan the peyne/ By lengthe of pleynte'. Each time, Chaucer precedes the words of lament with a set-piece description of woe; complaint is used as ritualised action, not only speech. This action develops the story on the plane of high tragedy and culminates in the death-like swoon of Criseyde which leaves Troilus complaining over her body and contemplating his own suicide:

> So after that he longe hadde hire compleyned,
> His hondes wrong and seyde that was to seye,
> And with his teeris salt hire breest byreyned . . .
> He gan hire lymes dresse in swich manere
> As men don hem that shal ben layde on beere.
> And after this with sterne and cruel herte,
> His swerd anon out of his shethe he twighte,
> Hym self to slen . . .   (IV, 1170–2, 1182–6)

Chaucer's addition of the ceremony of complaining over the corpse shows his sense of complaint as part of a pattern of behaviour, recognised in *Il Filostrato* and interpreted in a high rhetorical vein as one way of perceiving the situation of the lovers. Briefly they are envisaged as the players in a tragic drama, which Shakespeare later echoes in *Romeo and Juliet*, where describing the act of lament, with the words unspoken, is the equivalent of a stage-direction. One possible ending of the tale is briefly acted through as Troilus determines to follow Criseyde and, bidding farewell to Troy and his father and mother, addresses Fate and his beloved:

> 'Atropos, make redy thow my beere.
> And thow Criseyde, O swete herte deere,
> Receyve now my spirit.' (IV, 1208–10)

Criseyde, recovered from her swoon, completes the pattern when, seeing Troilus' sword, she makes her own promise not to have survived him even

> 'to han ben crowned Queene
> Of al that lond the sonne on shyneth sheene.
> But with this selve swerd which that here is,
> My selve I wolde han slayne.' (IV, 1238–41)

This is as far as Chaucer goes down that path; he expands the speech of Criseyde that follows to make it not only a practical response to the prospect of separation but an explicit rejection of the rhetorical, tragic road of complaint:

> 'Lo, herte myn, wel woot ȝe this,' quod she,
> 'That if a wight alwey his wo compleyne,
> And seketh nought how holpen forto be,
> It nys but folie and encresse of peyne.' (IV, 1254–7)

And so the movement towards the tragic end is halted and postponed; lamentation is again reined in, put into the perspective of a 'reasonable' seeking of remedies.[23] This brush with death is the nearest Criseyde comes to fulfilling one literary idea of the noble heroine of a love story; the implicit comparison with Thisbe or Alcyone or good Alceste creates the effect in the passage of Criseyde's rejection of a proffered role.

Two significant thematic and structural elements in Chaucer's fourth book are identifiable in this sequence of scenes of rhetorical extremity and its culmination in a potential suicide scene from which the heroine withdraws. One is the poet's creation of an alternation of feeling between complaint and argument, between monologue and dialogue, between acceptance that all is at an end and hope of some continuity. The other is Chaucer's opening up of the reader's moral judgment by means of suggested alternatives to the lovers' actions. I shall consider these in turn.

The first complaint of Troilus and the subsequent exchange with Pandarus establishes the pattern of lament, which is then first countered by practical opposition and subsequently reinforced by argument. The complaint itself (260–336) begins as a complaint against Fortune for her envy and changeable violence, but already Troilus sees himself as a 'combre-world' and introduces the death-wishing strain which runs through the following seven stanzas of address to the God of Love, to his own wretched wandering spirit, his woeful eyes, to Criseyde, all lovers and, finally, with a curse, to Calchas. The prospect Troilus sees is of a life of ceaseless, unsatisfied sorrow needlessly prolonged by the delay of a hoped-for death.[24] The succession of questions—'What shal I don?', 'Why nyltow fleen . . . ?', 'What shal ȝe doon . . . ?', 'who shal now ȝeven comfort . . . ?'—might alone accumulate into an impression of plaintive

155

emptiness but to most of them come answers direct or oblique, which identify life-long complaint as the bitter occupation of the wretched solitary:

> 'I shal, while I may dure
> On lyve in torment and in cruwel peyne,
> This infortune or this disaventure
> Allone as I was born, iwys, compleyne.'   (IV, 295–8)

The soul will lurk in woe, the eyes will weep themselves blind, no being will give comfort; the answers fill the void with physical images of sorrow, the blind Oedipus, the restless soul which yet clings to the nest of his miserable heart, the light of Criseyde's eyes extinguished, the imagined tomb by which lovers will pass. Through this sequence of questions, images and addresses Troilus' thought moves from the arraigning of Fortune to blame of the human agent who began the train of events, the 'unholsum and myslyved' Calchas, the explicit mean through which Fortune has worked her malice. The effect is of a natural dramatic sequence of thoughts and impulses rather than of a patterned lyric, a mixture of resentment, sorrow and fatalism, plaintive but incomplete.

Chaucer uses Pandarus, as he had in response to Troilus' laments in Book I, as a contrary voice, accepting Troilus' condemnation of Fortune but resisting his outbursts of grief:

> 'Swich is this world: forthi I thus diffyne:
> Ne trust no wight to fynden in fortune
> Ay propretee—hire ȝiftes ben comune.
> But telle me this, whi thow art now so mad
> To sorwen thus?'   (IV, 390–4)

Troilus should be glad that he has at least enjoyed his love and there are other women. Chaucer's plucking of the supposed authority Zanzis 'that was ful wys', from some unknown encyclopaedia to bolster up the platitudinous thought that 'The newe love out chaceth ofte the olde' identifies for the reader the shallow insensitivity. At this point in the poem Pandarus, hitherto at least making up in skill and worldly humour for a lack of honour and principle, begins to sound the inadequate voice. Chaucer mitigates the effect by adding a stanza (428–34) on Pandarus' motives, excusing the 'unthrift' of what he says by the intention to comfort, but then strengthens Troilus' reply (435–518), which is essentially a rejection of Pandarus' advice. Pandarus' speech is more important as a stimulus to this dramatic response than as a point of view in itself—indeed Pandarus' arguments sound more definite in Troilus' rejection of them than in Pandarus' own speech—but Chaucer is echoing the earlier structural pattern of placing the hero's negatives and questionings in debate with Pandarus' positive assertions and accepted wisdoms. Only now, the proverbial answers are not merely too pat but also wrong:

> 'O leve Pandare, in conclusioun
> I wol nat ben of thyn opynyoun
> Touchyng al this . . .'   (IV, 452–4)

The speech is significant in showing Troilus' making a moral judgment of Pandarus' arguments, seeing that to follow his advice would be an act of betrayal and of falsity to his word:

> 'syn I have trouthe hire hight,
> I wol nat ben untrewe for no wight.'   (IV, 445–6)

Pandarus' own standards of judgment are vividly characterised as having the arbitrariness of a game:

> 'But kanstow playen raket to and fro,
> Nettle in, dok out, now this, now that, Pandare?'
>                                                             (IV, 460–1)

or the artificiality of a constructed argument which has no basis in the experience of real life:

> 'Thow hast here made an argument . . .
> Whi gabbestow . . . ?
> O where hastow ben hid so longe in muwe,
> That kanst so wel and formely arguwe?'
>                                                  (IV, 477, 481, 496–7)

The vigorous bitterness of this speech turns the complaining Troilus into a stronger, more justified figure than he has seemed at any earlier point in the poem; the idealism has more substance now that the pragmatism which counters it has adversity to cope with and can do no better than assume that one woman is as good as another. Troilus' final plea to death to release him (501–18) develops Boethius' image of kindly death coming, often called, to wretches grieving not in sweet times but in bitter pain, by means of the language of love poetry; the fire of sorrow needs to be extinguished by the cold stroke of death or quenched in tears, which Chaucer envisages distilled in a chemical retort; through the alchemy of grief Troilus becomes *lacrimae rerum*. The exchange does not end there but the countering of Pandarus' arguments and the poet's use of intensifying lyric language makes it clear that whatever Pandarus now says, he is at a different level of apprehension from Troilus. Complaint has again been 'answered' but this time has asserted its truth. The rest of the conversation turns to the other theme of possible alternatives to Troilus' behaviour, which I shall return to later.

Complaining as an action inevitable in a situation of stress is just as markedly attibuted to Criseyde in the parallel scene which follows. Like Troilus she has to wait until other people can be excluded before she can fully express her feelings 'sobbyng in hire compleynte' (742). The words of her lament (743–9, 757–98) are offered by the poet as a mere indication of her distress, the extent of which is indescribable:

> my litel tonge,
> If I discryven wolde hire hevynesse,
> It sholde make hire sorwe seme lesse
> Than that it was, and childisshly deface
> Hire heigh compleynte, and therfore ich it pace.   (IV, 801–5)

This gesture towards the idea of an appropriately high strain of rhetoric to reinforce Criseyde's lament again identifies Chaucer's sense of formal complaint as a necessary means of registering the significance of events. The rest of life must be cleared away so that this ceremony may be properly performed. Fortune's blows need time to resound on the resonant gong of the characters' sensibilities and the decorum which the poet observes with regard to the process establishes for the reader a measure of priorities: circumstances are arbitrary and changeable and their significance in poetry becomes merely incidental in comparison with the inevitability of the human reaction, the sorrow and high rhetoric of its expression. Her actual complaint, like that of Troilus, is a weaving together of rhetorical questions and determinations towards death; a life of sorrow, 'compleynt and abstinence' will prepare for the joining of her soul with that of Troilus 'to compleyne/ Eternaly'. She renews the lament to Pandarus (828–47) in a passage added by Chaucer, asserting that all love and joy end in sorrow and offering herself as the mirror of all sorrows and all harms.

It is again Pandarus' role to resist the impulse towards death and the self-immolation, with questions about immediate action and repeated assertions of the uselessness of endless weeping:

> 'Bet is a tyme of cure ay than of pleynte.'   (IV, 931)

Criseyde is not given Troilus' tough reasoning power with which to refuse Pandarus' too easy solutions; her woeful appearance and readiness to sink her sorrow into that of Troilus leave her balanced between the two, afflicted and as incapable as Troilus of overcoming her grief, but amenable and ready to attempt to restrain her weeping for Troilus' sake. So complaint here is not reversed or defeated by countering argument, but held in, waiting for fulfilment or change.

Chaucer's addition of Troilus' long soliloquy on Fortune, free will and predestination builds on to the pattern of lament and debate already established. Again solitary despair is pictured as if it were an event; the actions of the book are the states of mind which are given so much more weight than the political manoeuvrings, or any idea of a 'reality' to which Pandarus' comings and goings belong. The static quality of lyric lament is here given substance and philosophical justification. Troilus 'complains' and yet accepts that all must be. His opening declaration—

> 'For al that comth, comth by necessitee.
> Thus to ben lorn, it is my destinee'   (IV, 958–9)

is unaltered by what follows from Boethius V, prose 3. The exclusion of Philosophy's answers to the questionings leaves Troilus only with the troubled uncertainty of Boethius, which Chaucer turns into a perverse constancy. Chaucer here firmly identifies Troilus with a view of life which makes perpetual complaint, in this life at any rate, inevitable. The abstract concept of God's steadfastness is used to express Troilus' idealism and fidelity; that concept can only be retained by the antithesis of God's 'parfit clere wytynge' and 'we men that han doutous wenynge' (992).

To believe in the possibility of free choice and of man's judgment being sure would lead to hope of happiness at the price of the concept of stability in the world. The effect of this curious passage in *Troilus and Criseyde* is mixed.[25] It confirms the touches of scholastic debate in Troilus' and Criseyde's condemnation of Calchas as the agent of misfortune and in Criseyde's use of the Aristotelian language of causes in her complaining:

> 'Pandare first of ioies mo than two
> Was cause causyng unto me, Criseyde,
> That now transmewed ben in cruel wo.'   (IV, 828–30)

Book IV is the part of the poem where lament is woven in with theory. But the idea that reasoning justifies Troilus' sense of things is accompanied by the less logical aspect of the passage: the fact that from line 1002 onwards it so insistently harps on the idea of necessity gradually overwhelms the idea of 'fre chois' and the final insistence seems not so much the culmination of the argument as the obsessive reiteration of an idée fixe:

> 'Ek right so whan I woot a thyng comyng,
> So mot it come; and thus the bifallyng
> Of thynges that ben wist bifore the tyde
> They mowe nat ben eschued on no syde.'   (IV, 1075–8)

Chaucer describes the passage as Troilus' 'Disputyng with hym self in this matere' (1084) and clearly intends the reader to see the hero's 'hevynesse', the mood of complaint, as here fusing with the element of debate, extending the earlier-mentioned idea of an inner debate within Troilus between Desire and Reason (lines 572–4).

Pandarus' voice (1086–1120) adds little in this instance to the effect of lament countered, since Troilus' soliloquy has been expressed in the Boethian terms of a complaint of man's instability, helplessness and limitation, not of excess of feeling; the excess is in the determinism of outlook and that, in a sense, is answered by the concern of Pandarus with the immediate moment, the ignorant present that foresees nothing. A wise man, for him, does not think, but lives in the moment; ironically for Troilus to do so and to encounter Criseyde is inevitably to weep, and so Chaucer returns to the high rhetoric of lament, swoon and sword in the scene already discussed.

In the latter part of Book IV the countering of complaint is, however, taken over from Pandarus by Criseyde, in another of her disconcerting shifts of stance. Once the potential suicide scene has been lived through, complaining becomes folly (1257) and in the longest speech that Chaucer gives her in the whole poem (1254–1414) Criseyde becomes the spokesperson for practicality. This speech takes up the other strain of presenting alternatives to hopeless grief.

These alternatives cumulatively represent the contrary response to Fortune's blows and this response, in a sense, gradually overcomes despair, since Troilus has to accept Criseyde's proposal that they accede to the exchange of prisoners while she secretly will plot to return to Troy. Out of this narrative thread an interestingly complex perspective for the hero's actions and thoughts is created. Pandarus' 'unthrifty' suggestions that Troilus should shrug his shoulders and look for a replacement for Criseyde are vigorously rejected and used to give expression to Troilus' commitment to the ideal of truth and fidelity to the individual beloved. His rejection of Pandarus' arguments leads to the blunt presentation by Pandarus of the alternative:

> 'Go ravysshe here ne kanstow not for shame?
> And other lat here out of towne fare,
> Or hold here stille and leve thi nyce fare.'   (IV, 530–2)

Chaucer shows Troilus restraining his grief and returning a considered answer; he will not add to Troy's record for the ravishing of women. The honour of the city and of Priam are joined to the honour of Criseyde as motives for Troilus' need to control his own desire:

> 'Thus am I with desire and reson twight:
> Desire forto destourben hire me redeth.
> And reson nyl nat, so myn herte dredeth.'   (IV, 572–4)

Pandarus' response makes clear the selfish strain in his advice: honour, the city's opinion, what do they matter?—Troilus can exploit his rank to get what he wishes:

> 'Devyne nat in resoun ay so depe
> Ne corteisly, but help thi selve anon.'   (IV, 589–90)

Pandarus' dismissal of reason leaves clear the sense that grief and complaint are not only the signs of sensibility but also the language of thought and moral judgment. Pandarus becomes completely cynical as he suggests that Troilus has as much right to his love as Paris and, though Chaucer omits Boccaccio's even more cynical comment that Criseida could as well manage without honour as Helen, he accepts the argument that Criseyde would not think less of Troilus for acting the manly ravisher's part. Pandarus' pragmatism here reaches an extreme definition as the antithesis of Troilus' conduct:

> 'Lat nat this wrecched wo thyn herte gnawe.
> But manly sette the world on six and sevene,
> And if thow deye a martyr, go to hevene . . .
> And if the list here sterven as a wrecche,
> Adieu, the devel spede hym that it recche.'
>
> (IV, 621–3, 629–30)

The 'active' view holds contempt for emotion and thought; inaction is un-manly cowardice. Troilus nevertheless resists the advice, deferring to Criseyde's will, which Pandarus then, in a less contentious vein, advises him to consult. The striking feature of the latter part of this conversation is the impression of steady resistance in Troilus' grief to any unprincipled expedient, in contrast to Pandarus' readiness to shift his position, to be contemptuous or placatory by turns. The shallowness and instability undermine the sympathy which the reader has earlier been ready to feel for practical common sense in the face of extremity of emotion. If these slippery shruggings off of conscience and decency are the alternative, then grief and complaint come to seem a more positive and worthy choice of behaviour. The subject of their discussion makes it appear as a choice, not a mere lapsing into weak incapacity, because the alternative possibilities are identified and evaluated.

However, Pandarus is not portrayed (any more than the slighter figure of Pandaro in the Italian) as concerned with abstracts, but only with the art of the possible and so he settles at the lowest level of agreement with Troilus, that at least he should not remain grieving alone but should talk to Criseyde. In the corresponding scene with Criseyde the alternative to helpless weeping is more acceptably urged by Pandarus; he has the immediate prospect of meeting Troilus to offer and Criseyde is not characterised as having any steadfast view of her own with which to resist. So grief is overcome simply by the suggestion that there are alternatives, supported by flattery and busy helpfulness:

> 'Syn ʒe be wise and bothe of oon assente,
> So shapeth how destourbe ʒoure goynge,
> Or come aʒeyn soon after ʒe be wente—
> Wommen ben wise in short avysemente—
> And lat sen how ʒoure wit shal now availle,
> And what that I may helpe, it shal nat faille.'   (IV, 933–8)

To this the succeeding soliloquy of Troilus seems a closing of the door. Whether or not Chaucer imported the Boethian meditation in order to emphasise the 'entrapped hopelessness', as Geoffrey Shepherd called it,[26] which he identified as the keynote of the pre-Christian outlook, within the see-sawing of persuasive rhetoric in Book IV this passage functions as a debating point in answer to Pandarus and the active point of view: there is no alternative; necessity will be fulfilled. Since the reader has known from the beginning of the poem that this, from a historical perspective at least, is the case, Troilus' argument fascinatingly combines perversity with truth: his resistance to alternatives seems to possess a kind of insight, because it accepts the inevitable. Against this, Pandarus and Criseyde appear to be vainly battering against immovable forces; their words must be empty because they are to be proved wrong and yet they are in some ways 'natural' and vulnerable. In the latter part of Book IV the function of resisting the unavoidable crescendo of grief and protest passes from Pandarus to Criseyde and in her long speech to Troilus Chaucer greatly expands and develops her arguments to present a final version of the alternatives to hopeless submission to inevitable tragedy.

The 'remede' she offers is very much in Pandarus' terms: concentrate on what can be done; for parting substitute meeting and plan to that end and all is simple:

> 'that it may be so
> By alle right and in a wordes fewe,
> I shal ʒow wel an heep of weyes shewe.'   (IV, 1279–81)

All that is inevitable is the immediate parting but that can be borne as necessary temporary suffering and the Greek camp is only a stone's throw away. The elimination of difficulties and the reassuring rhetoric of her address to Troilus (as, for example, when she puts thoughts into his mind at 1317–18) identify the quality of the early part of the speech as belonging to familiar types

161

of consolation and would by itself fit comfortably within the idea of the heroine's role as feminine easer of the sharpness of the world's pains. But the argument then extends into an increasingly ill-based hopefulness; the speech begins to sound like wish-fulfilment when the irony of history is brought into play to reveal the illusion of it all:

> 'Ʒe sen that every day ek more and more
> Men trete of pees and it supposed is
> That men the queene Eleyne shal restore,
> And Grekis us restoren that is mys . . .
> Ʒe may the bettre at ese of herte abyde.'
>
> (IV, 1345–8, 1351)

If the idea that Criseyde will simply come back to Troy seems possible, the possibility becomes fantasy when it merges with a hopeful vision of free commerce between peaceful societies and finally is overwhelmed in the variety of ideas offered by Criseyde as she enlarges on Calchas' avarice as a motive for her return. The last stanzas accumulate references to the instability of words and the haphazardness of things—'what for o thyng and for other', 'speken in amphibologies', 'Made hym amys the goddes text to glose'—and they give the final touch to this collection of insubstantial possibilities in which Troilus has to be made to believe. Chaucer's added stanza affirming Criseyde's 'good entente' and her 'purpos evere to be trewe' neatly undermines itself in the final line, 'Thus writen they that of hire werkes knewe', to round off the ironic effect.

The speeches which bring Book IV to a close leave the antithesis between Troilus' passionate disbelief in anything but sorrow and the practical bowing to circumstances essentially undisturbed. Temporarily the hero 'took it for the beste' and their sexual pleasure is renewed, but this turns Troilus' thoughts to anxiety about Criseyde's fidelity, and so to a reopening of the debate, when he begins to question her reasoning, casting doubt on the prospects of peace and of Criseyde's being able to deceive her father; more likely is that he will arrange a Greek marriage for her and persuade her to cast in her lot with the sophisticated and conquering Greeks. Thus the realm of possibility is also shown through Troilus to be full of threat and potential pain and his earlier resolution to maintain Troy's and Criseyde's honour weakens with the thought that present happiness is something certain and available, where all else is uncertain. Chaucer elevates and philosophises the contrast between the bird in the hand and the chances of the bush into that between essential good and the non-essential, optional attendant circumstances:

> 'folie is whan man may chese,
> For accident his substaunce ay to lese.'  (IV, 1504–5)

The idea of their running away together has, in fact, fewer practical barriers than the idea of Criseyde's returning alone from the Greek camp, but Criseyde takes the suggestion in terms of the questioning of her fidelity and so answers in the exaggerated language of oaths and protestations; the ideas of Troy's need, Troilus' honour, future name, future shame support her argument for caution, for control of passion by reason and for turning the necessity which had earlier so dominated Troilus' thoughts into a virtue. Troilus' protests continue but are overborne and the lovers prepare to part with mutual swearings of their truth.

The irony is inescapable, since they are preparing the circumstances for faithlessness, but Chaucer leaves the ambiguities for the reader's own savouring. He transfers Troiolo's speech in which he tells Criseida why he loved her to Criseyde, so that it is she whose voice utters the epitaph for the beloved about to be lost and for the quality of his love, characterised by 'moral vertue grounded upon trouthe', by 'gentil herte and manhod' and by the fact that 'ȝoure resoun bridlede ȝoure delit'. The words are more designed to be appropriate to the image of the bereft, tormented hero with which the book closes, than to the reader's sense of what earlier had moved Criseyde about Troilus, but their dignity and nobility confer moral sensibility on the speaker as well as on Troilus himself. And so the ebb and flow of lament and argument in Book IV reaches the point of crucial separation. Little has changed at the end of the book from the narrative point reached at line 217 but the rest is all needed to assess and work through some of the ideas and emotions central to the work. At the end of the book the inevitable movement is seen with richness and complexity. The relentless pull of the subject towards tragedy and lament has been dramatised by the polarising effect of debate and conflict of attitude. The contrary forces of practicality themselves consist of a subtly balanced mixture of common sense and realistic alternatives on the one hand and on the other ironic self-deluding fantasies.


5. Complaint as Dominant Mode

The note of passionate protest is struck early in Book V and Troilus' outward restraint as he watches Diomede take Criseyde away is contrasted with the inner turmoil of his self-reproachful thoughts. The poet points the irony of Troilus' intense perusal of his lady, the source of all his joy, since he is never to see her again, before his passionate self-questioning:

> 'Allas,' quod he, 'thus foul a wrecchednesse,
> Whi suffre ich it, whi nyl ich it redresse?'   (V, 39–40)

Chaucer's suppression of the 4-stanza reproach of Jove and Fortune which Boccaccio gives to Criseyde at this point stresses Troilus' grief; Criseyde has merely an echo of it with the single word 'allas' before she must ride sorrowfully to the point of exchange. As with Book IV, the essential narrative elements (except for the very end) of Book V are contained in the first couple of hundred lines or so: Troilus is left in Troy; Diomede sees his opportunity and exploits Criseyde's situation from the start; she returns to her father. Chaucer supplements Boccaccio from Benoit to anticipate the successful courtship of Criseyde by Diomede and so increases the ironic perspective from which all of Troilus' anxiety is viewed. Once this is established and the exchange completed (by line 196), Chaucer settles to creating one continuous sequence of attenuated emotion and thought from the material of Parts 5–8 of *Il Filostrato*. It reads as a lyric drama in three scenes, an enclosing of Criseyde's decline and fall within the two phases of Troilus' grief. In each of the three sections (197–686, 687–1099 and 1100–764) there is a strong strain of complaint, ranging in effect from elegiac pathos to ironic self-assessment and bitter protest.

In the first of the three the speeches of Troilus form a sequence of lyric expressions of loss and pain. From the outcry of one word 'deth' (205) Troilus' subsequent utterances may be read as a continuous and developing complaint—that is, the speeches at 218–45, 295–322, 414–27, 465–7, 540–53, 565–81, 582–602, 606–16, 638–58 and 669–79. The intervening passages serve to vary the colouring and tone of the lament by providing new settings, the stimulus of Pandarus' contrary point of view, the sense of passing time, but the interest of the poetry is in the plangency and melancholy sweetness of Troilus' lonely memories and the bitterness of his regrets.

Chaucer prefaces the series with an elaboration of the description of Troilus' frenzy: the detailed identification of the gods he curses and the comparison of his night-long writhings to the torments of Ixion set the stage for the soliloquy of complaint with touches of epic heightening and formal ceremony. The opening lines of the lament similarly are given an appropriate rhetorical patterning:

> 'Wher is hire white brest, wher is it, where?
> Wher is myn owene lady lief and deere?
> Wher ben hire armes and hire eyen cleere,
> That 3esternyght this tyme with me were?'   (V, 218–21)

The apostrophes to Criseyde ('O herte myn! . . . O swete fo!') equally identify the stylised quality of courtly love lyric as the mode towards which Chaucer persistently directs the expression, as he extends the soliloquy by converting a speech to Pandaro into an enlargement of the pattern of rhetorical questioning. From 'where?' Troilus proceeds to 'how?', 'when?' and 'whi?' and then to repeated 'who?' and 'how?': so uncertainty of place, time, motive, relationship and behaviour all indicate the unsettled state of being which loss creates. The 4-stanza lyric, moving in itself, leads naturally into as long a gloss on these sorrow-torn words in the form of a description of his dreams and variations of mood. Again Chaucer adapts part of a speech to Pandaro to create a weightier effect and, in his only reference in *Troilus and Criseyde* to the poem's being read, invites the reader to add to that effect in the imagination:

> Who koude telle aright or ful discryve
> His wo, his pleynt, his langoure and his pyne?
> Naught alle the men that han or ben on lyve.
> Thow redere, maist thi self ful wel devyne
> That swich a wo my wit kan nat diffyne.   (V, 267–71)

Again Chaucer uses the strategy, as in Book IV, of creating a studied impression of grief by combining physical description of sorrowing stances and attributes with lamenting soliloquy.

The structural pattern created earlier is also echoed in the continuation of the complaint themes into a dialogue with a contrasting voice. But though Pandarus' words here remind the reader of earlier passages of debate between the two (e.g. 'as I have told the 3ore/ That it is folye forto sorwen thus'), there is not the same degree of resistance to the prevailing mood of lamentation. Pandarus can do no more than suggest diversion to pass the time until Criseyde's return, while at the same time privately expressing his disbelief in that return (505–8). The weight of the conversation is given to the continuation of the grieving strain, both in Troilus' planning of his own funeral (for which Chaucer draws on the death and funeral of Arcita in *Il Teseida*) and even more pointedly within Pandarus' long speech of 'comfort' (323–414). Pandarus' supposed rallying of his friend actually serves to augment Troilus' sorrow, by supplying images of the inevitable griefs of life:

> '. . . from his love, or ellis from his wif,
> A man mote twynnen of necessite . . .
> . . . alwey frendes may nat ben yfeere.'  (V, 338–9, 343)

The very virtues that Pandarus recommends—good hope, endurance, the curative property of time—have misery and pain as their prerequisite. Chaucer makes a substantial addition to the speech in the comments on Troilus' dreams: Pandarus is made to be scornfully dismissive of the idea that dreams may have significance or should be taken seriously, but Chaucer's summary of the three dream kinds, *coeleste*, *animale* and *naturale*, and references to other details of dream lore have the effect, as is usual with Chaucer on this theme, not of closing the possibilities but of opening them up; there seem even more foreboding and uncertain aspects in Troilus' dreams by the time Pandarus has finished than there were before. Pandarus' proposal that they should enjoy a 'lusty lif in Troie' seems particularly implausible after all this and Troilus' proclaiming of the inevitability of weeping and lament (414–27) firmly places the idea of this visit to Sarpedoun's house as a mere temporising palliative, not even bringing much temporary relief, since Troilus is to spend his time reading over old letters and counting the passing hours.

Another lyric addition is made by Chaucer's expansion of Boccaccio's image of Criseida's beauty as once the radiance of her now-darkened house into the 2-stanza apostrophe 'O paleys desolat . . .' (540–53); this is another passage which may be read as inset elegiac song, extending but interestingly varying the burden of feeling. The preceding stanzas lead up to the intensified poetry in direct speech, providing the occasion and the image of the house itself, viewed in chilling despair by the abandoned lover. As elsewhere Chaucer presents a double picture: the visual tableau effect followed by the dramatic monologue which by evocative use of apostrophe, imagery, repetition and cadenced phrasing becomes an enactment of the speaker's grief. Chaucer weaves together the aristocratic imagery of the house as once a crown, a precious ring, a sanctuary which is now only an empty shell with touching references to the actual place, the crowd in the street, the cold doors he would gladly kiss. The complaint theme of the contrast of present woe with past joy is imaginatively projected into the individual circumstances of the fiction.

The next link in the lyric chain is a trio of speeches (565–81, 582–602, 606–16) which together form a patterned sequence almost a complaint structure of its own. The central speech is an inner comment in Troilus' thoughts on his own situation; the two outer ones peruse the past through the memory of places, sights and sounds associated with his love. Troilus, like the Man in Black in *The Book of the Duchess*, finds some expression of grief in assembling images of lost joy and beauty and as he recalls the corner where he heard his lady 'So wommanly with vois melodious,/ Syngen so wel, so goodly and so cleere' (577–8), the effect is, as in the earlier poem, of eulogy of now dead beauty and happiness. The linking of places and memories simultaneously identifies Troilus' mental procedures as a conscious intellectual exercise, not a mere nostalgic drooling; the arts of memory treat the former experience as a branch of knowledge in which Troilus has been well-versed. The latter speech moves as far as the actual parting as if to record the very last notation in the book of spiritual *loci*.[27] The central mental soliloquy gives an interestingly self-conscious cast to these formal, gazetted processes of grief. The apostrophe to Cupid has the effect of the speaker watching himself and identifying his own procedures and seeing himself as an illustrative example:

> 'O blisful lord Cupide,
> Whan I the process have in my memorie
> How thow me hast wereyed on every syde,
> Men myght a book make of it lik a storie.' (V, 582–5)

But even as he complains of the god's treatment, he reaffirms his allegiance to Love and, sandwiched between the two speeches which sound almost as if Criseyde is dead, completes the internal lyric in prayer for her return. The triadic sequence is ambivalent: the central passage comments on the others, but the return to memory of loss after the prayer gives it an ironic frame.

Two further lyrics complete the series in this first scene. The first is identified as a song designed to express 'Th'enchesoun of his wo' (632), but to be sung in secret, 'whan he was from every mannes syghte,/ With softe vois'. For this *Canticus Troili*, identified in many manuscripts as an inset lyric, Chaucer substitutes for Boccaccio's five stanzas of remembered eyes, lovely womanhood, fair arms and death-longing a single stanza (638–44) addressing Troilus' lost star, which he then draws out into an address to the moon (650–8). The recurrence of the imagery of light and dark and of ships and steering makes the passage a denser, more cogent expression of emotion than the Italian equivalent; the sense of sequence in the lamenting passages is not merely of a linked chain of like regrets, but of a crescendo of feeling and of realisation. Troilus' situation is identified with grim finality in the image of the ship lost in darkness:

> 'O sterre, of which I lost have al the light,
> With herte soore wel oughte I to biwaille,
> That evere derk in torment nyght by nyght,
> Toward my deth with wynd in steere I saille;
> For which the tenthe nyght, if that I faille
> The gydyng of thi bemes bright an houre,
> My ship and me Caribdis wol devoure.' (V, 638–44)

The address to the moon forms a sad coda to this emblem of the lost star. Troilus' hope of Criseyde's return is linked to that ready symbol of change-ability, further made suggestive in her awaited new guise of newly springing horns. So Chaucer here moves on from the poignant, elegiac effects of Troilus' memories and his measuring of his own grief to the expression of loss through symbolism and to the punctuation of irony through image and association. The poet cogently brings together the immediate dramatic situation and the meaningful signs which the world of the poem provides as interpretative emblems; Troilus is standing there in the dark, between phases of the moon, at a particular time and place, but the scene is perceived as abstract through the timelessness of symbolism.

In the last speech of this first phase of Troilus' agonised solitude (669–79) Chaucer seizes on and enlarges Boccaccio's imagery, here of the sighs of Criseida seeming like breezes from the Greek camp; to Troilus they convey a sense of almost demented illusion as he imagines the air doing his soul good, the wind hour by hour increasing, the wind 'that sowneth so lik peyne', speaking to him with Criseyde's voice 'allas, whi twynned be we tweyne?' From that picture of continuing lament and illusory hope upon the walls of Troy, Chaucer is able to make a particularly ironic transition to Criseyde who is in more than one sense 'Upon that other syde' (687) and who, far from coming to 'stynten al his sorwe' is herself saying 'allas . . . That I was born' and placed immovably 'among the Grekis stronge.'

In this middle scene of Book V (687–1099) Chaucer threads together the continuing narrative of Criseyde's meetings with Diomede with elements of assessment, both by Criseyde herself and by the commenting narrator. The Diomede-Criseyde narrative consists of one main scene (771–1015, which is the material of *Il Filostrato*, Canto 6) into which Chaucer startlingly inserts descriptions of the characters of Diomede, Criseyde and Troilus (799–840), extended into a summary of the subsequent meetings between them, in which she presents to Diomede the bay steed and brooch, and the narrator's equivocal account of her feelings for Diomede. At the beginning and end of this sequence Criseyde is given opportunities to assess her own situation and behaviour and these passages (four of them—689–707, 731–65, 1016 ff, 1054–85), as with the speeches of Troilus in the first phase of Book V, form a set of laments, stated or implied.

In the first of her speeches (689–707) Chaucer makes Criseyde admit that her judgment of things was wrong and allows her to express her fear of attempting a return to Troy. Though later Chaucer gives to Criseyde added determination, at this stage her weakness and vulnerability are the basis for a gloomy envisaging of the likely outcome—that Troilus 'shal in his herte deme/ That I am fals'. Since we know that this is to be the outcome, the effect of her complaint is inevitably the tragic one of a character's correct foreseeing of their own fate and this ironic insight recurs to complicate one's judgment of Criseyde's actions. Criseyde rightly foresees that she is lost and that she shall 'have unthonk on every side' and so the complaint goes beyond the emotion of the immediate moment of her situation to identify the ambivalence, which Chaucer maintains to the end:

> 'I nam but lost, al be myn herte trewe—
> Now myghty god, thow on my sorwe rewe!'  (V, 706–7)

This speech, added by Chaucer, in a sense anticipates the soliloquy of complaint at lines 731–65, but the element of simple regret and recognition that all 'now is wors than evere ʒet I wende' adds greatly to the more formal expression of grief in the later passage. Here Chaucer conveys the impression of Criseyde's facing the consequences of her situation; her optimistic glosses on circumstances in her speech to Troilus at the end of Book IV are now relentlessly corrected by the real state of affairs:

> 'My fader nyl for no thyng do me grace
> To gon aȝeyn, for naught I kan hym queme.'   (V, 694–5)

It is clear here that she will fall prey to the first protective strength that offers and it is in the light of this admission of weakness that one reads the more rhetorical expressions of grief and determination in the lament that follows, which opens, if no more than that, in the manner of a betrayed heroine's lament.

For her Complaint Criseyde takes up a suitably statuesque posture, looking towards the towers and halls of Troy which she has left behind, and finding in them a suitable focus for the tragic contrast between past prosperity and present woe:

> 'Allas!' quod she, 'the plesance and the ioie,
> The which that now al torned into galle is,
> Have ich had ofte withinne the ȝonder walles.'   (V, 731–3)

The main impulse of her lament is regret that she did not take Troilus' view of things (rather than that of the Pandarine, pragmatic adjustment to circumstances) and the greatest strength of feeling is the recognition that it is now too late for remedies:

> 'But al to late comth the letuarie,
> Whan men the cors unto the grave carie.'   (V, 741–2)

Criseyde diagnoses her own failing as lack of foresight and this addition by Chaucer (743–9) invites the reader to view the rest of Criseyde's speech with irony. The one eye of Prudence which Criseyde lacks is the ability to envisage future time; how then can one take her plan for escape by night, 'bityde what bityde', as anything but a repetition of that failure? In a further added stanza (757–63) Chaucer extends the idea of the limitation of Criseyde's range of imagination into another analysis of her own condition: in Boccaccio's lines indicating Criseida's indifference to public opinion Chaucer finds one more ambiguous clue to her combination of weakness and self-assurance:

> 'For that that som men blamen evere ȝit,
> Lo, other manere folk comenden it.
> And as for me, for al swich variaunce,
> Felicite clepe I my suffisaunce.'   (V, 760–3)

While it is possible to see in this a strain of idealism, fitting her ostensible intention boldly to set out for Troy, if one reads it as implying that she will be satisfied with nothing less than true happiness, the ambiguity of the last line obviously leaves available to the reader the sense that her own immediate comfort is enough. The narrator does not allow her resolution 'To Troie I wole' (765) even to survive the stanza in which it occurs:

> For both Troilus and Troie town
> Shal knotteles thorugh-out hire herte slide,
> For she wol take a purpos for t'abide.   (V, 768–70)

So from the rhetorical posture of the regretful heroine, Criseyde's speech has been drawn out into self-knowledge and pitiable inadequacy; the note of grandiose regret is abandoned for a more subtle ironic juxtaposition of good intention and self exposure. Even more strikingly than with the scenes between Criseyde and Pandarus in Book II, Chaucer prepares the reader's ironic awareness for the scene between Criseyde and Diomede. To the indications of Criseyde's looking for her own 'suffisaunce' and the poet's assurance of the weakness of her resolve, Chaucer now adds a further element, by a few shifts of emphasis and rearrangement of material—the contrast between the sitting target and the skill and cunning of the huntsman, Diomede, ready to capture Criseyde's heart in his net or play her with hook and line. The combination of retrospective regret, self-assessment and ironic comparison is powerfully and startlingly built on by Chaucer's addition, between Diomede's thoughts and his actual conversation with Criseyde, of the three set portraits of Diomede, Criseyde and Troilus. Placed between the 'hardy, testif' Diomede, 'of tonge large' and the 'ʒong, fressh, strong' Troilus, 'trewe as stiel', Criseyde's mixture of a reputation for Paradisal beauty and a nature which is 'tendre-herted, slydynge of corage' appears at its most equivocal; we see her in suspense, about to be passed from one lover to another, a balance-sheet of her qualities presented. It is a curiously effective way of reminding the reader that her story is complete, over and done with in the distant past, even though we still have to observe the exact transition to the next phase of her life. It is also chilling, almost callous, in its distancing effect; Chaucer turns Diomede and Criseyde even further into actors in a mockingly arranged scene in which the inevitable process of Criseyde's treachery must be exhibited. The narrator and Criseyde herself become the observers of the stages of this process, surprised, regretful, even at moments appalled, and yet detachedly interested in identifying the details of the case-history.

So although Criseyde temporises with Diomede and wishes to be able again to see Troy 'in quiete and in reste' (1007), her indirectly reported reflections point immediately to her weakness and need:

> Retornyng in hire soule ay up and down
> The wordes of this sodeyn Diomede,
> His grete estat, and perel of the town,
> And that she was allone and hadde nede
> Of frendes help . . .   (V, 1023–7)

From this the narrator takes the reader with ruthless speed to her yielding of self, of Troilus' gifts and even possibly of her heart to Diomede. All that remains is Criseyde's own judgment of her conduct and her self, for which Chaucer draws on the soliloquy of regret of Briseida in Benoit's *Roman de Troie*.[28] Chaucer again chooses to use a formal complaint at a significant point, here (1054–85) to bring the direct narration of the heroine's story to a close. As in her earlier lament, the rhetoric is mixed. At the beginning the perspective is large and foresees the condemnation of the ages; the heroine is no longer betrayed but betraying, and regret for the act of treachery is enlarged into lamentation for the relentless verdict of history:

> 'Allas, of me unto the worldes ende
> Shal neyther ben ywriten nor ysonge
> No good word, for thise bokes wol me shende.
> O, rolled shal I ben on many a tonge;
> Thorugh-out the world my belle shal be ronge!'
>
> (V, 1058–62)

By making the character begin the very process of name-blackening which she self-reproachfully regrets, the poet allows a kind of tragic dignity to Criseyde. She accepts the price of her falsehood and pays tribute to Troilus, even as Chaucer accepts the necessity to become one of the chroniclers who will in books 'shende' the fair Criseyde. But Chaucer elects not to leave his heroine with her dignity, nor to maintain his own detached stance. From self-reproach the complaint descends to the weak self defence of 'To Diomede algate I wol be trewe' (1071) and the sinking into the helplessness of 'But al shal passe' (1085), while the poet's voice refuses to blame, tries to divert the punishing verdict to other pens, and would offer excuses if any were possible. The shift of focus in the lament from self-assessment to emotional justification and farewell lacks the poetic power of a full-scale complaint, but it is shaped to the needs of the as yet unfinished narrative of Troilus' double sorrow. Criseyde is not given any great scene of struggle and lyric intensity, but is allowed to assess her own failure before lapsing into a weak muddle of sentiment and attempts to make verbal amends. Chaucer compounds the mixture by his own slippery relaxation into sympathy before he completes the less pitying picture of betrayal and its effects in the final phase of the poem where attention returns to Troilus.

Whereas for Troilus in Book V the lamenting speech is the keynote or the identifying central current of feeling, in this middle scene Chaucer uses complaint as part of an ironic view of Criseyde's fate. He lets the time-scheme blur from Troilus' counting of the passing days before Criseyde's expected return into a general view of the course of things, and he mingles the brief but vivid realisation of Diomede's calculating exploitation of Criseyde's weakness with Criseyde's regrets and empty protests and the narrator's inconsistencies to handle this most shifty part of his story. Complaint itself tends to modulate from a high, elaborate expression of regret and judgment to a more intimate, shameless admission of weakness of resolve and instability of moral purpose. The high tragic role is indicated but is left unfulfilled, a set of gestures and beginnings lapsing into stammering apology.

> 'And certes, ȝow ne haten shal I nevere,
> And frendes love, that shal ȝe han of me,
> And my good word, al sholde I lyven evere,
> And trewely, I wolde sory be
> Forto seen ȝow in adversitee;
> And gilteles, I woot wel, I ȝow leve –
> But al shal passe, and thus take I my leve.' (V, 1079–85)

Again the turning from one scene to another emphasises the irony: from Criseyde's guilt and regret the picture changes to Troilus and Pandarus watching upon the walls all day for her return and to the conjunction of Troilus' illusory confidence ['She comth tonyght, my lif that dorste I laye' (1169)] and Pandarus' assessment of the situation ['farewel al the snow of ferne ʒere' (1176)].

In this last of the three main scenes of Book V the poem returns to the strain of woeful reproach. With the disappointment of Criseyde's failure to return Troilus' hope dies but it is only after the revelation of Criseyde's betrayal in the symbolic dream of her embracing the sleeping boar that his passionate protest bursts out. Chaucer omits Troiolo's identification of the boar and so makes the juxtaposition of the image and Troilus' feeling sharper; the hideous conjunction is simply read as the act of betrayal and that is more important than the identity. That she should find *any* reason is pain enough and this is the logic in Troilus' complaint, a succession of groping, self-exposing, speculative questions reaching out in all directions, of which 'who?' is only one:

> 'O my Criseyde, allas, what subtilte,
> What newe lust, what beaute, what science,
> What wratthe of iuste cause have ye to me?
> What gilt of me, what fel experience,
> Hath fro me raft, allas, thyn advertence?
> O trust, O feyth, O depe aseuraunce,
> Who hath me reft Criseyde, al my plesaunce?'   (V, 1254–60)

Chaucer condenses the hero's regrets here to good effect, combining this impression of astonished, but vigorous and imaginative truth with the poignant innocence of:

> 'Who shal now trowe on ony othes mo?
> God wot, I wende, O lady bright, Criseyde,
> That every word was gospel that ye seyde.'   (V, 1263–5)

and the determination to die rather than live in perpetual complaint. In the latter stages of *Troilus and Criseyde* Chaucer repeatedly uses the device of having the characters, particularly Troilus, see clearly the significance of things and the inevitable end, only to have the insight blurred and the end pushed further away. So the abbreviated complaint states all, but must then be undone and complicated by Pandarus' rejection of Troilus' interpretation of the dream and by the formulation of the next outpouring of Troilus' grief into the letter to Criseyde.

This *Litera Troili* (1317–421), set off in many manuscripts as an inset section, was interpreted by some fifteenth-century readers as a detachable lyric and by others as a model for the love poem of yearning reproach. Its length makes it the most substantial expression of Troilus' feelings in this last book. It clearly belongs to that strand within *Troilus and Criseyde* of lyric 'embellishments' to the narrative, or, to put it another way, of distillations into monologue or dialogue of the central emotions of the characters. The rhetorical purpose of the letter is explicitly identified so that one reads it simultaneously with an awareness of it as part of Pandarus' strategies of persuasion and yet with an acceptance of the open opportunity provided for the direct expression of Troilus' innocence and justified protest. Chaucer's adaptation of the material of Boccaccio's letter to the accepted formulae of fourteenth-century polite letter-writing[29] gives a further sense of framing, and the accepted patterns of writer's courtesy provide a structure more subtly useful in this instance to set off interplay between convention and emotion than the declarative and repetitive patterns of the ritualised complaint. Repeatedly the reader's sense of a 'normal' use of the formula lying behind the unique formulation of it in this particular circumstance gives a penetrating bite or sharp intensity of effect. The opening commendation of the recipient and the deferential expression of the humility of the writer is almost embarrassingly adaptable to the valuations of beloved and self by the abased lover:

> 'Right fresshe flour whos I ben have and shal
> Withouten parte of elles-where servyse,
> With herte, body, lif, lust, thought and al,
> I, woful wyght, in everich humble wise,
> That tonge telle or herte may devyse,
> As ofte as matere occupieth place,
> Me recomaunde unto ȝoure noble grace.'   (V, 1317–23)

The all-inclusiveness of 1319, the utterness of the reference in 1321–2, the absoluteness of the terms used throughout, all turn convention into a total commitment of expression which shames the casual use of such terms as mere forms. Similarly the conventional reference to the writer's own health is turned, in the perspective of the lover's suffering, into a bitter ironic joke:

> 'And if ȝow liketh knowen of the fare
> Of me whos wo ther may no wit discryve,
> I kan namore but, chiste of every care,
> At wrytyng of this lettre I was on lyve.'   (V, 1366–9)

Even the conventional lyric idiom of the eyes turned into the wells of salt tears takes on the guise of a painful literal conformity to the duty of reporting on details of ill-health. Between these blistering realisations, through the language of total allegiance and pain, of the niceties of the epistolary style Troilus' message emerges as a complaint of the most accusing kind, expressed in simple, forceful language. From the pattern of the letter Chaucer devises a more penetrating documentary basis than the 'Bill' of complaint drawn from the legal plea or accusation which he used in *The Complaint unto Pity*. Here directly from injured to injurer goes the protest straight as an arrow:

> 'ȝe me lefte in aspre peynes smerte,
> Whan that ȝe wente, of which ȝet boote non
> Have I non had, but evere wors bigon
> Fro day to day am I . . .'   (V, 1326–29)

Though this directness is embellished by references to tear-stained paper and by mollifying endearments, the sharp accusation keeps penetrating through the veneer of social language:

'If any servant dorst or oughte of right
Upon his lady pitously compleyne,
Thanne wene I that ich oughte be that wight,
Considered this, that ʒe thise monthes tweyne
Han taried ther ʒe seyden, soth to seyne,
But dayes ten ʒe nolde in oost soiourne.'   (V, 1345–50)

Such social pretence as is inherent in the linguistic forms of address is the basis for Troilus' leaving of escape routes for Criseyde. The desire for the recipient's welfare and for news of her well-being is the opportunity for pleading for answer and for contradiction. News of his own harm and woe leads by patterns of courtesy to the suggestions of remedy. So the shifting instability of Fortune's treatment of the lover may be illustrated –

'My song, in pleynte of myn adversitee;
My good in harm, myn ese ek woxen helle is;
My ioie in wo . . .'   (V, 1375–7)

– but the writer's conventional desire to see the recipient again can be turned into the lover's hope for redress:

'with ʒoure commyng hom aʒeyn to Troie
ᴣe may redresse, and more a thousand sithe,
Than evere ich hadde, encressen in me ioie.'   (V, 1380–2)

Thus the stances of complaint are newly shaped and coloured by the letter's forms to mix intensity with intimacy, directness with a shadowing of irony. At the end Chaucer returns to his opening effects of giving to daily politeness a timeless absoluteness by mixing common courtesies with lyric intensities:

'But wheither that ʒe do me lyve or deye,
ᴣet praye I god, so ʒeve ʒow right good day.
And fareth wel, goodly, faire, fresshe may,
As she that lif or deth may me comande;
And to ʒoure trouthe ay I me recomande.'   (V, 1410–14)

To this letter bestowing upon the receiver the power of life and death, Chaucer adds his own tart coda in the indirect report of Criseyde's dishonest reply: 'She wolde come, ʒe, but she nyste whenne.' That interjected 'ʒe' marks by its over-insistence the emptiness of the promise, and the following stanza leaves no doubt as Troilus interprets the words as 'botmeles bihestes'. The narrator's comment underlines the pathos of the letter as mere wasted breath:

But Troilus, thow maist now, est or west,
Pipe in an ivy lef if that the lest.
Thus goth the world; god shild us fro meschaunce,
And every wight that meneth trouthe avaunce.   (V, 1432–5)

Thus the grief of Troilus' last long complaint is made particularly forceful and painful by Chaucer's mingling the language of love-lyric with the normalising patterns of courteous discourse and by his modulation from pathos and injury to the undercutting platitudes of the world-weary observer.

In the latter part of Book V the current of complaint which has for so long been the dominant mode of the book is diverted into anger and diffused by a complexity of handling which prepares for the gradual detachment of the poet's voice from direct expression of the situations and feelings. Chaucer disrupts the course of Boccaccio's narrative in which Troiolo's sorrow becomes the subject of debate among the members of his family and Cassandra's scorn the occasion for his public denial of love, combined with a noble defence of Criseyde. Instead of the mocking sister Chaucer uses Cassandra's role as prophetess to turn the current of narrative towards a sense of history and the working out of destiny; her interpretation of Troilus' dream becomes a story of resentment, conflict and violence, of Diana's revenge and the strife of Thebes, so that Criseyde's betrayal appears the culmination of a tragic sequence, part of a fated history which Troilus can not avoid and which simply results in the fact that 'Diomede is inne and thow art oute' (1519). It is in the anger of rejecting this that Troilus' last significant resistance is made (1520–33). Instead of a defence of Criseyde's qualities Chaucer gives him a more ironic comparison of his 'slandered' lady to Alcestis. The note of irony once struck becomes the narrator's inevitable tone: summary inherently tends to reduce narrative to its antithetical postures and symbols and the return of Troilus' zeal for war has hardly time to be identified before the narrator envisages Fortune plucking out Troy's bright feathers. The last glimpse of Criseyde in the poem, her equivocal letter (1590–1631), is placed between a summary of the death of Hector and Troilus' fruitless attempts to see Criseyde again on the one hand and on the other his discovery on Diomede's captured coat-armour of the brooch he himself had given her. So the stages of Troilus' realisation are marked out as part of the fortunes of war, with grief and the prospect of doom clouding any lingering hope. In this atmosphere of instability, just before the settling of war, Chaucer gives a last speech to each of his three main characters, Criseyde's letter, Troilus' response to the clear evidence of Criseyde's betrayal (1674–1722) and Pandarus' comment (1731–43). The letter has been deliberately postponed, Chaucer preferring ironic summary at the earlier stage, and its late occurrence bestows upon it the effect of a farewell utterance; though making use of some expressions from the earlier omitted letters, Chaucer has made an addition here. The other two speeches are based on Part 8 of *Il Filostrato* with some significant changes of emphasis.

Despite his 'routhe' for Criseyde, Chaucer chooses to show her at last at her most compromised. He makes little use here of the conventional formulae of letters but the opening flourishes convey a dignity and pathos to Criseyde's picture of herself:

'I herteles, I sik, I in destresse . . .'   (V, 1594)

From this the letter declines into avoidance of issues and into resentment followed by half-apology:

'Nor other thyng nys in ȝoure remembraunce,
As thynketh me, but only ȝoure plesaunce.
But beth nat wroth and that I ȝow biseche . . .'   (V, 1607–9)

174

The slide accelerates into accusation, no sooner made than withdrawn, into promise, no sooner made than blurred and deferred, into meaningless assurances of friendship and irrelevant excuses. Chaucer has composed a brilliant piece of feeble rhetoric, perhaps the cruellest passage in the poem, conveying a personality disintegrating. The expression is embellished with empty flourishes— 'while that my lif may dure', 'Th'entente is al' and so on—which appear as clothing borrowed by the otherwise expressionless nullity to which circumstances have reduced her.

Troilus' final complaint begins in a traditional 'ubi sunt?' mode:

> 'O lady bright, Criseyde,
> Where is ʒoure feith and where is ʒoure biheste?
> Where is ʒoure love, where is ʒoure trouthe?'   (V, 1674–6)

From the theme of incredulity and injustice, expressing the pain which is complaint's main impulse, the speech passes to its function as a final statement of the hero's view and so to that note of assessment which Chaucer had earlier used for Criseyde herself. Again it is the verdict upon Criseyde's honour that takes precedence:

> 'allas, ʒoure name of trouthe
> Is now fordon, and that is al my routhe.'   (V, 1686–7)

But the over-all theme of the poem, the sorrow of Troilus, his 'aventure in lovyng', his allegiance to his own faith in love and his inevitable destiny to 'ben lorn' has the last word. Troilus accepts that all is lost but holds to his love:

> 'Thorugh which I se that clene out of ʒoure mynde
> ʒe han me cast, and I ne kan nor may,
> For al this world, withinne myn herte fynde
> To unloven ʒow a quarter of a day.'   (V, 1695–8)

Beyond that is the recurrent stance of complaint and of the central suffering figure whose role throughout has been to register the rise, fall and rise of the pressure of uncertainty and pain, the sense of injustice, of virtue expended but rejected.

> 'But trewely, Criseyde, swete may,
> Whom I have ay with al my myghte yserved,
> That ʒe thus doon, I have it nat deserved.'   (V, 1720–2)

The last of the three speeches is, oddly, the bitterest. Now that Pandarus has nothing to argue against and can no longer resist the tide of 'pleynt', the fact that he 'may do the namore' leaves him incapable of anything but hatred for Criseyde. So Chaucer follows Boccaccio in giving him the last word, but Chaucer turns it into an admission of emptiness, for after 'I hate, ywys, Criseyde' he dwindles away into 'I kan namore seye' (1743). All that is left to counter 'the sorwe and pleynte of Troilus' is the continuous current of Fortune and Chaucer briefly summarises its course, mingling in his own poet's farewells to his matter and drawing *Troilus and Criseyde* to its contrary close.

Once Chaucer has completed his self-imposed task of giving an account of Troilus' double sorrow, he is, up to a point, free to make of it what he will, before signing off. The impression of the last fifteen stanzas is that he applied most of the concluding formulae that medieval poets could think of, weaving them together with an intention that may be identified both as the desire for comprehensiveness and as the uncertain use of alternatives. The most clearly identifiable intention is that of rejecting Boccaccio's moral that all women are fickle: Chaucer discards the last section of Canto 8 of *Il Filostrato* and the whole of Canto 9 except for the general idea of the poet's saying farewell to his work and sending it forth into the world. Chaucer's nearest to the 'thus we see' ending comes when he returns to *Il Filostrato* at line 1828 after his insertion of the flight of Arcita's soul from *Il Teseida*, and, in place of Boccaccio's anti-feminism, refers back to the beginning of the love affair and the beginning of the poem and draws from his ironic over-all view the moral of the instability and the transitoriness of the world. Structurally Chaucer here (1828–41) completes the design which the opening stanzas of Book I had forecast and, poignantly enough, identifies the sad realisation which the unfolding of the story has enforced. But Chaucer did not want merely to convey a sense of reaching an inevitable narrative goal. His ending is designed also to act as a corrective: the plainest corrective purpose is that of putting the pagan view of things in its place (1849–55) and Chaucer identifies not only the limitation of moral view which was inevitable within this pre-Christian material but also the prevailing rhetoric in which that view was expressed:

> Lo here, the forme of olde clerkis speche
> In poetrie, if ye hire bokes seche.   (V, 1854–5)

Though the primary meaning here is that poetry whose essential principle is the celebration of worldly appetite must be valueless, there are other implications. Taken in conjunction with Chaucer's introduction of the passage from *Il Teseida*, the stanza must imply a rejection of Troilus' prevailing tone of lament. In an odd way Chaucer in his corrective epilogue takes over an aspect of Pandarus' earlier role—the resistance to complaint. Troilus' view of his worldly experience from the perspective of the eighth sphere is a reversal from sorrow to bliss and from weeping to laughter. The rejection of lament is pointedly made in the antithesis of:

> And in hym self he lough right at the wo
> Of hem that wepten for his deth so faste.   (V, 1821–2)

The positive exhortations to love of Christ and to thoughts of God and the final prayer introduce positive elements of rhetoric to act as replacements for the vanity of poetic lamentation. But the reader can not avoid the recognition that the closing stanzas of *Troilus and Criseyde*, like the *Retractions* at the end of *The Canterbury Tales*, are essentially a rejection of poetry altogether. Were it not for the fact that Chaucer is simultaneously concerned to preserve his poem (1793–9), to commend it to his peers (1856–7), to have it take a deserved place among the great poems of the past (1786–92) and to mediate with his audience for a sympathetic view of it (1765–85), one might read the end of the work as a kind of apology. What one perceives in the combination of elements is a typical

Chaucerian preference for doubleness of vision over simple moral judgments or demonstrative proofs.[30] Having developed a story of ancient treachery in terms of its sequence of complaint and debate, the poet accepts that its inevitable course pulls it back to the registration of grief and loss but can not bear to forgo his recurrent design whereby complaint is not enough in itself, indeed is never more than half of his sense of a satisfying literary statement. Though the pragmatism of Pandarus has been overwhelmed, the poet can still counter lament by philosophical enlargement, by changing the historical and ethical boundaries and by forcing human weeping to dwindle into an instance of that very transitoriness which is its occasion.

# CHAPTER SEVEN

# Complaint in Narrative III: The Franklin's Tale

## 1. Introduction

Although, like *The Knight's Tale* and *Troilus and Criseyde*, *The Franklin's Tale* is Chaucer's version of material from Boccaccio, here Chaucer was taking only an episode from a longer work, rather than interpreting the over-all quality of a substantial Italian piece. The debate, as to which, knight, lover or magician, showed the greatest liberality, was not even part of Boccaccio's main story in *Il Filocolo* (the tale of Floriz and Blauncheflour), but the fourth of a series of thirteen problems concerning the ethics of love.[1] The fact that *Il Filocolo* (1376) was the first Italian romance in prose explains the diffuseness of composition which allowed the introduction of such secondary episodes and the casual realism of presentation of the group of people seated in a garden telling stories and debating the *Tredici questioni d'amore*. Chaucer was presumably interested in the theme rather than the text of Boccaccio. *The Franklin's Tale* is not, that is, an instance of Chaucer's sentence by sentence or even section by section reshaping, refocussing, amplifying or abbreviating an existing work but an independent imagining of an illustrative narrative and the debating point which it exemplifies. In his handling of *Il Teseida* and *Il Filostrato* Chaucer is mainly using his poetic skills to enable the narrative fully to communicate the moral ideas and the emotional and dramatic pleasure which he has seen, either already expressed or in some degree undeveloped, in his source. Both narratives are spread out over a large space, so that though the stories of both are simple in outline, the rendering is ample in expression, complex in its details: lyric, debate, commentary encourage the reader to take up a considering position towards the unfolding of the emotional and philosophical history of the figures. One is conscious of it laid out in a long line along which one can pass, looking forward and looking back, stopping to peruse, to lament, to expect, to weigh and measure the feelings and the ethics, adjusting one's point of view and judging differently as the pattern is completed.

*The Franklin's Tale* shares characteristics with these two longer narratives: the mixed pagan and Christian world, the elevated poetic style, with astrological and classical references, the romance seriousness whereby narrative directs attention to moral themes, the use of inset complaints. Yet the effect of reading it is different, partly because it is shorter and the stages of the narrative therefore fewer, but also because Chaucer's greater freedom when he is merely using a broad idea of a woman's rash promise and comparison of the conduct of three male characters, is apparent in the creation of a layered narrative, rather than a strung out, variously orchestrated one. Chaucer's main embellishments of Boccaccio's theme were first the archaic layer of references to Breton tradition and ancient British names, secondly the idealism and didacticism of the opening presentation of the marriage of Arveragus and Dorigen and thirdly the lengthy rhetorical speeches in the manner of complaint, two for Dorigen and one for Aurelius. A fourth amplification is created by the references to magic and to Christian and pagan religion. A significant omission is of Boccaccio's concluding debate between Fiammetta, the queen of the assembly, and Menedon, the story-teller—the very point for which the tale is told. And a significant change is Chaucer's substitution of the idea of the removal of the threatening black rocks around the coast for the wife's original desire for a Maytime garden in January. The fusion of different literary forms, different styles, even different values greatly complicates the tale for the reader and, though the omission of the explicit passage of debate and judgment in response to the question about liberality may seem typical of Chaucer's preference for unresolved irony or for implicit complexity of moral attitude, the tale here works rather to provide a context for that final question; the reader is conscious of the enrichment of its meaning as much as the lack of an answer to it. Whatever impression the view of marriage in *The Franklin's Tale* may make in comparison with other tales in the Canterbury series, within the tale itself Chaucer seems to be making it difficult for the reader to judge, rather than using the story to present a clear-cut sustained view of ideal marriage. On the one hand, he accepts the story as a case-history, illustrating, or at least raising, points of ethical principle: so there is a sense in places that the characters are little more than their social status:

> 'Thou art a squier, and he is a knyght;
> But God forbede, for his blisful myght,
> But if a clerk koude doon a gentil dede
> As wel as any of yow, it is no drede!' *(CT*, V, 1609–12)

On the other hand, the figures are allowed moments of self-expression which develop them beyond their illustrative function: Dorigen's address to God over the 'grisly rokkes blake' is turned into a questioning of divine providence ('Why han ye wrought this werk unresonable?'); Aurelius prays to Apollo and, though his role as lover is treated unsympathetically in the tale as a whole, the central strain of hopeless love is expressed fervently enough to stir the reader's understanding:

> 'Lo, lord! my lady hath my deeth ysworn
> Withoute gilt, but thy benignytee
> Upon my dedly herte have som pitee.' (1038–40)

The most extreme example of such emotional extension of the figures is Dorigen's often criticised Complaint, when she is caught in the trap of her own making.

These passages of complaint have for some readers blurred the tale's effect, and objection to them has more than once been linked to an unfavourable over-all view of the work. A fairly recent instance offers the view that *The Franklin's Tale*

> . . . is commonly more admired than enjoyed . . . the extended apostrophes appear disproportionately long and doubtfully relevant, while . . . there appears to be a serious disjunction between the idealised character of Arveragus and the moral attitude he exhibits at the end of the tale. One has a sense of performance somehow falling short of intention.[2]

In the edition which stimulated this comment Gerald Morgan argued that the presence of lyrical passages of personal feeling belongs to Chaucer's conception of the tale as Breton lay,[3] but the interest shown by Chaucer in other works in combining complaint with narrative links *The Franklin's Tale* also with *Anelida and Arcite*, *The Complaint of Mars* and the long Boccaccian narratives. The conjunction of pagan material, a framework of war, contrast between Mars and Venus and the consequent antithesis between the spheres of masculine and feminine conduct, the theme of threat and vulnerability, questions of free will raised in philosophical complaints and extended into the social aspects of freedom and thraldom, the pairing of man's folly and woman's grief, all link *The Franklin's Tale* with patterns of thought which Chaucer had explored in other poems. This fits with other indications that in the period when he was writing *The Canterbury Tales* Chaucer looked back, making use of some older pieces of writing, revisiting some earlier ideas and using a range of narrative kinds both to do a review of his own practice and to provide a variety of modern and old-fashioned types of story-telling for the range of cultural types which he envisaged in the role of teller. The function of complaint within the new context of *The Franklin's Tale* is interestingly enmeshed in the various layers of the story which I distinguished above and to understand the presence of Dorigen's series of classical exempla one needs to consider how these layers combine to create moral complexity.

The Prologue which Chaucer gave to the Franklin asks the reader to accept the following tale as a piece of pastoral archaism. Despite the self-conscious rhetoric which, later in the story, he is to apply to his material, the note struck at the start is that of artless simplicity: a tale of olden times dressed in 'swiche colours as growen in the mede' is what we are led to anticipate. The short romances of the 'Breton' tradition presumably seemed to Chaucer from the examples in the Auchinleck manuscript to have a sufficiently distinctive character to make an appeal, as part of his Canterbury pot-pourri, to his audience's interest in sentiment, idealism, magic and testing. He gives substance both to the picturesque aspects of the type by his use of the coastal setting and to the idea of a chronicle of ancient adventures by his borrowing of names and associations from Geoffrey of Monmouth. If the themes of a loving marriage threatened, husband and wife separated, a rash promise and magic ally *The Franklin's Tale* to *Sir Orfeo*, the names of Arveragus and Aurelius, a feat involving the removal of rocks and some interesting resemblances make as suggestive a connection with the *Historia Regum Britanniae*.[4]

According to Geoffrey, Arvirargus was the second son of Cymbeline who took over the throne of Britain when Guiderius, his brother, was killed in battle against the Romans. The peace terms Arvirargus accepted from the Emperor Claudius included marriage to Claudius' daughter, Genvissa, and the marriage was a success:

> Once she had been united with him in lawful marriage, she inflamed the king with such burning passion that he preferred her company to anything else in the world.[5]

It is in 'memory of so happy a marriage' that the city of Gloucester (Kaerglou) is founded and later, when Arvirargus falls into dispute with Vespasian, Queen Genvissa acts as mediator. In a peaceful old age Arvirargus is praised for strength and generosity and he is celebrated after his death for his open-handedness. Chaucer may have borrowed only the name of Arvirargus, but ideal marriage and generosity were part of that name's history.

So too with the name Aurelius, who is not only the king for whom Merlin performed the 'impossible' task of moving the Giants' Ring from Ireland to Stonehenge, but also the son of Constantine whom Merlin, foreseeing the death of Vortigern, envisaged leaving the coast of Armorica with his brother Uther:

> 'Even as I speak they are leaving the coasts of Armorica and spreading their sails to cross the sea. They will make for the island of Britain . . . the two brothers Aurelius and Uther are landing . . .'[6]

Here are suggestions both of Arveragus' leaving Brittany to seek honour in Britain and of the young magician's meeting the two brothers as they approach Orleans:

> 'I knowe,' quod he, 'the cause of youre comyng.' (1176)

Other associations possibly lurking in Chaucer's mind come from other deeds of Merlin. He first appears in the *Historia* as a result of Vortigern's search for a boy without a father, as a boy who knows what other magicians do not. The inserted chapter concerning Merlin's prophecies describes overturnings of Nature during coming times of calamity: so the mountains of Armorica will erupt, the sea contract to a narrow channel, the Thames overflow the confines of its bed so that 'it will submerge nearby towns and overturn mountains in its course'.[7] The famous episode in which Merlin helps Uther Pendragon to enjoy Igaerne, wife of Gorlois, by means of a magic transformation of his appearance into that of Gorlois occurs shortly after the rock-moving exercise for Aurelius and it makes use of the sea-coast setting of Tintagel. Chaucer's Dorigen looking at the rocks off Brittany might be a picture of Igaerne supposedly safe in Tintagel while Gorlois is away; magic can bring a substitute husband there, in spite of sea, rocks, cliffs, walls, gates. Igaerne is one possible source for Dorigen, although the name itself resembles more closely that of the wife of Alain I of Brittany (888–907) which occurs in the forms Dorguen, Droguen, Dorigien. The fusion of the transformation of Uther's appearance with the moving of rocks for Aurelius, together with the motive of enjoying a woman's love, suggestively lie behind Chaucer's plot, and

181

there is even the basis of the figure of the brother/confidant in Ulfin who advises Uther:

'Who can possibly give you useful advice?' answered Ulfin, 'when no power on earth can enable us to come to her . . . ? If only the prophet Merlin would give his mind to the problem . . .'[8]

In search of authentication of his notion of an old-fashioned story of magic and high life, Chaucer has created a fascinating mixture of stock figures of contemporary literature—husband, wife, lover and knight, squire, clerk—and echoes of ancient chronicle and intrigue. Arveragus has greater weight than the anonymous husband in *Il Filocolo* partly because his ideals are more fully examined but partly because his name attributes to him some history and some tradition of power, devoted love and generosity. Aurelius has to fulfil a role which is at times comic, at others pathetic and penitent, but he too is made more dangerous in the imagination by the sense that he is attempting to re-enact an earlier royal usurpation of a husband's rights with the aid of a powerful wizard. Memory of the figure of Merlin in the characterisation of the 'philosopher' is, I suggest, one feature in the interestingly complex transformation by Chaucer of Boccaccio's Tebano, which I shall discuss more fully later.

## 2. The Ethical Argument

In Boccaccio's treatment of the story in the *Filocolo* the most interesting aspect is the judgment of conduct at the end. In the telling of the story the husband and wife are not named, the setting is, rather vaguely, Spain, but Tarolfo, the rival knight, searches all the lands of the west and eventually finds his magician, an aged herb-gatherer, at the foot of the mountains in Thessaly; the magician's supernatural journeys in a dragon-drawn chariot to gather ingredients include visits to Africa, Crete, the Caucasus, Libya, Lesbos, Colchos, Patmos, and the rivers Ganges, Rhine, Seine, Po, Arno, Tiber, Don and Danube; the tale assumes the character of a fantastic dream fable. When he used the story again in the *Decameron* (Day 10, Tale 5), Boccaccio made it more realistic and prosaic: in Udine in Friuli, Dianora, the beautiful wife of the rich Gilberto is loved by the noble baron Ansaldo Gradense, the highest-ranking character and famed for feats of arms and chivalry, while the anonymous magician's part is reduced; emphasis is directed more to the contrast between the intense cold of a snowy January and the fruit and flowers of the magic garden than to the performing of the transformation. Here it is the generosity of the hopeful lover, Ansaldo, which is praised most highly by the narrator, but Boccaccio indicates that Gilberto's claims are also debated. Though judgment is expressed only briefly, the structure of the *Decameron* stresses the illustrative point of each narrative. The theme of the tenth day is liberality; comparative judgment is running through the sequence of tales. The fifth tale is quite short and the only strikingly amplified moment is the husband's reaction to his wife's explanation of her distress at Ansaldo's fulfilment of her conditions. Gilberto explicitly reproves Dianora for opening her ears to unchaste messages but accepts the purity of her soul and instructs her to go to Ansaldo and 'do anything you can to free yourself from the promise, short of your chastity; and if that is impossible, for once you must yield him your body, but not your soul.'[9] Moral priorities are thus clearly indicated in this short version as in the more explicit treatment in the *Filocolo*. There is no suggestion in the latter case of leaving the question of liberality open to debate. Fiammetta defines the generosity of husband, lover and magician clearly: the first in respect of his honour, which is precious, the second in respect of his lustful will, which is best avoided anyway, and the third in respect of riches which, since they are troublesome to a virtuous life, are not to be desired. There is, therefore, no doubt that the husband's action (though less than *wise*) is the most liberal and he was also the leader, whose example the others followed. The story-teller, Menedon, questions the judgment and so brings the three actions again under review. In his opinion the husband gave up only what he could not deny, since he was bound by the lady's oath, while the lover, after long suffering, sought what seemed impossible and earned reward because of the wife's pledge, and he acted greatly in yielding. But even more liberal is the act of the poor man in giving up riches, lawfully earned, only to return to the state he had, in old age, sought with such toil to escape. These arguments stimulate an even closer analysis by Fiammetta of the rights and wrongs of the three men's circumstances. Menedon's preference for Tebano shows a weak understanding of the blessings of poverty, lack of fear, temptation and the envy of others; the magician was not liberal but wise. Tarolfo did no more than his duty, since we are bound by reason to avoid vice and to follow virtue, and men who uphold the honour of chastity and wifely virtue are beloved of God. The point about the husband and the oath founders because the oath could not be valid; husband and wife are one flesh and she could not make the oath without his will—if she did, it would be made void by her earlier marriage oath. Since the oath was not binding, the husband should not have sent her to Tarolfo unless he wished to and hence was liberal with his honour. Thus the tale itself in *Il Filocolo* is merely the exemplum from which moral analysis, debate and refinement are developed. The further the discussion goes the more explicitly Christian are the terms in which Boccaccio sees the moral comparison defined.

Chaucer's leaving all this out is of a piece with his tendency in many other parts of his work to avoid explicit moral definitions, to avoid condemnation, even judgment, and to avoid the constricting effect of messages and labels. This is obviously not true of *The Parson's Tale*, where moral definitions and judgments are the basic material, nor of his other piece of morality in prose, *Melibee*, but verse romance is a different matter. Yet in *The Franklin's Tale* Chaucer's additions and emphases show that his concern was for moral ideas and for some depth of treatment of conduct. He does not, that is, merely leave the question as to which of the men has behaved most liberally open for the reader to debate, but in his handling of the plot he makes it more difficult to reach a clear-cut conclusion.

The beginning of the tale (where Boccaccio moves straight from a brief account of the marriage to the second suitor's importunate addresses) gives importance to the idea of marriage and Chaucer consistently uses this in Dorigen's rejections of Aurelius later (984–5 and 1003–5), where not only determination on her part to be a faithful wife but the more prosaic aspect is expressed: what an absurd idea it seems to think of pleasure with the wife of another man who can enjoy her whenever he wishes. The lengthy treatment of marriage and the expression of Dorigen's anxiety turn the tale into a romance of security threatened, where the main feelings are of sorrow at parting and loss, of threat to peace of mind, of the sense of the value of married love (or, in other such tales, of kingship, patriotism, sworn oaths and so on). Much of the complexity (and resulting irony) in the tale comes from the combination of two strands of narrative: the story of Arveragus and Dorigen separated and of love threatened, where security is recovered by reunion and the defeat of threat; and the story of Aurelius as lover questing for favour and to achieve an imposed task, where, as in fairy tales of miller's youngest sons, completion of the task ought to win the hand of the beloved. The ironies of this combination include Dorigen's promise of adultery as a way of proving fidelity; the terms of the bargain contradict the moral principles by which Dorigen is supposedly motivated. To remove the dangers from her husband's path at the price of giving away the honour for which the dangers are incurred is a subtle moral idea which deserves fuller treatment than Chaucer finds time to give it in the tale. The other main ironic effect is the displacement of Aurelius' achievement of his task from what in some romances would be its 'heroic' position; here the young lover is the 'villain', or at least the fool, in the context provided by the story of husband and wife. Chaucer increases the moral weight within the story and more significance is given to Aurelius' realisation of his folly, which is the main moral development in the tale. Dorigen suffers but if she learns anything, it is implicit.

The main way in which Chaucer adds moral weight is by his opening amplification of the conditions of marriage between Arveragus and Dorigen. One effect of this passage is to undermine the reasoning which Boccaccio gave to Fiammetta in *Il Filocolo*. She argued that only with appropriate cause could the wife's oath even be considered to have any validity, since according to both reason and law the husband's permission is needed to give his wife the authority to swear oaths or bear witness.[10] Chaucer's definition of the marriage relationship makes it clear that the wife's responsibilities and rights are not limited to legal terms. Arveragus swears that he will not exercise a husband's authority against her will, nor be jealous, but will obey her and follow her will as lover to lady, except that, for the sake of honour among his equals, he requires the reputation of being lord and master. These terms give to Dorigen, within their private legal and moral system, the exercise of her free will, the right to undertake obligations, and swear oaths, as long as she does no public harm to his good name. Dorigen sees this as itself a sign of Arveragus' *gentillesse* and defines her own state:

'Ye profre me to have so large a reyne.' (755)

The narrator's comments insist that Love continues only in freedom: women (and men too) naturally—'of kynde' (768)—wish not to be 'constreyned as a thral'. The development of this into the antithesis between patience and rigour glosses the concept of freedom as the husband's willingness to tolerate weakness, error and even wrong; he offers her 'suffrance' and she swears to have no 'defaute'. Finally the marriage is defined as a combination of 'lordshipe and servage' and though this is stated from the husband's point of view, Dorigen's promises to be humble and faithful, not to cause strife, to allow him 'the name of soveraynetee' and so on imply the mutuality of the conditions. It

184

is perhaps natural that it is the moral role of Arveragus that is explicitly defined, since that is the more unusual, but it could also be a sign of Chaucer's reaction to the analysis of the husband's liberality in *Il Filocolo*. Chaucer removes the legal constraints in marriage and so lessens the element of *acte gratuit* in the husband's behaviour at the end. Arveragus' liberality is registered as consistent with his earlier promises. Chaucer's narrative is more tautly held together than Boccaccio's: not only is the task given to Aurelius one that relates to the situation and motives of husband and wife but the progress of the narrative is eventually perceived as a putting to the test of ideas propounded in the initial stages.

Dorigen's Complaint lays bare the dilemma not only of wife but also of husband: given that honour has exacted such a high price in the tales of old, what now will the husband do? The long suspension heightens the audience's speculations and allows us to envisage the possibility that Arveragus will revert to tyrant lord, to jealous blusterer, to judge. So, although Chaucer diminishes Boccaccio's effect of abstract liberality in the husband's behaviour, giving up honour which he could not recover when he was not bound to do so, he develops an equally interesting moral argument and one more ingeniously woven into the tale. There is a strong element of honour between men in the Italian (even clearer in the Decameron version), but in Chaucer's version the liberality is really in the opening conditions of marriage, in the husband's allowing freedom while reasonably requiring the outward signs of conformity. At the end he is shown to be a man of principle in sticking to these terms: though he is grieved, he swears that no sign of his woe will be betrayed; he reasonably requires secrecy according to the second marriage condition; he does not merely allow but urges on his wife the independent validity of her oath. The principle of 'trouthe' is highest in the hierarchy of conflicting priorities. He allows her sovereign will to prevail; she is not to be 'constreyned' by her husband's authority (though Dorigen's words 'as my husband bade' show that this is how she takes it), but only by her own free choice and the need to be honourable. Thus all three of the principles of the marriage are demonstrated.

Chaucer's treatment of the material suggests a desire to give a much denser idea of marriage than he found in *Il Filocolo*. He creates special terms for the marriage, possibly out of countering Fiammetta's arguments: it is as if he were imagining a situation that would resist, in which the wife's oath *is* valid, because the husband has yielded his right to be lord—will the husband *then* accept adultery as the price of principle? This more penetrating consideration of the ethical problem is supported by other aspects which are more densely treated; Chaucer envisages more circumstances of the marriage, Arveragus' absences, Dorigen's friends and her anxieties, the earlier and later phases of their relationship, and so on.

The nature of Dorigen's actual oath has often been seen as an instance of Chaucer's imaginative transformation of his sources:[11] instead of a challenge which has an element of the random about it, Dorigen gives Aurelius a task which is specifically related to the conditions of the Tale, her earlier expressed fears for her husband's safety. Aurelius is asked to bring about something which Dorigen desires as part of the existing love relationship, the one she does care about. Even in her moment of 'pley', Chaucer gives his heroine a desperate sincerity. That, at least, is how the surface of the tale works. If one looks further, then what Chaucer has done may be stated in several different ways. He has replaced an image which stood only for the wife/lover relationship by a more complex one which involves all three characters: the figure of changing winter to spring symbolises the lover's change of the wife's coldness to warmth, an unwelcome change registering the disturbing stirrings towards adultery which Boccaccio explicitly identifies and reproves in his Decameron version; Chaucer's idea of removing the rocks around the coast ingeniously expresses not only the urge towards adultery but the anxiety and guilt as well. If the lover removes the rocks, he removes the obstacle to his own desire; to the lover the rocks are the excluding barrier of Dorigen's married state. To the wife the rocks are thus a protection as well as an expression of existing anxiety; loving concern for the husband's welfare is focussed through an image of threat which registers also unease at his absence, and the sense that the smooth, safe, plain sailing of the marriage envisaged at the start is at hazard. The anxiety is amplified in Dorigen's first complaint into a questioning of Providence, which brings in another layer of meaning.

The symbolism is thus richly suggestive. The rocks may be seen as the external dangers that threaten and Brewer sees the moral of the story as that of learning acceptance of threat as a condition of life.[12] Beyond that one could see that the illusion of making the rocks disappear is an act of untruth, falsification, even of blasphemy in the distortion of God's created order. To suppress or disguise danger is equivalent to adultery within the circumstances of the tale; to retain the rocks is the way of fidelity, the actual experience of the complexities of the married condition.

From another angle it could be said that Dorigen expresses the unconscious wish to substitute a present Aurelius for an absent Arveragus, because she wants marriage without anxiety and separation. If Aurelius can remove threats, he is a more satisfactory lover: love is togetherness and security. But Dorigen will not face the consequences of her unconscious logic (and Arveragus is back by then anyway) and so dramatises herself as wronged virtue. She is forced to face the fact that what she has wished upon herself would destroy her marriage; to want a 'rockless' marriage is something false to her original vows. She is finally let off the hook and accepts the implications of danger.

From the lover's point of view, Aurelius has to find a way of neutralising the husband's power to control the wife's conduct. The rocks bind her to her marriage; they are the external appearance of sovereignty which Arveragus required. But the liberal conditions of marriage allowed Dorigen not to be bound by the reality of 'rules' of marriage. These rocks, one might say, are not really there at all; the free marriage does not provide that restriction, nor the protection. From this angle the magic trick exposes the weakness of equal marriage, which must depend on the generosity of others for its preservation. This would explain why Dorigen in her second complaint reaches out for the rules and constraints of traditional marriage, of long-established ethical codes.

Chaucer's redefining of the relationship of husband and wife thus leads to the introduction of interesting tensions and resonances within the material. The treatment of the wife is also more probing of the ethics of her behaviour. Boccaccio's character is quite cool in visiting the burgeoning garden, picking flowers and fruit and calmly promising Tarolfo that she is ready to visit him when discreet opportunity offers. Privately she tries to think of ways of avoiding keeping her promise and 'finding no lawful excuse she became more sorrowful', which her husband then sees. The husband tells her to give herself to Tarolfo liberally—he has earned it! Dorigen is less sophisticated; first astonished, then feeling threatened, bewildered and distressed, she becomes incapable of rational thought. Arveragus' judgment of her situation leaves her in this state 'half as she were mad', crying 'allas!' as she goes unwillingly to keep her word. Thus it is in bitter suffering followed by relief that Dorigen learns that the exercise of her freedom may damage the granter of the freedom and the relationship within which it was to operate, as well as cause suffering to herself. The narrator (either himself or through Aurelius) has to make the point briefly at the risk of sounding didactic to make clear the moral scheme of the tale:

> But every wyf be war of hire beheeste!
> On Dorigen remembreth atte leeste.   (1541–2)[13]

Presumably this could apply to all of her promises, not just the one to Aurelius.[14]

The question about liberality is thus made a more complicated one by Chaucer. By creating special conditions within the marriage and emphasising the historical setting, he excludes from the world of the narrative the normal fourteenth-century social and religious criteria about binding oaths. By developing Dorigen's capacity to suffer (the anxieties before Aurelius arrives on the scene, the astonishment of being caught in her own jest and the mental distress of her realisation of the consequences), Chaucer has made the heroine's vulnerability a sounding-board for the liberality of the male characters. It is not such an easy affair as that of honour among men in Boccaccio, where, though the wife is praised as 'valorosa donna', she is not much stirred by her situation; she is more practical, capable even of enduring adultery if she knew her husband would not be harmed or angry. Dorigen is treated by Chaucer as much less independent than the terms of her marriage allow. She gets no satisfaction from the proof that Arveragus accepts her independence; she merely feels trapped by one man and ordered to do what is humiliating by the other. She does not come into direct contact with Aurelius' brother or the magician but both reinforce the idea of threat against the weak woman. The brother says of her:

> 'Thanne moste she nedes holden hire biheste,
> Or elles he shal shame hire atte leeste.'   (1163–4)

Thus, as in romances turning on slander, the 'shaming' of an innocent woman is envisaged as a possible part of the excitement of a love plot. Even more suggestively the magician shows Aurelius in magic illusion the sight of his lady dancing, as if he had power to command her appearance, and in his 'routhe' for Aurelius he does his work so that 'she and every wight sholde wene and seye/ That of Britaigne the rokkes were aweye.' At the end he asks 'Hastow nat had thy lady as thee liketh?' In each of these references there is just enough of the suggestion of presumption to accumulate into a passing impression of callousness and manipulation. Hence Dorigen's speeches are appropriately emotional, to fulfil the role of feminine vulnerability and expose the imprisoning nature of the attitudes and actions of the male characters. It is striking that in the final scene Aurelius tells the magician not only of Arveragus' *gentillesse* in the service of 'trouthe' but also of Dorigen's sorrow and innocence and her unwillingness to be wicked:

> The sorwe of Dorigen he tolde hym als;
> How looth hire was to been a wikked wyf,
> And that she levere had lost that day hir lyf,
> And that hir trouthe she swoor thurgh innocence,
> She nevere erst hadde herd speke of apparence.
> 'That made me han of hire so greet pitee . . .'    (1598–1603)

The moving virtue of the woman is thus given as important a place in the moral denouement as the liberality of the man.

The judgment asked of the reader at the end is of complex and unlike things. Aurelius recognises his 'cherlyssh wrecchednesse' but is given a substantial speech to Dorigen and another to the magician (as well as a report of his thoughts) in which the reader comes to see that adverse judgment is mitigated by the evidence that he is able to learn from his experience. Arveragus' honourable liberality is a matter of fulfilling a principle (under three headings) and has been turned from a free choice into an insistence on honour despite personal pain, which may still be more liberal than the behaviour of the others but is not nearly such a clear-cut case of action on a different moral plane. Menedon's point in *Il Filocolo* that the husband was bound by the lady's oath (and so he gave up only what he could not deny) has more validity here. Arveragus was still 'liberal with his honour' but he retains the reader's sympathy only because Chaucer indicates his hope for a happy outcome; by behaving generously and honestly he hopes that 'It may be wel' and his hope is fulfilled. Similarly Chaucer associates Arveragus' wish that Dorigen may 'kepe and save' her 'trouthe' with his own 'verray love' for her; the passage shows a return to Christian religious references (e.g. in lines 1470, 1471, 1475) so that 'verray love', 'trouthe' and so on are given religious colouring and associated with the qualities of innocence and virtue which elsewhere distinguish Arveragus and Dorigen from the other characters. True love and honesty are persuasively enough linked for the reader to accept the paradox that yielding to another man may be a sign of love for her husband. The third element in the question about generosity, the magician, is also a difficult case to judge; though the figure is completely different from Tebano, Chaucer may have been influenced by Menedon's opinion that the man who gave up financial reward was the most liberal of the three—at least in a practical, realistic sense. Chaucer makes the debating point less clear-cut and by subsuming what judgment there is (of Aurelius mostly) into the denouement of the tale he has created a rich nucleus of controversy, analytical and delicate.


3. Complaint

A significant element in the richness of the tale is provided by yet another layer of treatment, Chaucer's creation of three rhetorical passages of direct speech: Dorigen's address to God on the subject of providence (865–93), Aurelius' appeal to the gods (1031–79) and Dorigen's address to Fortune (1355–1456).

All three develop from the figure of apostrophe, used as an expression of grief or indignation, and they add substantially to the moral seriousness of the tale.[15]

The first of the three is the closest to Chaucer's use of inset complaints elsewhere. Dorigen's address to God on the subject of evil recalls Palamon's invocation 'O cruel goddes that governe/ This world'; both draw on passages in Boethius. The opening words combine the approach to God as 'governour, governynge alle thynges by certein ende' in *De Consolatione* Book I, metrum 5 with the discussion of 'purveiance' in Book IV, prose 6;[16] other Boethian reminiscences provide the subsequent themes of apparent injustice in human affairs (Book IV, prose 5), which has simply to be accepted by the ordinary Christian, and the antithesis between the 'fair werk' of mankind and man's troubles and death (Book I, metrum 5).[17] The passage is the climax of the part of the tale dealing with Dorigen's sorrow at her husband's absence and combines an emotional intensification with the symbolism of the 'grisly, fiendly rokkes blake', which contrast sharply with the following image of the Maytime garden, which survives from Boccaccio's narrative as the setting for Aurelius' love for Dorigen. The effect is of a moving meditative lyric opposing an innocent, even if accusing, human questioning to the inscrutability of divine purposes. It convinces the reader of Dorigen's seriousness of nature and of the depth of her love. Most persuasively it registers the unintellectual quality of mind by which Chaucer characterises his heroine's vulnerability: the images are of the confusion of appearances and any claim to understand 'argumentz' is denied; the climax is a hapless wish for her lord's safety and the sinking of the black rocks. At this stage of the story the rocks represent the flaw in God's creation; 'this werk unresonable' threatens man, exposes his weakness and identifies God's treatment of man as uncharitable. From Dorigen's own situation, as from Palamon's, Chaucer envisages a complaint against the human condition; God foresees and governs but devises the means for men's harm. The argument is on a familiar medieval theme; Chaucer does not here spell out the rest of it, as he does in *Troilus and Criseyde*, the problem of man's free will and God's provision of man's potentiality for sin, but the question of freedom emerges as the central moral theme of *The Franklin's Tale*; this complaint's rhetoric explores one aspect of it. Dorigen's freedom in marriage is, as the tale reveals, dependent on the 'proces of nature' which includes the black rocks of life. But here the complaint has only reached the stage of opening up the conflicting elements, the antithesis between the thought that 'Love is a thyng as any spirit free' (767) and the disconcerting realisation that apparent love may include danger and death:

> 'Thanne semed it ye hadde a greet chiertee
> Toward mankynde; but how thanne may it bee
> That ye swiche meenes make it to destroyen,
> Which meenes do no good, but evere anoyen?'  (881–4)

Aurelius' complaint and prayer similarly combine evocative symbolism with an emotional intensity which extends the range of the tale and develops the figures beyond any mere exemplifying function. This passage too relates to the operations of natural law and superficially it confirms Dorigen's wish that the black rocks be banished. But Aurelius' prayer is to Apollo and Lucina and, though they are addressed primarily as governors of the seasons of the earth and the movements of the waters, they are identified also as the divinities of light. The irony that Aurelius invokes Apollo just after the sun has gone down is signalled to the reader by Chaucer's touch of comedy:

> For th'orisonte hath reft the sonne his lyght—
> This is as muche to seye as it was nyght! (1017–8)

The bathos prepares an element of scepticism for Aurelius' 'ravyng . . . orisoun' which follows. Within his speech the contrast is made between the operation of natural laws (expressed in terms of limitations and desires, 1049–54) and the suspension of those laws by supernatural agency for which Aurelius pleads. In literal and metaphorical darkness Aurelius asks the gods of light either to provide a continual full moon and its spring tides or the sinking of every rock into the darkness of Pluto's realm; either extreme will do equally well, an excess of light or an excess of dark. Aurelius is willing to create cosmic chaos for the sake of the fulfilment of his desire.

Thus Aurelius' love for Dorigen is expressed in terms which demonstrate that it is out of harmony with the principles of the created order of being; the association between the threatened marriage and divine stability is a significant undercurrent in the fable. The cosmic aspect of the tale is still in Chaucer's mind at the end of the poem, which is set in winter at a time when Apollo's influence is slight:

> Phebus wax old and hewed lyk laton,
> That in his hoote declynacion
> Shoon as the burned gold with stremes brighte;
> But now in Capricorn adoun he lighte,
> Where as he shoon ful pale, I dar wel seyn.
> The bittre frostes, with the sleet and reyn,
> Destroyed hath the grene in every yerd. (1245–51)

But Chaucer puts more emphasis on the unsympathetic, even absurd, aspects of the complaint; prefaced by bathos, it is finished off by dismissive scorn:

> Dispeyred in this torment and this thoght
> Lete I this woful creature lye;
> Chese he, for me, wheither he wol lyve or dye. (1084–6)

The over-all effect therefore is of complaint unreasonably used, a desperate prayer for a pagan, unnatural miracle. The images have literal relevance to the physical laws of tides and seasons (so that one sees the daily phenomena of sea and light pictured and dramatised as personal relationships of the gods) but bring with them the exaggerations of love poetry, where lovers express their yearning and despair by picturing themselves as the centre of universal motions. All is to turn on Aurelius' desire and the overwhelming egoism of love is well expressed in his naive request:

> 'Lord Phebus, dooth this miracle for me.' (1065)

Yet Chaucer can not but convey a note of pathos even within this piece of moral distortion, so attuned is his verse to the plangency natural to complaint, as in lines 1038–40 quoted earlier, or in

> 'Lord Phebus, se the teeris on my cheke,
> And of my peyne have som compassioun.'  (1078–9)

As in *Troilus and Criseyde* Chaucer frames the actual speech between pictures of appropriate postures and gestures, a sense of setting and dramatic highlighting; alone he returns to his house, where

> For verray wo out of his wit he breyde.
> He nyste what he spak, but thus he seyde;
> With pitous herte his pleynt hath he bigonne
> Unto the goddes . . .  (1027–30)

At the end the grief is frozen into a tableau as he falls into a trance on the ground, to be discovered by his brother; between the bathos and the scorn which indicate the necessary moral placing, Chaucer gives to the speech itself the full operatic treatment.

Dorigen's long Complaint to Fortune is the most controversial of the three emotional amplifications. Many readers have disliked it or ignored it as inessential to the tale, largely because after the initial arraignment of Fortune it is expressed mainly in terms of classical instances and it turns into a catalogue of ancient heroines. It has had its defenders, though. Sledd argued for its unity and an effect as 'a deliberate bit of rhetorical extravagance, intended as an assurance that all shall yet go well', but he does not take it seriously.[18] Morgan argues more strongly that the complaint shapes moral truths in the terms of rhetorical tradition and that each exemplum has relevance to the pattern of moral exposition in the tale.[19] He sees the exempla as falling into three groups, illustrating chastity (1364–1423), fidelity (1424–41) and fame (1442–56). He makes two other substantial points: that the complaint is protracted in order to demonstrate that the moral dilemma is insoluble, and that the accusation of Fortune is a way of expressing the important idea that the removal of the rocks is a piece of injustice, since it implies abolition of providential order. Whether or not the reader finds this passage of complaint acceptable or significant depends on earlier response to the speeches of Dorigen and Aurelius and on the consequent recognition of the layered nature of the tale, and on the wide stretch of style which is needed to encompass the different levels at which Chaucer is imagining his material. I am in broad agreement with Morgan's view that the passage is a major indicator of how the reader should see the moral sense of the story.

The idea of this passage is of reaching out from a state of disorder (where the laws of nature have been overturned and the rules of marriage are threatened) for fixed rules and patterns of behaviour. The world Dorigen calls up in her examples is, because bookish and looking to the past, something deliberately limited in effect in comparison to magic. Chaucer presents us with two ways of knowing. If, according to one, experience can be contradicted by appearance, in the sphere of the other (the moral patterns Dorigen envisages) behaviour is determined by example, precedent, repetition of what is already known.

Contradiction of the process of nature has trapped Dorigen in her own words and this is reflected in the image of imprisonment with which her Complaint begins: wrapped in Fortune's chain Dorigen can think of no escape routes but the two impossible exits of death or dishonour; it behoves her to choose one of these and of the two clearly death is the way of nobility according to the ancient examples. (This is another point where Chaucer leaves aside the remedies of Christian teaching: there is no thought of confession, repentance, and so on.) Dozens of instances remind her of chaste maidens who died rather than be defiled, of wives who were true to their husbands, of examples of perfect wifehood. Her very multiplication of pressing examples, all reinforcing the unavoidable conclusion, postpones and works against the fulfilment of the judgment. The Complaint is a suspension of action, expressing strength of feeling, the moral significance of the moment, and the sense of a suspended moral question waiting to be debated and resolved. Arveragus' return resolves the tension, but the longer the speech itself lasts, the more Chaucer makes the reader aware of the unresolvedness and of the aspects of womanhood and wifeliness that may be in question.

At the same time the passage heightens the significance of what follows, preparing for the seriousness of the ethical point about 'trouthe' and teaching us in what company Dorigen's potential adultery would belong; for all his longing and youthful intensity, Aurelius is a potential violator of chastity, marriage and honour. The range of names does not (as lists of examples sometimes do) enrich the poetry, because the instances all prove the same point, if with variations; they reinforce and accumulate, rather than complicate.

What the reader perceives about Dorigen is Chaucer's sense of her as incapable of resolving the situation; he makes her represent the innocent wife made vulnerable by lack of caution, even possibly by that very freedom which the opening of the tale presented as a benefit. Because she is given independence, Arveragus accepts that she can make an oath and be held accountable for it. But freedom has exposed her to the consequences from which her married state would 'normally' have protected her. Another way of putting it is that Fortune has trapped her into the rigour of moral patterns based on precedent which is a denial of her freedom to choose her actions—to speak in 'pley' among other things. She takes on all the examples of moral virtue she can find; they are the imprisoning chain and she numbers over the links, wondering 'what shall I say of you?'; the answer is 'Nothing', since each instance is just another nail in the coffin. What from one point of view has often seemed to readers a tedious list, from another makes a significant point by means of the very rhetoric of repetition; all occasions inform against Dorigen and close in her vision of life. The precedents of the past are worse than the black rocks, which by now seem part of the stability of the process of nature. The uniqueness of Dorigen's marriage seems, at this point, to be coming to an end; she must apparently now join the list of examples of wifely virtue (or worse, not even contemplated, join the other unnamed company of wicked wives). Through the painful counting over of the virtuous paragons of the past the unspoken question runs of whether a way can be found of being honourable without dishonouring her pledge, or alternatively, if she must, of being dishonourable and yet retaining her honour as a wife, which was the source of her foolish promise.

Chaucer's organisation of the Complaint is partly the familiar one of preparatory description, as Dorigen 'wepeth, wailleth . . . And swowneth that it routhe was to see', identification of the intention to complain and opening declaration:

> 'Allas!' quod she, 'on thee, Fortune, I pleyne,
> That unwar wrapped hast me in thy cheyne.'   (1355–6)

After that opening flourish the pattern is more unusual, a combination of the series of brief instances and intermittent protests of sincere intent. The series recalls *The Legend of Good Women* and Dorigen's position resembles that of the poet having to expiate his folly, but the parts of the series are even more reduced to miniature pictures seen through the wrong end of a telescope. Punctuating these are Dorigen's early declaration:

> 'yet have I levere to lese
> My lif than of my body have a shame,
> Or knowe myselven fals, or lese my name.'   (1360–2)

and the intermediate reinforcement:

> 'I wol be trewe unto Arveragus.'   (1424)

That there is no crescendo of faithful protest marks the Complaint as incomplete; Arveragus' return dramatically releases Dorigen from what might have become perpetual self-flagellation by exempla into the powerfully condensed statement of Dorigen's real, helpless sense of her dilemma:

> 'Allas!' quod she, 'that evere was I born!
> Thus have I seyd,' quod she, 'thus have I sworn.'   (1463–4)

The three long complaints further illustrate Chaucer's sense of the intensifying and focussing power of the lamenting and protesting speech. All three are stages in the working out of an interestingly complex fable and all three (even this last example) seem to me well integrated into the story. None of them represents a final state of thought; all extend the meaning of the moment at which they occur in a way that enriches the subsequent stages. In the latter part of *The Franklin's Tale* brief echoes of the earlier expressions of longing and uncertainty keep the strain of complaint in play; Arveragus' promise of restraint ('As I may best, I wol my wo endure'), Dorigen's 'allas! allas!' and Aurelius' lament ('Allas, that I bihighte/ Of pured gold a thousand pound of wighte/ Unto this philosophre! How shal I do?'), all sound the recurrent note of unease which keeps the tale's sensibility alert to the end. But each receives a resolving answer which completes each layer of the tale in turn, so that complaint is seen in the final stages as part of a dialogue in which anxiety is eased and generosity rewarded. Serious narrative for Chaucer needs the suspensions and enlargements of complaint both to draw out from the material its moral implications or aspects of its argument and to give time for the story to have its due weight and operative power for the reader. In *The Franklin's Tale* complaints seem to me to be worked into the narrative with particularly subtle and dense effect.

193

## 4. Pagan and Christian

Boccaccio's tale contains only one passage where religious ideas are specifically treated, when Tebano the magician warns Tarolfo that the place he is wandering in is an uncanny haunt of evil spirits and Tarolfo replies: 'God is everywhere equally powerful, here as elsewhere; He holds my life and my honour in His hands'. Otherwise references are classical-pagan in the identification of Tarolfo as a lover who follows the precepts of Ovid, and particularly in the striking passage on Tebano's magic spells and prayers, which are dependent on Ovid's description of the magic rites of Medea when she 'renewed old Aeson' (*Metamorphoses* VII). Further, there are invocations of Hecate and Ceres and echoes of the magic in Virgil's Eighth Eclogue (which had already influenced Ovid) with reference to reversals of Nature and the hastening or slowing of the moon's course. The imitation by Boccaccio makes Tebano's performance equivalent to the pagan sorcery of Medea, which was seen as diabolic in the Middle Ages, but there is no explicit recognition in Boccaccio's story-teller that Tebano is performing unholy rites. In Boccaccio's commentary in Fiammetta's discussion with Menedon, although the examples referred to are classical (or at least Roman, taken from Valerius Maximus), the moral terms become more and more explicitly those of medieval Christian teaching about worldly and spiritual values, about chastity and poverty.

In Geoffrey of Monmouth there is also a mixture of Christian and pagan loyalties and notions from which Chaucer could possibly have derived a sense of ancient Brittany as a place where invocations to classical gods might co-exist with condemnation of pagan magic. So, when Vortigern has by guile got the throne by manoeuvring the death of one son of Constantine and driving the others into exile, Hengist and Horsa invade Kent and contrast is made between Vortigern's belief in 'God himself' and Hengist's worship of 'Saturn, Jove and others who rule over this world, especially Mercury whom we in our language call Woden'. Later we are told that 'Satan entered the heart' of Vortigern when he fell in love with Hengist's daughter.[20] Missionaries come to Britain because the Christian faith has been corrupted both by pagans and by the Pelagian heresy. By the time Aurelius arrives from Brittany, Vortigern and the Saxons have devastated churches and Aurelius is seen as the restorer of Christianity. The suspected diabolic origin of Merlin provides another source of ambivalence.

In *The Franklin's Tale* Chaucer creates an inexplicable fusion of elements. Despite the reference to the God of Love, the first impression is of a Christian society; the echoes of the Form of Solemnisation of Marriage in the terms of the marriage of Arveragus and Dorigen,[21] the terms in which Dorigen addresses Arveragus and in which her friends pray to her, and Dorigen's prayer 'Eterne God . . .' only make sense if the reader assumes that the context is medieval Christian civilisation. The contrary element enters with Aurelius, 'servant to Venus', though he too speaks of 'God that this world made' (967) and so on, and the conversation he has with Dorigen is markedly liberal with such references in the words of Dorigen herself (lines 983, 989, 1000). But at nightfall Aurelius' prayer to Apollo and Lucina shifts the terms to those of the gods. Chaucer here draws in a general way on the kind of material Boccaccio had used for Tebano's prayer. Though Chaucer employs the astrological aspect of the classical gods so that one can think of planets rather than deities, such a line as 'Thy temple in Delphos wol I barefoot seke' (1077) seems to belong literally to the classical pagan world.

Chaucer's most significant change from Boccaccio is the shift from the Italian poet's raving, white-haired, naked sorcerer riding in a sky-chariot drawn by dragons to the professional young illusionist of Orleans, with a touch of Merlin in the otherwise smooth, computer-wise operator of nature. The impression is that some ancient tradition of *sathrapas, walkyries, devinores of demorlaykes*, and *sorzers of exorsismus*[22] through which medieval magic kept in touch with classical stories of entranced pythonesses and readers of cryptic entrails has been taken over by the Orleans department of psychical research. Chaucer's aiming for an ancient Breton effect in some parts of the tale is quite at odds with his choice of a 'modern' magician; the new learning of the universities is an intriguing intrusion of professionalism into a world of amateurs—no wonder Dorigen is left gasping 'It is agayns the proces of nature'. Chaucer treats the magic as modern intellectual paganism, a 'super-sticious cursednesse' which is mere folly to the faithful son of the church but necessary for

> swiche illusiouns and swiche meschaunces
> As hethen folk useden in thilke dayes.   (1292–3)

When 'thilke dayes' were is impossible to decide: the magic is based on ancient knowledge, but the clerk is a modern philosopher, no poor herb-gatherer but the more sophisticated figure of the wise man who consults esoteric books, some of quite recent date. The demonstrations of the clerk's power similarly combine the diabolic arts of one who can command spirits to produce illusions with the scientific precision of one who can impress others simply by knowing a lot more.

The esoteric knowledge is shared to some extent by the character of Aurelius' brother, added by Chaucer and given the function of making the transition from Brittany to Orleans by means of the role of helpful, practical confidant to the distressed lover (the Pandarus touch) and his memory of illusions. Chaucer effectively makes one part of the story overlap with the other; the astrologer is a new character entering the story at a late stage but here given a prepared area of another's experience. Aurelius, the brother and the magician compose an intriguing sequence in Chaucer's presentation of the magic and planetary astrology in the tale. Aurelius knows little but turns to Sun and Moon for aid, suggesting an instinctive recourse in his frenzy to primitive forces of nature, a reversion to heathen worship in the hours of darkness. The brother provides the link to 'magyk natureel' (1125) and the association of 'craft' and 'subtile tregetoures' with appearances. The astrologer is the polished expert. Together they oppose Arveragus and Dorigen who represent love, marriage, honour, simplicity and trust, an innocent directness of feeling and reaction in the early part of the tale, with a strong religious colouring in the language applied to them. The other three characters become representative of a subtle combination of unreason and sophistication. Aurelius, motivated by unreasoning passion, wildly and foolishly seeks the upheaval of natural forces; the pagan aspect in his praying is associated with going 'out of his wit'. The brother is a cleric, not identified with belief in magic, but motivated by brotherly affection to tolerate elements lurking in his own past knowledge. The astrologer is no down-at-heel conjurer, but a man comfortably off, a well-appointed host in his own house giving a consultation like some free-lance surgeon or barrister exacting a good fee from a client and then performing a competent professional job. In the later references to him, though still 'this subtil clerk', he is Aurelius' 'maister' and 'this philosophre'. We know little of his inner mind; he has 'swich routhe' of Aurelius that he helps him and finally he responds to the 'gentil' behaviour of the other two. There is no explicit judgment of him, beyond what is implied in the terms used to describe his skills.

Thus, at the end, the reader's thoughts about this character too are complex. Chaucer has removed the poverty/riches element from the question about liberality. The clerk drives a hard bargain for a stiff fee. His liberality is the yielding of a legal claim to an earned payment:

> 'For, sire, I wol nat taken a peny of thee
> For al my craft, ne noght for my travaille.' (1616–7)

Even the social comparison of knight, squire and clerk has been complicated by the impression Chaucer has created of the clerk as propertied host and the squire as naive suppliant and apologetic debtor. It contributes a wry irony to *The Franklin's Tale* that the clerk seems the most successful, impressive figure, free of wasteful, self-torturing agonies about love, honour and danger, sensibly mindful of a good supper and the payment of his expenses. For him truth is fair dealing. Chaucer's interest in this figure contributes significantly to the unsettled religious condition of the tale, the shifts in the sense of ancient and modern and the openness of the question about generosity at the end.

Of course, there are two endings really, by means of which Chaucer, as is his wont, has it both ways. One of them does make judgments and settle questions and fits into a comprehensible Christian scheme of thought. Aurelius is moved by Dorigen's distress and Arveragus' sense of honour to an examination of his own conduct and an explicit moral judgment of his intentions as:

> 'so heigh a wrecchednesse
> Agayns franchise and alle gentillesse!' (1523–4)

This realisation releases Dorigen and Arveragus from confusion and pain. Generosity is given the power to promote self-questioning and repentance and the world is allowed to seem at ease again, leaving only the slightly comic coda of the release from the debt.

But the other ending is the question, all that remains of that close examination of conduct and comparison of different kinds of obligation in *Il Filocolo*. For analytical debate Chaucer has substituted complicating undercurrents, in the treatment of the marriage, in the development of the moral sensibility and the mental activity of the characters and in the imagining of particular aspects within the dramatic life of the narrative. The tale begins with the close relationship of two people, the confines of the Breton court and Dorigen's private anxieties. But the challenge of the potential lover becomes associated with the tale's moving out into the wider prospects of a changing world, of knowledge, of wonder, subtle craft, varied times and experiences; Aurelius' journey to Orleans becomes a mental as well as a physical one, a disguised quest which extends life's possibilities and, though the narrator punctuates this with warning notes about 'japes', 'wrecchednesse' and so on, Aurelius' attempts to outwit reality achieve a greater substance and imaginative appeal in the tale than Arveragus' quest for 'worshipe and honour'. At the end of the story the moral judgment of Aurelius is associated with a return to Brittany and the narrower concerns of private ethics.

The sense of a wider world comes particularly through the character of the clerk and the associations of Orleans both with modern, scientific, intellectual command over the forces of life and with literature and grammar (developing from rivalries among thirteenth-century rhetoricians and reactions to the anti-literary forces of Parisian dialectic). Chaucer's mixed feelings about the character of the magician—his curious balancing act between condemnation and varied envisaging of his magic powers–suggest that the kinship between magic and poetry was too strong for him to maintain a simple line of argument. In the narrative voice he devised for *The Franklin's Tale* Chaucer combined sensibility with down-to-earthness, romantic and realistic touches working together.[23] Such a mixed style is consistent with a view of the clerk as the sensibly 'free' man in a world of romantic emotional amateurs; to use the agent of magic to provide the undercutting irony of a pragmatic presence casts a sceptical light on those who live according to 'trouthe' rather than appearance. The professional magician, like the poet, must be on the side of the power of illusion, though he does not insist on being paid for it, when it has no practical result.

Opposite the bizarre mixture of the clerk's modern subtlety of art and calculation and Aurelius' 'ancient', nature-worshipping lack of civilised measure, Arveragus and Dorigen are associated with traditional ideas of knighthood, marital fidelity, honesty, truth, Christian virtues, and yet with a sense of innovation in their devising individual rules of marriage. Both are concerned in the latter part of the tale with right behaviour. Dorigen in her confused and disconcerted self-questioning, looks to ancient models for a formula, but not to follow it, rather to provide a context by which her own uncertainty is defined. Chaucer exposes the weakness in Arveragus' position too in that weeping but consistent moment of telling Dorigen to be 'true' but to conceal the falsity that it involves. 'Ah!' the reader may well think, 'that's the concealed rock beneath this apparently high-minded morality.' Between the desperate sentimentalist, whose insistence betrays Dorigen into folly, and the cool modern intellectual, whose manipulation pins her against the wall, husband and wife are caught. The tale lets them off, but they no longer seem the bold free-thinkers of the opening. Decency has limitations, whereas Aurelius and the clerk in their different ways envisage the impossible. All Dorigen can do in distress is think of precedents and all Arveragus can do is think of principles; but then that is what enhances their quality of ideal virtue.

So in *The Franklin's Tale* complaints are interestingly worked in to the fabric of the tale and are resolved in a process of continuing moral debate and exploration; experience exposes Dorigen to moral danger and quells protest and confronts Aurelius with suffering and high principle to teach him to moderate his own will. The structural problems of uniting complaint and narrative seem to be solved in the positive mutual good behaviour which ends the tale in harmony and a friendly challenge to distinguish among kinds of virtue. But, once start trying to answer the question and to sort out Chaucer's sense of what it is to be 'fre', and the transformation of Boccaccio's moral fable is clear.

CHAPTER EIGHT

# Beyond Complaint

Reading Chaucer's Boccaccian narratives demonstrates the English poet's association between complaint and his characters' moral sensibility. For Palamon and Arcite, to consider their situation in prison and in love is to complain, not only of their immediate circumstances but of the human lot. For Troilus, to become vulnerable to love is to become sensitive to grief, embarrassment, fear and awareness of death; to gain love is to anticipate its loss; to lose love is to become aware of the necessity of mutability. For Dorigen and Aurelius, complaint raises questions of order and justice besides registering the anxieties of separation, frustration and shock. There is both a naturalistic and a philosophical cast to Chaucer's sense of the usefulness of complaint within narrative, despite the rhetorical formality associated with the genre, and the threat of its seeming merely an automatic ritual. His reliance on lamenting speeches suggests that Chaucer found the opportunities for dramatic lyricism, and for the ethical debates to which such lyricism was attached, particularly stimulating in the Italian's work. At the same time, Boccaccio's use of ancient material gave Chaucer the chance to try his hand at creating a period perspective of the pagan past by means of a statuesque style, particularly appropriate to the studied articulation of intense states of mind. All three of the works considered integrate complaint into narrative so that the lament becomes part of a complex process within which it is variously qualified, questioned, resisted or extended, answered or dissipated. One can see in this use of the idea lines of development in Chaucer's sense of literary structure, though this development may be interpreted in different ways.

Brewer, for example, sees Chaucer's movement from the dream poems to his adaptation of *Il Filostrato* as expressing a 'developing preference for impersonal narrative',[1] and his treatment of Boccaccio's poem as a removal of the first-person element; yet to express the underlying 'deep sense of loss and betrayal' in the story Chaucer needs to set up 'a process of interactions' and to give verbal realisation to feelings and responses.[2] The mould of complaint may thus be seen as providing part of the necessary machinery of realisation, impersonal, yet acting out the fluctuating states of mind. David Wallace sees Boccaccio's *Filocolo* as 'experimenting with the tension between lyric and narrative components' as well as exploring the relationships between ancient pagan material and the 'modern' Christian authorial stance.[3] His comments identify qualities apparent also in *The Knight's Tale*, in *Troilus and Criseyde* and in *The Franklin's*

*Tale.* Where one view sees impersonality, another tensions, a third might associate the use of meditative lyric within narrative with the movement from action towards the 'increasingly reflective cast of mind in the English characters', which Barry Windeatt sees in *Troilus and Criseyde*;[4] as he says, the lovers 'hope and speak so much more yet can act so much less'.[5] But, yet again, complaint is also recognisable as part of a 'convention of extreme emotion, a heightening of tension together with images of violence and darkness [which] fill *The Knight's Tale* with sound and fury';[6] Chaucer's complaints within narratives, that is, may be viewed as a sign of bravura exaggeration of Boccaccio's measured grandeur by one reader in one place, while, elsewhere, another reader is taking it as a token of Chaucer's move towards internalisation of narrative. The variation of reaction at least supports the idea that Chaucer learned flexibility in his use of the plaintive speech.

By the time Chaucer came to compile the material for *The Canterbury Tales* he had experimented with complaint over a long period. Perhaps the attempt to make a poem from a series of pathetic tales in *The Legend of Good Women* ended his interest in it as a major rhetorical pattern: *Troilus and Criseyde* and *The Legend of Good Women* between them had explored the uses of the idea far-reachingly, in the former extending the adaptability of the lamenting, protesting speech to a variety of situations, and, in the latter, working through some of the possibilities of variation within a patterned series. That the substantial instances within *The Canterbury Tales* occur in romances dealing with ancient or remote material and emphasising traditional ideals suggests that in his last years Chaucer associated complaint with the past, still useful in the right context, but something which he had worked through. Some minor examples seem to confirm this, as when complaint is associated with an older character such as John the carpenter in *The Miller's Tale*:

> 'Allas, my wyf!
> And shal she drenche? allas, myn Alisoun!'
>
> (*CT*, I, 3522–3)

Other passages show Chaucer's sense of complaint as belonging with violent, melodramatic action, as when Phoebus in impetuous anger kills his unfaithful wife in *The Manciple's Tale* and then curses the tell-tale crow and reaches for some resonant rhetoric to express the appropriate regret for his action:

> 'Allas, that I was wroght! why nere I deed?
> O deere wyf! o gemme of lustiheed!
> That were to me so sad and eek so trewe,
> Now listow deed, with face pale of hewe,
> Ful giltelees, that dorste I swere, ywys!
> O rakel hand, to doon so foule amys!
> O trouble wit, o ire recchelees,
> That unavysed smyteth gilteles!'
>
> (*CT*, IX, *The Manciple's Tale*, 273–80)

The setting of this within a short moral fable stresses the exemplary nature of the state of mind: the reader is not invited to be moved by the outburst, but simply to recognise a demonstration of illustrative passion.

There are places in *The Canterbury Tales* where one might expect complaint to play a larger part than it does. *The Man of Law's Tale*, in particular, provides many occasions when the heroine might well have uttered impassioned accusations and reproaches addressed to Fortune and to her various oppressors and detractors. Chaucer does, as I pointed out at the start, draw on the tradition of Marian lament to express the pathos of Constance's situation, but he uses her voice comparatively rarely. *The Man of Law's Tale* is much more consistently narrative in the handling of the melodramatic plot than either *Troilus and Criseyde* or *The Knight's Tale*; instead of changes of direction into a lyric mode of expression Chaucer attributes the apostrophising function to the narrator and so embellishes the tale with a rhetorical commentary rather than dramatised thought and feeling in the voices of the characters. Innocence outraged in *The Physician's Tale* merely makes a gesture towards the death-lament. In *The Clerk's Tale*, though, the whole moral argument is based on the idea of Griselda's restraint. Complaint is held in to touches of rueful pathos:

> 'I have noght had no part of children tweyne
> But first siknesse, and after, wo and peyne.'
>
> (*CT*, IV, 650–51)

In the heroine's longest speech (814–89) the point is Griselda's overcoming of any element of 'pleynt' and Chaucer subtly moves the reader by the controlled expression of complaint's themes:

> 'O goode God! how gentil and how kynde
> Ye semed by youre speche and youre visage
> The day that maked was oure mariage!
> But sooth is seyd—algate I fynde it trewe,
> For in effect it preeved is on me—
> Love is noght oold as when that it is newe.
> But certes, lord, for noon adversitee,
> To dyen in the cas, it shal nat bee
> That evere in word or werk I shal repente
> That I yow yaf myn herte in hool entente!' (852–61)

Chaucer very successfully here makes the reader aware of the occasion for lament and creates a powerful effect from refusing to allow the rhetoric to blossom. The idea of steadfast Christian faith stopping the flow of bitter sorrow is as appropriately but less inventively present in the other religious tales, most explicitly in *The Parson's Tale* where 'the angwissh of troubled herte' is simply identified as the damnable sin of Accidie. Patience is obviously alien to the spirit of complaint.

The subject of complaint and objections to it is most specifically treated by Chaucer in *The Monk's Tale* and the comments on it in the *Prologue* to *The Nun's Priest's Tale*. The series of tragedies which make up *The Monk's Tale* obviously has some resemblance to the pattern of composition in *The Legend of Good Women*. Instead of complaints against the faithlessness of men, this is bound together by complaints against the mutability of Fortune. Some of these are brief, such as that of Ugolino:

> 'Allas, Fortune, and weylaway!
> Thy false wheel my wo al may I wyte.' (*CT*, VII, 2445–6)

Others are more obvious flourishes of generalising rhetoric, as with the narrator's comment on the fall of Alexander:

> Who shal me yeven teeris to compleyne
> The deeth of gentillesse and of franchise,
> That al the world weelded in his demeyne,
> And yet hym thoughte it myghte nat suffise?
> So ful was his corage of heigh emprise.
> Allas! who shal me helpe to endite
> False Fortune, and poyson to despise,
> The whiche two of al this wo I wyte?   (2663–70)

The repeated accusations of Fortune affirm the declared intention of the piece and of the narrator: the *Prologue* includes one of Chaucer's definitions of tragedy and the narrator announces in his opening words, 'I wol biwaille'. Though Chaucer interrupts the series after a mere sixteen instances, he also rounds off the set with a definition:

> Tragedies noon other maner thyng
> Ne kan in syngyng crie ne biwaille
> But that Fortune alwey wole assaille
> With unwar strook the regnes that been proude;
> For whan men trusteth hire, thanne wol she faille,
> And covere hire brighte face with a clowde.   (2761–6)

Tragedy will always illustrate Fortune's instability and that, as much as the relentless succession of the actual stories, is sufficient reason for calling a halt. The definitions turn *The Monk's Tale* into an examination of a literary genre and the comments of the Knight and Host into part of an assessment of the value of different types of narrative which runs through *The Canterbury Tales*. If Chaucer had any thought of the contents of *The Knight's Tale* when attributing opinions to the Knight here, he must have been concentrating on the ending, on Palamon's eventual good fortune and on Theseus' positive philosophy; the element of protest against Fortune is repudiated as is the interest of Arcite's 'sodeyn fal'. Perhaps the most believable aspect of Chaucer's giving to the Knight the desire for happy rags-to-riches narrative is the sense that Chaucer conceived of his character as unintellectual. More predictably the Host is used as an opponent of bewailing, though his reaction to *The Physician's Tale* showed him elsewhere responsive to the power of 'a pitous tale for to heere'. Here the attitude is impatient and dismissive:

> > 'this Monk he clappeth lowde.
> He spak how Fortune covered with a clowde
> I noot nevere what; and als of a tragedie
> Right now ye herde, and, pardee, no remedie
> It is for to biwaille ne compleyne
> That that is doon, and als it is a peyne,
> As ye han seyd, to heere of hevynesse.'   (2781–7)

201

The Host shares the idea of the uselessness of lamenting what can not be altered with the practical philosophy of life which Chaucer used to characterise Pandarus, but Chaucer also identifies the resistance to complaint relevant within the context of *The Canterbury Tales* in connection with the idea of tale-telling as a game. The Host objects to gloomy stories because 'therinne is ther no desport or game'.

Thus two strong resistant forces to complaint are given expression in *The Canterbury Tales*, patience and 'game'. The relationships between instances of sufferance and of indulgence and between earnest and game are visible in what was completed of the tales as themes for contrary narratives and debate among the story-tellers—two more themes not fully developed in the unfinished work.

Yet, though the interest in comedy and the invention of a tale-telling contest in which stories have to offer pleasure as well as instruction create a context in which complaint is inevitably a minor element, there are still signs in *The Canterbury Tales* of Chaucer's sense of its peculiar qualities. *The Knight's Tale*, *The Franklin's Tale* and *The Clerk's Tale* are concerned, in their different ways, with the adequate valuation of virtue and the expression of protest against injustice or the uncertainties of life. Adapted to the particular situation and moral scope of each tale, complaint is a token of the poet's taking the subjects seriously. Chaucer's rejection of 'hevynesse' through the voice of the Host is well enough, but one would hardly want *The Canterbury Tales* to consist entirely of fabliaux in order to keep Harry Bailly awake. In the exchange between Host and Monk, it is the Monk who has the last word and his declaration 'I have no lust to pleye' is a motto for the serious artist and one Chaucer himself was ready to observe at times. The stylistic range is simply wider in *The Canterbury Tales* than in any other of Chaucer's works and so complaint, like romance, like dreams, like exempla and so on, is taken seriously in places but seen in its absurdity elsewhere. The stylistic variation and self-consciousness produce burlesque and parody and push complaint into a mock-heroic role in Pertelote's repeated 'Allas!' and the narrator's desire for Geoffrey de Vinsauf's learning—

> Thanne wolde I shewe yow how that I koude pleyne.
>
> (*CT*, VII, 3353)

But Chaucer does allow his characters to 'pleyne' and asks us to take them seriously when they do so:

> 'Deeth, allas! ne wol nat han my lyf.
> Thus walke I, lyk a restelees kaityf,
> And on the ground, which is my moodres gate,
> I knokke with my staf, bothe erly and late,
> And seye, "Leeve moder, leet me in!
> Lo how I vanysshe, flessh, and blood, and skyn!
> Allas! whan shul my bones been at reste?"'   (*CT*, VI, 727–33)

The structural influence of complaint in combination with narrative is, nevertheless, probably more far-reaching in *The Canterbury Tales* than the direct contribution of the mode itself to expression within the tales. As I suggested in discussing dual forms, the conjunction of prologue and tale develops in a few of the tales that juxtaposition of two different perspectives which Chaucer first explored in linking passionate direct speech to narrative settings. The essence of the problem of creating a satisfying literary experience from such a juxtaposition is how to shift from one perspective to another and how to resolve the contradictions of attitude or the split between two voices which resulted. The prologue which explores temperament or opinion or social ambition, followed by the narrative which, in some way, extends or reflects on that material is a design which Chaucer found more adaptable than the classical narrative extended into lyric. Both, however, are based on a linking of the narrating and the confessional, self-assessing voice. What Chaucer seems, by the time he was composing *The Canterbury Tales*, to have learned from experience is how to develop the voice from one phase to another in a more meaningful, subtle and ironic way. At the same time he was exploring ways of working his juxtaposed moods towards a resolving conclusion. Several of the Canterbury narratives may be described as layered narratives, tales which go through a number of phases, passing through a sequence of stances or voices: first comes some expression of personality or circumstance or viewpoint; secondly there follows a narrative illustration; thirdly comes an element of rhetorical enlargement into judgment or philosophical perspective or general-isation of experience. It is a pattern within which can still be seen the vague outline of the dream-poems and *dits* on which he cut his teeth.

Take the case of *The Canon's Yeoman's Tale*. Here Chaucer composed three sections, each of which opens up the subject further. The dramatic incursion of the Canon and his Yeoman provides the starting point for the exploration, which proceeds by means of the Host's questioning of the Yeoman and moves from the first cheery welcome to the observation of the poverty and grubbiness of his clothes. So one begins with a sense of stages: the facade presented by Canon and Yeoman and then the reality of their furtive life in the back alleys of some suburb. It is here, in explaining his discoloured face, that the Yeoman first uses the key word *multiplie* (669), which indicates their occupation, the supposed transmutation of base metal, but which acquires some richness of association by repetition, and which, in a sense, describes the literary process in which Chaucer is engaged. The 'Prima Pars' of the tale extends the picture of the Canon's way of life by means of accumulation of technical language and anecdotal detail and by means of a typifying picture of alchemists gathering around the broken crucible, grubbing around in the sieved rubbish. The chemical language both authenticates the picture—this is the place where Chaucer most enthusiastically engages in the local colour aspect of dramatic monologue—and also contributes to the characterisation. The impression is of increasing loquacity, a pouring forth of all the knowledge the Yeoman has accumulated. The 'Secunda Pars' moves on supposedly to another Canon and so to a further layer of experience in which the tricks of the deceiving trade are revealed by more anecdotal illustration and by, eventually, a narrative. This is a mere anecdote of the Canon's deception of a young moneyed priest, told as a case-history in the manner of a moral exemplum. The voice of the narrator develops with the material. It reaches a stage of moral demonstration and the style stretches from the early stumbling naiveté to touches now of charac-terising *sentence*:

Trouthe is a thyng that I wol evere kepe   (*CT*, VIII, 1044) or of diagnostic shrewdness:

> in ech estaat
> Bitwixe men and gold ther is debaat.   (1388–9)

The range of expression becomes allusive and satirical with reference to conventional romance motifs:

> This sotted preest, who was gladder than he?
> Was nevere brid gladder agayn the day,
> Ne nyghtyngale, in the sesoun of May,
> Was nevere noon that luste bet to synge;
> Ne lady lustier in carolynge,
> Or for to speke of love and wommanhede,
> Ne knyght in armes to doon an hardy dede,
> To stonden in grace of his lady deere,
> Than hadde this preest this soory craft to leere.   (1341–9)

The narrator is even capable now of ironic pungency:

> A man may lightly lerne, if he have aught,
> To multiplie, and brynge his good to naught!   (1400–1)

Given this ability of the narrative to find the voice it needs, it is not really any disruption or inconsistency that is visible in the explicit didacticism of the end, nor even in the bookishness and erudition of the references to alchemical texts and the figures they discuss—to Hermes, the *Secreta Secretorum*, Plato. This acknowledgement of the philosophical tradition linked with alchemy enlarges the otherwise narrow, condemnatory perspective of the tale. Though it remains clear that the man who does 'bisye hym this art for to seche' (1462) is seen as one who 'maketh God his adversarie' (1476), yet alchemy as secret knowledge is permitted by God 'where it liketh to his deitee/ Men for t'enspire' (1469–70). The dramatic monologue of theory, morality and instance may be seen at the end as enlarged by philosophical amplification. The voice of the speaker responds to the rhetorical need for wider comment, regardless of any idea of dramatic consistency. *The Canon's Yeoman's Prologue and Tale* has the quality of a layered structure where each section overlaps with the previous one but extends the view: it moves from colloquial dramatic realism to become a genre painting of grotesque images of ruthless greed and then a narrative exemplification of the themes, from which an over-riding intellectual view of the subject is drawn. The tale is the furthest Chaucer develops the social complaint; a piece of satire against folly and vice needs both dramatic and intellectual perspective. The former is provided by the useful device of the voice of the ignorant observer, drawn in by his servant status and so representing a kind of innocent normality against which the extremity of obsession and exploitation in others can be measured. But for the intellectual, theoretical perspective on alchemy, its adherents and its victims, Chaucer needs a more detached and knowledgeable voice. He works up to it skilfully by means of the layering of the narrative, though some readers have seen the end of the tale as 'dramatically undigested' or as evidence that the Pars Secunda was originally an independent piece which has been imperfectly adapted.[7]

There are many points of comparison between this tale and the two tales with lengthy prologues, which I considered earlier as dual forms, those given to the Pardoner and the Wife of Bath. In all three Chaucer shows an interest in developing, with variations, a 'spoken' style. The Wife of Bath's diffuseness, digressions, repetitions, clichés, breakings off, interjections and so on show Chaucer fully in command of supposedly impromptu expression. The Yeoman's Prologue is an extended piece in the style of the Link-passages in *The Canterbury Tales*, mainly a dialogue for Yeoman and Host written as heightened conversation. The Pardoner's Prologue is a guide to his favoured rhetorical techniques and so directs the reader's attention to elements of a spoken style used to persuade. The three tales move from this interest in oral effects to conclusions which include explicit didacticism and a degree of literary purpose beyond the range of merely imitative, naturalistic devices. The reader perceives the layers of *The Pardoner's Prologue and Tale* in terms of the ironic relationship between the speaker's corrupt purpose in preaching and the vivid moral efficacy of his tale—that is, primarily as a dual form. The quarrel between Pardoner and Host which rounds off the tale could be said to turn it into a composite or layered experience. The tale itself works as complaint 'against the times' of the sort that lies behind the morality plays. Human actions are composed into an almost mathematical proof of man's folly and vice, displayed in the framework of an antithesis of life and death. The figure of the old man utters his version of man's complaint against life's limitations. Finally the speaker has to move into a strain of higher rhetoric:

> And Jhesu Crist, that is oure soules leche,
> So graunte yow his pardoun to receyve,
> For that is best; I wol yow nat deceyve.   (*CT*, VI, 916–8)

He has convinced some readers but the Host's rejection of his relics leaves us with the effect of one type of complaint being tested by Chaucer in the market-place and found wanting. He gives his dual form an extra dimension as a way of placing it in context.

With the Wife of Bath's case Chaucer shows complexity of intention both in the dual pattern he makes from prologue and tale and by the strategy within the tale itself. This is another example of layered narrative in the sense that the reader is aware of different voices at different stages of the tale and conscious too of the story being used merely as a framework for the exploration of attitudes and ideas. The attention is deflected from any unnecessary concern with mere matters of suspense, narrative outcome, character and so on by the swift identification by Chaucer of the disparity between the matter and the voice of the narrator, between once-upon-a-time romance and the insistent perspective of experience. The grafting of the wedding-night instruction onto the tale of the knight's quest for an answer to the court's question produces a hybrid of romance adventure and teaching dialogue. The attitude moves from the pragmatic story-teller's purpose to entertain the audience to the spokesperson for woman's partisan interest in the quest and to the apotheosis of womanly wisdom in the old wife's lengthy sermon on social ideals. In this, as in *The Pardoner's Tale* and *The Canon's Yeoman's Tale*, there is an element of social complaint, though the teaching here accompanies its exposures of the weaknesses of the rich and noble with positive Christian advocacy for virtuous

205

poverty. The dual pattern of prologue and tale thus overlaps in some respects with the composite or layered narrative.

The other powerful example of the development of layered narrative is *The Merchant's Tale* where the three stages I distinguished earlier are visible in, first, the long speech on marriage near the beginning, which creates the viewpoint, secondly the composite story, including elements of debate, fabliau, allegorical fable, satire, lyric and mock-heroic, and, thirdly, the element of judgment or philosophical perspective brought in by the supernatural observers Pluto and Proserpine in their contest between masculine and feminine values. The simple story and fictional world of elderly Italian merchant, wife and servant, city, house and garden, involved in a plot based on sexual appetite and ready wit, is transformed by speeches, opinions and the narrator's high-flown glosses into an exemplum for moral debate. The actual scenes are presented constantly as observed from outside. The narrator offers the tale as an illustration of marriage and prepares the reader's mind for irony by the mock innocence of the opening praise of wives. The voices of Placebo and Justinus expose January's intentions as arrogant, foolish and self-deluding. From a layer of knowledge even more remote from the supposed world of the fiction, the Wife of Bath's opinion is cited as a point of reference. The appearance of Venus and Hymen at the wedding makes the reader see it all as a scene parodying ancient seasonal ceremony and Pluto and Proserpine watch the end as if from a box at the theatre. The characters are treated as puppets and the narrator at times seems to be performing an act of ventriloquism in describing them; so the complaint makes a fleeting appearance as a stock identifying feature for the young lover, but in the narrator's mouth rather than that of the cardboard Damian:

> Now wol I speke of woful Damyan,
> That langwissheth for love, as ye shul heere;
> Therfore I speke to hym in this manere:
> I seye, 'O sely Damyan, allas!
> Andswere to my demaunde, as in this cas,
> How shaltow to thy lady, fresshe May,
> Telle thy wo?'   (*CT*, IV, 1866–72)

The answer is that 'in a lettre wroot he al his sorwe/ In manere of a compleynt or a lay', but the poet does not bother to compose the words of it. Similarly the narrator has to supply the appropriate outburst of rhetoric against the treachery of household servants (1783 ff.) and, of course, to complain against Fortune:

> O sodeyn hap! o thou Fortune unstable! . . .
> O brotil joye! o sweete venym queynte!
> O monstre . . .
> Why hastow Januarie thus deceyved?   (2057, 2061–2, 2065)

The mock-heroic effect directs attention not to the characters of husband, wife and lover but to the voices of the knowing commentators. The tale unfolds as a progression from the tongue-in-cheek commendation of the wife who 'seith nat ones "nay" when he seith "ye"./ "Do this," seith he; "Al redy, sire," seith she', to the wry reasonableness of Justinus who 'woot best where wryngeth me my sho', and to Pluto's and Proserpine's provision of the intelligent husband/ wife dialogue to accompany the farcical scenes from married life which end the tale. Scattered among these variously detached observers, the narrator's attitudes dodge from pungent satire to gleeful complicity. As Robert Jordan puts it, 'the tale as a whole is an extremely varied and discordant mixture of many of the voices which Chaucer habitually uses'.[8] The structural basis is the combination of narrative with commentary, but the commentary here is shared by several voices, so that, again in Jordan's words, 'there is no single viewpoint governing the narrative'. Between them the commenting voices compile a sort of medley of complaint, concerning women, marriage and fairness, but the ingenuity with which Chaucer weaves this into his story of greed, self-delusion and beguiling is a good deal more sophisticated in literary intention than a simple pairing of narrative with complaint.

Nevertheless the layered or many-voiced narrative is, in some sense, an extension of that simple pairing. Chaucer seems throughout his writing career to look for a composite quality in his literary structures. Narrative and complaint led him to other pairings, to sequences and series. Boccaccio stimulated interest in the possibilities of given historical narrative, within which insertions and expansions could create varieties of stance and emphasis. The scheme of *The Canterbury Tales* made an even larger frame capable of holding varied content as well as a mixture of stylistic levels and narrative voices. At all stages of this development of interest in composite narrative there are signs of uncertainty about the right way of bringing the mixture to an end. Not only did Chaucer leave more works unfinished than any other major English author, but many of the works that he did complete are test cases of the idea that 'th'ende is every tales strengthe', or, as a modern critic puts it, that 'the sense of closure is a function of the perception of structure'.[9] The creation of composite works made the question more acute for Chaucer than it would have been for more modest medieval writers, since his mixture of literary kinds goes beyond the limits of endings appropriate for a particular literary type.

Medieval theorists did not provide much help in this, since scholarly compilers and writers on rhetoric assumed compatibility of subject-matter and unity of treatment and were not catering in their analyses and prescriptions for writers who liked heterogeneous yokings together. In any case, as Curtius points out, classical ideas of the appropriate topics for the conclusion of an oration were not necessarily appropriate for poetry. Where classical orations were supposed to review the principal points of the argument and then appeal to the emotions of the audience, classical poets sometimes preferred the abrupt ending without conclusion (as with the death of Turnus at the end of the *Aeneid*) or a mere indication that 'the game is over' (Ovid at the end of *Ars Amandi*).[10] The brief concluding formula was often used in the Middle Ages and the waking at the end of a dream-poem is one version of it. Chaucer follows that model for the brief ending of *The Book of the Duchess* and the last few lines of *The Parliament of Fowls*, and he was confident enough elsewhere (in the fabliaux in *The Canterbury Tales* particularly) in applying actual formulae for rounding things off, such as the three types of ending recommended by Geoffrey de Vinsauf: reviewing the material and drawing a summing-up idea from it, applying a proverb as a summing up of the meaning, or using an exemplum for the same purpose.[11] But about the larger architectural sense of resolving tensions within the material of a poem, the theorists can offer no more guidance than the grand over-all plan which Geoffrey de Vinsauf envisages at the beginning of the *Poetria Nova*, part of which Chaucer attributes to Pandarus in *Troilus and Criseyde* (Book I, 1065–9):

> If anyone is to lay the foundation of a house, his impetuous hand does not leap into action: the inner design of the heart measures out the work beforehand, the inner man determines the stages ahead of time in a certain order; and the hand of the heart, rather than the bodily hand, forms the whole in advance, so that the work exists first as a mental model rather than as a tangible thing.[12]

On the basis of this idea of the archetype, one might argue that in shaping the arc of Troilus' fortune from the material of *Il Filostrato* Chaucer followed Geoffrey de Vinsauf's stress 'on the organic nature of the work of art, on the need for every aspect of the work to be functional, to bear an intrinsic relation to the whole'.[13] But the ending of *Troilus and Criseyde* goes beyond the completion of the scheme of Troilus' double sorrow and seems to scuttle the whole enterprise, illustrating rather the notion that 'Medieval poets never heard of organic form, and they did quite well without it'.[14]

Whether Chaucer ever found a completely satisfying way of combining narrative and lyric is an aspect of the larger question of closure.[15] Complaints proved for Chaucer an adaptable way of exploring the emotional and moral aspects of narrative, but they tend to raise questions or create expectations which lie beyond the scope of the narrative frame. Nevertheless Chaucer sought, especially in his later work, to stretch the scope of particular narrative material and of literary genre. Voices and stances shift and change; styles are juxtaposed; parody, burlesque and the mock-heroic look askance at modes of expression. The result is that endings become more equivocal, except within the local narrative units of simpler types of fiction. Many commentators have puzzled over the uncertainties of Chaucer's endings, especially the 'palinode' to *Troilus and Criseyde* and the 'Retractions' to *The Canterbury Tales*, seeing them variously as 'qualified endings' which offer 'a double perspective of guilt and grace',[16] or as 'suspended judgments' which play off the final judgments of the author against the interim judgments of the narrator,[17] or as transitions from the fictional to the factual world,[18] and so on. Perhaps it gets nearer the mark to accept that Chaucer is not comfortable with the sense of closure, whether of ideas and themes or of experience, his discomfort perhaps coming, as Crampton suggests, from a sense of 'the density that the poet wants to grasp in his fictions; there seems to be no end'; Chaucer could simply think of too many possibilities.[19]

The best that Chaucer could do in his longer works was an enlargement of the envoy of the ballade, a twist or turn to his audience and an involvement by plea of his hearers in his own uncertainties. This is a self-protective way of ending and in tune with the note of apology and correction that one hears in Chaucer's completions; to end a work was, among other things, an occasion for putting things right. The successful worldly endings (in *The Merchant's Tale* and the Envoy to *The Clerk's Tale*) offer, in their own way, similar adjustments of perspective. But the complaint could not always be put right, since at its heart was a recognition of injustice, and of the pains and inevitabilities of love and of life. Inherent in every complaint is the theme of death, though Chaucer often keeps it at bay by humour and irony. The force of the inevitable patterns of life—the succession of the Ages of Man, the turn of Fortune's wheel, the end of the pilgrimage—provides a strong sense of movement towards completion in Chaucer's writing. But there is also a strong resistance to it, a feeling that the unreached conclusion is the stuff of life. Once the retractions close in, the poetry has to stop. But the poet, like the swan, 'Ayens his deth begynneth for to synge'. Hence the recurrence of complaint, in which the poet dramatises his protest and invites us all to join him:

> The proudest of yow may be mad ful tame;
> Wherfore I pray yow, of your gentilesse,
> That ye compleyne for myn hevynesse.

# Abbreviations

| | |
|---|---|
| Boitani and Mann | *The Cambridge Chaucer Companion*, eds. Piero Boitani and Jill Mann (Cambridge, 1986) |
| Brewer (ed) 1974 | *Writers and Their Background: Geoffrey Chaucer*, ed. Derek Brewer (London, 1974) |
| *ChauR* | *Chaucer Review* |
| *CL* | *Comparative Literature* |
| Clemen | W. Clemen, *Chaucer's Early Poetry* (London, 1963) |
| *CT* | *The Canterbury Tales* |
| *EC* | *Essays in Criticism* |
| *ELH* | *English Literary History* |
| *JEGP* | *Journal of English and Germanic Philology* |
| Kean | P. M. Kean, *Chaucer and the Making of English Poetry*, 2 Vols. (London, 1972) |
| Kolve | V. A. Kolve, *Chaucer and the Imagery of Narrative: the First Five Canterbury Tales* (London, 1984) |
| *MAe* | *Medium Aevum* |
| *M&H* | *Medievalia et Humanistica* |
| *MLQ* | *Modern Language Quarterly* |
| *MP* | *Modern Philology* |
| Norton-Smith, *GC* | J. Norton-Smith, *Geoffrey Chaucer* (London, 1974) |
| Payne | Robert O. Payne, *The Key of Remembrance: A Study of Chaucer's Poetics* (New Haven/London, 1963) |
| Pearsall | Derek Pearsall, *The Canterbury Tales* (London, 1985) |
| *PQ* | *Philological Quarterly* |
| *PBA* | *Proceedings of the British Academy* |
| *PMLA* | *Publications of the Modern Language Association* |
| *RES* | *Review of English Studies* |
| Robinson | F. N. Robinson (ed.), *The Works of Geoffrey Chaucer*, 2nd edition (London, 1957) |
| SATP | Société des Anciens Textes Français |
| *SP* | *Studies in Philology* |
| Wimsatt | James I. Wimsatt, *Chaucer and the French Love Poets: the Literary Background of The Book of the Duchess* (Chapel Hill, N. Carolina, 1968) |
| Windeatt | B. A. Windeatt (ed.), Geoffrey Chaucer, *Troilus and Criseyde* (London, 1984) |
| Windeatt, *S&A* | B. A. Windeatt, *Chaucer's Dream-Poetry: Sources and Analogues* (Cambridge, 1982) |

# Notes and References

*Chapter One: The Order of Complaint*

1 See Clemen, 175–9.

2 See Douglas Gray, 'Chaucer and "Pite"', in *J. R. R. Tolkien, Scholar and Storyteller*, edd. M. Salu and R. T. Farrell (Ithaca/London, 1979), 173–203.

3 See Kean, Vol. 2, 190–3.

4 John Peter, *Complaint and Satire in Early English Literature* (Oxford, 1956), 59. Paul Miller would not agree, since in his view 'complaint and satire were distinct literary types': to my mind there is an overlap and I do not share Miller's confidence in the separability of medieval genres. See Paul Miller, 'John Gower, Satiric Poet', in *Gower's Confessio Amantis: Responses and Reassessments*, ed. A. J. Minnis (Cambridge, 1983), 79–105, particularly p. 89.

5 Peter, op. cit., p. 60 (and the whole of Chapter 4). Miller, op. cit., p. 87, distinguishes three sub-species of medieval satire: (i) against single vices; (ii) against single estates; (iii) comprehensive surveys of society and its vices.

6 Anna Crabbe, 'Literary Design in the *De Consolatione Philosophiae*', in *Boethius, His Life, Thought and Influence*, ed. Margaret Gibson (Oxford, 1981), 237–74.

7 Alanus de Insulis, *De Planctu Naturae*, in *Patrologia Latina*, ed. J. P. Migne, Vol. 210. Alain of Lille, *The Plaint of Nature*, translation and commentary by J. J. Sheridan (Toronto, 1980).

8 Nancy Dean, 'Chaucer's Complaint: A Genre descended from the *Heroides*', CL, 19 (1967), 1–27.

9 Payne, p. 185, following E. Faral's discussion of amplification in *Les Arts poétiques du XIIe et du XIIIe siècle* (Paris, 1923).

10 The theory of vernacular lyric forms was developing in the latter part of the fourteenth century as is clear from Deschamps' *L'Art de Dictier*, which lists *complainte* along with *ballade, chant royal, motet, lai, débat* and so on. *Oeuvres Complètes de Eustache Deschamps*, Vol. 7, SATP (Paris, 1878–1903). See R. P. Parr, Introduction to Geoffrey of Vinsauf, *Documentum de Modo et Arte Dictandi et Versificandi* (Milwaukee, Wisconsin, 1968), 21–4.

11 James I. Wimsatt, *Chaucer and the French Love Poets* (Chapel Hill, N. Carolina, 1968).

12 *Li Romanz de la Poire* of Messire Thibaut, publié par F. Stehlich (Halle, 1881).

13 *Le Fablel dou Dieu d'Amours*, ed. I. C. Lecompte, MP, 8 (1910–11), 663 ff. See also C. Oulmont, *Les Débats du Clerc et du Chevalier* (Paris, 1911).

14 *De Venus la Déese d'Amour*, ed. W. Foerster (Bonn, 1880).

15 *Oeuvres de Guillaume de Machaut*, ed. F. Hoepffner, SATP, 3 vols (Paris, 1908–21). *Oeuvres de Froissart: Poésies*, ed. A. Scheler, 3 vols (Brussels, 1870–2). *L'Espinette amoureuse*, ed. A. Fourrier (Paris, 1974).

16 See Wimsatt, 104–7.

17 Janet Coleman, *English Literature in History 1350–1400: Medieval Readers and Writers* (London, 1981), Chapter 3.

18 Coleman, p. 97.

19 J. A. Burrow, *Medieval Writers and their Work: Middle English Literature and its Background 1100–1500* (Oxford, 1982), p. 38, points out the importance of the petitionary mode: poets 'are discovered, as it were, upon their knees . . . Their usual tone is one of complaint and of entreaty.'

*Chapter Two: Complaints Simple and Compound*

1 The poem occurs in only 2 Shirley MSS where it is described as 'By Chaucier'. Norton-Smith, *GC*, p. 20, n. 2, casts doubt on its authenticity.

2 Clemen, p. 186.

3 The poem's lack of rhetorical figures and the 'speaking voice' are noted by Paul M. Clogan, 'The Textual Reliability of Chaucer's Lyrics: *A Complaint to His Lady*', *M&H*, ns 5 (1974), 183–9.

4 E.g. by J. E. Cross, 'The Old Swedish *Trohetsvisan* and Chaucer's *Lak of Stedfast-nesse*—A Study in Medieval Genre', *Saga-Book*, 16 (1965), 283–314.

5 See Geoffrey Shepherd, 'Religion and Philosophy in Chaucer', in Brewer (ed.) 1974, 262–89 (quotation from p. 267). V. J. Scattergood, 'Social and Political Issues in Chaucer: An Approach to *Lak of Stedfastnesse*', *ChauR*, 21 (1987), 469–75, stresses Chaucer's fusion of the traditional complaint of the evils of the age and the particular significance of contemporary occasion—the events of 1387.

6 See Kean, Vol. 1, 34–42.

7 See V. J. Scattergood, 'Chaucer's curial satire: the *Balade de bon conseyl*', *Hermathena*, 133 (1982), 29–45.

8 Clemen, p. 197.

9 E. Vasta, '*To Rosemounde*: Chaucer's "Gentil" Dramatic Monologue', in *Chaucerian Problems and Perspectives*, edd. E. Vasta and Z. P. Thundy (Notre Dame/London, 1979), 97–113, describes it as 'at once an argument, an encomium, a complaint, a proclamation, a play of doctrine and an exercise in the manipulation of poetic convention' (p. 101).

10 A. V. C. Schmidt, 'Chaucer and the Golden Age', *EC*, 26 (1976), 99–115.

11 Norton-Smith traces the poetic impulse not to Boethius but to Seneca: J. Norton-Smith, 'Chaucer's *Etas Prima*', *MAe*, 32 (1963), 117–24.

12 A. V. C. Schmidt. 'Chaucer's Nembrot: A Note on *The Former Age*', *MAe*, 47 (1978), 304–7.

13 See Douglas Kelly, *Medieval Imagination* (Madison, Wisconsin, 1978), 182–7.

14 Haldeen Braddy, *Chaucer and the French Poet Graunson* (Louisiana, 1947). Wimsatt, Chapter 8. A. Piaget, 'Oton de Grandson, sa vie et ses poésies', *Mémoires et Documents publiés par la Société d'Histoire de la Suisse Romande*, 3rd series, Vol. 1 (Lausanne, 1941).

15 James I. Wimsatt, *Chaucer and the Poems of 'Ch'* (Woodbridge, Suffolk, 1982).

16 Clemen, p. 182.

17 Norton-Smith, *GC*, p. 21.

18 M. Pittock, 'Chaucer: "The Complaint unto Pity"', *Criticism*, 1 (1959), 160–8.

19 Charles J. Nolan Jr, 'Structural Sophistication in "The Complaint unto Pity"', *ChauR*, 13 (1978–9), 363–72.

20 James Reeves (ed.), *Chaucer: Lyric and Allegory* (London, 1970), p. 160.

21 V. A. Kolve, 'Chaucer and the Visual Arts' in Brewer (ed.) 1974, p. 304.

22 This could be the origin of Shirley's note in MS Ashmole 59 that the poem was 'translated out of ffrenshe into Englisshe by þat famous Rethorissyen Geffrey Chaucier'. See A. Brusendorff, *The Chaucer Tradition* (London/Copenhagen, 1925), 241–5. J. I. Wimsatt, 'Chaucer, *Fortune* and Machaut's "Il m'est avis"', in *Chaucerian Problems and Perspectives*, 119–31, points out the French trappings of *Fortune* and argues for de Machaut as a source.

23 *Boece*, Book 1, metrum 4, for example.

24 See B. L. Jefferson, *Chaucer and the Consolation of Philosophy of Boethius* (Princeton, 1917), 57–60. J. J. Mogan, *Chaucer and the Theme of Mutability* (The Hague/Paris, 1970), 81–5.

25 See J. D. Burnley, *Chaucer's Language and the Philosophers' Tradition* (Cambridge, 1979), 37, 39–40, 78.

26 J. Norton-Smith, 'Chaucer's Boethius and *Fortune*', *Reading Medieval Studies*, 2 (1976).

*Chapter Three Dual Forms*

1 J. I. Wimsatt, '*Anelida and Arcite*: a Narrative of Complaint and Comfort', *ChauR*, 5 (1970–71), 1–8.

2 Michael D. Cherniss, 'Chaucer's *Anelida and Arcite*: Some Conjectures', *ChauR*, 5 (1970–71), 9–21.

3 J. Norton-Smith, 'Chaucer's *Anelida and Arcite*', in *Medieval Studies for J. A. W. Bennett*, ed. P. L. Heyworth (Oxford, 1981), 81–99.

4 Clemen, 197–209.

5 J. I. Wimsatt, 'Guillaume de Machaut and Chaucer's Love Lyrics', *MAe*, 47 (1978), 66–87.

6 Norton-Smith quotes from a Florentine poem *L'Intelligenza*: 'La bella Analida e lo bono Ivano', op. cit., p. 81, n. 2.

7 Clemen, p. 199.

8 Compare *The Wife of Bath's Prologue*, *CT* III, 386, where a variant of this line is effectively amplified in the following line: 'I koude pleyne, and yit was in the gilt.'

9 Clemen, 205–6.

10 Norton-Smith, *GC*, p. 28.

11 As Gardiner Stilwell points out: 'Convention and Individuality in Chaucer's *Complaint of Mars*', *PQ*, 35 (1956), 69–89.

12 Clemen, p. 195.

13 See Wimsatt, 57–67.

14 See Haldeen Braddy, *Chaucer and the French Poet Graunson* (Louisiana, 1947) and Windeatt, *S and A*, 120–4.

15 See Norton-Smith, *GC*, p. 28.

16 Clemen, p. 192. Charles A. Owen Jr, 'The Problem of Free Will in Chaucer's Narratives', *PQ*, 46 (1967), 433–56, sees Mars and Venus as exemplary figures in a mechanical universe; the combination of astrology and myth results in Chaucer's 'most deterministic poem' (p. 435).

17 Reflection of particular poems by de Machaut is proposed by Wimsatt: article cited in n. 5 above, 73–6.

18 See J. P. McCall, *Chaucer among the Gods: the Poetics of Classical Myth* (Pennsylvania, 1979), 33–90 and Norton-Smith, *GC*, 32–4.

19 See A. J. Minnis, *Medieval Theory of Authorship: Scholastic Literary Attitudes in the Later Middle Ages* (London, 1984), especially the section on Chaucer in Chapter 5, for discussion of the influence of Aristotelian causes on medieval literary theory.

20 Spenser's interpretation of the tale as one of disruption of brotherly concord (i.e. a variation on *The Knight's Tale*) is discussed by A. Kent Hieatt, '*The Canterbury Tales* in *The Faerie Queene*', in *Spenser and the Middle Ages 1976* (Kalamazoo, Michigan, 11th Conference on Medieval Studies, 1976), 216–29. See also A. Kent Hieatt, *Chaucer, Spenser, Milton: Mythopoeic Continuities and Transformations* (Montreal, 1975). A full account of the history of interpretation of *The Squire's Tale* is given in Chapter 5 of David Lawton, *Chaucer's Narrators* (Cambridge, 1985).

21 Charles Larson, '*The Squire's Tale*: Chaucer's Evolution from the Dream Vision', *Revue des Langues Vivantes*, 43 (1977), 598–607.

22 Jennifer R. Goodman, 'Chaucer's *Squire's Tale* and the Rise of Chivalry', *Studies in the Age of Chaucer*, 5 (1983), 127–36.

23 J. Burke Severs (ed.), *A Manual of Writings in Middle English 1050–1500*, Vol. 1, Romances (New Haven, 1967), Section 10, Miscellaneous Romances by L. H. Hornstein: II Composites of Courtly Romance, 147–58. See also Dorothee Metlitzki, *The Matter of Araby in Medieval England* (New Haven, 1977), p. 136 ff. on the combination of family romance, magic and orientalism.

24 See Gardiner Stilwell, 'Chaucer in Tartary', *RES*, 24 (1948), 177–88, for an often-quoted view of Chaucer's 'excessive use of whimsical *occupatio*' in the tale.

25 Lawton, op. cit., p. 111 ff.

26 Ibid., 118–23.

27 See J. Burke Severs, *The Literary Relationships of Chaucer's Clerkes Tale* (New Haven, 1942).

28 See Kean, Vol. 2, 126–8, for a sensitive discussion of the presentation of Griselda.

29 See Anne Middleton, 'The Clerk and his Tale: Some Literary Contexts', *Studies in the Age of Chaucer*, 2 (1980), 121–50, for an intelligent demonstration of the sophistication of the tale.

30 Richard Firth Green, *Poets and Princepleasers: Literature and the English Court in the Late Middle Ages* (Toronto, 1980).

31 Green, p. 143.

32 Anne Middleton, 'Chaucer's "New Men" and the Good of Literature in the *Canterbury Tales*', in Edward W. Said (ed.), *Literature and Society*, Selected Papers from the English Institute, 1978, new series 3 (Baltimore, 1980), 15–56.

33 B. A. Windeatt, 'Literary Structures in Chaucer', in Boitani and Mann, 195–212, sees Chaucer as exploiting 'the devices of interruption and of pairing' (p. 207).

*Chapter Four: Sequence and Series*

1 Or, as D. S. Brewer puts it, 'these love-visions may well be regarded as narratively expanded first-person lyrics': 'Towards a Chaucerian Poetic', first published in *PBA*, 60 (1974), 219–52, reprinted in D. S. Brewer, *The Poet as Storyteller* (London, 1984), 54–79 (quotation from p. 57).

2 See Windeatt, *S&A*, 3–70.

3 On the art of the compiler and Chaucer see A. J. Minnis, 'Chaucer and Comparative Literary Theory', in *New Perspectives in Chaucer Criticism*, ed. Donald M. Rose (Norman, Oklahoma, 1981), 53–69, and A. J. Minnis, *Medieval Theory of Authorship* (London, 1984).

4 Chaucer, *The Book of the Duchess*, ed. Helen Phillips (Durham & St Andrews Medieval Texts, no. 3, 1982), p. 16.

5 Payne. In a later essay Payne argues that Chaucer's structures develop organically from the first-person narrator and his relationship with his audience: R. O. Payne, 'Chaucer's Realization of Himself as Rhetor', in *Medieval Eloquence: Studies in the Theory and Practice of Medieval Rhetoric*, ed. J. J. Murphy (Berkeley, 1978), 270–87.

6 Helen Phillips (ed.), *The Book of the Duchess*, p. 47.

214

7 A. C. Spearing, *Medieval Dream Poetry* (Cambridge, 1976), 53–4, 62–3, and Clemen, p. 30. The concept of Chaucer's structures as 'inorganic' and Gothic is elaborated by Robert M. Jordan, *Chaucer and the Shape of Creation: the Aesthetic Possibilities of Inorganic Structure* (Cambridge, Mass., 1967).

8 See particularly J. A. W. Bennett, *The Parlement of Foules: An Interpretation* (Oxford, 1957) and Piero Boitani, *Chaucer and the Imaginary World of Fame* (Cambridge, 1984).

9 See Wimsatt.

10 Not all commentators would agree, obviously. See B. G. Koonce, *Chaucer and the Tradition of Fame* (Princeton, 1966); Sheila Delany, *Chaucer's House of Fame and the Poetics of Skeptical Fideism* (Chicago, 1972); J. A. W. Bennett, *Chaucer's Book of Fame* (Oxford, 1969); Boitani, op. cit.

11 See Windeatt, *S&A*, 127–35. Nicole de Margival, *Le Panthère d'Amours*, ed. H. A. Todd, SATP (Paris, 1883).

12 J. A. W. Bennett, *Chaucer's Book of Fame*, Chapter 5, especially 171–2.

13 Bennett, op. cit., and L. K. Shook, '*The House of Fame*', in Beryl Rowland (ed.), *Companion to Chaucer Studies* (Oxford, 1979), 341–54. P. Boitani, 'Chaucer's Labyrinth: Fourteenth-Century Literature and Language', *ChauR*, 17 (1982–3). 197–220.

14 Alain of Lille, *The Plaint of Nature*, translated by J. J. Sheridan (Toronto, 1980). See Winthrop Wetherbee, 'The Theme of Imagination in Medieval Poetry and the Allegorical Figure "Genius"', *M&H*, ns 7 (1976), 45–64.

15 Examinations of Chaucer's treatment of this material include R. W. Frank Jr, *Chaucer and The Legend of Good Women* (Cambridge, Mass., 1972) and Lisa J. Kiser, *Telling Classical Tales: Chaucer and The Legend of Good Women* (Ithaca, 1983).

16 Peter L. Allen, 'Reading Chaucer's Good Women', *ChauR*, 21 (1987), 419–34, goes as far as to say 'we are explicitly warned that these stories may be false, and that as interpreters we are on our own' (p. 422).

17 R. O. Payne, 'Making His Own Myth: the Prologue to Chaucer's *Legend of Good Women*', *ChauR*, 9 (1975), 197–211, sees the G-Prologue as a search for an *ars poetica* (p. 210).

18 W. P. Ker in his introduction to Lord Berners' translation of *Froissart's Chronicles* (London, 1901–3), Vol. 1, p. lxxviii.

19 See Chapter One above.


*Chapter Five: The Knight's Tale*

1 N. R. Havely, *Chaucer's Boccaccio* (Cambridge, 1980).

2 See Howard Schless, 'Transformations: Chaucer's Use of Italian', in Brewer (ed.) 1974, 184–223.

3 Robert A. Pratt, 'The Knight's Tale', in W. F. Bryan & G. Dempster, *Sources and Analogues of Chaucer's Canterbury Tales* (London, 1941), 82–105, amplified in R. A. Pratt, 'Chaucer's Use of the *Teseida*', *PMLA*, 62 (1947), 598–621. A closer examination is P. Boitani, *Chaucer and Boccaccio*, Medium Aevum Monographs, ns 8 (Society for the Study of Medieval Language and Literature, Oxford, 1977).

4 W. C. Curry, *Chaucer and the Medieval Sciences* (New York, 1926) is the starting-point.

5 N. F. Blake, *The Textual Tradition of the Canterbury Tales* (London, 1985), p. 143.

6 Helen Cooper, *The Structure of The Canterbury Tales* (London, 1983), 94–5.

7 Kolve.

8 Also Ecclesiastes 3.18 (quoted in *De Contemptu Mundi*).

9 Elizabeth Salter, *Fourteenth-Century English Poetry* (Oxford, 1983), 153 ff.

10 Robinson, p. 670.

11 See Maurice Keen, *Chivalry* (New Haven, 1984), p. 193.

12 See S. Robertson, 'Elements of Realism in the *Knight's Tale*', *JEGP*, 14 (1915), 226–55. H. M. Cummings, 'The Indebtedness of Chaucer's Works to the Italian Works of Boccaccio', University of Cincinnati Studies, Vol. X, pt. 2 (Cincinnati, 1916), 144–6.

13 R. A. Pratt, 'Chaucer's Use of the *Teseida*'.

14 Robinson, note on lines 1426–43, citing J. L. Lowes, '*The Franklin's Tale*, the *Teseida* and the *Filocolo*', *MP*, 15 (1917–18), p. 692, n.

15 Juliet Vale, *Edward III and Chivalry: Chivalric Society and its Context 1270–1350* (Woodbridge, Suffolk, 1982), p. 142.

16 Maurice Keen, op. cit., p. 191.

17 D. S. Brewer, *Chaucer and his World* (London, 1978), p. 98.

18 Juliet Vale, op. cit., 45–6.

19 Ibid., 64–5.

20 Sumner Ferris, 'Chronicle, chivalric biography and family tradition in fourteenth-century England' in *Chivalric Literature*, edd. Larry D. Benson and John Leyerle (Michigan, 1980), 25–38.

21 R. F. Green, *Poets and Princepleasers* (Toronto, 1980), Chapter 5.

22 D. S. Brewer, *Chaucer and his World*, 125–8.

23 For example, the similarity between Arcite's accident and the subsequent mourning to the account in Higden's *Polychronicon* of the death of the 17-year old Earl of Pembroke as the result of a jousting accident: *Polychronicon Ranulphi Higden*, ed. J. R. Lumby (London, 1886), 9, 219–20, quoted in E. Rickert, *Chaucer's World* (New York, 1948), p. 216, and G. R. Crampton, *The Condition of Creatures* (New Haven, 1974), p. 82. Again, a parallel has been seen between Froissart's description of the capture of the King of France by the Black Prince at Poitiers in 1358 and his subsequent imprisonment at Windsor and Theseus' treatment of Palamon and Arcite: see Kolve, 100–1.

24 Paul Strohm, 'Chaucer's Audience', in *Literature and History*, 5(1977), 26–41.

25 D. A. Pearsall, *Old English and Middle English Poetry* (London, 1977), 191–7.

26 Green, op. cit., p. 111.

27 Vale, op. cit.

28 Ibid., 73–4.

29 Thomas Walsingham, *Historia Anglicana*, ed. H. T. Riley, Rolls Series (London, 1863–4), Vol. II, 156, quoted by Patricia J. Eberle, 'The Politics of Courtly Style at the Court of Richard II', in *The Spirit of the Court*, edd. Glyn S. Burgess & Robert A. Taylor (Cambridge, 1985), 168–78.

30 V. J. Scattergood, 'Literary Culture at the Court of Richard II', in *English Court Culture in the Later Middle Ages*, edd. V. J. Scattergood and J. W. Sherborne (London, 1983), 29–43.

31 In V. J. Scattergood (ed.), *The Works of Sir John Clanvowe* (Cambridge, 1975).

32 See Robinson: note on lines 2155–86, and W. C. Curry, op. cit., 130 ff.

33 A. C. Spearing (ed.), Chaucer, *The Knight's Tale* (Cambridge, 1966), p. 178.

34 D. Everett, *Essays on Middle English Literature* (Oxford, 1955), p. 141.

35 Chaucer had already used this grove as the place where the lists were erected, of course—a change from *Il Teseida*.

36 As Spearing points out: *The Knight's Tale*, p. 189.

37 Represented, for instance, by C. F. Muscatine, 'Form, Texture and Meaning in Chaucer's *Knight's Tale*', *PMLA*, 65 (1950), 911–29 and such essays as W. Frost, 'An Interpretation of Chaucer's *Knight's Tale*', *RES*, 25 (1949), 290–304, reprinted in R. J. Schoeck & J. Taylor (edd.), *Chaucer Criticism: The Canterbury Tales* (Notre Dame, Indiana, 1960).

38 Richard Neuse, 'The Knight: The First Mover in Chaucer's Human Comedy', *U. of Toronto Quarterly*, 31 (1961–2), 299–315.

39 E.g. H. J. Webb, 'A Reinterpretation of Chaucer's Theseus', *RES*, 23 (1947), 289–96.

40 John Reidy, 'The Education of Chaucer's Duke Theseus', in *The Epic in Medieval Society: Aesthetic and Moral Values*, ed. Harald Scholler (Tübingen, 1977), 391–408 (quotations from p. 404).

41 Reidy depends on Maurice Keen, *The Laws of War in the Late Middle Ages* (London, 1965). Keen himself reacts to Terry Jones, *Chaucer's Knight, the Portrait of a Medieval Mercenary* (London, 1980), in his 'Chaucer's Knight, the English Aristocracy and the Crusade', in *English Court Culture in the Later Middle Ages*, 45–61. Chaucer is seen as celebrating knighthood and warfare also by Elizabeth Porter, 'Chaucer's Knight, the Alliterative *Morte Arthure*, and the Medieval Laws of War: A Reconsideration', *Nottingham Medieval Studies*, 27 (1983), 56–78.

42 A. J. Minnis, *Chaucer and Pagan Antiquity* (Cambridge, 1982): quotations from pp. 121, 128, 131.

43 Pearsall sees them as elemental beings (Pearsall, p. 130). Robertson calls them 'statements of principle': D. W. Robertson Jr, *A Preface to Chaucer: Studies in Medieval Perspectives* (Princeton, 1962), p. 270.

44 W. C. Curry, op. cit., 119–63.

45 D. Brooks & A. Fowler, 'The Meaning of Chaucer's *Knight's Tale*', *MAe*, 39 (1970), 123–46.

46 Kolve, p. 86.

47 Ibid., p. 105.

48 Kean, Vol. 2.

49 Minnis, op. cit., 140–1.

50 Elizabeth Salter, *Chaucer's The Knight's Tale and The Clerk's Tale* (London, 1962) and *Fourteenth-Century English Poetry*.

51 Pearsall, 115–38.

52 Ibid., p. 125.

*Chapter Six: Troilus and Criseyde*

1 N. R. Havely, *Chaucer's Boccaccio* (Cambridge, 1980), p. 25.

2 David Wallace, *Chaucer and the Early Writings of Boccaccio* (Woodbridge, Suffolk, 1985), Chapter 5.

3 It is surprising to me that more interest has not been shown in this aspect of the poem: Alice R. Kaminsky, *Chaucer's Troilus and Criseyde and the Critics* (Ohio, 1980), says that 'Too much is made of the lyrics and the narrative commentary at the expense of the characterization' (p. 96), but my impression is that it is the other way round.

4 Payne, 184–5. ('Few readers would miss the ten lyrics if they were omitted', says Kaminsky, op. cit., p. 95; perhaps she should avoid poetry.)

5 See J. I. Wimsatt, 'Guillaume de Machaut and Chaucer's *Troilus and Criseyde*' *MAe*, 45 (1976), 277–93.

6 Payne, p. 186.

7 William Godwin, *Life of Chaucer* (1803), quoted in Derek Brewer (ed.), *Chaucer: The Critical Heritage*, Vol. 1, 1385–1837 (London, 1978), p. 241.

8 Compare C. S. Lewis, 'What Chaucer Really Did to "Il Filostrato"', *Essays and Studies*, 17 (1932), 56–75, reprinted in *Chaucer's "Troilus": Essays in Criticism*, ed. Stephen A. Barney (London, 1980), 37–54, and Barry Windeatt, 'Chaucer and the Filostrato', in Piero Boitani (ed.), *Chaucer and the Italian Trecento* (Cambridge, 1983), 163–83.

9 B. A. Windeatt (ed.), Geoffrey Chaucer, *Troilus and Criseyde* (London, 1984), p. 87. Quotations throughout this chapter are from this edition, hereafter identified simply as Windeatt.

10 Windeatt, p. 115.

11 My translation.

12 Windeatt, p. 119.

13 *CT*, V, 1356. Bondage in *Troilus and Criseyde* is discussed in Stephen A. Barney, 'Troilus Bound', *Speculum*, 47 (1972), 445–58.

14 Havely, op. cit., p. 34.

15 In Books II and IV of *Troilus and Criseyde* 65 per cent and 70 per cent of the lines respectively are in direct speech, compared to about 52 per cent in the other three books.

16 Pandarus has 687.5 lines (39 per cent of Book II), to Criseyde's 49 speeches occupying 287.5 lines (16.4 per cent of the book) and Troilus' 11 speeches occupying 43 lines (2.4 per cent of the book). In Book IV fewer separate speeches account for 1194 lines of direct speech (out of 1701 lines), and by then it is Pandarus who has least to say and Troilus most. The main characters are nearly equal in Book III: Pandarus has 40 speeches and 365 lines (20.1 per cent of the book), Troilus 27 speeches and 307.5 lines (16.9 per cent) and Criseyde 35 speeches and 264.5 lines (14.5 per cent).

17 Jill Mann interestingly suggests that Chaucer 'wanted the comparison of the two scenes to reveal human efforts as negligible when weighed against the role of chance': 'Chance and Destiny in *Troilus and Criseyde* and the *Knight's Tale*', in Boitani and Mann, 75–92.

18 The fusion of motifs from several poems indicates Chaucer's interest in the general style rather than the particular substance: see Wimsatt, *MAe*, 45.

19 Not that this is as simple as I make it sound. The passage may be read as ironic: e.g. 'To give the hymn to Troilus is to reveal how misdirected is his love, since the very terms of the hymn make clear that the "holy bond of love" must exclude a love that had become an end in itself': I. L. Gordon, *The Double Sorrow of Troilus* (Oxford, 1970), p. 36.

20 See Alan T. Gaylord, 'Gentilesse in Chaucer's *Troilus*', *SP*, 61 (1964), 19–34, and Gordon, op. cit., 115–7.

21 Winthrop Wetherbee describes 'the steady descent from vision into materiality' in this part of Book III and explores the narrator's self-doubt and the effect of anti-climax in 'The Descent from Bliss: *Troilus* III, 1310–1582', in *Chaucer's "Troilus": Essays in Criticism*, 297–317.

22 Troilus has 466.5 lines (27 per cent of Book IV) and Criseyde 421.5 lines (25 per cent).

23 Mark Lambert suggests that the scene represents 'a ghost ending' or an 'averted ending' and that 'this pseudo-death scene' is 'a moment of major transition': 'Telling the story in *Troilus and Criseyde*', in Boitani and Mann, 59–73—quotes from 68–70.

24 Winthrop Wetherbee describes the effect of the passage as that of Troilus 'wilfully declining into the role of the conventional abandoned lover': *Chaucer and the Poets: An Essay on Troilus and Criseyde* (Ithaca, 1984), p. 209.

25 The passage has often been discussed, of course: it is analysed in the context of Chaucer's interest in 'the fatalistic pagan' and his use of Trevet's commentary on Boethius by A. J. Minnis, *Chaucer and Pagan Antiquity* (Cambridge, 1982), 95 ff.

26 G. T. Shepherd, 'Religion and Philosophy in Chaucer', in Brewer (ed) 1974, 262–89.

27 Susan Schibanoff, 'Prudence and Artificial Memory in Chaucer's *Troilus*', *ELH*, 42 (1975), 507–17.

28 Windeatt, p. 505.

29 Norman Davis, 'The "Litera Troili" and English Letters', *RES*, ns. 16 (1965), 233–44, reprinted in *Chaucer's Troilus: Essays in Criticism*, 145–58. See also John McKinnell, 'Letters as a type of the formal level in *Troilus and Criseyde*', in *Essays on Troilus and Criseyde*, ed. Mary Salu (Cambridge, 1979), 73–89.

30 Among recent explorations of the 'lack of definitive authority' in this much discussed ending see Monica McAlpine, *The Genre of Troilus and Criseyde* (Ithaca, 1978), 177–81, 235–46, and David Aers, *Chaucer, Langland and the Creative Imagination* (London, 1980), 138–42.

*Chapter Seven: The Franklin's Tale*

1 See Germaine Dempster & J. S. P. Tatlock, 'The Franklin's Tale', in W. F. Bryan & G. Dempster, *Sources and Analogues of Chaucer's Canterbury Tales* (London, 1941), 377–97.

2 Nicolas Jacobs, review of Gerald Morgan (ed.), *The Franklin's Tale* (London, 1980), *MAe*, 52 (1983), 126–31.

3 Morgan, op. cit., p. 87.

4 Bryan & Dempster, op. cit., 383–5.

5 Geoffrey of Monmouth, *The History of the Kings of Britain*, translated by Lewis Thorpe (London, 1969), p. 102.

6 Ibid., p. 163.

7 Ibid., p. 158.

8 Ibid., 182–3.

9 Boccaccio's *Decameron*, translated by Richard Aldington (London, 1955), p. 261.

10 The nature of oaths and vows in the tale is discussed, from a different point of view, by Gerald Morgan, 'Boccaccio's *Filocolo* and the Moral Argument of *The Franklin's Tale*', *ChauR*, 20 (1986), 285–306.

11 E.g. Pearsall, p. 154, describes it as Chaucer's 'most brilliant single stroke in his rehandling of the narrative'.

12 D. S. Brewer in several places: e.g. *Chaucer*, 3rd edition (London, 1973), p. 179 and *English Gothic Literature* (London, 1983), p. 122.

13 These lines are given to Aurelius in most mss. but the view that 1541–4 (and 1000–6 and 1493–8) are late additions which have been misplaced and should be given to the narrator is very plausible. See J. M. Manly & E. Rickert, *The Text of the Canterbury Tales* (Chicago, 1940), Vol. II, 314. Also R. Woolf, 'Moral Chaucer and Kindly Gower', in *J. R. R. Tolkien, Scholar and Storyteller*, edd. M. Salu and R. T. Farrell (Ithaca, 1979), 221–45, especially 241–2.

14 R. Woolf, op. cit., p. 240, points out that promises to commit a sinful act were not binding.

15 As is recognised with particular point by Gerald Morgan in his edition of the tale and elsewhere (see Notes 2 and 9 above) and by M. W. Bloomfield, 'The Franklin's Tale: A Story of Unanswered Questions', in *Acts of Interpretation: the Text in its Contexts 700–1600*, edd. M. J. Carruthers and E. D. Kirk (Norman, Oklahoma, 1982, 189–98.

16 See Phyllis Hodgson (ed.), *The Franklin's Tale* (London, 1960), 84–5.

17 Gerald Morgan (ed.), *The Franklin's Tale*, 93–4.

18 James Sledd, 'Dorigen's Complaint', *MP*, 45 (1947–8), 36–45 (quotation from p. 42).

19 Gerald Morgan, 'A Defence of Dorigen's Complaint', *MAe*, 46 (1977), 77–97, and *The Franklin's Tale*, 33–44.

20 Geoffrey of Monmouth, translated Thorpe, 135–8.

21 See R. P. Miller (ed.), *Chaucer: Sources and Backgrounds* (New York, 1977), 373–84.

22 Terms used in *Cleanness*, 1576–9. M. Andrew and R. Waldron (edd.), *The Poems of the Pearl Manuscript* (London, 1978), p. 175.

23 See John B. Beston, 'How Much Was Known of the Breton Lai in Fourteenth-Century England?', in *The Learned and the Lewed*, ed. L. D. Benson (Cambridge, Mass., 1974), 319–36, especially 329–30.

*Chapter Eight: Beyond Complaint*

1 D. S. Brewer, 'Towards a Chaucerian Poetic', *PBA*, 60 (1974), 219–52, reprinted in D. S. Brewer, *Chaucer: The Poet as Storyteller* (London, 1984), 54–79 (quotations from p. 58).

2 Ibid., 66–7.

3 David Wallace, 'Chaucer and Boccaccio's Early Writings', in Piero Boitani (ed.), *Chaucer and the Italian Trecento* (Cambridge, 1983), 141–62. (Quotation from p. 148.)

4 Barry Windeatt, 'Chaucer and the *Filostrato*', in *Chaucer and the Italian Trecento*, 163–83 (quotation from p. 170).

5 Ibid., p. 173.

6 Piero Boitani, 'Style, Iconography and Narrative: the Lesson of the *Teseida*', in *Chaucer and the Italian Trecento*, 185–99 (quotation from p. 197).

7 Pearsall, p. 113.

8 Robert M. Jordan, 'The Non-Dramatic Disunity of the *Merchant's Tale*', *PMLA*, 78 (1963), 293–9, reprinted in Robert J. Blanch (ed.), *Geoffrey Chaucer: Merchant's Tale* (Columbus, Ohio, 1970), 81–93.

9 B. H. Smith, *Poetic Closure: A Study of How Poems End* (Chicago,1968), p. 4.

10 E. R. Curtius, *European Literature and the Latin Middle Ages*, translated W. R. Trask (Original German 1948, translation Princeton, 1953, 1967), Chapter 5, Section 5, 'Topics of the Conclusion'.

11 Geoffrey of Vinsauf, *Documentum de Modo et Arte Dictandi et Versificandi*, translated Roger P. Parr (Milwaukee, Wisconsin, 1968), 95–6.

12 *Poetria Nova*, 43–8, in E. Faral, *Les arts poétiques du XIIe et du XIIIe siècle* (Paris, 1924), 197–262, translated by Ernest Gallo, *The Poetria Nova and its Sources in Early Rhetorical Doctrine* (The Hague, 1971).

13 Peter Dronke, 'Medieval Rhetoric', p. 327, in *Literature and Western Civilization: The Medieval World*, edd. David Daiches and Anthony Thorlby (London, 1973), 315–45.

14 Ernest Gallo, 'The *Poetria Nova* of Geoffrey de Vinsauf', in *Medieval Eloquence: Studies in the Theory and Practice of Medieval Rhetoric*, ed. J. J. Murphy (Berkeley, 1978), 68–84 (quotation from p. 84).

15 This question is interestingly explored by B. A. Windeatt 'Literary Structures in Chaucer', in Boitani and Mann, 195–212.

16 Michael Holahan, ' "Swich fyn . . . Swich fyn": Senses of Ending in Chaucer and Spenser', in *Classical, Medieval, Renaissance and Modern: Spenser 1977*, 12th Conference on Medieval Studies (Kalamazoo, Michigan, 1977), 116–31 (quotations from 117 and 126).

17 Tony Millns, 'Chaucer's Suspended Judgments', *EC*, 27 (1977), 1–19.

18 Gale C. Schricker, 'On the Relation of Fact and Fiction in Chaucer's Poetic Endings', *PQ*, 60 (1981), 13–27.

19 Georgia Ronan Crampton, 'Other Senses of Ending', in *Classical, Medieval, Renaissance and Modern: Spenser 1977*, 132–42 (quotation from p. 141).

# Bibliography

*Editions of Chaucer*

Hodgson, Phyllis, (ed.), Chaucer, *The Franklin's Tale* (London, 1960)
Morgan, Gerald, (ed.), Chaucer, *The Franklin's Tale* (London, 1980)
Phillips, Helen, (ed.), Chaucer, *The Book of the Duchess* (Durham & St Andrews Medieval Texts, no. 3, 1982)
Reeves, James, (ed.), *Chaucer: Lyric and Allegory* (London, 1970)
Robinson, F. N., (ed.), *The Works of Geoffrey Chaucer*, 2nd edition (London, 1957)
Spearing, A. C., (ed.), Chaucer, *The Knight's Tale* (Cambridge, 1966)
Windeatt, B. A., (ed.), Geoffrey Chaucer, *Troilus and Criseyde* (London, 1984)


*Secondary Sources*

Aers, David, *Chaucer, Langland and the Creative Imagination* (London, 1980)
Aers, David, (ed.), *Medieval Literature: Criticism, Ideology and History* (Brighton, 1986)
Alain, de Lille, *De Planctu Naturae*, translated J. J. Sheridan (Toronto, 1980)
Allen, Peter L., 'Reading Chaucer's Good Women', *ChauR*, 21 (1987), 419–34
Allen, J. B., *The Friar as Critic* (Nashville, 1971)
Baldwin, C. S., *Medieval Rhetoric and Poetic* (Gloucester, Mass., 1959)
Barney, Stephen A., 'Troilus Bound', *Speculum*, 47 (1972), 445–58
Barney, Stephen A., (ed.), *Chaucer's 'Troilus': Essays in Criticism* (London, 1980)
Bennett, J. A. W., *The Parlement of Foules: An Interpretation* (Oxford, 1957)
Bennett, J. A. W., *Chaucer's Book of Fame* (Oxford, 1969)
Beston, John B., 'How Much was Known of the Breton Lai in Fourteenth-Century England?', in *The Learned and the Lewed*, ed. L. D. Benson (Cambridge, Mass., 1974), 319–36
Birney, Earle, *Essays on Chaucerian Irony*, ed. Beryl Rowland (Toronto, 1985)
Bishop, Ian, *Chaucer's Troilus and Criseyde: A Critical Study* (Bristol, 1981)
Blake, K. A., 'Order and the Noble Life in Chaucer's *Knight's Tale*', *MLQ* 24 (1973), 3–19

Blake, N. F., *The Textual Tradition of the Canterbury Tales* (London, 1985)

Bloomfield, M. W., '*The Franklin's Tale*: A Story of Unanswered Questions', in *Acts of Interpretation: the Text in its Contexts 700–1600*, edd. M. J. Carruthers & E. D. Kirk (Norman, Oklahoma, 1982), 189–98

Boitani, Piero, *Chaucer and Boccaccio*, Medium Aevum Monographs, new series VIII (Oxford, 1977)

Boitani, Piero, *English Medieval Narrative in the 13th and 14th Centuries*, translated J. Krakover Hall (Cambridge, 1982)

Boitani, Piero, 'Chaucer's Labyrinth: Fourteenth-Century Literature and Language', *ChauR*, 17 (1982–3), 197–220

Boitani, Piero, (ed.), *Chaucer and the Italian Trecento* (Cambridge, 1983)

Boitani, Piero and Torti, Anna, (edd.), *Literature in Fourteenth-Century England* (Cambridge, 1983)

Boitani, Piero, *Chaucer and the Imaginary World of Fame* (Cambridge, 1984)

Boitani, Piero and Mann, Jill, (edd.), *The Cambridge Chaucer Companion* (Cambridge, 1986)

Braddy, Haldeen, *Chaucer and the French Poet Graunson* (Louisiana, 1947)

Brewer, D. S., *Chaucer*, 3rd edition (London, 1973)

Brewer, Derek, (ed.), *Writers and Their Background: Geoffrey Chaucer* (London, 1974)

Brewer, D. S., 'Towards a Chaucerian Poetic', *PBA*, 60 (1974), 219–52, reprinted in *The Poet as Storyteller* (London, 1984), 54–79

Brewer, D. S., *Chaucer and his World* (London, 1978)

Brewer, D. S., (ed.), *Chaucer: The Critical Heritage* (London, 1978)

Brewer, D. S., *Tradition and Innovation in Chaucer* (London, 1982)

Brewer, D. S., *English Gothic Literature* (London, 1983)

Brewer, D. S., *Chaucer: The Poet as Storyteller* (London, 1984)

Brooks, D. & Fowler, A., 'The Meaning of Chaucer's *Knight's Tale*', *MAe*, 39 (1970), 123–46

Brusendorff, A., *The Chaucer Tradition* (London/Copenhagen, 1925)

Bryan, W. F. & Dempster, G., *Sources and Analogues of Chaucer's Canterbury Tales* (London, 1941)

Burnley, J. D., *Chaucer's Language and the Philosophers' Tradition* (Cambridge, 1979)

Burnley, J. D., *A Guide to Chaucer's Language* (London, 1983)

Burrow, J. A., *Medieval Writers and their Work* (Oxford, 1982)

Burrow, J. A., 'Chaucer's *Knight's Tale* and the Three Ages of Man', in *Essays on Medieval Literature* (Oxford, 1984), 27–48

Calin, W., *A Poet at the Fountain: Essays on the Narrative Verse of Guillaume de Machaut* (Kentucky, 1974)

Carruthers, Mary J., 'The Gentilesse of Chaucer's Franklin', *Criticism*, 23 (1981), 283–300

Cherniss, Michael D., 'Chaucer's *Anelida and Arcite*: Some Conjectures', *ChauR*, 5 (1970–71), 9–21

Clemen, Wolfgang, *Chaucer's Early Poetry* (London, 1963)

Clogan, Paul M., 'The Textual Reliability of Chaucer's Lyrics: *A Complaint to his Lady*', *M&H*, ns 5 (1974), 183–9

Coleman, Janet, *English Literature in History 1350–1400: Medieval Readers and Writers* (London, 1981)

Cooper, Helen, *The Structure of The Canterbury Tales* (London, 1983)

Cosman, M. P. & Chandler, Bruce, (edd.), *Machaut's World: Science and Art in the Fourteenth Century* (New York, 1978)

Crabbe, Anna, 'Literary Design in the *De Consolatione Philosophiae*, in *Boethius, His Life, Thought and Influence*, ed. Margaret Gibson (Oxford, 1981), 237–74

Crampton, G. R., *The Condition of Creatures* (New Haven/London, 1974)

Crampton, G. R., 'Other Senses of Ending', in *Classical, Medieval, Renaissance and Modern: Spenser 1977*, 12th Conference on Medieval Studies, (Kalamazoo, Michigan, 1977)

Cross, J. E., 'The Old Swedish *Trohetsvisan* and Chaucer's *Lak of Stedfastnesse*: A Study in Medieval Genre', *Saga-Book*, 16 (1965), 283–314

Cummings, H. M., 'The Indebtedness of Chaucer's Works to the Italian Works of Boccaccio', *University of Cincinnati Studies*, Vol. X, pt 2 (Cincinnati, 1916)

Curry, W. C., *Chaucer and the Medieval Sciences* (New York, 1926)

Curtius, E. R., *European Literature and the Latin Middle Ages*, translated W. Trask (Princeton, 1953)

David, Alfred, *The Strumpet Muse: Art and Morals in Chaucer's Poetry* (Bloomington, Indiana/London, 1976)

Davis, Norman, 'The "Litera Troili" and English Letters', *RES*, ns 16 (1965), 233–44

Dean, Nancy, 'Chaucer's Complaint: A Genre Descended from the *Heroides*', *CL*, 19 (1967), 1–27

Delany, Sheila, *Chaucer's House of Fame and the Poetics of Skeptical Fideism* (Chicago, 1972)

Dronke, Peter, 'Medieval Rhetoric' in *Literature and Western Civilization: The Medieval World*, edd. David Daiches and Anthony Thorlby (London, 1973), 315–45

Eberle, Patricia J., 'The Politics of Courtly Style at the Court of Richard II', in *The Spirit of the Court*, edd. Glyn S. Burgess and Robert A. Taylor (Cambridge, 1985), 168–78

Everett, D., *Essays on Middle English Literature* (Oxford, 1955)

Ferris, Sumner, 'Chronicle, Chivalric Biography and Family Tradition in Fourteenth-Century England', in *Chivalric Literature*, edd. Larry D. Benson and John Leyerle (Michigan, 1980), 25–38

Ferster, Judith, *Chaucer on Interpretation* (Cambridge, 1985)

Fichte, Joerg O., *Chaucer's 'Art Poetical': A Study in Chaucerian Poetics* (Tübingen, 1980)

Frank Jr, R. W., *Chaucer and The Legend of Good Women* (Cambridge, Mass., 1972)

Frost, W., 'An Interpretation of Chaucer's *Knight's Tale*', *RES*, 25 (1949), 290–304

Fyler, John M., *Chaucer and Ovid* (New Haven/London, 1979)

Gallo, Ernest, *The Poetria Nova and its Sources in Early Rhetorical Doctrine* (The Hague/Paris, 1971)

Gallo, Ernest, 'The *Poetria Nova* of Geoffrey de Vinsauf', in *Medieval Eloquence*, ed. J. J. Murphy (Berkeley, 1978), 68–84

Gaylord, Alan T., 'Gentilesse in Chaucer's *Troilus*', *SP*, 61 (1964), 19–34

Gaylord, Alan T., 'The Role of Saturn in the *Knight's Tale*', *ChauR*, 8 (1974), 171–90

Geoffrey, de Vinsauf, *Documentum de Modo et Arte Dictandi et Versificandi*, translated R. P. Parr (Milwaukee, Wisconsin, 1968)

Geoffrey of Monmouth, *The History of the Kings of Britain*, translated Lewis Thorpe (London, 1969)

Golding, M. R., 'The Importance of Keeping "Trouthe" in *The Franklin's Tale*', *MAe*, 39 (1970), 306–12

Goodman, Jennifer R., 'Chaucer's *Squire's Tale* and the Rise of Chivalry', *Studies in the Age of Chaucer*, 5 (1983), 127–36

Gordon, I. L., *The Double Sorrow of Troilus* (Oxford, 1970)

Gray, Douglas, 'Chaucer and "Pite"', in *J. R. R. Tolkien, Scholar and Storyteller*, edd. M. Salu and R. T. Farrell (Ithaca/London, 1979), 173–203

Green, Richard Firth, *Poets and Princepleasers: Literature and the English Court in the Late Middle Ages* (Toronto, 1980)

Havely, N. R., *Chaucer's Boccaccio* (Cambridge, 1980)

Hieatt, A. Kent, *Chaucer, Spenser, Milton: Mythopoeic Continuities and Transformations* (Montreal, 1975)

Hieatt, A. Kent, '*The Canterbury Tales* in The Faerie Queene', in *Spenser and the Middle Ages 1976*, 11th Conference on Medieval Studies (Kalamazoo, Michigan, 1976)

Hieatt, C. B., 'Une Autre Forme: Guillaume de Machaut and the Dream Vision Form', *ChauR*, 14 (1979–80), 97–115

Holahan, Michael, '"Swich fyn . . . swich fyn": Senses of Ending in Chaucer and Spenser', in *Classical, Medieval, Renaissance and Modern: Spenser 1977*, 12th Conference on Medieval Studies (Kalamazoo, Michigan, 1977), 116–31

Jefferson, B. L., *Chaucer and the Consolation of Philosophy of Boethius* (Princeton, 1917)

Jordan, Robert, M., 'The Non-Dramatic Disunity of the *Merchant's Tale*, *PMLA*, 78 (1963), 293–9

Jordan, Robert M., *Chaucer and the Shape of Creation: the Aesthetic Possibilities of Inorganic Structure* (Cambridge, Mass., 1967)

Kaminsky, Alice R., *Chaucer's Troilus and Criseyde and the Critics* (Ohio, 1980)

Kane, George, 'Chaucer, Love Poetry and Romantic Love', in *Acts of Interpretation: the Text in its Contexts 700–1600*, edd. M. J. Carruthers and E. D. Kirk (Norman, Oklahoma, 1982), 237–55

Kean, P. M., *Chaucer and the Making of English Poetry*, 2 vols. (London, 1972)

Keen, Maurice, *The Laws of War in the Late Middle Ages* (London, 1965)

Keen, Maurice, 'Chaucer's Knight, the English Aristocracy and the Crusade', in *English Court Culture in the Later Middle Ages*, edd. V. J. Scattergood and J. W. Sherborne (London, 1983)

Keen, Maurice, *Chivalry* (New Haven, 1984)

Kelly, Douglas, *Medieval Imagination* (Madison, Wisconsin, 1978)

Kiser, Lisa J., *Telling Classical Tales: Chaucer and the Legend of Good Women* (Ithaca, 1983)

Knight, Stephen, 'Rhetoric and Poetry in *The Franklin's Tale*', *ChauR*, 4 (1969–70), 14–30

Kolve, V. A., 'Chaucer and the Visual Arts' in Brewer (ed) 1974

Kolve, V. A., *Chaucer and the Imagery of Narrative: the First Five Canterbury Tales* (London, 1984)

Koonce, B. G., *Chaucer and the Tradition of Fame* (Princeton, 1966)

Lambert, Mark, 'Telling the Story in *Troilus and Criseyde*', in Boitani and Mann, 59–73

Larson, Charles, '*The Squire's Tale*: Chaucer's Evolution from the Dream Vision', *Revue des Langues Vivantes*, 43 (1977), 598–607

Lawton, David, *Chaucer's Narrators* (Cambridge, 1985)

Lenaghan, R. T., 'The Clerk of Venus: Chaucer and Medieval Romance, in *The Learned and the Lewed*, ed. L. D. Benson (Cambridge, Mass., 1974), 31–43

Lewis, C. S., 'What Chaucer Really Did to *Il Filostrato*', *Essays and Studies*, 17 (1932), 56–75

Manly, J. M. and Rickert, E., *The Text of the Canterbury Tales* (Chicago, 1940)

Mann, Jill, *Chaucer and Medieval Estates Satire: the Literature of Social Classes and the General Prologue to the Canterbury Tales* (Cambridge, 1973)

Mann, Jill, 'Chance and Destiny in *Troilus and Criseyde* and *The Knight's Tale*', in Boitani and Mann, 75–92

Mathewson, E. J., 'The Illusion of Morality in *The Franklin's Tale*', *MAe*, 52(1983), 27–37

McAlindon, T., 'Cosmology, Contrariety and *The Knight's Tale*', *MAe*, 55 (1986), 41–57

McAlpine, Monica E., *The Genre of Troilus and Criseyde* (Ithaca, 1978)

McCall, John P., *Chaucer among the Gods: the Poetics of Classical Myth* (Pennsylvania, 1979)

Mehl, Dieter, *Geoffrey Chaucer: an Introduction to his Narrative Poetry* (Cambridge, 1986)

Metlitzki, Dorothee, *The Matter of Araby in Medieval England* (New Haven, 1977)

Middleton, Anne, 'The Clerk and his Tale: Some Literary Contexts', *Studies in the Age of Chaucer*, 2 (1980), 121–50

Middleton, Anne, 'Chaucer's "New Men" and the Good of Literature in *The Canterbury Tales*', in *Literature and Society*, Selected Papers from the English Institute, 1978, ns 3, ed. Edward W. Said (Baltimore/London, 1980), 15–56

Miller, Paul, 'John Gower, Satiric Poet', in *Gower's Confessio Amantis: Responses and Reassessments*, ed. A. J. Minnis (Cambridge, 1983), 79–105

Miller Robert P., *Chaucer: Sources and Backgrounds* (New York, 1977)

Millns, Tony, 'Chaucer's Suspended Judgments', *EC*, 27 (1977), 1–19

Minnis, A. J., 'Chaucer and Comparative Literary Theory', in *New Perspectives in Chaucer Criticism*, ed. Donald M. Rose (Norman, Oklahoma, 1981), 53–69

Minnis, A. J., *Chaucer and Pagan Antiquity* (Cambridge, 1982)

Minnis, A. J., *Medieval Theory of Authorship: Scholastic Literary Attitudes in the Later Middle Ages* (London, 1984)

Mogan, J. J., *Chaucer and the Theme of Mutability* (The Hague/Paris, 1970)

Morgan, Gerald, 'A Defence of Dorigen's Complaint', *MAe*, 46 (1977), 77–97

Morgan, Gerald, 'Boccaccio's *Filocolo* and the Moral Argument of *The Franklin's Tale*', *ChauR*, 20 (1986), 285–306

Moseley, C. W. R. D., *Geoffrey Chaucer, The Knight's Tale* (Harmondsworth, 1987)

Murphy, J. J., *Rhetoric in the Middle Ages* (Berkeley/London, 1974)

Murphy, J. J., (ed.), *Medieval Eloquence: Studies in the Theory and Practice of Medieval Rhetoric* (Berkeley, 1978)

Muscatine, C. F., 'Form, Texture and Meaning in Chaucer's *Knight's Tale*', *PMLA*, 65 (1950), 911–29

Neuse, Richard, 'the Knight: The First Mover in Chaucer's Human Comedy', *University of Toronto Quarterly*, 31 (1961–2), 299–315

Nolan Jr, Charles J., 'Structural Sophistication in "The Complaint unto Pity"', *ChauR*, 13 (1978–9), 363–72

Norton-Smith, J., 'Chaucer's *Etas Prima*', *MAe*, 32 (1963), 117–24

Norton-Smith, J., *Geoffrey Chaucer* (London, 1974)

Norton-Smith, J., 'Chaucer's Boethius and *Fortune*', *Reading Medieval Studies* (1976)

Norton-Smith, J., 'Chaucer's *Anelida and Arcite*', in *Medieval Studies for J. A. W. Bennett*, ed. P. L. Heyworth (Oxford, 1981), 81–99

Olson, G., 'Deschamps' *Art de Dictier* and Chaucer's Literary Environment', *Speculum*, 48 (1973), 714–23

Owen Jr, Charles A., 'The Problem of Free Will in Chaucer's Narratives', *PQ*, 46 (1967), 433–56

Payne, F. Anne, *Chaucer and Menippean Satire* (Madison, Wisconsin, 1981)

Payne, Robert O., *The Key of Remembrance: A Study of Chaucer's Poetics* (New Haven/London, 1963)

Payne, Robert O., 'Making His Own Myth: the Prologue to Chaucer's *Legend of Good Women*', *ChauR*, 9 (1975), 197–211

Payne, Robert O., 'Chaucer's Realization of Himself as Rhetor', in *Medieval Eloquence*, ed. J. J. Murphy (Berkeley, 1978), 270–87

Pearsall, D. A., *Old English and Middle English Poetry* (London, 1977)

Pearsall, Derek, *The Canterbury Tales* (London, 1985)

Peck, Russell A., *Chaucer's Lyrics and Anelida and Arcite: An Annotated Bibliography 1900–80*, The Chaucer Bibliographies (Toronto, 1983)

Pelen, M. M., 'Machaut's Court of Love Narratives and Chaucer's *Book of the Duchess*', *ChauR*, 11 (1976–7), 128–55

Peter, John, *Complaint and Satire in Early English Literature* (Oxford, 1956)

Piaget, A., 'Oton de Grandson, sa vie et ses poésies', *Mémoires et Documents publiés par la Société d'Histoire de la Suisse Romande*, 3rd series, Vol. 1 (Lausanne, 1941)

Pittock, M., 'Chaucer: "The Complaint unto Pity"', *Criticism*, 1 (1959), 160–8

Porter, Elizabeth, 'Chaucer's Knight, the Alliterative *Morte Arthure*, and the Medieval Laws of War: A Reconsideration', *Nottingham Medieval Studies*, 27 (1983), 56–78

Pratt, Robert A., 'Chaucer's Use of the *Teseida*', *PMLA*, 62 (1947), 598–621

Reidy, John, 'The Education of Chaucer's Duke Theseus', in *The Epic in Medieval Society: Aesthetic and Moral Values*, ed. Harald Scholler (Tübingen, 1977), 391–408

Robertson, S., 'Elements of Realism in the *Knight's Tale*', *JEGP*, 14 (1915), 226–55

Rowland, Beryl, (ed.), *Companion to Chaucer Studies* (Oxford, 1979)

Ruggiers, Paul G., *The Art of the Canterbury Tales* (Madison/London, 1967)

Salter, Elizabeth, *Chaucer: The Knight's Tale and The Clerk's Tale* (London, 1962)

Salter, Elizabeth, *Fourteenth-Century English Poetry* (Oxford, 1983)

Salu, Mary, (ed.), *Essays on Troilus and Criseyde* (Cambridge, 1979)

Saul, Nigel, 'The Social Status of Chaucer's Franklin: A Reconsideration', *MAe*, 52 (1983), 10–26

Scattergood, V. J., (ed.), *The Works of Sir John Clanvowe* (Cambridge, 1975)

Scattergood, V. J., 'Chaucer's curial satire: the *Ballade de bon conseyl*', *Hermathena*, 133 (1982), 29–45

Scattergood, V. J., 'Literary Culture at the Court of Richard II', in *English Court Culture in the Later Middle Ages*, edd. V. J. Scattergood and J. W. Sherborne (London, 1983)

Scattergood, V. J., 'Social and Political Issues in Chaucer: An Approach to *Lak of Stedfastnesse*', *ChauR*, 21 (1987), 469–75

Schaar, Claes, *Some Types of Narrative in Chaucer's Poetry*, Lund Studies in English, 25 (Lund, 1954)

Schibanoff, Susan, 'Prudence and Artificial Memory in Chaucer's *Troilus*', *ELH*, 42 (1975), 507–17

Schless, Howard, 'Transformations: Chaucer's Use of Italian', in Brewer (ed) 1974, 184–223

Schmidt, A. V. C., 'Chaucer and the Golden Age', *EC*, 26 (1976), 99–115

Schmidt, A. V. C., 'Chaucer's Nembrot: A Note on *The Former Age*', *MAe*, 47 (1978), 304–7

Schricker, Gale C., 'On the Relation of Fact and Fiction in Chaucer's Poetic Endings', *PQ*, 60 (1981), 13–27

Severs, J. Burke, *The Literary Relationships of Chaucer's Clerkes Tale* (New Haven, 1942)

Severs, J. Burke, and Hartung, A. E., (edd.), *A Manual of Writings in Middle English* (New Haven, 1967)

Shepherd, Geoffrey, 'Religion and Philosophy in Chaucer', in Brewer (ed) 1974, 262–89

Shook, L. K., '*The House of Fame*, in Beryl Rowland (ed.), *Companion to Chaucer Studies* (Oxford, 1979)

Sledd, James, 'Dorigen's Complaint', *MAe*, 45 (1947–8), 36–45

Smith. B. H., *Poetic Closure: A Study of How Poems End* (Chicago, 1968)

Spearing, A. C., *Medieval Dream Poetry* (Cambridge, 1976)

Steadman, John M., *Disembodied Laughter: Troilus and the Apotheosis Tradition* (Berkeley/London, 1972)

Stilwell, Gardiner, 'Chaucer in Tartary', *RES*, 24 (1948), 177–88

Stilwell, Gardiner, 'Convention and Individuality in Chaucer's *Complaint of Mars*', *PQ*, 35 (1956), 69–89

Strohm, Paul, 'The Origin and Meaning of Middle English *Romaunce*', *Genre*, 10 (1977), 1–28

Taylor, P. B., 'Chaucer's "Cosyn to the Dede"', *Speculum*, 57 (1982), 315–27

Vale, Juliet, *Edward III and Chivalry: Chivalric Society and its Context 1270–1350* (Woodbridge, Suffolk, 1982)

Varty, K., 'Deschamps' *Art de Dictier*', *French Studies*, 19 (1965), 164–7

Vasta, Edward, '*To Rosemounde*: Chaucer's "Gentil" Dramatic Monologue', in *Chaucerian Problems and Perspectives: Essays presented to Paul E. Beichner*, edd. E. Vasta and Z. P. Thundy (Notre Dame/London, 1979), 97–113

Wallace, David, 'Chaucer and Boccaccio's Early Writings', in P. Boitani (ed.), *Chaucer and the Italian Trecento* (Cambridge, 1983)

227

Wallace, David, *Chaucer and the Early Writings of Boccaccio* (Woodbridge, Suffolk, 1985)

Webb, H. J., 'A Reinterpretation of Chaucer's Theseus', *RES*, 23 (1947), 289–96

Wenzel, Siegfried, 'Chaucer and the Language of Contemporary Preaching', *SP*, 73 (1976), 138–61

Wetherbee, Winthrop, 'The Theme of Imagination in Medieval Poetry and the Allegorical Figure "Genius"', *M&H* ns 7 (1976), 45–64

Wetherbee, Winthrop, 'The Descent from Bliss: *Troilus* III, 1310–1582', in *Chaucer's "Troilus": Essays in Criticism*, ed. S. A. Barney (London, 1980)

Wetherbee, Winthrop, *Chaucer and the Poets: An Essay on Troilus and Criseyde* (Ithaca/London, 1984)

Wimsatt, James I., *Chaucer and the French Love Poets: the Literary Background of The Book of the Duchess* (Chapel Hill, 1968)

Wimsatt, J. I., '*Anelida and Arcite*: a Narrative of Complaint and Comfort', *ChauR*, 5 (1970–71), 1–8

Wimsatt, J. I., 'Guillaume de Machaut and Chaucer's *Troilus and Criseyde*', *MAe*, 45 (1976), 277–93

Wimsatt, J. I., 'Guillaume de Machaut and Chaucer's Love Lyrics', *MAe*, 47 (1978), 66–87

Wimsatt, J. I., 'Chaucer, *Fortune* and Machaut's "Il m'est avis"', in *Chaucerian Problems and Perspectives: Essays presented to Paul E. Beichner*, edd. E. Vasta and Z. P. Thundy (Notre Dame/London, 1979), 119–31

Wimsatt, J. I., *Chaucer and the Poems of 'Ch'* (Woodbridge, Suffolk, 1982)

Windeatt, B. A., *Chaucer's Dream Poetry: Sources and Analogues* (Cambridge, 1982)

Windeatt, B. A., 'Chaucer and the *Filostrato*', in P. Boitani (ed.), *Chaucer and the Italian Trecento* (Cambridge, 1983), 163–83

Windeatt, B. A., 'Literary Structures in Chaucer', in Boitani and Mann, 195–212

Woolf, Rosemary, 'Moral Chaucer and Kindly Gower', in *J. R. R. Tolkien, Scholar and Storyteller*, edd. M. Salu & R. T. Farrell (Ithaca, 1979) 221–45

# Index

229

MSS (*contd.*)
  Shirley MSS 212
  Univ. of Pennsylvania MS French 15 16
Muscatine, C. F. 216

narrative 7–9, 24–9, 32–3, 40, 42–3, 55, 61,
    64, 74, 91–197 *passim*, esp. 106–15
Neuse, R. 216
Nolan, C. J. 19, 212
Norton-Smith, J. 18, 23–4, 32, 212–13

*occupatio* 42–3, 46, 80, 87, 94, 111, 120–2,
    126–7
Ovid 4–5, 14, 32–3, 35, 60, 63, 67–70, 74–5,
    77, 82, 84, 86, 194, 207
  *Fasti* 75, 84
  *Heroides* 5, 25, 75, 86, 136, 211
  *Metamorphoses* 14, 34, 67, 75, 194
  *Tristia* 4
*Ovide moralisé* 34, 75
Owen, Charles A. Jr 213

Palamon/Palemone 12, 38, 91–128 *passim*, 140,
    189, 198, 201, 216
Pandarus 23, 72, 130–77 *passim*, 195, 202, 208,
    218
Pardoner 58–60, 205
*Parliament of the Three Ages, The* 63
*Partonope of Blois* 41–2
Paul, St 59
Payne, R. 6, 64, 130, 211, 214–15, 217
*Pearl* 63
Pearsall, Derek 107, 126, 216–17, 219–20
Peter, John 4, 211
Petrarch 60, 130, 133–4
Philippa, Queen of Edward III 106–7
Phillips, Helen 64, 214
Physician 51
Pittock, M. 212
plaintiff, see complaint as legal plea
*planctus* 4
Plato 5, 204
Plutarch 75
Porter, Elizabeth 217
Pratt, R. A. 106, 215–16
prologue 33, 47, 50–1, 55–8, 60, 74–87, 93,
    202–6

Reeve 51
Reeves, James 20, 213
Reidy, John 124, 217
Richard II 11, 16, 21, 53, 106, 108–10, 124
Rickert, E. 216, 219
Robertson, D. W. 217
Robertson, S. 216
Robinson, F. N. 30–1, 79, 102, 215–16
*Roman de la Rose, Le* 7, 21–2, 34, 56, 60, 62–3,
    68
*Romanz de la Poire* 6, 211

Salter, Elizabeth 101, 126, 215, 217
Scattergood, V. J. 109, 212, 216
Schibanoff, Susan 218
Schless, Howard 215

Schmidt, A. V. C. 14, 212
Schricker, Gale C. 220
*Secreta Secretorum* 108, 204
Seneca 12, 21
Severs, J. Burke 214
Shakespeare 79, 154
Shepherd, Geoffrey 161, 212, 218
Shook, L. K. 215
*Sir Degrevant* 41
*Sir Gawain and the Green Knight* 93
*Sir Orfeo* 180
Sledd, J. 191, 219
Smith, B. H. 220
Socrates 21
*Somnium Scipionis* 63, 73
Spearing, A. C. 64, 111, 215–16
Spenser, Edmund 40–1, 214
Squire 41, 46, 51
*Squire of Low Degree, The* 41
Statius 25, 39, 60, 92
Stilwell, Gardiner 213
St George's Chapel, Windsor 106–8
St Stephen's, Westminster 107
Strohm, Paul 107, 216

Tatlock, J. S. P. 219
*Teseida*, see Boccaccio
*Thebaid* 25, 27, 92
Theseus/Teseo 26, 28, 32, 42, 86, 91–128
    *passim*, 201, 216
Tristram 13, 102
Troilus 23, 36, 38, 48, 72, 128, 129–77 *passim*,
    198, 208, 218

Vache, Philip de la 12–13
Vale, Juliet 108, 216
*Valentine and Orson* 41–2
Vasta, E. 212
Vegetius, *De Re Militari* 107–8
Venus 5, 7, 33–7, 39–40, 45, 50, 56, 61, 68,
    70–3, 91–2, 96, 98, 109, 113, 115–18,
    127, 144–5, 147–8, 152, 180, 206
Virgil 70, 81–2, 86, 104, 194
  *Aeneid* 68–9, 75, 85, 92, 207
Virginia 5

Waldron, R. A. 219
Wallace, David 129, 198, 217, 220
Walsingham, Thomas, *Historia Anglicana* 109,
    216
Webb, H. J. 216
Wetherbee, Winthrop 215, 217
Wife of Bath 52, 55–7, 60, 205–6
Wimsatt, James I. 6–7, 16, 24–5, 211–13, 215,
    217–18
Windeatt, B. A. 131, 134, 199, 214–15, 217–
    18, 220
Windsor Castle 106
*Winner and Waster* 108
woman's lamenting role 5–6, 9, 15–18, 23–34,
    40, 69, 72, 75–87, 94–5, 140–2, 148–9,
    153–4, 157–8, 168–70, 179–80, 185, 187–
    9, 191–3
Woolf, R. 219

232